SIMPLY K

A Developmental Approach to Kindergarten

Carrie Bailey

Author: Carrie Bailey

Master Books Creative Team:

Editor: Laura Welch

Design: Terry White

Cover Design: Diana Bogardus

Copy Editors:
Judy Lewis
Willow Meek

Curriculum Review:
Laura Welch
Kristen Pratt
Diana Bogardus

First printing: August 2019
Fourth printing: July 2021

Master Books®, P.O. Box 726, Green Forest, AR 72638

Master Books® is a division of the New Leaf Publishing Group, Inc.

ISBN: 978-1-68344-171-7
ISBN: 978-1-61458-721-7 (digital)

Unless otherwise noted, Scripture is from the New International Version (NIV) of the Bible.

All images are istock.com and Carrie Bailey except for:
Shutterstock - pages 102, 105, 162, 164, 180, 183, 201, 216, 242
Wikimedia Commons (PD-US) - page 62

Please consider requesting that a copy of this volume be purchased by your local library system.

Printed in the United States of America

Please visit our website for other great titles:
www.masterbooks.com

For information regarding author interviews, contact the publicity department at (870) 438-5288.

About the Author

CARRIE BAILEY is a Christian homeschool mom to three boys. She has a degree in early childhood education and has also taught students with special needs in the public school system. She and her husband, Jesse, work in their church, serving in many capacities from media to curriculum decisions. Carrie has a passion for helping others on their journey and encouraging other moms.

In addition to *Simply K*, she has written *Stepping Stones*, a book for teaching preschoolers, and has teamed up with author Angela O'Dell on *Math K* in the popular *Math Lessons for a Living Education* series from Master Books.

TABLE OF CONTENTS

QUICK START GUIDE

SIMPLY K was created to be an open and go curriculum. To assist in this process, we've included this Quick Start Guide to help teachers understand how to make the most of the course.

SCOPE & SEQUENCE

The combined Scope & Sequence and schedule in the front of the book summarizes the lesson basics for each day, including the four areas of focus, memory verses, and more.

A lesson prep page begins each lesson and makes it easy to see what is needed and what is being taught. It provides a weekly supply list, an objectives summary, the week's memory verse, and extended activities you might wish to do. Start your week here and you'll be ready for everything the lesson introduces.

Simply K also includes: 26 Alphabet Mini-books; Reference Charts: ABC's, Letter Tracing, Emotions, Weather; Alphabet Cards; Book Suggestions; and a Kindergarten Diploma.

THERE ARE 4 AREAS OF FOCUS IN EACH LESSON:

Bible — learning lessons from God's Word and how we can live for Him. Bible stories, character, and memory verses are used to lay a biblical foundation.

Rhyme Time — learning poetry and new vocabulary words, too

Life Skills — learning how to do important things around the house

ABC's and More — learning the alphabet and basic reading skills

ELEMENTS IN THE COURSE:

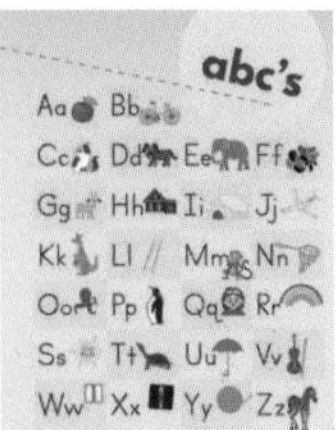

ABC chart — this will be used daily so the student will develop a visual memory association with letters and sounds. You can laminate this or place it in a sheet protector.

ABC cards — these cards are used in games throughout the course alongside the ABC chart. You can laminate them or store in a small box.

Please see the Teacher Resource Page in the back of the book for tips and videos with pertinent information. It is vital that you read this before you begin teaching the course. **Videos available: https://www.masterbooks.com/classroom-aids.**

Mini books — Each letter has its own mini book to help the student learn "concepts about print," such as left to right and top to bottom progression. It is recommended to keep a "book basket" so the student can use these later on for "independent" reading if so desired. (These can also be used alongside *Foundations Phonics* by Master Books.)

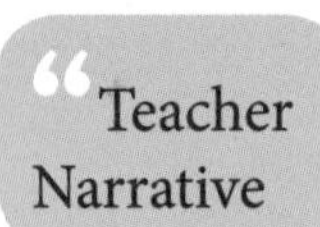

Teaching is kept simple by using color coding. The dark yellow portions are what the teacher says to teach the student. The text on the lighter yellow background is for additional instruction tips and guidance. Student pages/activities are found throughout the book in-between the teaching text.

After Lesson 26, students will begin to learn about sounds (beginning and ending) in words and words that rhyme.

THINGS TO KNOW:

If there is something in the course, such as a recipe, that you do not want to do or do not have the funds to do, then simply skip it or find an alternative, such as having your child help with a meal you are already doing. This course is meant to create a love for learning and setting the child up for future success.

This course is a tool and guide for you. You are the teacher guiding your child and you choose what works and what does not. You can do this and be successful!

Watch your child for fatigue. Children at this age have a short attention span. Each child develops differently, and we never recommend exceeding 20 minutes at a time for learning concepts at this age. Hands-on activities, such as cooking or games, do not have to be included in the 20 minutes. If you see your child getting restless or showing fatigue, please take a break. The course is designed so you can easily break and come back to an activity.

SCOPE & SEQUENCE

Week	Letter	Life Skills	Rhyme	Bible	Due Date
1	Aa	Understanding weather terms, review colors, cutting skills, tracing	"ABC Tumble Down D;" "Now Take This Little Ball"	Noah's Ark and a rainbow promise; A colorful coat	
2	Bb	Understanding weather terms, overview of seasons, color sorting, tracing	"Baa, Baa, Black Sheep"	The Good Shepherd: Sheepfold	
3	Cc	Understanding weather terms & learning to use the weather chart, seasons, color sorting, tracing	"I Am the Wind"	Grace: It's amazing! (2 Cor. 12:9; Eph. 2:8; Eph. 4:7-8)	
4	Dd	Folding a T-shirt, weather: dressing appropriately, cutting & gluing	"Hey Diddle Diddle"	Jesus riding on a donkey (Matt. 21:1-11); Jesus calms the storm (Mark 3:35-41); Appreciating Creation (Gen. 1:1)	
5	Ee	Emotions (chart daily), sizes (big, little, tall, short)	"Little Boy Blue"	Joyful noise (Ps. 98:6); Sad: Adam & Eve (Gen. 3); Excited: Jesus heals Bartimaeus	
6	Ff	Emotions (chart daily), sizes (teeny tiny, ginormous, wide, deep)	"Good Night, Sleep Tight"	Angry: Jesus clears the Temple (Mark 11:15-19); Scared: Mary & Joseph; Scared or full of faith: Shadrach, Meshach, & Abednego	
7	Gg	5 senses, All About Me: name, birthday	5 Senses Songs (3 songs)	Armor of God	

Week	Letter	Life Skills	Rhyme	Bible	Due Date
8	Hh	5 senses, All About Me: name, birthday	5 Senses Songs (3 songs)	Armor of God	
9	Ii	Kinds of food, writing name	"Little Miss Muffet"	Jesus feeds the 5,000; Raining bread (Exod.16); Storehouses of food (Gen. 41-43)	
10	Jj	Where does it belong?, food sorts	"Jack and Jill"	Bigger barns; Ruth; Woman at the well	
11	Kk	Sorting laundry	"Lucy Locket"	Widow's coin; Lost sheep; The prodigal	
12	Ll	Matching & mating socks	"Little Worm"	New creations! (2 Cor. 5:17) (life cycles & salvation)	
13	Mm	Manners (setting table, please, thank you, yes/no sir, yes/no ma'am, may I ___)	"I'm a Little Teapot"	Thankful-Noah's family (Gen. 8:20–22, 9:12–17); Attitude of gratitude! (Luke 17:11-19)	
14	Nn	Manners, social settings: patriotism, opening doors, elevators	"Yankee Doodle"	Blessed nation (Ps. 33:12-22); Honor (1 Peter 2:17); Be strong & courageous (Josh. 1:9)	
15	Oo	Health: basic hygiene	"Come Little Leaves"	Fearfully & wonderfully made (Ps. 139); Leper (Mark 1:40-45)	
16	Pp	Health: basic hygiene	"Apples Ripe"	Blessing others: do unto others (stuffing socks)	
17	Qq	Learning address and phone number	"Quack Quack Little Duck"	Jesus: Birth to the Cross	
18	Rr	Safety: natural disasters, emergencies, seat belts/car seats	"Row, Row, Row Your Boat"	Jesus: Birth to the Cross	
19	Ss	Understanding street signs	"Do You Know How Many Stars?"	The Way, Truth, Life	
20	Tt	Tying shoes, sewing a button	"Star Light, Star Bright"	Obedience: Noah, Joshua; Obedience, Promise	

Week	Letter	Life Skills	Rhyme	Bible	Due Date
21	Uu	Cleaning: sweeping, dusting, wiping spills/ messes	"Mary Had a Little Lamb"	Mary & Martha; The children come (Mark 10:13-16); A young example (1 Tim. 4:12)	
22	Vv	Making a bed	"I Should Like to Build Today"	Take up your bed & walk; Jesus heals the little girl; Tower of Babel	
23	Ww	Sorting: toys, clothes	"A Little Bird Made a Nest"	12 disciples; walking on water; Triune God	
24	Xx	Cleaning the table after eating, which shoe goes on this foot?	"Pat-a-Cake"	Prayer: 4 main kinds (praise, thanks, repentance, & request)	
25	Yy	Animal/plant care	"Yik Yak Yam"	Animal & plant kinds; How much He cares for you (Matt. 6:26-30)	
26	Zz	Snaps, zippers, buttons, and belts	"I Am a Busy Bee"	Story of David: shepherd to king (weight of armor)	
27	Rhyming & Review letters using ABC Chart	Social skills: personal space, waiting your turn/ not interrupting	"Down by the Bay"	Sequencing; Samuel; God's Calling; Days of Creation	
28	Rhyming & Review letters using ABC Chart	Following 3-step directions	"Down by the Bay"	10 Commandments	
29	Rhyming & Review letters using ABC Chart	Questions or statements?, putting away dishes	"Over Field & Meadow"	10 Commandments	
30	Beg. Sounds & ABC Chart	Communication, electronic manners	"Lizards"	Women of the Bible: Ruth, Esther, Priscilla	
31	Beg. Sounds & ABC Chart	Social skills: good sport, taking turns	"To and Fro the Ball"	Kind: Good Samaritan; Kind to others; Islanders show Paul kindness	

Week	Letter	Life Skills	Rhyme	Bible	Due Date
32	Beg. Sounds & ABC Chart	Cooperation: working together & communicating	"The Church Door & Window"	1 Corinthians: love	
33	Ending Sounds & ABC Chart	Good stewards: staying on budget (grocery shopping, electricity, water, tithing)	"The Child's World"	Love: unlovable Zacchaeus; Good Samaritan: notice others	
34	Ending Sounds & ABC Chart	Hospitality: be a host/hostess	Pick a poem you have learned to share with your friend(s)	Relationships (Matt 22:37-40); Jesus first, others second	
35	Ending Sounds & ABC Chart	Opening containers & straws	"The Snail"	Miracles: POSSIBLE WITH GOD! Parting a sea; Jesus heals the boy blind from birth; Raising Lazarus from the dead	
36	Ending Sounds & ABC Chart	Understanding first, second, third	YOU PICK your favorite	First: John 1:1—The beginning; 1st man/2nd man; Seek first the kingdom of God (Matt. 6:33)	

COURSE SUPPLIES

These are supplies that will be used regularly throughout the course for different activities. It would be helpful if you gather them in a labeled storage container and keep it in the area where you are teaching the lessons. Each lesson has a supply list, but they will list items other than those from this list that are needed.

You Will Need:

- ☐ ABC Chart
- ☐ Book basket/bin/tub
- ☐ Bible
- ☐ Highlighter (or highlighting tape)
- ☐ Crayons
- ☐ Glue sticks
- ☐ Scissors
- ☐ Construction paper
- ☐ White cardstock
- ☐ Watercolors
- ☐ Playdough
- ☐ Colored pencils
- ☐ Dry erase marker(s)
- ☐ Sheet protectors or laminator

REMINDER: The author has made videos available on how to teach components of the course. They contain very helpful information. It is important you watch the videos before starting the course. Videos are available: https://www.masterbooks.com/classroom-aids.

LESSON 1
Prep Page

Supply List

- ☐ Weather Chart (daily, life skills)
- ☐ White paper (day 1, Bible)
- ☐ Ball (daily, rhyme time)

Look Ahead*

- ☐ Ink pad/paint (thumbprints)
- ☐ Small rocks (from outside)
- ☐ Small sticks (from outside)
- ☐ Cotton balls

Objectives

Letter of the week: Aa

Skills/Concepts: Understanding weather terms, review colors, cutting skills, tracing

Memory Verse

Deuteronomy 6:5

Love the LORD your God with all your heart and with all your soul and with all your strength.

Extended Activities

Allow them to cut more, even if you draw lines on the edge of a paper for them to "fringe" the edges.

Play a board game for 1-1 correspondence, color recognition, and number recognition, such as Chutes & Ladders®, Sorry®, Trouble®, Candy Land®, etc.

* The "Look Ahead" section of the prep page is so you can prepare for future activities beyond this lesson.

LESSON 1
Day 1

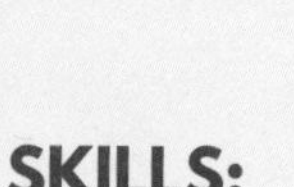

LIFE SKILLS:

Show the student the weather chart on page 430.

"Weather impacts how we dress each day. We have all kinds of weather, don't we? Some days it is sunny, while other days it is rainy. Different times of the year and different places we live affect the temperature. We have cold, which is like snowy weather. We have cool, which is not as cold, but you still might need a light jacket. Then we have warm, which is not sweating, but we wouldn't need a jacket, either. Last, we have hot. If it is hot outside, we will definitely be sweating. What is our weather like today?

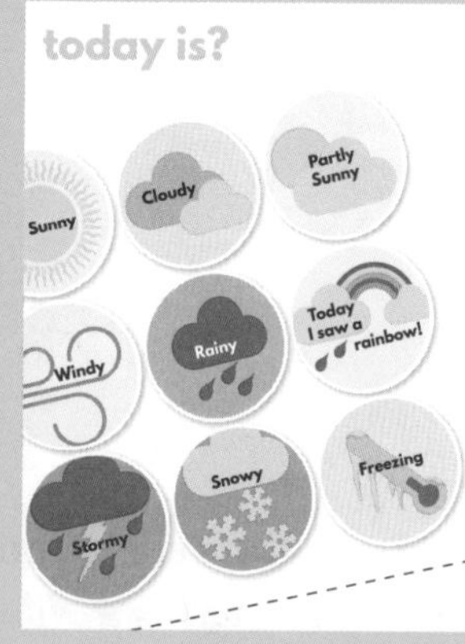

BIBLE:

Read Genesis 6:9–9:17.

"In Genesis, we learn that Noah was a man faithful and obedient to God. Many others were not doing what was right. God told Noah to build an Ark, which is a really big boat, and that He would send a flood to destroy those that were not on the Ark. Noah did as God commanded. Noah and his family all boarded the Ark and God sent animals of all kinds onto the Ark as well. Then, God shut the door of the Ark. It began to rain. It rained for 40 days and 40 nights! Once it stopped raining, Noah waited 40 days. Noah sent a dove out and when the dove did not return, Noah knew it was safe to remove the covering of the Ark. God told him, his family, and the animals to go out onto dry land.

"Let's review our colors now as we remember God's promise. If we look at this rainbow, we can see there are 7 colors. We have red, orange, yellow, green, blue, indigo (which is a mix of blue and purple), and violet (which is a true purple). Let's color a rainbow!

Use paper and let your child make a rainbow.

"Noah loved God. I know a verse in the Bible that tells me we should love the Lord, too. I want us to learn that verse this week. You repeat me as I say parts of it. This is called echo reading. Let's read the memory verse!

Echo read the verse. Add motions.

Love  the Lord your God

With all your heart 

And with all your soul 

And with all your strength. 

"Now let's add motions so we can remember it even better!

"I am so proud of you! You have done a fantastic job! You are showing me how much you care about learning. Being caring is such a great quality to have! I love how much you care!

LESSON 1
Day 1

Read "A B C Tumble Down D."

"That rhyme is funny! It says "The cat's in the cupboard." Do you know what a cupboard is?

Give explanation if they do not know; if they know, have them explain or show you. A cupboard is a cabinet with shelves, like in our kitchen. Take them and show them.

A B C Tumble Down D

A B C tumble down D.
The cat's in the cupboard
And can't see me.

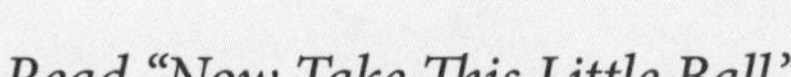

Read "Now Take This Little Ball."

It would be more fun if you added a ball into this and had them toss it back and forth to you as you read it.

"I am so proud of you! You have done a fantastic job! You are showing me how much you care about learning. Being caring is such a great quality to have! I love how much you care!

BREAK if needed — see the beginning section on signs your child is tiring.

Now Take This Little Ball

Now take this little ball
and do not let it fall,
balls of yellow, red, and blue,
some for me and some for you.
Now take the little ball
and do not let it fall.

Hold it in your hand,
then quite still let it stand,
balls of yellow, blue, and red,
you are round just like my head.
Hold it in your hand,
then quite still let it stand.

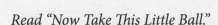

LESSON 1
Day 1

ABC'S AND MORE:

TIPS: See instructional video for this and the instructions in the beginning of the book. See Teacher Resource Section for pertinent information.

See Teacher Resource Page.

Chant the ABC chart.

Sing the ABC song.

See Video 1 for instructions. The URL is on page 5. You point to a letter/its image and say the letter as the student is seeing it. The student will learn to apply that information and do it too.

“An apple is kind of like a circle. Did you know the word “apple” begins with the letter A? We will use your ABC chart to chant the letters and pictures. Echo, or repeat, what I say. Make sure you touch each letter and picture like I do.

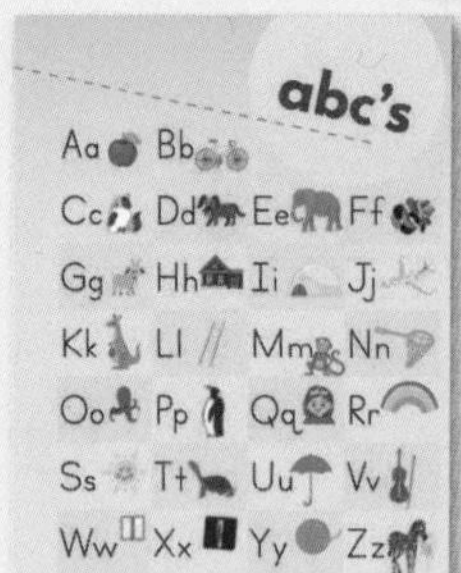

Go through the chart saying each letter like “A, a, apple.” The student should repeat it. Then move to the next “B, b, bike” as you work your way through all the letters. A helpful way to remember the process is simply: say, see, do.

“Did you notice how each picture has two letters by it? Like this one for the apple (*point as you are telling them*) see the A, this is a capital A. Then, this a is a lowercase a. Each letter has a capital letter or big letter and a lowercase letter or small letter.

“Today, we will learn how to write the letter Aa.

Show the child on the ABC chart.

“Remember that we have capital letters and lowercase letters.

Point to the capital A.

“This is a capital A.

Point to the lowercase a.

“This is a lowercase a.

Practice writing Aa's.

“A: (slant up, slant down, across in the middle)
Start at the bottom line, slant up and in toward the top line (slant up).
Slant down and out to the right bottom line (slant down).
Then, we cross it at the middle (cross in the middle)

LESSON 1
Day 1

"a: (over around, up, and down)
You start the lowercase a on the middle line.
Go over and around (over around).
And back up toward the middle line (up).
And then down to the bottom line (down).

Trace the Aa's below.

"Now, let's play a game! I am going to say silly words and we are going to see if you can hear the first sound in the word.

Tips: Emphasize the beginning sounds. Do not show words or letters to them. This is for hearing sounds in isolation.

"If I say zzzipper . . . I hear a zzzz sound like a buzzing bee! Can you act like a bee?

"G-g-g-giraffe . . . What sound do you hear first when I say g-g-giraffe?

They should say /j/, but if they do not, please say the word again and then tell them the sound.

"sssssnake . . . What sound do you hear first when I say sssssnake? /s/ Can you make a sound like a snake?

"fffffrog . . . What sound do you hear first when I say fffffrog? /f/ Can you hop like a frog?

"Great job! You did so well hearing those sounds and pretending to be animals!

See the Teacher Resource Page.

Do a picture walk.

Read the book to the student pointing to each letter/word.

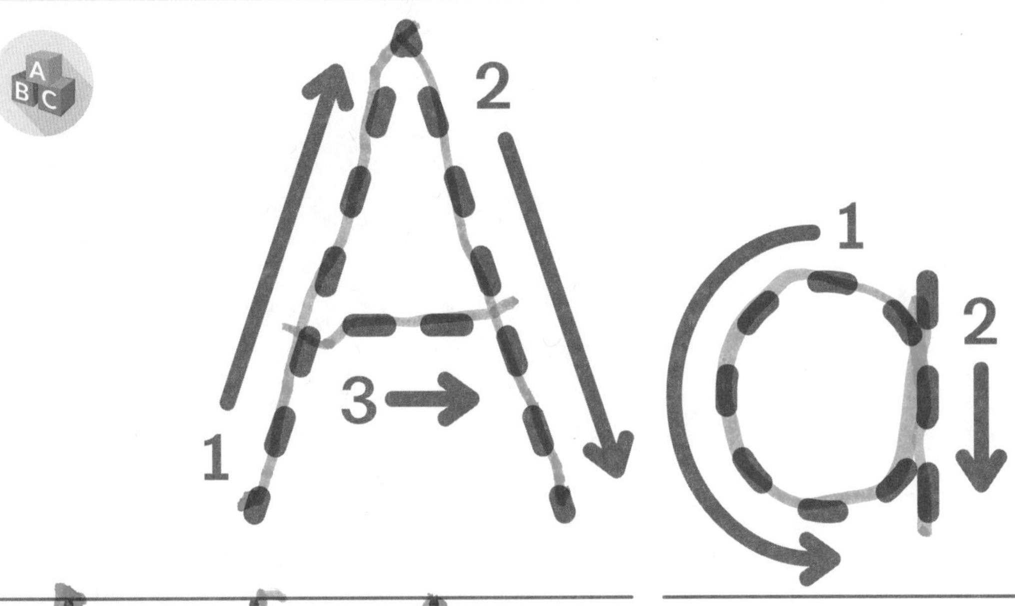

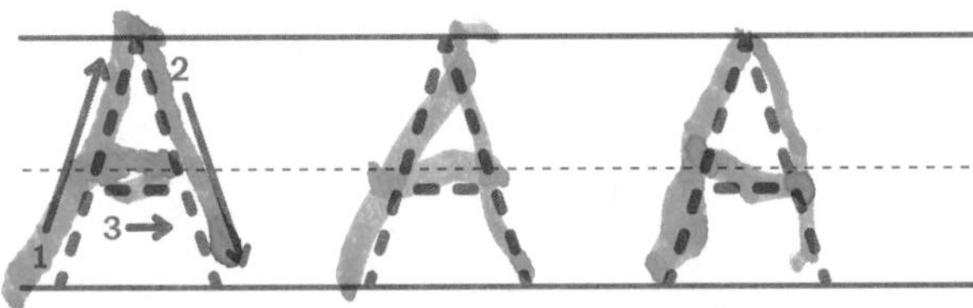

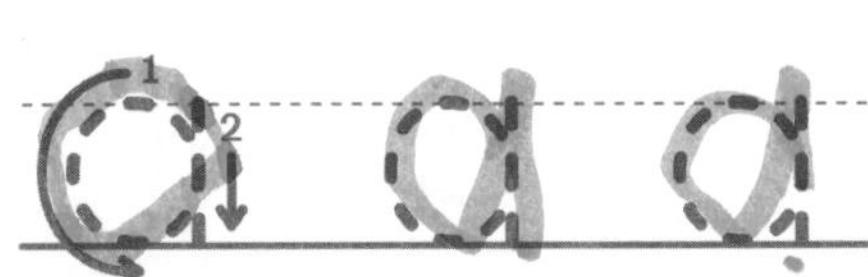

LESSON 1
Day 2

LIFE SKILLS:

"Let's learn how to use scissors.

Model the steps below for the student as you do it:

"Hold the scissors by the handle, not the sharp end.

"Remember, we never run with scissors in our hands, and we only cut what I give you to cut.

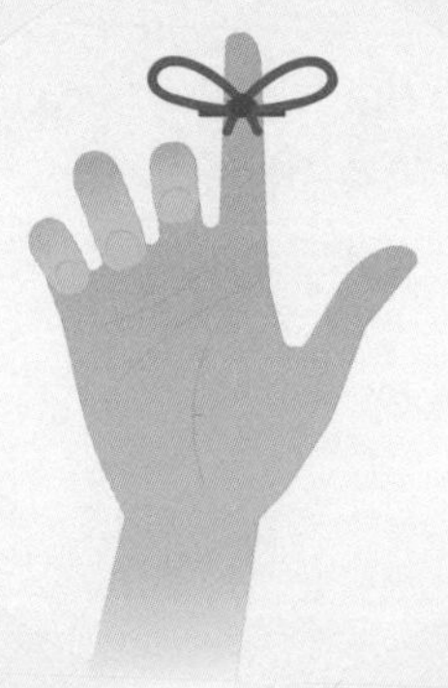

"Open and close like an alligator chomp.

"Great job! I think you are ready for cutting!

BIBLE:

"Let's color Noah's ark and make waves by doing the Bible activity on the next page. Then we will do our rhyme time and read a mini book!

"Do you remember about Noah and the rainbow promise? What can you tell me about that promise?

Review memory verse on page 12.

"That's right, the promise of the rainbow was that God would not destroy life on earth again with a flood. You are doing great at remembering what you learned. Today, I want us to do some more art, but I also want us to use scissors to make the art. We are going to make waves like the waves during the flood of Noah.

"Find a blue crayon and color the waves on the next page blue and then cut on the lines. It will be your waves.

Start the Bible activity on the next page.

"Color the Ark picture on page 19 and tell me which colors you are using each time.

"Paste the waves to the bottom for layered waves.

Finish the Ark activity on page 19.

TIP: If you start at the base of the Ark first and then paste the waves toward the bottom of the page you will see the wave lines.

LESSON
Day 2

RHYME TIME:

"Remember our poems and rhymes from yesterday? Let's get that back out and read those again.

Read "ABC Tumble Down D" and "Now Take This Little Ball" on page 13.

"Can you remember what a cupboard is? Right! It is a cabinet with shelves.

MINI-BOOK A:

"Here is our letter Aa book for this week. Now, watch as I read this book again.

Aa
mini book

Read the letter book to the student.

Have the student highlight the capital and lowercase letter of the week.

"Use a highlighter to make a dot on the A's and a's in the book.

Paste the waves here.

LESSON 1
Day 2

ABC'S AND MORE:

"We will use your ABC chart to chant the letters and pictures. Echo, or repeat, what I say. Make sure you touch each letter and picture like I do.

See Teacher Resource Page.

Sing the ABC song.

Chant the ABC chart.

"Remember that we have capital letters and lowercase letters.

Point to the capital A.

"This is a capital A.

Point to the lowercase a.

"This is a lowercase a.

Practice writing Aa's.

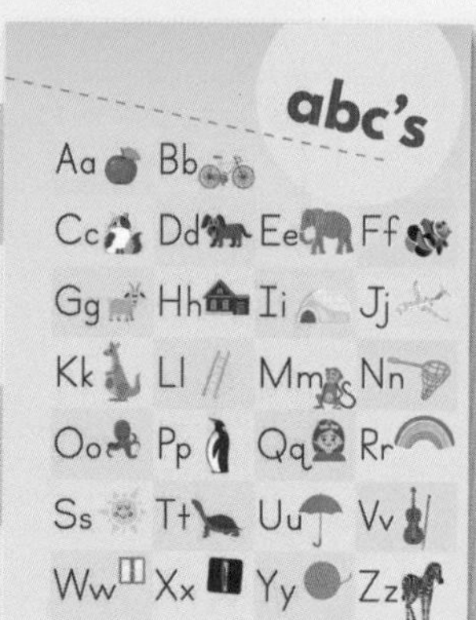

"A: (slant up, slant down, across in the middle)
Start at the bottom line, slant up and in toward the top line (slant up).
Slant down and out to the right bottom line (slant down).
Then, we cross it at the middle (cross in the middle).

"a: (over around, up, and down)
You start the lowercase a on the middle line.
Go over and around (over around).
And back up toward the middle line (up).
And then down to the bottom line (down).

Trace the Aa's below.

"You have done a fantastic job today! I am so proud of you for showing that caring attitude about your work! When you care, you pay attention to details and do your best work! I love how much you care.

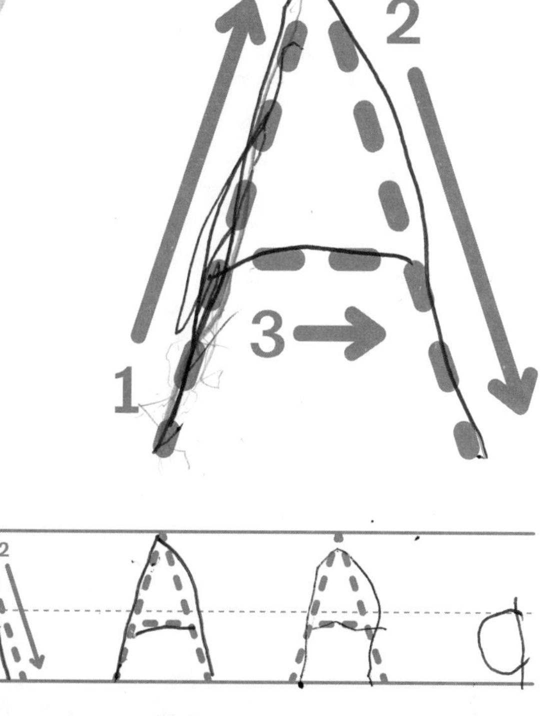

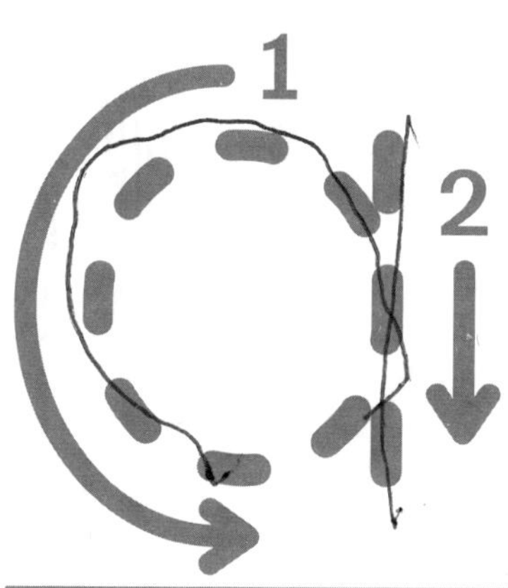

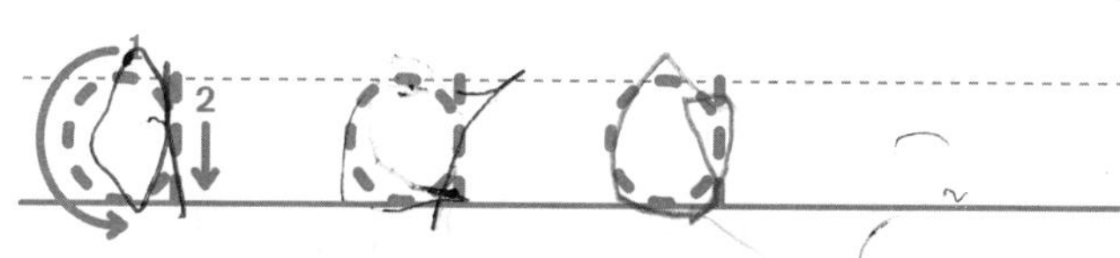

LESSON 1
Day 2

Try to catch your child showing this caring attitude other times and praise them.

"You did so well playing that game yesterday with the sounds and animals that we are going to play it again!

"Remember, I am going to say silly words and we are going to see if you can hear the first sound in the word.

"Rrrrain . . . what sound do you hear first? */r/* Great! Now, if we gently pat on our legs then we can make it kind of sound like rain!

Alternate patting hands on each leg.

"B-b-b-boom . . . What sound do you hear first when I say b-b-boom? Yes! */b/* Okay, now thunder makes booming sounds, can you stomp around to make booms like thunder?

"Sssnow . . . What sound do you hear first when I say sssnow? */s/* Okay, snow falls gently. Can you walk as you make your arms gently move up and down?

"W-w-w-wind . . . What sound do you hear first when I say w-w-wind? */w/* Can you spin around like a leaf flying in the wind?

Note: These are optional images/words you will see throughout the course as space allows. These can be incorporated into the lesson for extra practice and letter recognition. We recommend that you read the word to the student and point out the first letter.

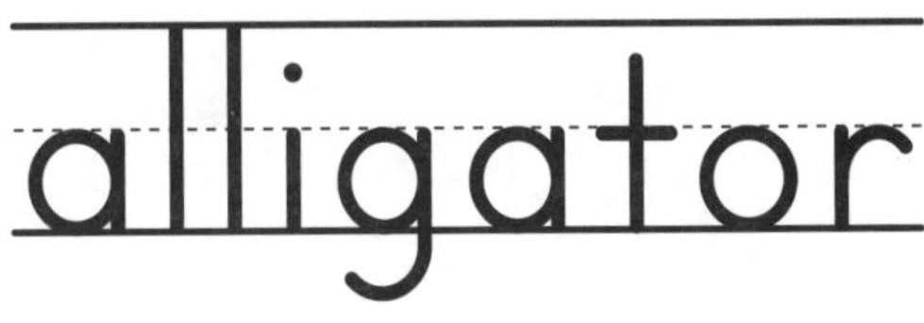

LESSON 1
Day 3

LIFE SKILLS:

"You know, you have done so well on showing how much you care about your work this week. I was so impressed with how well you did using your scissors yesterday that I wanted to have you cut some more today. Remember your safety rules for scissors? Let's review those. Show me how to hold the scissors.

Allow them to show you/help them to hold them correctly. Do the same for how to hold them while walking.

"Now, if you wanted to walk with these, how do you hold them?

"Great! Now you are ready for cutting more things. You showed great care in your cutting skills and doing your best! I am so proud of you!

Cutting will be done during Bible activity.

"Have you noticed the weather this week? Was each day the same? I love your observation skills. Observation means to look closely and pay attention to details. That is what you are doing when you observe the weather. What are some other things you can observe?

RHYME TIME:

Read "ABC Tumble Down D;" "Now Take This Little Ball."

"We are going to do our poems before our Bible today.

"Use a highlighter to dot the letters A and a in the poems. Be sure to find capital and lowercase A's.

Use the poems from Rhyme Time Day 1 on page 13.

BIBLE:

"Our rhyme talks about colors of yellow, red, and blue. Do you know a story in the Bible that talks about a colorful coat?

Read the account of Joseph and his colorful coat in Genesis 37:2–34.

"The coat Joseph had was very special. It would have been made using what we call dyes. Just like we use food coloring to dye icing on cakes, there is a dye you can use to color clothing. "The Bible only mentions four colors of dye. It talks about purple, blue, crimson (a dark purplish-red), and scarlet (a bright red). The dyes would have come from natural items like shellfish, insects, and plant roots." (from the *Illustrated Family Bible Stories*, p. 34)

"Color Joseph's coat. Then, make the bottom edge of the coat have fringe by cutting slits up from the bottom.

"Joseph loved God very much, and God made him very wise and gave him dreams. God loves you, too! We have been learning a verse this week that God has given us a command to love Him. Do you remember with what we are supposed to love the Lord? With all our…

(Wait for answer, but help if needed.)

Review your memory verse on page 12.

BREAK if needed. See front for suggestions on signs your child is tiring and needs a break.

Name

LESSON 1
Day 3

ABC'S AND MORE:

See the Teacher Resource Page.

Chant the ABC chart.

Sing the ABC song.

"Now, let's look at our ABC chart. Use your ABC chart to find the capital letters for F, J, P, R, K. Use your ABC chart to find the lowercase letters for e, o, x, n, j.

"Great job! You are really showing a caring attitude and paying attention. Before we read our book again, let's sing the ABC song.

"We will use your ABC chart to chant the letters and pictures. Echo, or repeat, what I say. Make sure you touch each letter and picture like I do.

**Remember: This is you modeling for independent use later on. Please use the following guide carefully as this sets a foundation to build upon later on.*

"Today, we will review how to write the letter Aa.

Show the child on the ABC chart and on the next page.

"Remember that we have capital letters and lowercase letters.

Point to the capital A.

"This is a capital A.

Point to the lowercase a.

"This is a lowercase a.

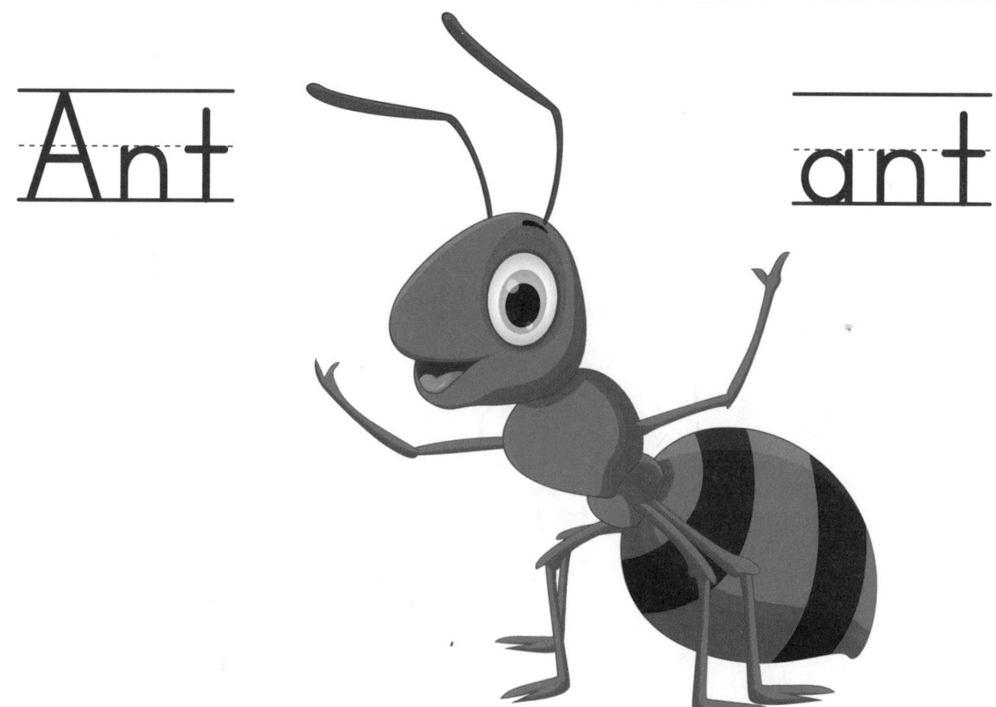

Bottom of Page blank for cutting.

LESSON 1
Day 3

Practice writing Aa's.

"A: (slant up, slant down, across in the middle)
Start at the bottom line, slant up and in toward the top line (slant up).
Slant down and out to the right bottom line (slant down).
Then, we cross it at the middle (cross in the middle).

"a: (over around, up, and down)
You start the lowercase a on the middle line.
Go over and around (over around).
And back up toward the middle line (up).
And then down to the bottom line (down).

"Here is our letter Aa book for this week. Let's read it again.

Read the letter book again.

Advanced K — see if your child can read the book to you. Read the letter mini book.

Trace the Aa's below.

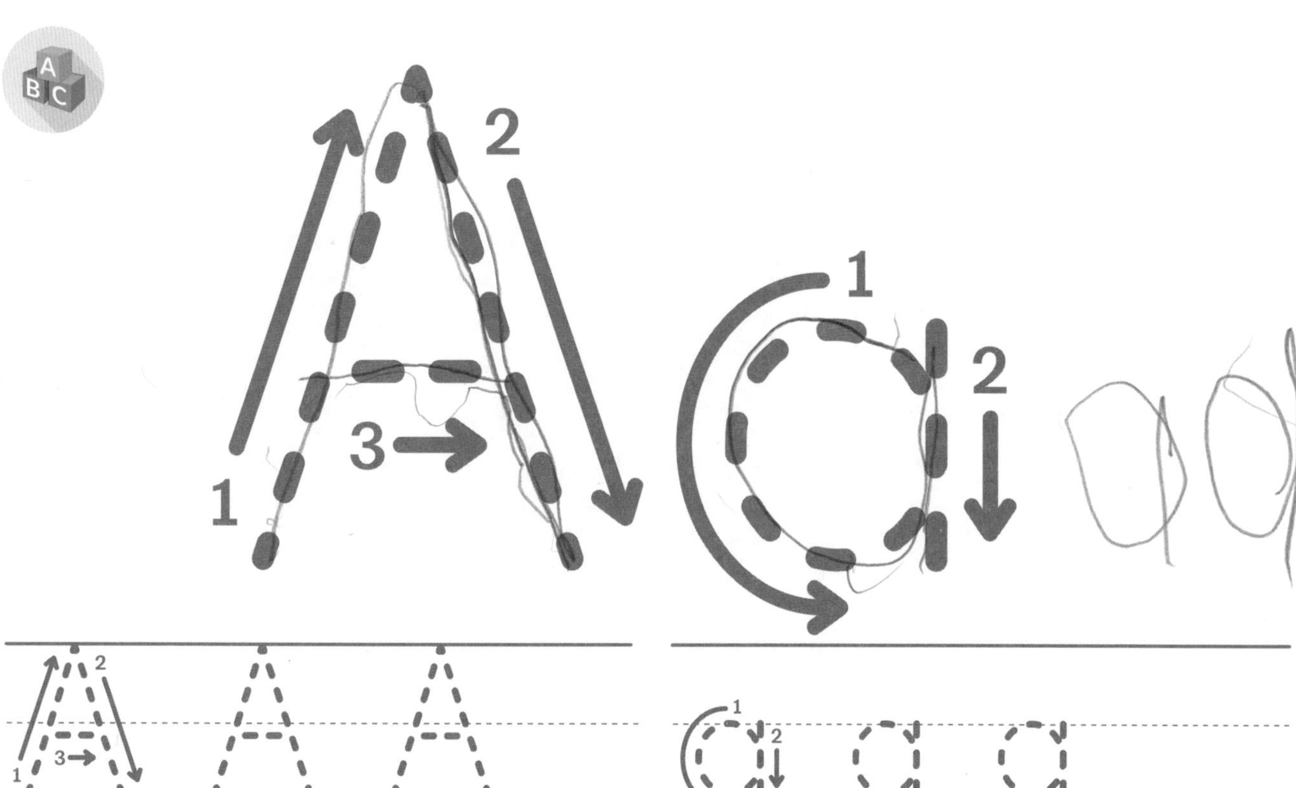

LESSON 2
Prep Page

Supply List

- ☐ Blank paper (day 2, life skills)
- ☐ Small rocks (day 3, Bible)
- ☐ Small sticks (day 3, Bible)
- ☐ Playdough (optional, day 3, Bible)

Objectives

Letter of the week: Bb

Skills/Concepts: Understanding weather terms, overview of seasons, color sorting, tracing

Memory Verse

John 10:14

I am the good shepherd; I know my sheep and my sheep know me.

Extended Activities

Allow them to cut more, even if you draw lines on the edge of a paper for them to "fringe" the edges.

Watch the weather and then let them pretend to be a weather reporter. Record them if you want. You can use a U.S. map for them to stand in front of.

Play a board game for 1-1 correspondence, color recognition, and number recognition, such as Chutes & Ladders®, Sorry®, Trouble®, Candy Land®, etc.

LESSON 2
Day 1

LIFE SKILLS:

"One thing that affects the weather in different places is called seasons. Some people even have rainy or dry seasons. In most of the United States, there are four different seasons in a year. The four seasons are winter, spring, summer, and fall (or autumn). Some places in the world do not have four true seasons. Each season has a difference in temperature and what you see. For example, in fall (or autumn) in Arkansas, leaves would be changing colors and the temperature would be turning mild or cooler. If you lived in the Amazon Rainforest, you would not have a winter. If you lived at the North Pole, winter would be freezing and the sun would not shine much at all. In San Diego, California, winter is chilly with shorter days. We will focus on the four main seasons and what that looks like in this chart.

"I love the beautiful leaves of fall. Let's review our colors.

Play a game of "I spy," using colors. (I spy something that is: red, blue, orange, brown, pink, purple, yellow, green, white, black.)

BIBLE:

"In the Bible, it talks a lot about shepherds. What do you know about a shepherd? Shepherds take care of sheep. Jesus is known as the Good Shepherd and we are known as His sheep. In our memory verse, John 10:14, it says:

Echo read the verse. Add motions.

I am the good  shepherd

I know  My sheep

And my sheep know me .

"What do you think that means? Jesus says He is the Good Shepherd. Well, if He is the shepherd, the shepherd takes care of whom? *(sheep)* And we are His sheep, right? *(yes)* So that means that He takes care of us! It also says He knows us and we know Him. What is a way we can know Him better?

LESSON 2
Day 1

RHYME TIME:

"Our poem this week is called "Baa, Baa, Black Sheep." Let's read it now.

Read "Baa, Baa, Black Sheep."

Baa, Baa, Black Sheep

Baa, baa, black sheep,
have you any wool?
Yes sir, yes sir, three bags full.
One for the master,
and one for the dame,
and one for the little boy
who lives down the lane.

ABC'S AND MORE:

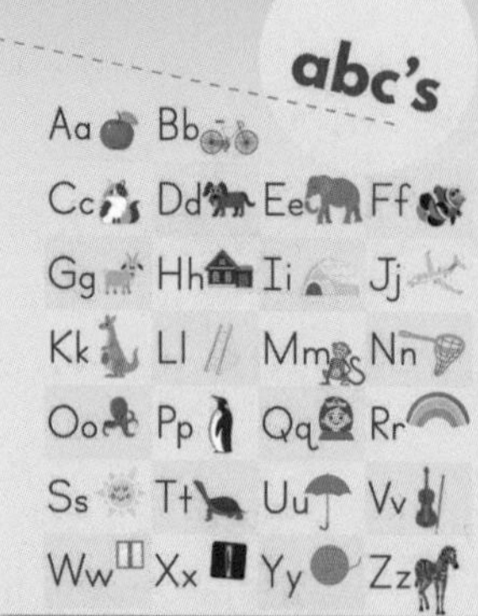

TIPS: See instructional video for this and the instructions in the beginning of the book. See Teacher Resource Section for pertinent information.

See the Teacher Resource Page.

Chant the ABC chart.

Sing the ABC song.

"Today, we will learn how you write the letter B.

Show the child on the ABC chart and on the next page.

"Remember we have capital letters and lowercase letters.

Point to the capital B.

"This is a capital B.

Point to the lowercase b.

"This is a lowercase b.

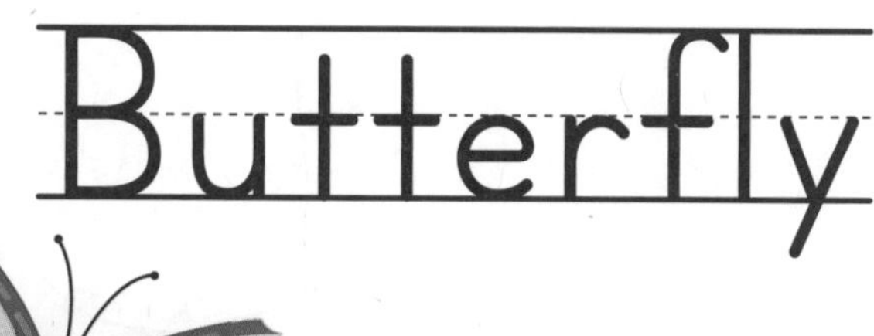

LESSON 2
Day 1

Practice writing B's and b's.

"B: (down, up around, around)
Start at the top line, go down (down) to the bottom line.
Then, go back up that line, and around to the middle line (around).
And around to the bottom line (around).

"b: (down, up, around)
Start at the top line, go down to the bottom line (down).
Go up to the middle line (up) and around to the bottom line (around).

Trace the Bb's below.

"Today we will play the sounds game again. Remember, I am going to say silly words and we are going to see if you can hear the first sound in the word.

"Sh-sh-sh-sheep . . . what sound do you hear first when I say sh-sh-sheep? **/sh/** What sound do sheep make?

"Mmmmonkey . . . What sound do you hear first when I say monkey? Yes! **/m/**! What sound do monkeys make?

"D-d-d-duck . . . What sound do you hear first when I say duck? **/d/** What sound does a duck make? Great job!

MINI-BOOK B

See the Teacher Resource Page.

Do a picture walk.

Read the book to the student.

"Now, watch and follow along as I read this book to you.

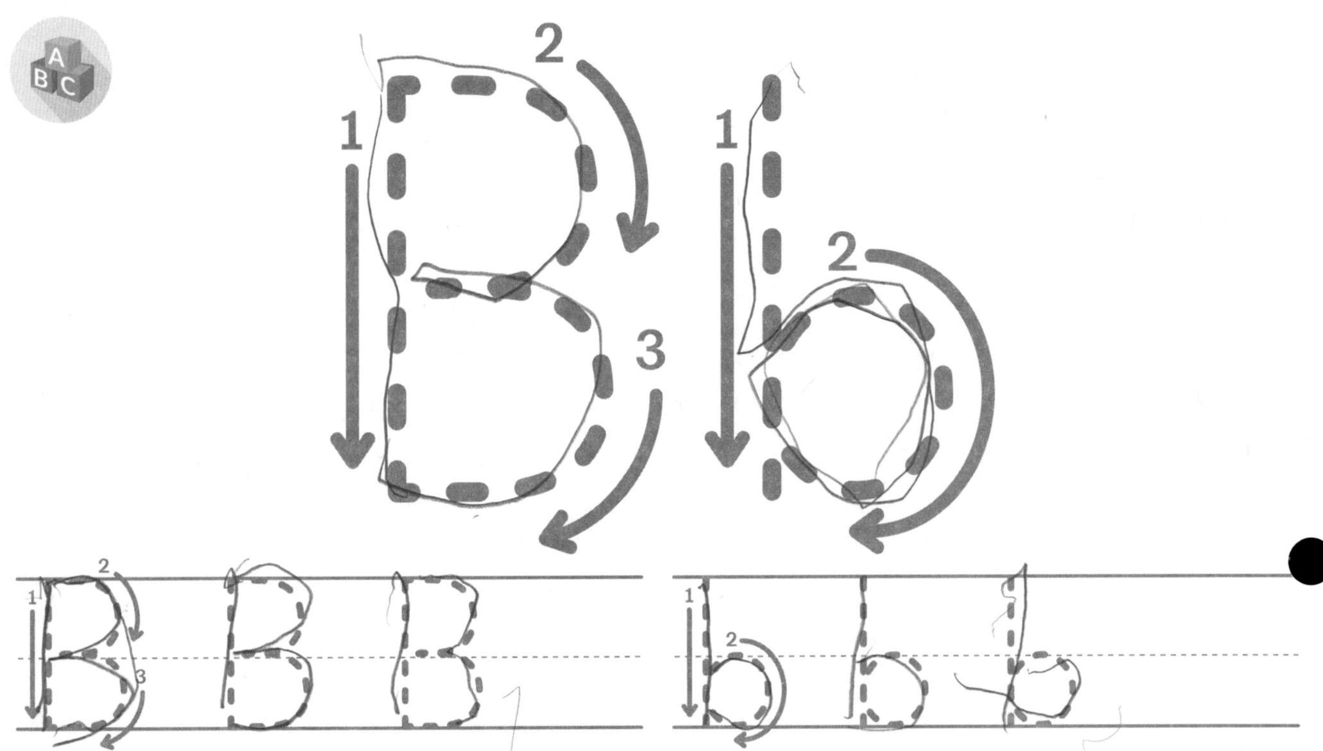

LESSON 2
Day 2

LIFE SKILLS:

"Let's look at seasons again today. I want you to draw a picture of the season we are in now. If we look at our chart on seasons, we can see right now it is most like _____ season outside.

Give the student a blank sheet of paper for their drawing.

"Draw a picture of the season it currently is.

Play a game of "I spy" using colors. (I spy something that is: red, blue, orange, brown, pink, purple, yellow, green, white, black.)

"You will practice colors more on the next page. Look at the color of each paint bucket. Match it with the object that also has the same color.

Do the color matching activity on the next page.

BIBLE:

"Yesterday, we talked about the Good Shepherd and how Jesus is the Good Shepherd.

Review your memory verse on page 28.

"There is another Scripture that talks about a sheepfold. A sheepfold is kind of like a pen for the sheep. It has a door or gate, and it surrounds the sheep to help give them protection as well as keep them inside. Can you picture a sheepfold? Let's read John 10:1–5 in our Bible.

Gate Keeper Game: (You need three people total to play or use a pretend voice.)

"Jesus talks about being the "gate keeper." Let's pretend that I am the gate keeper. Remember, it said His sheep know His voice. If it isn't His voice, the sheep run away. So, come get in my sheepfold (make a pretend one or designate an area to be one). Then, if I call you, you will come to me. If someone else calls you, you run! (Play this taking turns as gate keeper.)

RHYME TIME:

"Let's read our poem "Baa, Baa, Black Sheep" again!

Read "Baa, Baa, Black Sheep" on page 29.

Optional: Draw a picture to illustrate the poem on a separate piece of paper.

Lesson 2
Day 2

Name

Match the paint bucket to the correct color object.

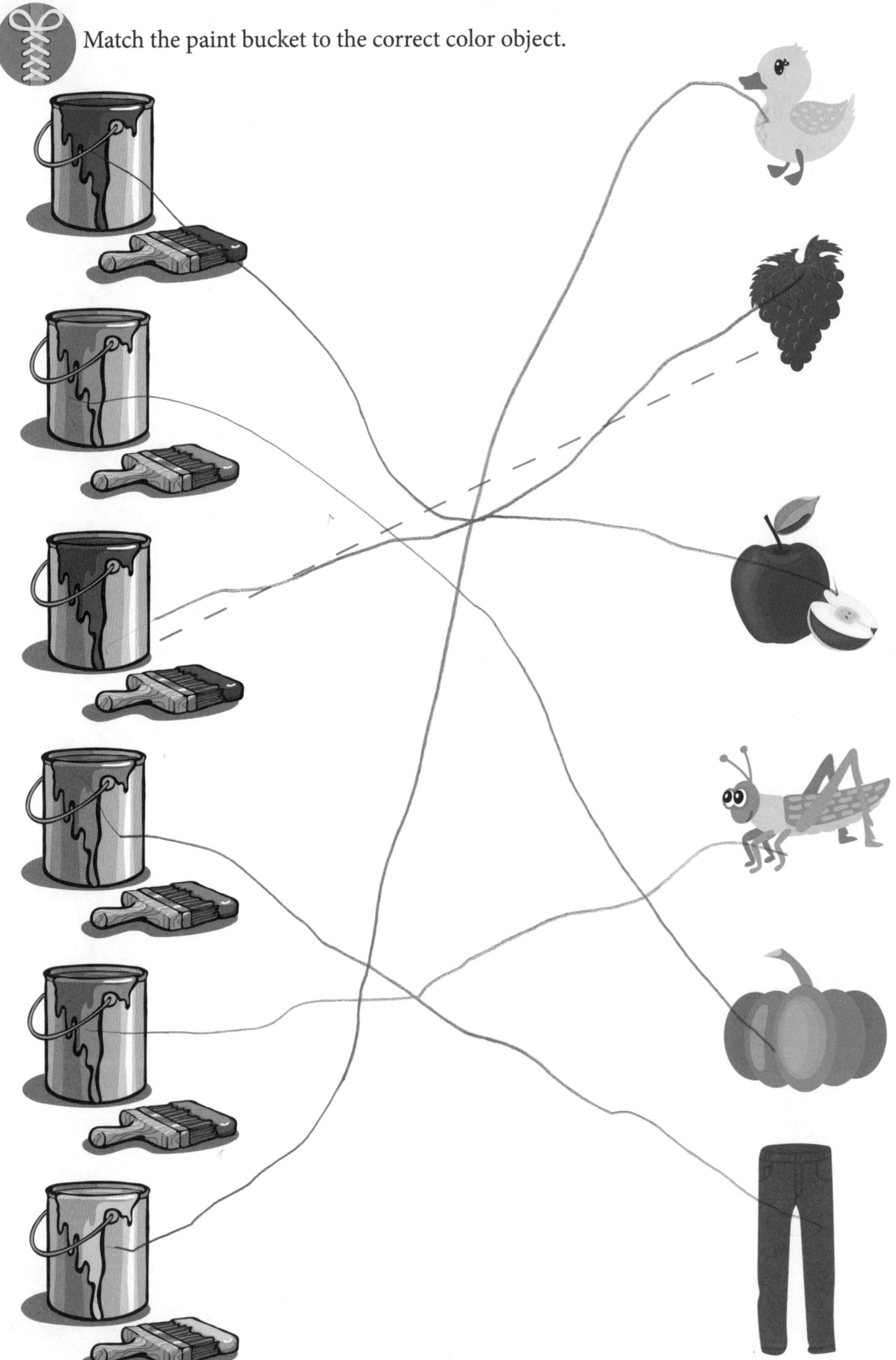

LESSON 2
Day 2

ABC'S AND MORE:

Chant the ABC chart.

Sing the ABC song.

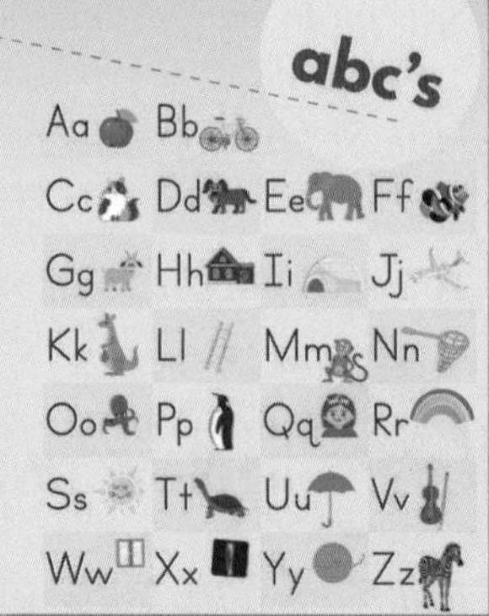

"Today, we will review how you write to letter B.

"Remember, we have capital letters and lowercase letters.

Point to the capital B. Point to the lowercase b.

"This is a capital B. This is a lowercase b.

Practice writing B's and b's.

"B: (down, up around, around)
Start at the top line, go down (down) to the bottom line.
Then, go back up that line, and around to the middle line (around).
And around to the bottom line (around).

"b: (down, up, around)
Start at the top line, go down to the bottom line (down).
Go up to the middle line (up) and around to the bottom line (around).

Trace the Bb's below.

MINI-BOOK B

Read the letter book to the student.

Have the student highlight the capital and lowercase letter of the week.

"Now, watch and follow along as I read this book to you.

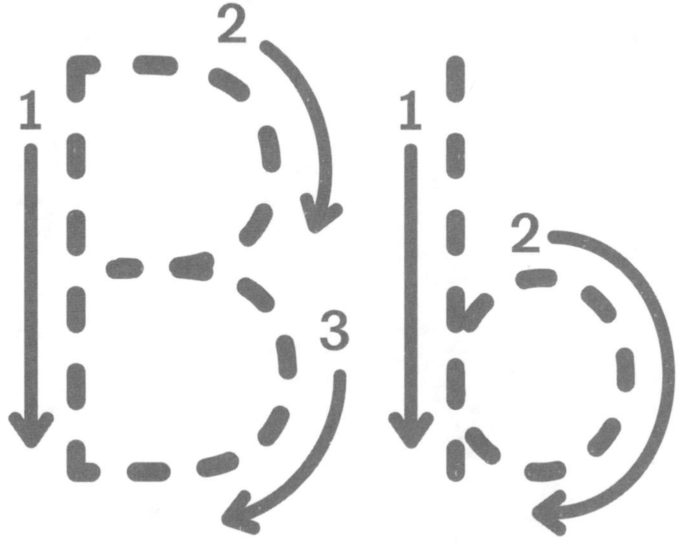

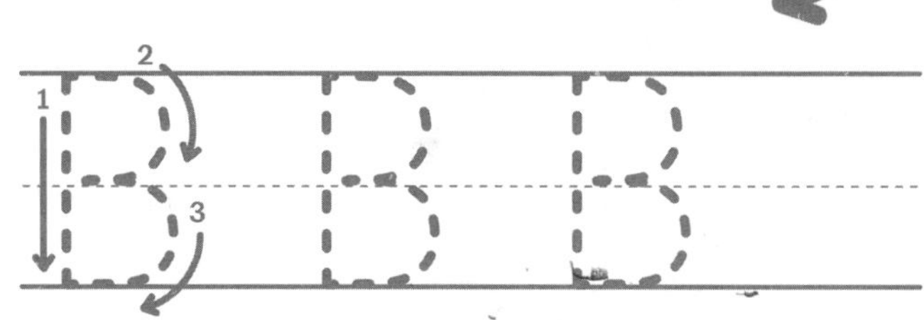

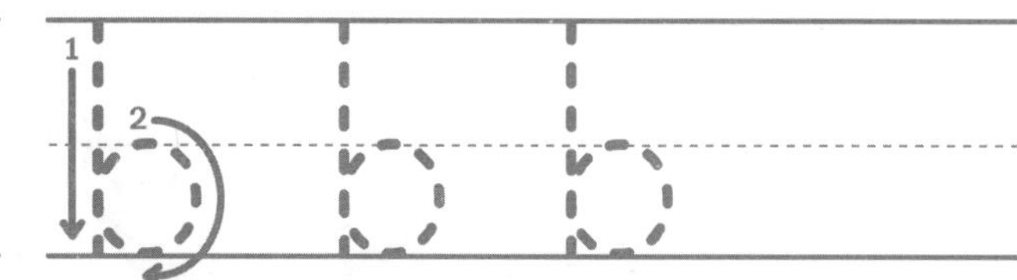

LESSON 2
Day 3

LIFE SKILLS:

"Do you remember that we learned about the four seasons this week? Look on the next page in your book. The four seasons are listed and there are pictures of kids doing fun things throughout the year. See if you can choose the season that each child's activity is taking place during the year.

Do the matching activity on the next page.

Play a game of "I spy" using colors. (I spy something that is: red, blue, orange, brown, pink, purple, yellow, green, white, black.)

BIBLE:

Review your memory verse on page 28.

"Remember the sheepfold? It has a door or gate, and it surrounds the sheep to help give them protection as well as keep them inside. Let's read John 10:1–5 in our Bible again.

Sheepfold — Gather rocks from outside to make a sheepfold. Use sticks as the "gate." Narrate how Jesus is the Good Shepherd and the Gate Keeper.

You may choose to use playdough instead.

RHYME TIME:

Read "Baa, Baa, Black Sheep."

"Highlight the B's and b's in the poem.

Baa, Baa, Black Sheep

Baa, baa, black sheep,
have you any wool?
Yes sir, yes sir, three bags full.
One for the master,
and one for the dame,
and one for the little boy
who lives down the lane.

Bicycle bicycle

Name

Match the pictures with the correct season by drawing a line from one to the other.

Winter

Spring

Summer

Fall

LESSON 2
Day 3

ABC'S AND MORE:

See the Teacher Resource Page.

Use the ABC chart to chant the letters and pictures.

Sing the ABC song.

"Today, we will review how you write the letter B.

"Remember we have capital letters and lowercase letters.

Point to the capital B.

"This is a capital B.

Point to the lowercase b.

This is a lowercase b.

Practice writing B's and b's.

"B: (down, up around, around)
Start at the top line, go down (down) to the bottom line.
Then, go back up that line, and around to the middle line (around).
And around to the bottom line (around).

"b: (down, up, around)
Start at the top line, go down to the bottom line (down).
Go up to the middle line (up) and around to the bottom line (around).

Trace the Bb's below.

MINI-BOOK B

Read the letter book again.

Advanced K — see if your child can read the book to you.

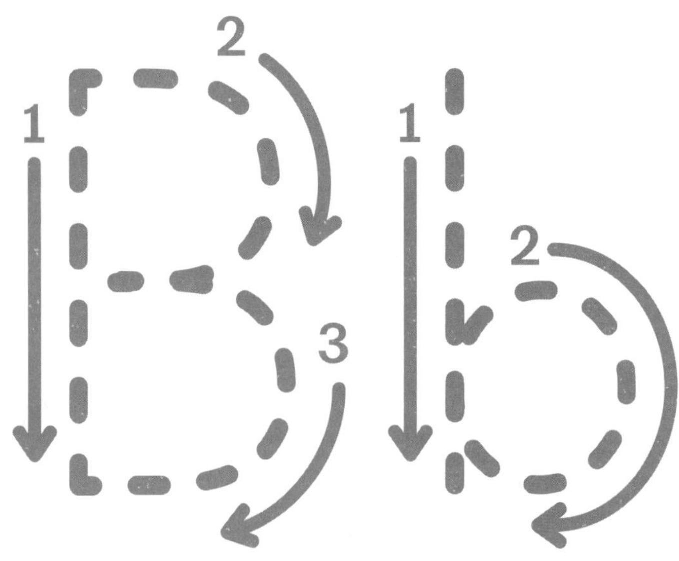

LESSON 3
Prep Page

Supply List

- ☐ Blank paper (day 1, Bible)
- ☐ Mini post-it notes (day 1, Bible)
- ☐ Real or plastic butter knife (optional)

Look Ahead

Day 1 – Draw a large cross outline on the blank piece of paper for Bible time.

Day 2 – Gift package with word GRACE inside

Objectives

Letter of the week: Cc

Skills/Concepts: Understanding weather terms, overview of seasons, color sorting, tracing

Memory Verse

John 3:16

For God so loved the world that he gave his one and only Son, that whoever believes in him shall not perish but have eternal life.

Extended Activities

String Cheerios on yarn for extra-fine motor control.

LESSON 3
Day 1

LIFE SKILLS:

"Ready for some fun? Let's see if you can stay between the lines on the worksheet on the next page! Be sure to try and do your best! Then we will learn our memory verse.

Trace inside the lines on the next page.

Color Game: Have the students get several items from around the house and sort them into piles based on color.

BIBLE:

"In our memory verse this week in John 3:16:

Echo read the verse. Add motions.

For God  so loved the world  that

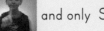

he gave his one and only Son,

that whoever believes  in him

shall not perish but have eternal life  .

"I am so thankful for Jesus! This week, I want you to think about how much God loves us and how we can show grace and forgiveness to others. Being forgiving is a great way to be like Christ. If someone hurts you by accident, then you can forgive them. If your brother/sister breaks your toy, you can forgive them. Look for ways to show forgiveness to others.

"In 2 Corinthians 12:9, it says: "But he said to me, 'My grace is sufficient for you, for my power is made perfect in weakness.' Therefore I will boast all the more gladly about my weaknesses, so that Christ's power may rest on me."

"We can use post-it notes to write down different sins. Sin is anything that separates us from God… like lying or hitting others. Help me think of some sins.

Write each one on a post-it note and stick it on you and the child.

"We are covered with sins we wrote. But grace entered in when Jesus died on the Cross for our sins. When we ask Him to forgive us, He takes each one of these sins *(remove them one at a time and start to place on the Cross)*, and now, we are free through the blood of Jesus! Isn't that amazing?! It sure is amazing grace!

""My grace is sufficient." Sufficient is a big word that means "enough." An example would be that the amount of blocks I have is sufficient for both of us. Or the amount of blocks I have is enough for both of us. So, this verse is God speaking and saying His grace is sufficient. Grace is amazing. Grace is when God favors us or is kind when we don't deserve or earn it.

RHYME TIME:

"Our poem this week is called "I Am the Wind." Let's read it now.

Read "I Am the Wind" on the next page.

Name

Trace inside the lines below. Be sure to not touch the sides and stay between the lines.

I Am the Wind

I am the wind, and I come very fast,
thro' the tall woods I can blow a loud blast.
Sometimes I am soft as a sweet, gentle child,
I play with the flowers, am quiet and mild.

And then out so loud all at once I can roar.
If you wish to be quiet, close window and door,
for I am the wind, and I come very fast,
thro' the tall woods I can blow a loud, loud blast.

LESSON 3
Day 1

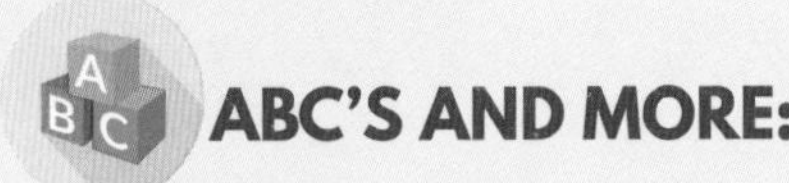

ABC'S AND MORE:

TIPS: See instructional video for this and the instructions in the beginning of the book. See Teacher Resource Section for pertinent information.

See the Teacher Resource Page.

Chant the ABC chart.

Sing the ABC song.

"Today, we will learn how you write the letters C and c.

Show the child on the ABC chart and here.

"Remember, we have capital letters and lowercase letters.

Point to the capital C. Point to the lowercase c.

"This is a capital C. This is a lowercase c.

Practice writing Cc's.

"C: (over around, leave it open)
Start a little below the top line, go over and around (over around).
And before you get to the middle line, stop and leave it open (leave it open).

"c: (over around, leave it open)
Start a little below the middle line, go over and around (over around).
And just after the bottom line, stop and leave it open (leave it open).

Trace the Cc's below.

MINI-BOOK C

See the Teacher Resource Page.

Do a picture walk.

Read the book to the student, pointing to each letter/word.

"Follow along as I read this book to you.

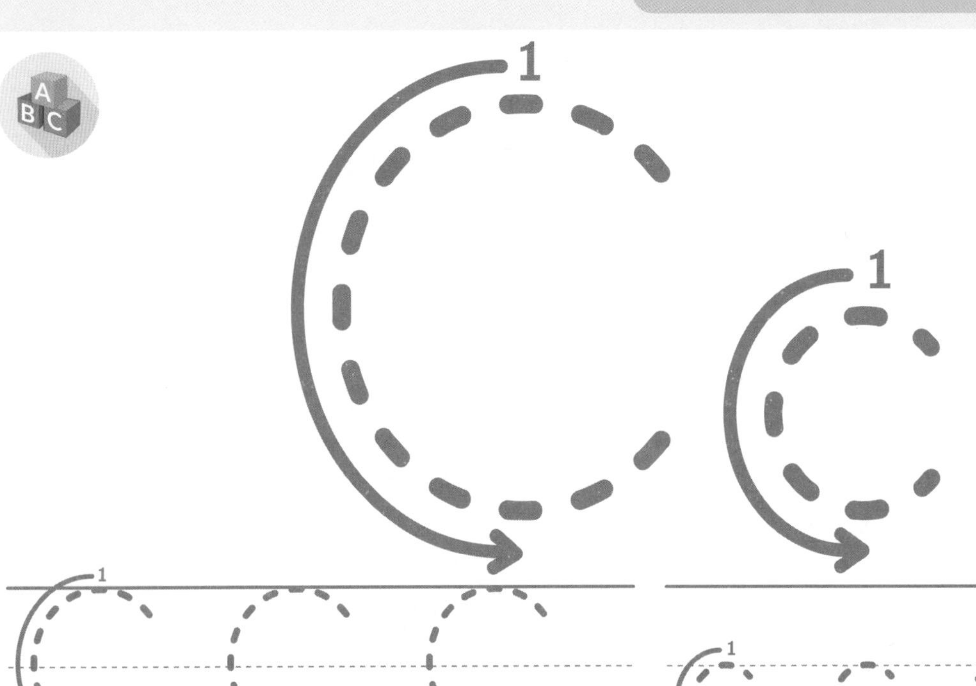

LESSON 3
Day 2

LIFE SKILLS:

"What is your favorite color? I want you to find three objects of that color.

"Color this picture using as many colors as you can or only use your three most favorite. When you are done, we will do our memory verse and rhyme time!

Color the picture below.

Color this picture using as many colors as you can!

LESSON 3
Day 2

BIBLE:

"We are talking about grace this week.

Hand them the gift (see supplies). As they open it, tell them the verse.

"In Ephesians 2:8, it says: "For it is by grace you have been saved, through faith — and this is not from yourselves, it is the gift of God." Remember, grace is not earned. It is not even something we should have, but we do because God wants to give us the gift of grace so we can be saved and live with Him forever. Grace is amazing!

Review your memory verse on page 38.

"Do you remember that being forgiving is a great way to be like Christ? Do you remember what it means to forgive someone? You know, forgiving someone helps us. It helps us not hold on to hurt which can make us feel bad. We can forgive, even if the other person doesn't ask us to. It's like that gift we talked about. What are some ways you have been able to show forgiveness to others this week?

RHYME TIME:

"Let's read our poem again.

Read "I Am the Wind."

I Am the Wind

I am the wind and I come very fast,
thro' the tall woods I can blow a loud blast.
Sometimes I am soft as a sweet, gentle child,
I play with the flowers, am quiet and mild.

And then out so loud all at once I can roar.
If you wish to be quiet, close window and door,
for I am the wind and I come very fast,
thro' the tall woods I can blow a loud, loud blast.

LESSON 3
Day 2

ABC'S AND MORE:

Use the ABC chart to chant the letters and pictures.

See the Teacher Resource Page.

Chant the ABC chart.

Sing the ABC song.

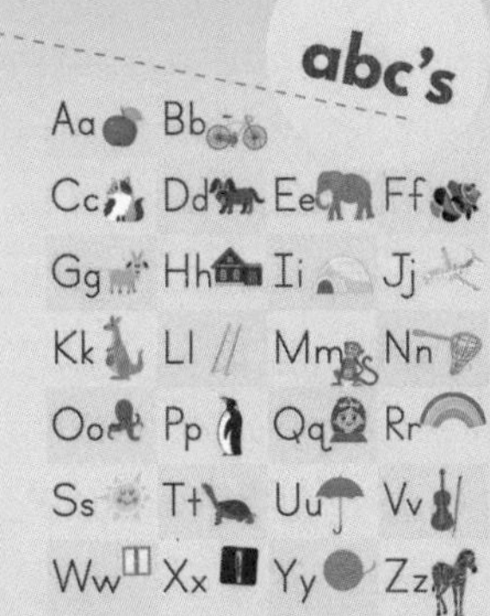

"Today, we will review how you write the letters C and c.

Point to the capital C. Point to the lowercase c.

"Remember, we have capital letters and lowercase letters. This is a capital C. This is a lowercase c.

Practice writing Cc's.

"C: (over around, leave it open)
Start a little below the top line, go over and around (over around). And before you get to the middle line, stop and leave it open (leave it open).

"c: (over around, leave it open)
Start a little below the middle line, go over and around (over around).
And just after the bottom line, stop and leave it open (leave it open).

Trace the Cc's below.

MINI-BOOK C:

Read the letter book to the student.

Have the student highlight the capital and lowercase letter of the week.

"Now, watch and follow along as I read this book to you.

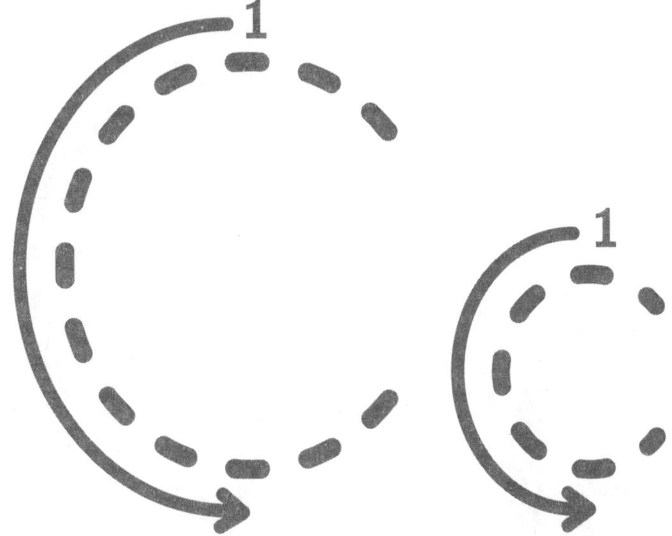

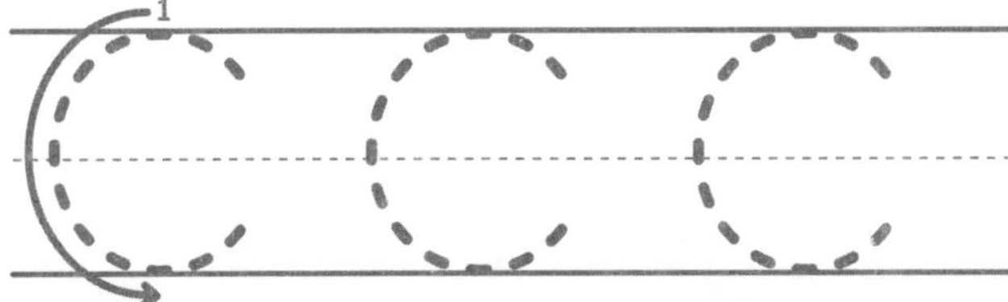

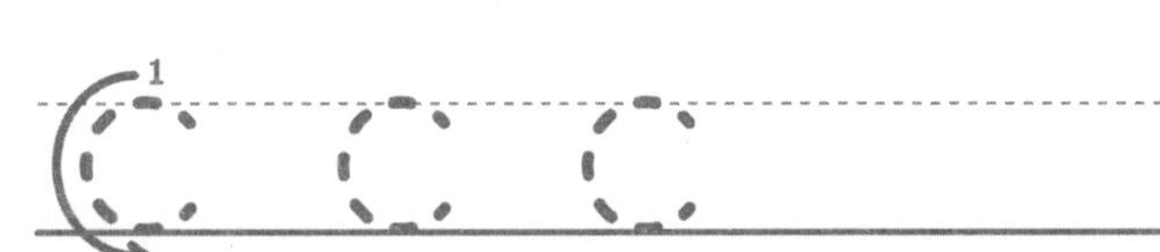

LESSON 3
Day 3

LIFE SKILLS:

"Today we will be helping the mouse get to his paint bucket.

"For more fun on the next page, match the tree from each season with the picture related to it on the next page. Then we will learn more about the Bible.

Complete both activities on the next page.

BIBLE:

"We are continuing our talk about grace this week. Ephesians 4:7 says, "But to each one of us grace has been given as Christ apportioned it."

"Jesus Christ gives each one of us the gift of grace. It is by grace we are saved through our faith in Jesus Christ. Grace makes it possible for us to have salvation. It does not matter who you are or where you are from, the gift of eternal life is for all! Jesus died for everyone.

"Remember, grace is not earned. It is not even something we should have, but we do, because God wants to give us the gift of grace so we can be saved and live with Him forever. Grace is amazing!

Review your memory verse on page 38.

"Forgiveness is what we were working on this week. What are some ways you have been able to show forgiveness to others this week? Remember, we should forgive others, just as Jesus Christ forgives us!

RHYME TIME:

Read "I Am the Wind."

"Highlight the C's and c's in the poem.

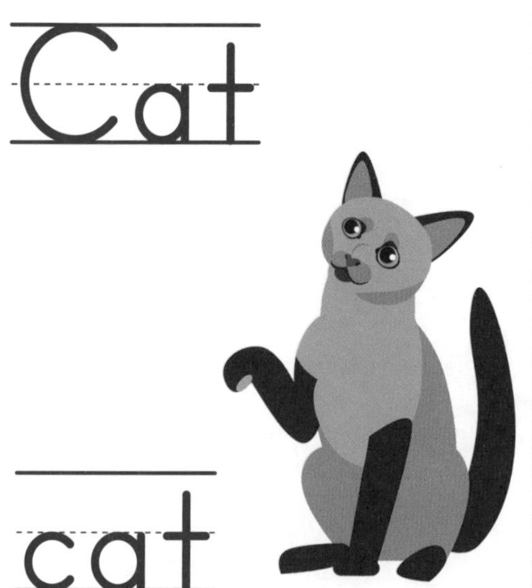

I Am the Wind

I am the wind and I come very fast,
thro' the tall woods I can blow a loud blast.
Sometimes I am soft as a sweet, gentle child,
I play with the flowers, am quiet and mild.

And then out so loud all at once I can roar.
If you wish to be quiet, close window and door,
for I am the wind and I come very fast,
thro' the tall woods I can blow a loud, loud blast.

Name

Help the mouse get to the bucket. Trace each path with your finger to find the right one. Then use a pencil.

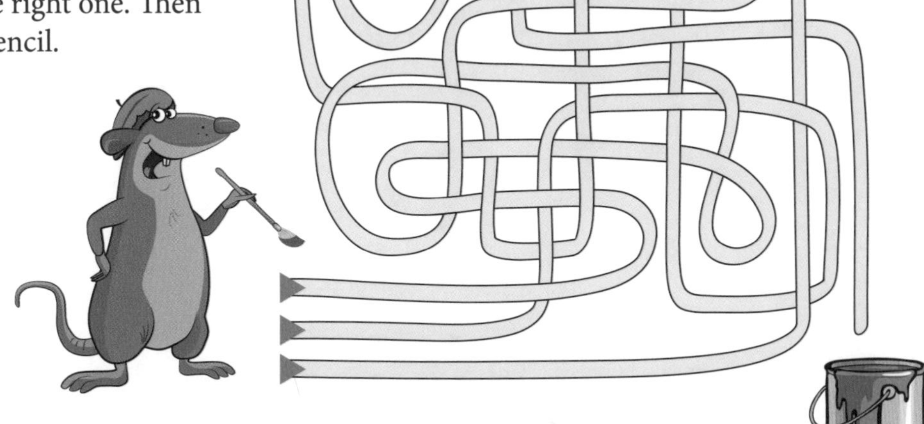

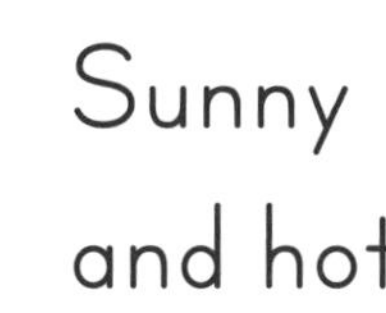

Match the tree with the weather.

Sunny and hot

Snowy

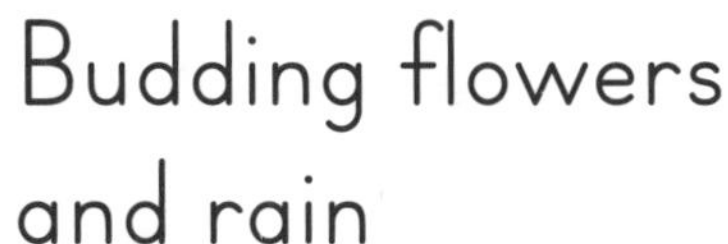

Budding flowers and rain

Fall leaves

LESSON 3
Day 3

ABC'S AND MORE:

See the Teacher Resource Page.

Chant the ABC chart.

Sing the ABC song.

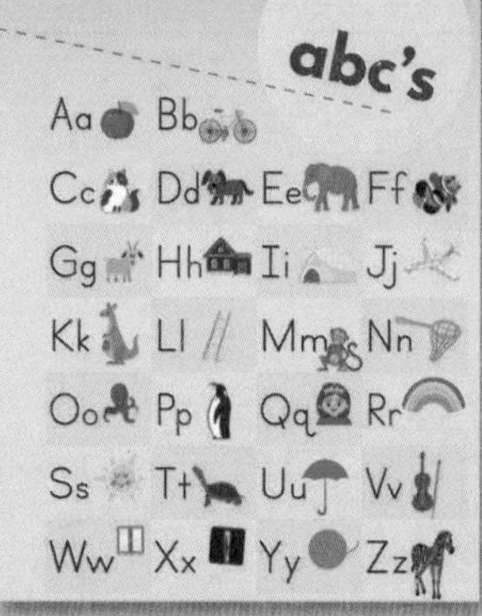

"Today, we will review how you write the letters C and c.

Have them show you the capital and lowercase c.

Practice writing Cc's.

"C: (over around, leave it open)
Start a little below the top line, go over and around (over around).
And before you get to the middle line, stop and leave it open (leave it open).

"c: (over around, leave it open)
Start a little below the middle line, go over and around (over around).
And just after the bottom line, stop and leave it open (leave it open).

Trace the Cc's below.

MINI-BOOK C:

Read the letter book again.

"Now, watch and follow along as I read this book to you.

Advanced K — see if your child can read the book to you.

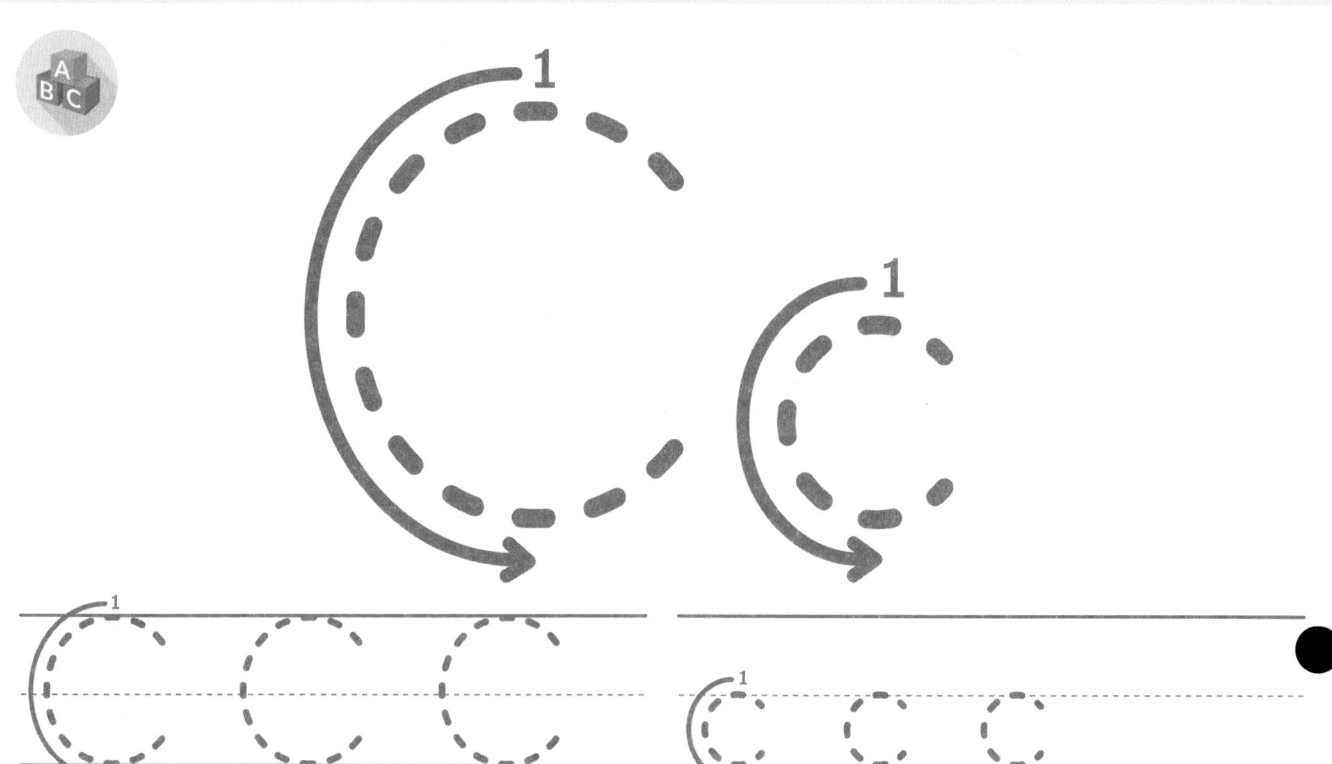

LESSON 4
Prep Page

Supply List

- ☐ Closet of clothing for life skills game
- ☐ 2 T-shirts
- ☐ Small bag or suitcase (optional)

Objectives

Letter of the week: Dd

Skills/Concepts: Folding a T-shirt, weather: dressing appropriately, cutting & gluing

Memory Verse

Psalm 13:6

I will sing the LORD's praise, for he has been good to me.

Extended Activities

Play the weather packing game each day with variations.

Pick a location in the world that has a different climate/temps than your area. Record the temperature there and your hometown. Name clothing that you might wear in each place.

Have the student dress a doll and explain why they chose the clothing they did based on the weather. (They can say because the doll went to the North Pole and so they put a hat and gloves on him/her even if it is hot where you are — pretend play is vital at this age!)

LESSON 4
Day 1

LIFE SKILLS:

"Let's play a game! We will go to your closet and pretend we are packing a bag and staying in a hotel in your town. What would you pack for today?

Help your child, with explanations, to pick appropriate clothing for the weather. Keep out two T-shirts.

"Since we have some clothing items out, let's learn how to fold shirts today!

Model how to fold and then practice.

"I am so proud of you! Do you know what it means to persevere?

Wait on answer — if no, respond like stated below; if yes, then praise them for showing perseverance.

"To persevere or perseverance is a fancy word for keeping on trying even when it is hard. Not giving up! You did that today! You showed perseverance, and I am so proud!

BIBLE:

"Did you know that Jesus rode on a donkey? Most kings would have ridden on a horse or a camel, but Jesus chose a donkey. This was a sign to them that He came in peace. Let's read this in our Bible in Matthew 21:1–11.

"Just like those people praised God in this story, we can also praise Him now. One way we can praise Him is by knowing His Word. The Bible tells us in Psalms 119 to hide God's Word in our hearts so we will not sin. The Word of God is mighty and powerful, and it helps us become better Christians.

"Complete the maze of the palm leaf on the next page, but try to not touch the walls of the maze.

"This week we will learn a verse from the Bible found in Psalm 13:6:

Echo read the verse. Add motions.

I will sing 

the LORD's praise ,

for He has been

good  to me.

RHYME TIME:

"Today, I am so excited because we get to read a new poem called "Hey Diddle Diddle"!

Read "Hey Diddle Diddle" on the next page. You can even put it to a rhythm or a song.

Name

Complete the palm leaf maze.

Hey Diddle Diddle!

Hey, diddle, diddle,
the cat and the fiddle,
the cow jumped over
the moon;
the little dog laughed
to see such sport,
and the dish ran away
with the spoon.

LESSON 4
Day 1

ABC'S AND MORE:

"Now, let's look at our ABC chart.

See Teacher Resource Page.

Chant the ABC chart.

Sing the ABC song.

Practice writing D's and d's.

"D: (down, up, curve around)
Start at the top line go down (down) and hit the bottom line. Up, to the top line (up).
Curve around and stop (curve around).

"d: (over around, up, down)
Start at the middle line, go over around and hit the bottom (over around) and go back passing the middle and hitting the top line (up).
Down and stop at the bottom line (down).

Trace the Dd's below.

MINI-BOOK D:

See the Teacher Resource Page.

Do a picture walk.

Read the book to the student, pointing to each letter/word.

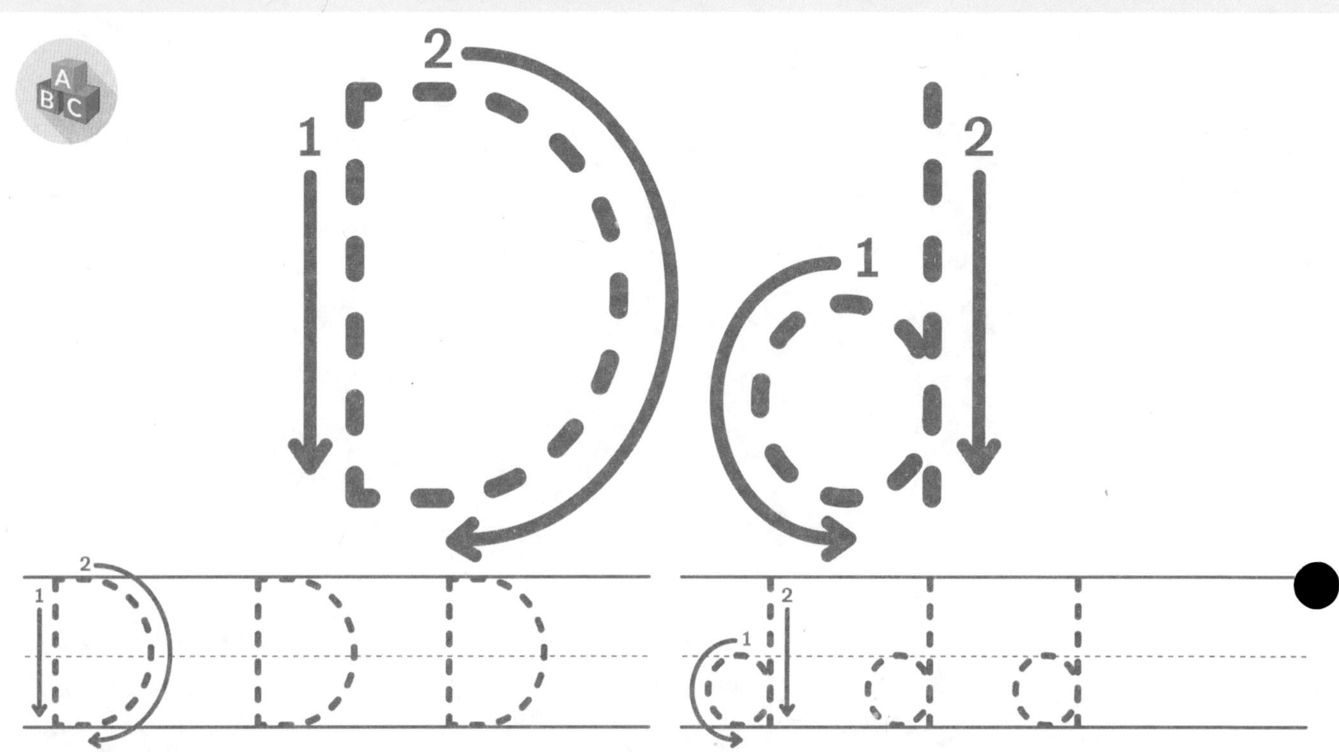

LESSON 4
Day 2

LIFE SKILLS:

Practice folding a T-shirt and putting it away.

"Today, we are going to be discussing more on weather and how to be safe in a storm. You know, even though storms might be scary, our Bible tells us that we can trust God in every situation and that He will protect us. He also gives us tools to help us, like the chart on the next page.

Review the safety tips on the next page with your student and then display later as a reminder.

BIBLE:

"Have you ever been in a storm? Were you scared or afraid?

"Did you know that in the Bible in the Book of John it tells about Jesus calming a storm? Can you imagine walking outside and telling the wind and rain to stop and be quiet and then it did? Let's read to see what really happened in Mark 4:35–41.

Be dramatic in your reading.

Review your memory verse on page 48.

"WOW! That is amazing isn't it? That just shows you how big and powerful God really is!

RHYME TIME:

Read poem "Hey Diddle Diddle" on page 49.

"Now let's read "Hey Diddle Diddle" again and see if you can say it with me.

Allow for student response to the following questions.

"Wow . . . umm . . . what jumped over the moon? *(the cow)* Can you imagine a little dog laughing or a dish running away with a spoon?

"Create a drawing that shows what you picture in your head when you hear the rhyme. Let me read it again so you can close your eyes and play a movie in your mind that you can then illustrate. Illustrate means to be the artist and draw to show what you see.

Remember, praising them for the effort and persevering (even when frustrated) is important.

Dinosaur dinosaur

LIGHTNING SAFETY

Seek shelter in building

Do NOT swim, get out of water

Do NOT carry umbrella

HURRICANE SAFETY

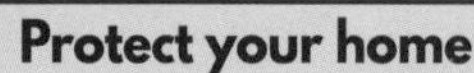

Protect your home

Stay on the news

Plan evacuation route

EARTHQUAKE SAFETY

Get under desk or table and hold on

Cover your neck and head

Do not stand in doorway

TORNADO SAFETY

Seek shelter in interior room with no windows or storm shelter

Keep a flashlight and water

Cover your neck and head

LESSON 4
Day 2

ABC'S AND MORE:

Chant the ABC chart.

Sing the ABC song.

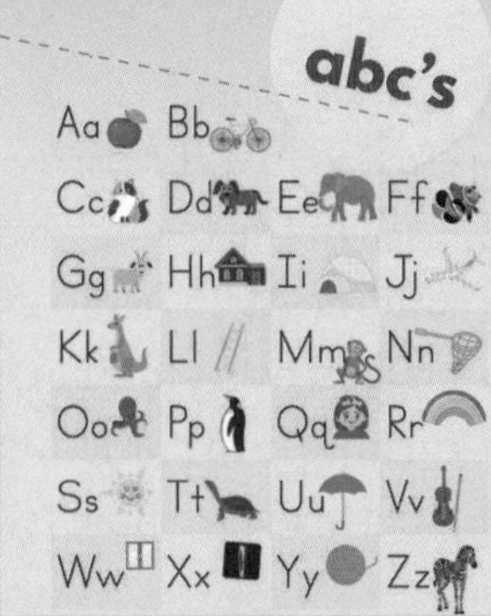

"Use your ABC chart to find ANY five capital letters. Use your ABC chart to find five lowercase letters.

"Let's review writing the letter Dd.

Point to the capital D. Point to the lowercase d.

"Remember there is both a capital D and a lowercase d.

Practice writing D's and d's.

"D: (Down, up, curve around)
Start at the top line go down (down) and hit the bottom line. Up, to the top line (up).
Curve around and stop (curve around).

"d: (over around, up, down)
Start at the middle line, go over around and hit the bottom (over around) and go back passing the middle and hitting the top line (up).
Down and stop at the bottom line (down).

Trace the Dd's below.

Read the letter book to the student.

Have the student highlight the capital and lowercase letter of the week.

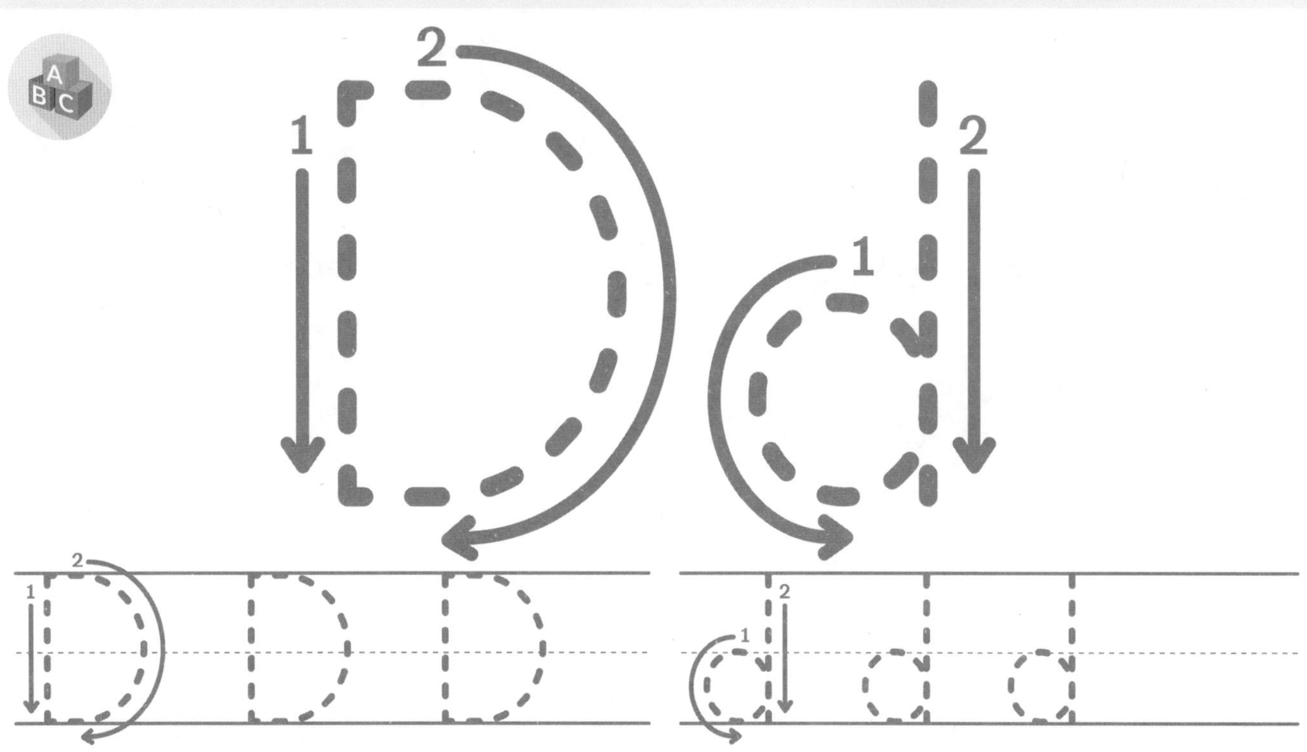

LESSON 4
Day 3

LIFE SKILLS:

“Show me how good you are at folding T-shirts.

Have them narrate (talk through the steps) to you as they do it, offering assistance or clues if/when needed. Praise them for persevering in the task.

BIBLE:

“A few ways we can praise and honor God is by reading and memorizing His Word.

Review your memory verse on page 48.

“Do you enjoy being outside? You know what I love about being outside?

If not raining, go outside and find nature to observe.

“I love that I can see all the things God created just for us! The Bible says in Genesis 1:1, “In the beginning God created the heavens and the earth.” About 6,000 years ago, He created everything! Can you imagine nothing turning into something so beautiful? You know what else the Bible tells me?

“That God created you and me in HIS image. Isn't it amazing how special He thinks we are? I think you are special, too. This week you have shown such perseverance and you have tried new and hard things, but you have persevered and that makes me proud that you have tried your best even when it was hard.

RHYME TIME:

“Our poem this week is “Hey Diddle Diddle.”

Read “Hey Diddle Diddle.”

“While we have our listening ears on, let's say our rhyme of “Hey Diddle Diddle.” Highlight letters D and d.

Duck

duck

Hey Diddle Diddle!

Hey, diddle, diddle,
the cat and the fiddle,
the cow jumped over the moon;
the little dog laughed
to see such sport,
and the dish ran away with the spoon.

LESSON 4
Day 3

ABC'S AND MORE:

See the Teacher Resource Page.

Chant the ABC chart.

Sing the ABC song.

"Let's review writing Dd's.

Practice writing D's and d's.

"D: (down, up, curve around)
Start at the top line go down (down) and hit the bottom line. Up, to the top line (up).
Curve around and stop (curve around).

"d: (over around, up, down)
Start at the middle line, go over around and hit the bottom (over around) and go back passing the middle and hitting the top line (up).
Down and stop at the bottom line (down).

Trace the Dd's below.

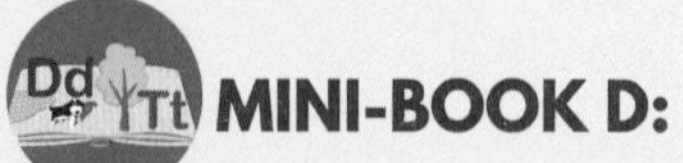

MINI-BOOK D:

Read the letter book again.

Advanced K — see if your child can read the book to you.

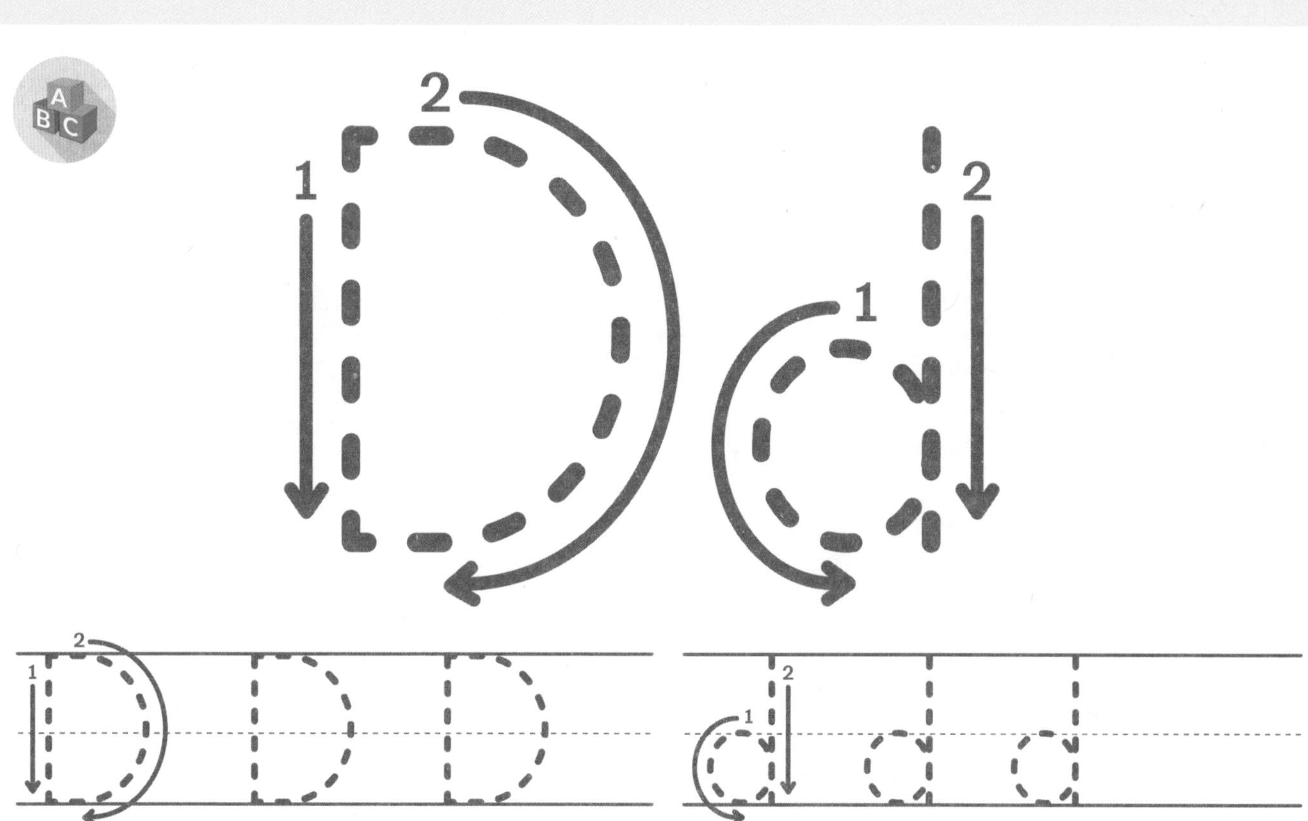

LESSON 5
Prep Page

Supply List

- ☐ 1-4 straws (day 2, Bible)
- ☐ Mirror (day 2, life skills)
- ☐ 3 small treats
- ☐ Emotions chart (daily, life skills)

Objectives

Letter of the week: Ee

Skills/Concepts: Emotions (chart daily), sizes (big, little, tall, short)

Memory Verse

Proverbs 16:32

Better a patient person than a warrior…
One with self-control…
Than one who takes a city…

Extended Activities

Teach them to fold towels and talk about how they are the shape of a rectangle.

LESSON 5
Day 1

LIFE SKILLS:

"This week will be talking about emotions.

Show the child the emotions chart on page 427.

"We have a really neat chart that helps us understand emotions. We were created by God to be emotional! We have several emotions. Sometimes, emotions are difficult to explain. Let's look at this chart to discuss each one and when you might feel that way.

BIBLE:

"You know the Bible talks about emotions. It even tells us Jesus cried in John 11:35. We have to be able to show self-control. Self-control is being able to be boss of our emotions. We cannot let our emotions be the boss and take control. The Bible tells us to be angry, but do not sin. God knew we would become angry over things, but if we throw fits and yell, hit, and say mean things, then our anger is being the boss, not us. If we become angry, and use our words to say "I am angry," but we keep ourselves from throwing a fit, then that is self-control. This week, we will be practicing self-control when we go about our day. Not just with anger, but in all emotions. Let's help each other remember to use self-control throughout this week.

"The Bible is such a good tool for us. In Proverbs 16:32, it says:

Echo read the verse. Add motions.

Better a patient  person than a warrior  one with self-control  than one who takes a city.

"I love how that verse tells me it is better to be a person with self-control. Some emotions are more positive emotions, like excitement! I know a story in the Bible about a man who got really excited. He was also persistent! Let's look at this story about this man named Bartimaeus…you can call him Blind Bart.

Read Mark 10:46-52. Read this with enthusiasm as if you were Bartimaeus and were desperate to be healed.

"You see, when Blind Bart heard Jesus was coming, he became excited because he knew Jesus could heal him. Then, when the crowd told him to be quiet, Blind Bart was persistent because he so desperately wanted to see. Then, when they told Blind Bart to come to Jesus, He was so excited that he jumped up on his feet and went to Jesus. Then, he followed Jesus. This emotion of excitement was a good or positive emotion.

Use the emotions chart.

"Looking back at our emotion chart, how do you think you would feel if you were Blind Bart?

LESSON 5
Day 1

RHYME TIME:

"We have a new nursery rhyme this week called "Little Boy Blue." Let's read it.

Read poem "Little Boy Blue."

"Do you know why it says "little boy blue"? Blue is a color, but the word blue can also mean sad. Have you ever been sad? Tell me about a time when you were sad. Was there anything anyone did to help you be happy?

Eagle

eagle

Little Boy Blue

Little Boy Blue, come blow your horn,
the sheep's in the meadow, the cow's in the corn.
Where is the boy who looks after the sheep?
He's under a haystack, he's fast asleep.
Will you wake him? Oh no, not I,
for if I do, he'll surely cry.

LESSON 5
Day 1

ABC'S AND MORE:

"Now, let's look at our ABC chart."

See the Teacher Resource Page.

Sing the ABC song.

Chant the ABC chart.

"Let's learn to write our Ee's today! Don't forget, there are capital letters and lowercase letters. Let's review them."

Point to the capital E. Point to the lowercase e.

"Here is the capital E and the lowercase e."

Practice writing E's and e's.

"E: (down, out, out, out)
Start at the top line, go down to the bottom line (down)
Go out at the top line (out)
Go out at the middle line (out)
Go out at the bottom line (out)"

"e: (out, over around, leave it open)
We learned a c, and this is kind of like that. First, you start between the middle line and bottom line. Make a line out (out)
Then, go over around (like a c, over around).
And leave it open a little past the bottom line (leave it open)."

Trace the Ee's below.

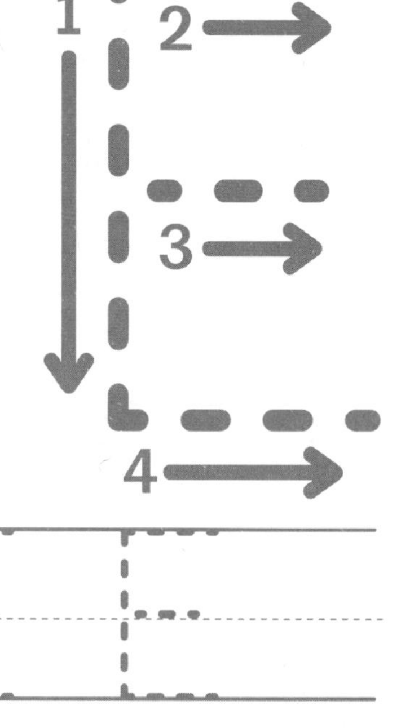

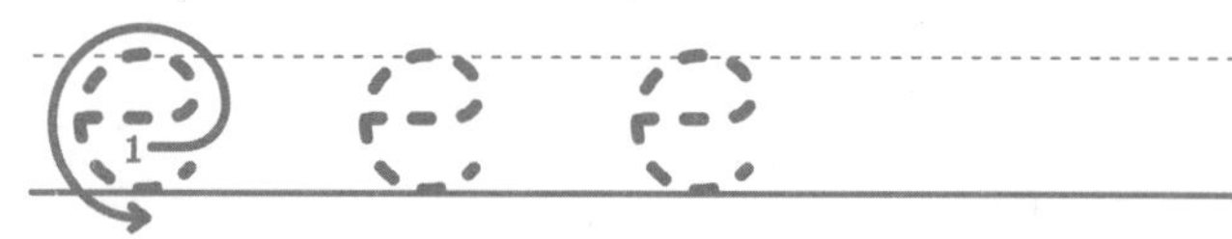

LESSON 5
Day 1

MINI-BOOK E:

See the Teacher Resource Page.

Ee
mini book

Do a picture walk.

Read the book to the student, pointing to each letter/word.

" Now, watch as I read this book.

Eggs eggs

LESSON 5
Day 2

LIFE SKILLS:

Use the emotions chart to play the Mimic Game:

"I want to play a little game using our Emotions chart. We need to get to a mirror. We will try to make the same faces that are on our chart and check our faces in the mirror.

BIBLE:

"Joy is another word for happy, but it is not just being happy in a moment. An example is when you get a new toy for your birthday. In that moment, you are happy, but joy is being able to be happy all the time, or most of the time. The Bible tells us in Psalms 98:6, "with trumpets and the blast of the ram's horn — shout for joy before the Lord, the King."

"Today we will use straws to make an instrument to make a joyful noise!

FLUTES: Flatten one end of a straw and cut the edges into a V-shape tip. Then, place it between your lips (one point on top, other on the bottom), seal your lips around it, begin to blow as you slowly pull it out until it begins to vibrate and make the noise. (kind of sounds like a kazoo)

TIPS: If you want to, you can do this with more straws and cut off some length to see the difference in sounds. The shorter the straw, the higher the pitch.

"We are talking about self-control this week. Do you remember what self-control is?

"Right, it's you being the boss of your emotions. Have you shown self-control anytime this week? What about in showing self-control in your schoolwork? Or playing with ____?

Review your memory verse on page 58.

RHYME TIME:

"Do you remember why it says "Little Boy Blue"?

Read poem "Little Boy Blue."

"Blue is a color, but the word blue can also mean sad. Can you show me on our chart the sad emotion?

Little Boy Blue

Little Boy Blue, come blow your horn,
the sheep's in the meadow, the cow's in the corn.
Where is the boy who looks after the sheep?
He's under a haystack, he's fast asleep.
Will you wake him? Oh no, not I,
for if I do, he'll surely cry.

LESSON 5
Day 2

ABC'S AND MORE:

"Now, let's look at our ABC chart.

Chant the ABC chart.

Sing or play the ABC song.

"Let's write our Ee's again!

Point to the capital E.
Point to the lowercase e.

"Remember the capital E and the lowercase e.

Practice writing Ee's.

"E: (down, out, out, out)
Start at the top line, go down to the bottom line (down)
Go out at the top line (out)
Go out at the middle line (out)
Go out at the bottom line (out)

"e: (out, over around, leave it open)
Remember, you start between the middle line and bottom line. Make a line out (out)
Then, go over around (like a c, over around)
And leave it open a little past the bottom line (leave it open)

Trace the Ee's below.

MINI-BOOK E:

Read the letter book to the student.

Have the student highlight the Ee's.

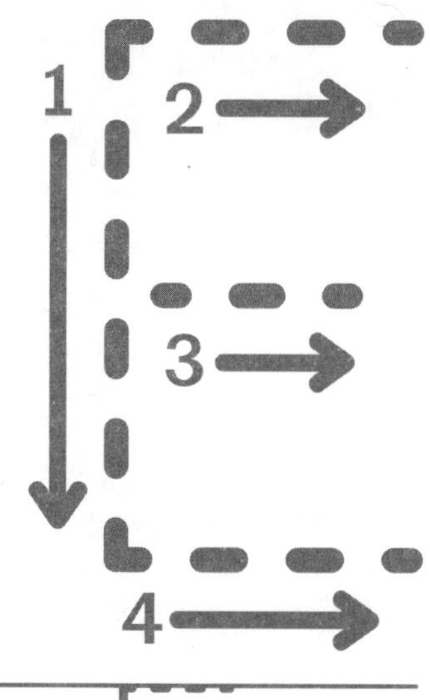

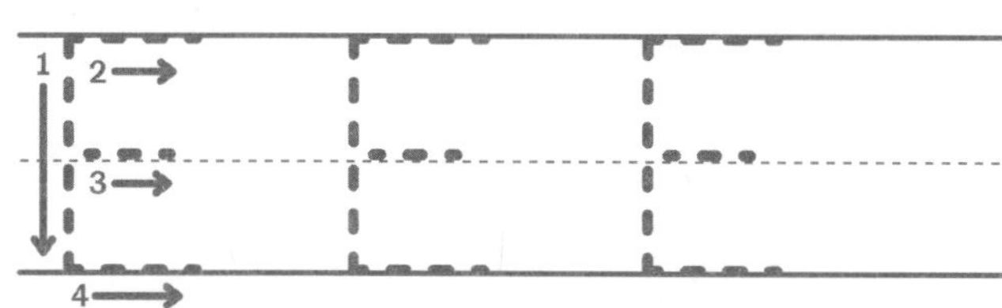

LESSON 5
Day 3

LIFE SKILLS:

Emotions Game: (use emotions chart).

"I will tell you a story and you will find the emotion on our chart that shows how you think you would feel.

"Hayden was coloring his schoolwork. Someone bumped his arm and made him make a huge mark across the page. How do you think that made Hayden feel? Show me the face you think Hayden was making.

Answers will vary, but it should be appropriate. If not, you should discuss a possible answer.

"Katie had been trying to learn to tie her shoes. Her older brother helped her learn how. How do you think Katie feels?

"Josiah and Sarah were listening to the weatherman as he talked about a tornado. Later, at bedtime, it began to storm, and Sarah did not want to go to her room. How do you think Sarah was feeling?

"Josie had asked for a new pet. She asked for a puppy dog a few weeks before, but her mom said no. Today is her birthday and she woke up to find a new puppy. How do you think Josie feels?

BIBLE:

"I know a story in the Bible where I think two people felt sad. I will read a brief description of this story.

Or you may read the story as it is in Genesis chapters 2–3.

"Adam and Eve were in a beautiful garden that God made just for them. He told them they could eat from any tree, except one, or they would die. A serpent came to Eve and told her that she would not die if she ate from that tree, but that it would open her eyes and she would be like God and know good from evil. Eve listened to the serpent and disobeyed God, then she gave the same fruit to Adam and he also disobeyed God. God was upset and sent Adam and Eve out of the Garden of Eden forever. He even put angels to guard the entrance of the garden so Adam and Eve could not enter again.

"Do you think Adam and Eve were sad that they had to leave the Garden of Eden? I think they were. Now, color the following page that shows Adam and Eve leaving the Garden of Eden.

Color the picture on the next page.

"We are talking about self-control this week. Do you remember what self-control is? Right — it's you being the boss of your emotions. Do you think Adam and Eve showed self-control?

Set out the treats (candy or some other treat they would really want).
Tell them they can have one now, or if they wait until you come back, they can have all three. Leave the room for three minutes, saying nothing else.

"Waiting on something we really want is difficult. We all want what we want NOW. Self-control is when we can control ourselves, or be the boss, long enough to get the reward.

Review your memory verse on page 58.

Name

Color this picture.

LESSON 5
Day 3

RHYME TIME:

"Let's read our poem again!

Read "Little Boy Blue" on page 59.

ABC'S AND MORE:

"Now, let's look at our ABC chart. Show me three capital letters.
Show me three lowercase letters.

See Teacher Resource Page.

Chant the ABC chart.

Sing the ABC song.

"Let's review how we write our Ee's!

Practice writing Ee's.

"E: (down, out, out, out)
Start at the top line, go down to the bottom line (down).
Go out at the top line (out).
Go out at the middle line (out).
Go out at the bottom line (out).

"e: (out, over around, leave it open)
First, you start between the middle line and bottom line. Make a line out (out).
Then, go over around (like a c, over around)
And leave it open a little past the bottom line (leave it open).

Trace the Ee's below.

MINI-BOOK E:

Read the letter book again.

Advanced K — see if your child can read the book to you.

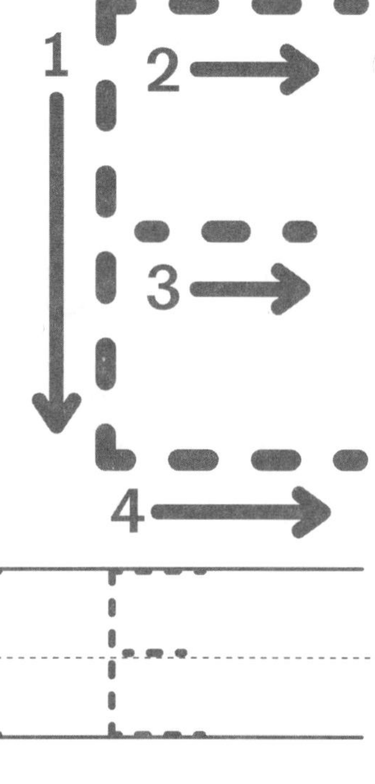

LESSON 6
Prep Page

Supply List

- ☐ Emotions chart (daily, life skills)

Look Ahead

Please look ahead to Lesson 7 supply list. There is a project and 2 hearts from black/red paper to make.

Objectives

Letter of the week: Ff

Skills/Concepts: Emotions (chart daily), sizes (teeny tiny, ginormous, wide, deep)

Memory Verse

3 John 1:11

Dear friend, do not imitate what is evil but what is good. Anyone who does what is good is from God. Anyone who does what is evil has not seen God.

Extended Activities

Use the emotions chart to help them throughout the day with their emotions and being able to express which one they are feeling/expressing at different times.

LESSON 6
Day 1

LIFE SKILLS:

Emotions Match: Match the emotion with its picture.

Match the words and faces from the chart to things that might cause those emotions: A storm might make you scared (storm=scared). For example, playing with friends might make you happy (playing with friends=happy). Now look at the others and come up with some on your own!

BIBLE:

"Remember last week I told you about how the Bible says to "be angry and sin not"? Well, one time, Jesus even became angry. Let's read about that now in John 2:13–17.

"Jesus was angry because they were taking money from the people for their sacrifices. Jesus knew this was not right. The temple is a holy place. Jesus made them all leave and told them to stop using the temple in that way. (Temple is another word for House of God.) Then, everyone was in shock, wanting to know who He was that He could tell them what to do. Jesus knew how important a sacrifice was because He was going to be the sacrifice for everyone's sins when He died on the Cross. He didn't want them to think His sacrifice meant nothing or for it to be a way for them to make money. He wanted it to be a way for people to come to Him and live in heaven with him.

"The Bible is such a good tool for us. In 3 John 1:11, it says:

Echo read the verse. Add motions.

Dear friend, do not  imitate what is evil but what is good . Anyone who does what is good  is from God. Anyone who does what is evil  has not seen  God.

LESSON 6
Day 1

RHYME TIME:

"I really like our poem this week since it reminds me of what our verse says and about making good choices.

"Our poem this week is "Good Night, Sleep Tight." I will read it to you.

Read "Good Night, Sleep Tight."

Good Night, Sleep Tight

Good night, sleep tight,
wake up bright
in the morning light,
to do what's right
with all your might.

Frog frog

LESSON 6
Day 1

ABC'S AND MORE:

"Now, let's look at our ABC chart. Show me three capital letters. Show me three lowercase letters.

See the Teacher Resource Page.

Chant the ABC chart.

Sing the ABC song.

"Let's learn to write Ff's today!

Point to the capital F. Point to the lowercase f.

"First, look at the capital and lowercase Ff's.

"F: (down, out, out)
Start at the top line, go down to the bottom line (down).
Go out at the top line (out).
Go out at the middle line (out).

"f: (curve up, down, across in the middle)
Start between the middle line and the top line
Curve up to the top line (curve up).
Down to the bottom line (down)
Cross it at the middle line (across in the middle).

Trace the Ff's below.

MINI-BOOK F:

See the Teacher Resource Page.

Do a picture walk.

Read the book to the student, pointing to each letter/word.

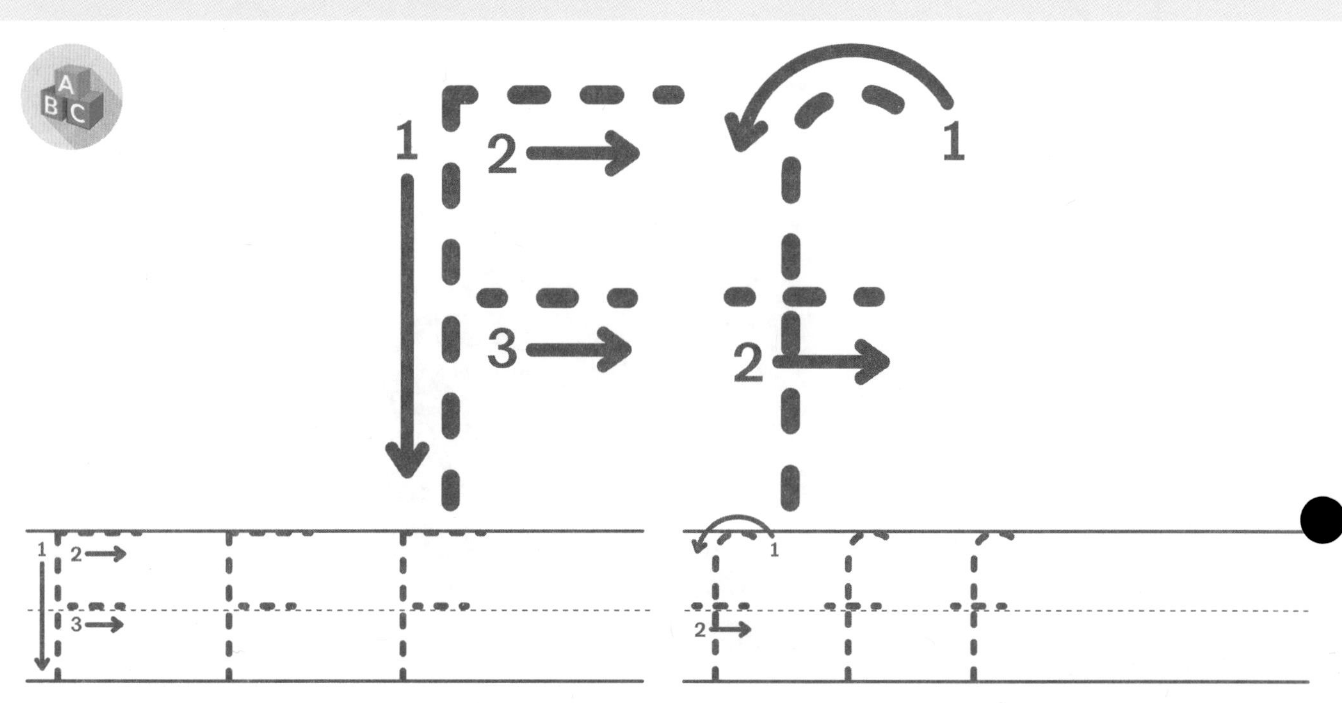

LESSON 6
Day 2

LIFE SKILLS:

"First, let's review what we have learned about emotions. We often see and use emojis to represent emotions. On the next page, you will select the correct emoji that matches the emotion shown by each picture.

"Now, this week I want us to focus on "doing what is right." Sometimes, doing what is right is not fun. Sometimes doing the right thing is not easy. It takes a lot for us to make the right choice. It is like taking self-control a small step further. We have to decide to be kind, thankful, show grace, love, tell the truth, and so on. I know that you can show me ways that you choose to make the right choices this week. Let's think of a way you can do what is right. If your brother/sister takes your toy, would the right thing be to hit them or ask for the toy back? Yes! Doing what is right also takes patience. I know this is a difficult concept, but I know you can do the right thing this week! Let's practice that every day this week.

BIBLE:

"Do what's right! Let's read the story of Mary and Joseph in Matthew 1:18–25.

"Mary and Joseph were afraid or scared. It took an angel of the Lord to calm their fear. See, Joseph was not really sure what the right thing was. It was also scary to Joseph. He couldn't see God's plan and did not understand that he would be the earthly father of God's son. The angel showed Joseph. Joseph did the right thing even though it was not the easy thing to do. He married and protected Mary so God's plan and salvation through Jesus Christ could be for all people. I know that you too can make good choices. One way we can know our choices are good is to pray and ask for God's help. He will help us.

Review your memory verse on page 68.

"The memory verse says do not imitate what is evil, but what is good. Imitate means to copy someone's actions or words.

Play the mimic game again from page 62. Take turns or add siblings.

RHYME TIME:

"Our poem this week is "Good Night, Sleep Tight." Let's read it now.

Read poem "Good Night, Sleep Tight" on page 69. You can even put it to a rhythm or song.

Lesson 6
Day 2

Name

Circle the emoji under each picture that matches best the emotion in the picture above it. (Hint! Look for clues in the pictures!)

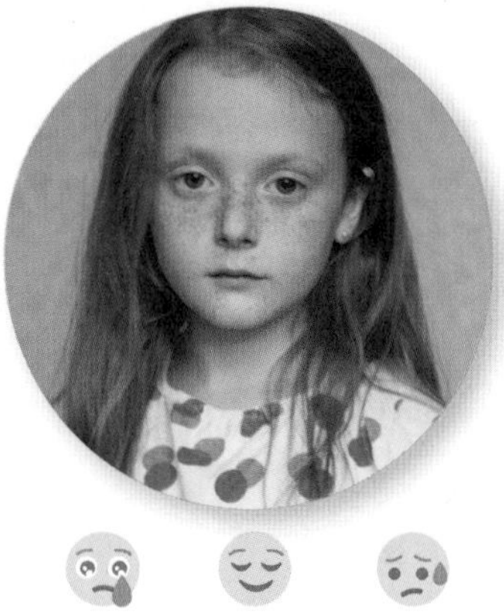

LESSON 6
Day 2

ABC'S AND MORE:

"Now, let's look at our ABC chart. Show me three capital letters. Show me three lowercase letters.

Sing the ABC song.

Chant the ABC chart.

"Let's write our Ff's!

"Remember that we have capital letters and lowercase letters.

Point to the capital F. Point to the lowercase F.

"This is the capital F. This is the lowercase F. Can you point each one out like I just did?

Practice writing Ff's.

"F: (down, out, out)
Start at the top line, go down to the bottom line (down).
Go out at the top line (out).
Go out at the middle line (out).

"f: (curve up, down, across in the middle)
Start between the middle line and the top line
Curve up to the top line (curve up)
Down to the bottom line (down)
Cross it at the middle line (across in the middle)

Trace the Ff's below.

MINI-BOOK F:

Read the letter book to the student.

Have the student highlight the capital and lowercase letter of the week.

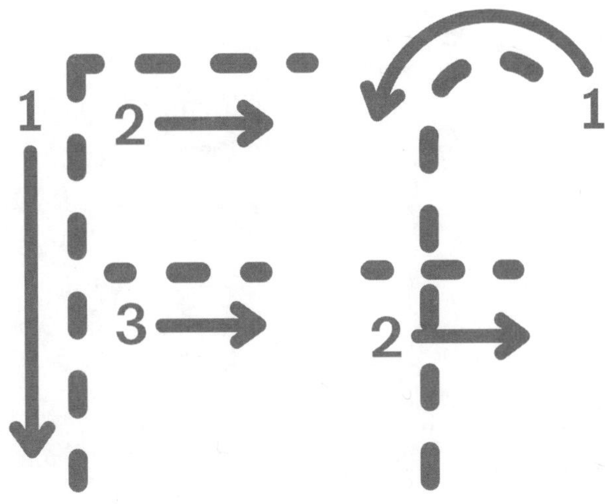

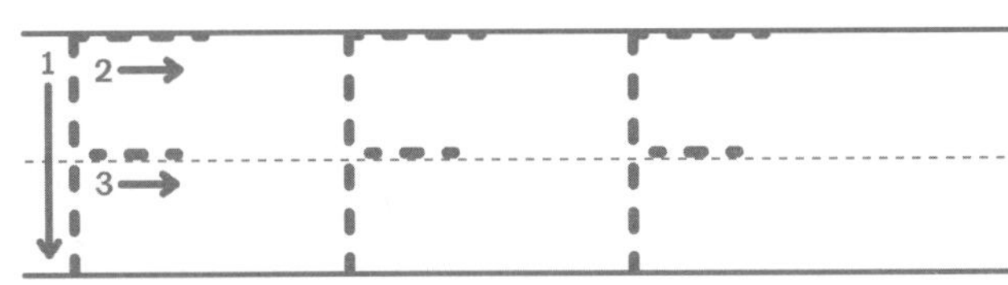

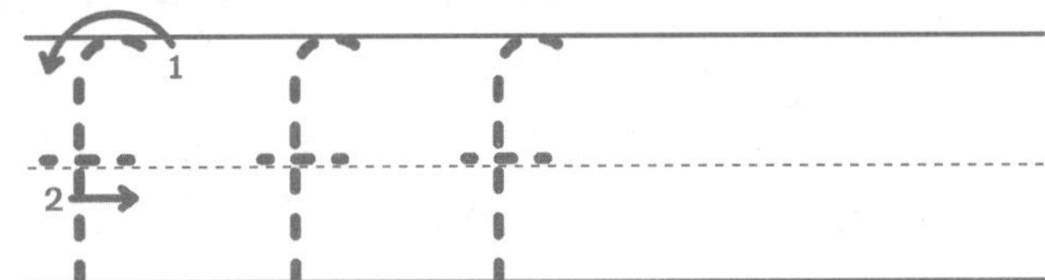

LESSON 6
Day 3

LIFE SKILLS:

Using the Bible stories we have talked about the past two weeks, match them with the emotion the people felt.

Adam/Eve kicked out of garden=sad
Blind Bart healed=excited
Jesus angry in temple=angry/mad
Mary/Joseph=scared

BIBLE:

"You know, there were times in the Bible when some people should have been afraid, but instead they showed courage and bravery! They did the right thing! Here is a story of three men who did what was right. It is found in Daniel 3. Daniel and his three friends, named Shadrach, Meshach, and Abednego, should have been afraid or scared, but they knew they served a mighty God, and instead they showed courage. The king during that time had a dream, and no one could tell him what it meant. So he became angry and was going to have all the wise men killed. This included Daniel and his three friends. So the four men prayed to God and he gave them the meaning of the king's dream. Then, about 15 years later, the king built a tower of a golden statue that was 90 feet tall. He commanded everyone to bow down and worship that golden statue. If people refused to worship the statue, they would be thrown into a fiery furnace. Shadrach, Meshach, and Abednego were three of the king's officials and they refused to bow to the statue because they served God!

"The king gave them a warning, and the men still refused to bow to the statue, and they said God would save them. That shows faith, not fear. This made the king even more angry. He had the fire turned up to seven times hotter than normal. He had soldiers put Shadrach, Meshach, and Abednego into the furnace. All of a sudden, they could see four men walking around in the fire! The king ordered that they all come out and everyone was amazed that Shadrach, Meshach, and Abednego were not harmed and didn't even smell like the fire! Then, the king praised God. Shadrach, Meshach, and Abednego did what was right, but it sure was not easy, was it? They had to stand up to the king and go against his orders to follow God and do what was right. They showed great courage and bravery.

(Adapted from on "Shadrach. Meshach, and Abednego," *10 Minute Bible Journey,* p. 121–122)

Review the memory verse on page 68.

LESSON 6
Day 3

"It says do not imitate what is evil, but what is good. Imitate means to copy someone's actions or words. If Shadrach, Meshach, and Abednego would have bowed down like the king said, they would be imitating others instead of imitating Christ. We need to make sure that we always obey and follow God, not man.

"Let's read our poem now.

Read poem "Good Night, Sleep Tight."

"There are not any F's to highlight in the poem, so highlight the F's and f's in the following story:

Funny Freddie Forrester gave Wilma Fortson a frog named Fred. She fidgeted while she held him between her fingers. The frog licked Wilma's face. She screamed as she jumped and the frog flew through the air. Funny Freddie Forrester's frog gave Wilma Fortson quite a fright.

LESSON 6
Day 3

ABC'S AND MORE:

"Now, let's look at our ABC chart.

See Teacher Resource Page.

Chant the ABC chart.

Sing the ABC song.

"Let's review how we write our Ff's!

Point to the capital F.
Point to the lowercase f.

"Now, you point to the capital F. Point to the lowercase f.

Practice writing Ff's.

"F: (down, out, out)
Start at the top line, go down to the bottom line (down).
Go out at the top line (out).
Go out at the middle line (out).

"f: (curve up, down, across in the middle)
Start between the middle line and the top line
Curve up to the top line (curve up).
Down to the bottom line (down),
Cross it at the middle line (across in the middle).

Trace the Ff's below.

Do the Letter Hunt activity on the next page.

MINI-BOOK F:

Read the letter book again.

Advanced K — see if your child can read the book to you.

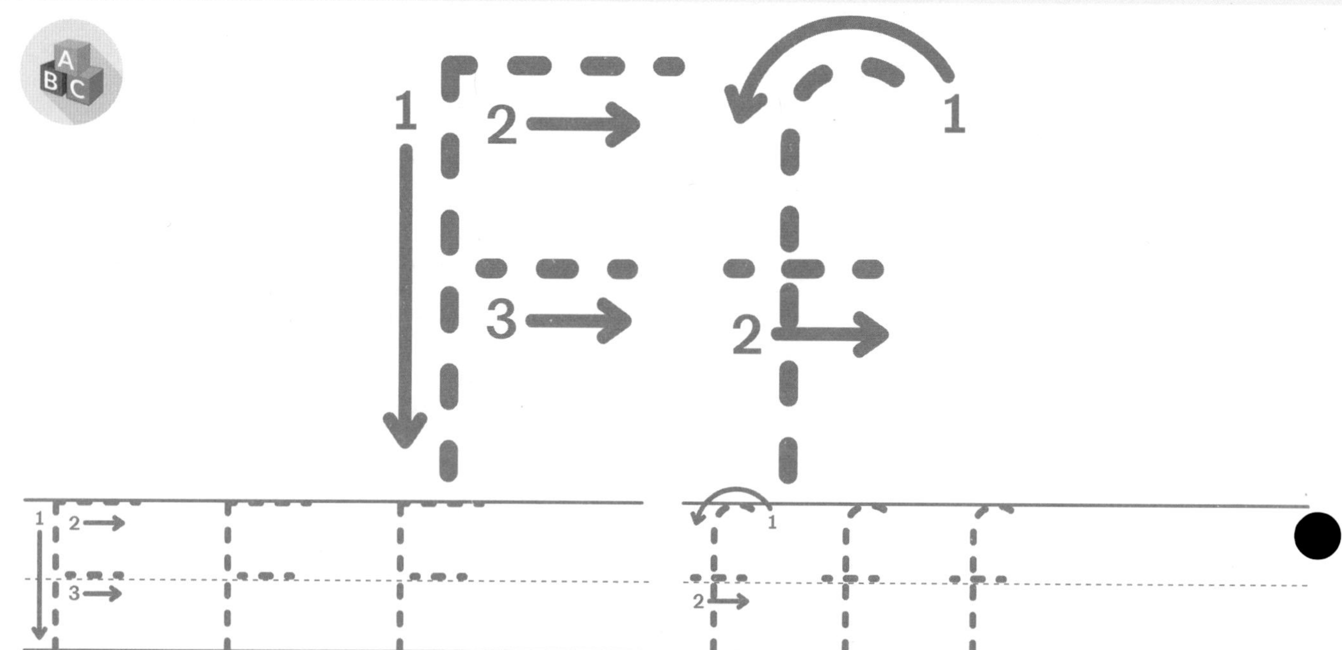

Name

Letter Hunt! Find the letter F's below and highlight each one.

F	Q	L	M	H	Q	F	I
P	D	F	N	Y	W	S	O
O	Z	I	V	B	E	D	F
I	X	U	C	U	D	G	P
U	F	Y	L	I	D	J	K
F	C	F	K	O	F	F	P
H	V	H	J	P	R	S	N
J	B	N	F	S	E	A	F

Forks forks

LESSON 7
Prep Page

Supply List

- ☐ Gather items to taste (day 1, rhyme time) sour = lemon juice, fruit = sweet, salt = bitter, cinnamon candy = spicy/hot
- ☐ Blindfold (day 1 & 2, life skills)
- ☐ Belt (day 1, Bible)
- ☐ Flashlight (day 1, life skills)
- ☐ Papers for outline (day 2, life skills)
- ☐ Painter's tape (day 2, life skills)
- ☐ Red/black construction paper (day 2, Bible)
- ☐ Touch objects (day 2, rhyme time) (ex: furry or fuzzy like fur or fuzzy blanket, pokey or prickly like a pinecone, slimy like grapes with skin removed or cooked noodles, hard like a rock or apple, soft like tissues)
- ☐ Stuffed animal, toys (day 3, life skills)
- ☐ Magnetic letters/tiles (day 2, life skills)
- ☐ Shoes (day 3, Bible) (too big boots, high heels, flip flops, sandals, their tennis shoes)

Look Ahead

See items for smelling in lesson 8.

Prepare the ABC cards.

Project

Gather a picture of them, a poster board, and old magazines. Let them create their own All About Me poster. Use magazine clippings for things that are their favorite color or foods, etc. Let them be creative! You can let them work on this throughout the week. It might be neat to spell their name with clipped magazine letters.

Objectives

Letter of the week: Gg

Skills/Concepts: 5 senses, all about me (name/birthday)

Memory Verse

Ephesians 6:10

Be strong in the Lord and in his mighty power.

Extended Activities

Lacing a shoe is a great fine motor task that will help them build up hand stamina (not tying it yet, just lacing).

LESSON 7
Day 1

RHYME TIME:

"The next two weeks we will be doing our poem right before our Life Skills because those two go together. We will be talking all about you, and one thing God gave us that is really neat — our five senses! Our five senses are touch, taste, smell, sight, and hearing. We use all of these senses every day!

"Today, we will focus on tasting. Each day we will have a poem on one of the five senses. We have motions with our poem, too! Today, our poem is "Tasting."

Read poem "Tasting."

"Let's play a tasting game!

Gather items of varying tastes. Blindfold the student and have them taste different things. They may want a glass of water after some.

LIFE SKILLS:

"This week is ALL ABOUT YOU! This week we will be creating a page all about you! One thing you need to know is your birthday. You were born on ________________. Be sure to include information about your favorite color, food, toy, things to do, and even friends.

On a blank sheet of paper, write the student's birthday. Be sure to keep this page for future lessons this week.

TIP: This is a great time to tell them about the day they were born or how they came to be a part of your family if you want to share.

"The Bible tells us that we were made in the image of God (Gen. 1:27). That makes us set apart, special, or unique! You are special to God. Go outside and find your shadow.

Tasting

Your little mouth now open,
and taste well what I bring;
then guess its name,
and praises we will gladly, gladly sing.

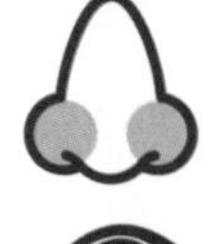

LESSON 7
Day 1

If it is not sunny, try using a flashlight in a dark room.

"Let's find our shadows. Do you see your shadow? Do you see mine? Come stand in my shadow. This is kind of like how God made us in his image. This shadow is an image of me. If you stand still in my image, you cannot even see your image. That is because in God's image, He made us to be like Him. He made us unique and special.

BIBLE:

"We are going to talk about the armor of God and how important it is for us to use the things God has given us to protect ourselves from sin. The Bible tells us in Ephesians 6:10:

Echo read the verse. Add motions.

Be strong  in the Lord 

and in His mighty power .

"A long time ago, a warrior would wear armor like in the picture on the next page. They had pieces to protect the vital organs of their body, like their brain or heart, and other important parts of their body, like their feet. Let's read Ephesians 6:13–17 about the armor of God. There are six pieces to the armor of God.

"Each day for this week and next week we will discuss one piece of the armor. Today, we will talk about the belt of truth. Here is a belt, let's put it on you so you can remember what we are learning.

"The belt would be buckled around the warrior's waist, like we have done to you. This belt of truth reminds us that God's Word, the Bible, is truth. We must always remember that the Bible is the truth and everything else is compared to the Word of God. We know that all Scripture is true, and that is how we know if something is true. Satan likes to try to trick us or tell us lies to get us to sin. If we do not have truth, we are lost. The Bible says in John 14:6 that Jesus is the way, the TRUTH, and the life, and that no one comes to the Father except through Jesus. This piece of armor, the belt of truth, is really what holds it all together. The belt of a Roman soldier was not a simple leather strap like we wear today. It was a thick, heavy leather and metal band with a protective piece hanging down from the front of it. The belt held the soldier's sword and other weapons. It is what holds what we need to fight against Satan. We must know Jesus to know truth and be able to be like a mighty warrior for Christ.

PARENT NOTE: Children's hearts are tender and sensitive; this study would be a great way to talk to your child about salvation and what it means to really know Christ.

Color the belt of truth on the image of the Armor of God on the next page.

You will be learning about the Armor of God during the next two weeks. You will need to keep this page for future lessons.

Armor of God

Ephesians 6:13–17

LESSON 7
Day 1

ABC'S AND MORE:

"Now, let's look at our ABC chart.

See Teacher Resource Page.

Chant the ABC chart.

Sing the ABC song.

Point to the capital G.

"This the capital G.

Point to the lowercase g.

"This is the lowercase g. Let's try writing it!

Practice writing Gg's.

"G: (over around, in)
Start a little below the top line, and go over around like a C (over around).
When you get to the middle line, you make a line in (in).

"g: (over around, up, down and curve)
Starting at the middle line, just like you make a lowercase a, go over around (over around) back up to the middle line (up).
And then down but keep going below the bottom line and curve (down and curve).

Trace the Gg's below.

Using the tracing ABC page in the back of the book, review writing letters A-F.

MINI-BOOK G:

See the Teacher Resource Page.

Do a picture walk.

Read the book to the student, pointing to each letter/word.

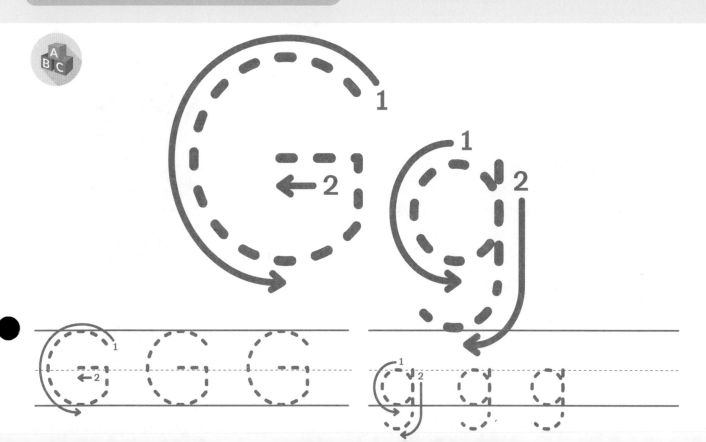

LESSON 7
Day 2

RHYME TIME:

"Do you remember what our five senses are?

"Touch, taste, smell, sight, and hearing. We use all of these senses every day! Today, we will focus on touch. Remember, each day we will have a poem on one of the five senses. Today, our poem is "Touching."

Read poem "Touching."

LIFE SKILLS:

"Let's play another game called "What's That?"

Gather materials for touching after they are blindfolded.

"You are going to be blindfolded again. I will put something in your hand as I say our rhyme and you have to try to guess what it is.

"We will continue making a page this week that is ALL ABOUT YOU! Your name is _______. We write it like this: __________________.

TIP: Get a blank piece of paper and use a highlighter to write their name three times and have them trace inside the highlighted text. Or write their name twice, once each on two notecards. Cut one apart for them to match the letters in their name and build it (only first names).

Continue working on the blank page from Day 1 of this week, adding the student's name.

"I want to discuss your All About Me project.

Ask them questions about themselves using the project as a guide. For example, what is your favorite color? Or point to a photo, or a favorite toy and ask them to tell you about it.

Touching

Though your little eyes are blinded,
your little hands can feel;
now take the thing I give you,
and quick its name reveal.

LESSON 7
Day 2

“Remember, the Bible tells us that we were made in the image of God (Gen. 1:27). That makes us set apart, special, or unique! You are special to God.

“We will make a profile picture today of you using your shadow.

Tape a blank piece of paper to a wall. Shine a flashlight from a distance. Have your child sit in front of the paper so you can use a marker to trace their silhouette of the head down to their neck. Cut this out (or have your child cut it out). They can tape it on the wall.

BIBLE:

“We are continuing to discuss the armor of God and how important it is for us to use the things God has given us to protect ourselves from sin.

Review memory verse on page 81.

“Let’s read Ephesians 6:13–17 about the armor of God again. There are six pieces to the armor of God.

“Each day for this week and next week we will discuss one piece of the armor. What piece of armor did we talk about yesterday? Yes, the belt of truth! Today, we will be talking about the breastplate of righteousness.

“The breastplate would have protected the vital organs, like our heart and lungs. It was made of overlapping metal pieces with leather and flexible fabric so they could still move, but also be protected. The stronger the breastplate, the better it was at protecting against the hits of the enemy. A breastplate of righteousness is what helps us not be affected by the hits of the enemy. The word righteousness means making the right choices and obeying what is in the Bible. If a person is righteous, it means they are obedient to God, always making the right choice. Jesus was righteous, but a special righteous, because He NEVER sinned — he never made wrong choices.

“Color the breastplate of righteousness on your Armor of God page.

(Get a black heart and a red heart, glue them together so you can flip it from black to red.)

“Our hearts are like this black heart when we sin. It is dead without Jesus. Satan wants our hearts to stay like this. We can change this though. If we pray to God and ask him to forgive us of our sins, He will forgive us and make our hearts clean. It is kind of like washing off the dirt. We can have a new clean heart like this (flip to red).

PARENT NOTE: Children’s hearts are tender and sensitive; this study would be a great way to talk to your child about salvation and what it means to really know Christ.

LESSON 7
Day 2

ABC'S AND MORE:

"Now, let's look at our ABC chart. Show me two capital letters. Show me two lowercase letters.

Sing the ABC song.

Chant the ABC chart.

"Let's practice writing our Gg's again.

Point to the capital G. Point to the lowercase g.

"This is the capital G and this is the lowercase g. Let's write them!

Practice writing Gg's.

"G: (over around, in)
Start a little below the top line, and go over around like a C (over around).
When you get to the middle line, you make a line in (in).

"g: (over around, up, down and curve)
Starting at the middle line, just like you make a lowercase a, go over around (over around) back up to the middle line (up).
And then down but keep going below the bottom line and curve (down and curve).

Trace the Gg's below.

Using the tracing ABC page in the back of the book, review writing letters A-F.

MINI-BOOK G:

Read the letter book to the student.

Have the student highlight the capital and lowercase letter of the week.

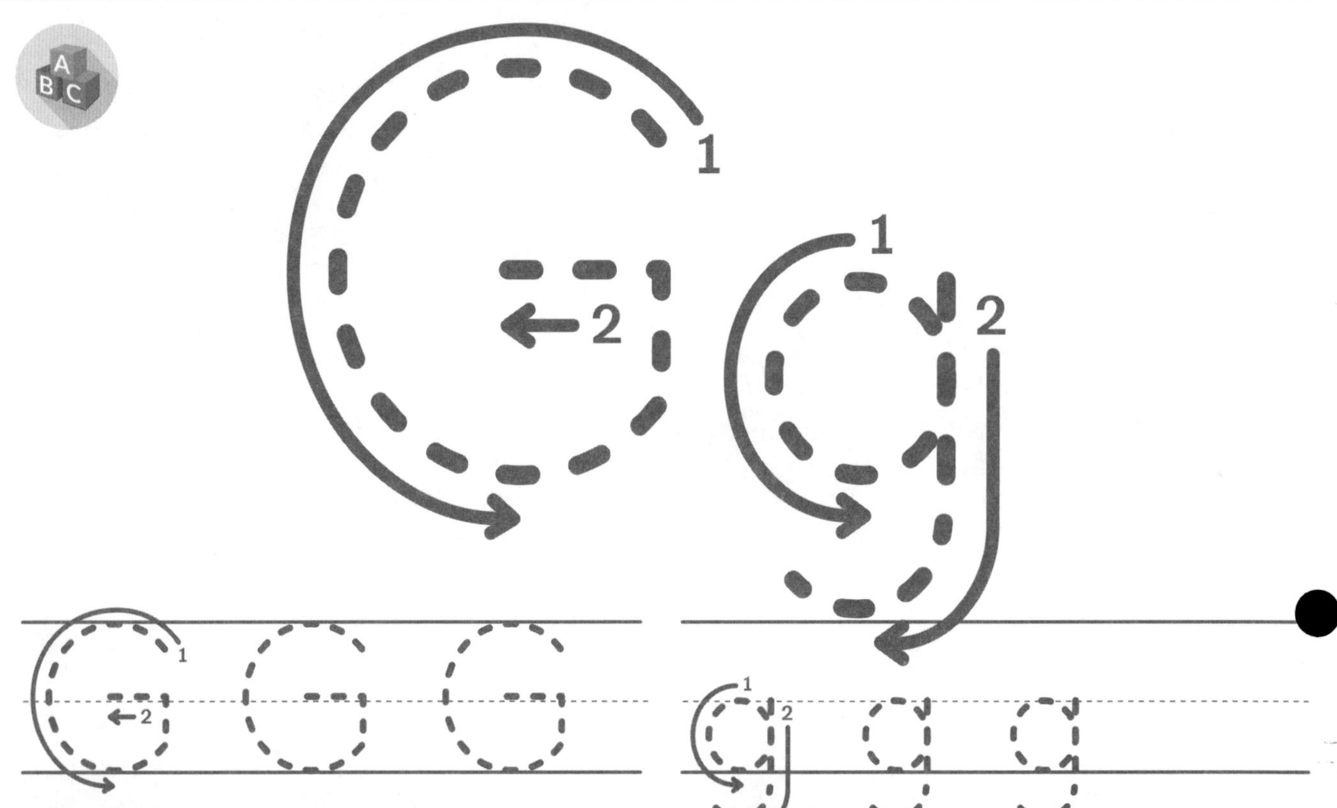

LESSON 7
Day 3

RHYME TIME:

"Do you remember what our five senses are?

"Touch, taste, smell, sight, and hearing. We use all of these senses every day! Today, we will focus on sight. Remember, each day we will have a poem on one of the five senses. Today, our poem is "Seeing."

Read poem "Seeing" below.

"Highlight the Gg's in the poem below.

LIFE SKILLS:

"Where am I? We will play hide and seek using a stuffed animal. There are a few rules. Rule #1: You must leave part of the stuffed animal where it can be seen.

"Rule #2: You must only hide it in ______ room and ________ room.
I will hide it first, and you will try to find it.
Then, you can hide it and I will try to find it.

Remind them of the rules as they search and hide.

"Can you see light? What if it is nighttime and we are in the car? Can you see the lights of the city from far away? Yes, a light is a powerful thing to the darkness. Just like we should shine our lights for others to see! That means we should show Jesus to others.

"Remember, the Bible tells us that we were made in the image of God (Gen. 1:27). That makes us set apart, special, or unique! You are special to God.

Seeing

When we're playing together,
we are happy and glad,
we don't care for the weather,
and we never grow sad;
one of us has disappeared,
you shall guess which one it is,
and shall heartily be cheered,
if your guess is not a-miss.

LESSON 7
Day 3

Shadow puppets: Go in a dark room. Have your child sit close to the wall facing it. You will need to be farther away and have a flashlight set up where you can put objects between the flashlight and the wall for your child to guess what image it is. Use some of their favorite toys.

“Since we have been discussing being made in the image of God, we will play “Guess what image I am” using shadow puppets.

BIBLE:

“We are continuing to discuss the armor of God and how important it is for us to use the things God has given us to protect ourselves from sin.

Review memory verse on page 81.

See supplies list to gather shoes on page 79.

“Let’s read Ephesians 6:13–17 about the armor of God again. There are six pieces to the armor of God. What pieces of armor have we talked about?

“Yes, the belt of truth and breastplate of righteousness! Today, we will be talking about having shoes of peace. Do you know what peace is? Peace is freedom from trouble. If our feet are ready with shoes of peace, then we can know we will be free from trouble. If you were going on a journey over a mountain, which of these shoes would you want to wear? Try on each pair. Why would you not want to wear these heavy shoes that are too big? Why wouldn’t you wear flip flops? Right — if you have your feet ready with the right shoes, then you can go farther on your journey and be better protected. We have to have our feet protected. If we were warriors, we would walk a lot and have special sandals that were light and comfortable for walking. They would also have to be able to walk over rough ground and avoid anything the enemy put in our path. Just like the warrior had to watch for things that might trip them up, we must watch for things that might cause us to not follow God.

“Color the shoes of peace on the Armor of God page.

goldfish

LESSON 7
Day 3

ABC'S AND MORE:

"Now, let's look at our ABC chart.

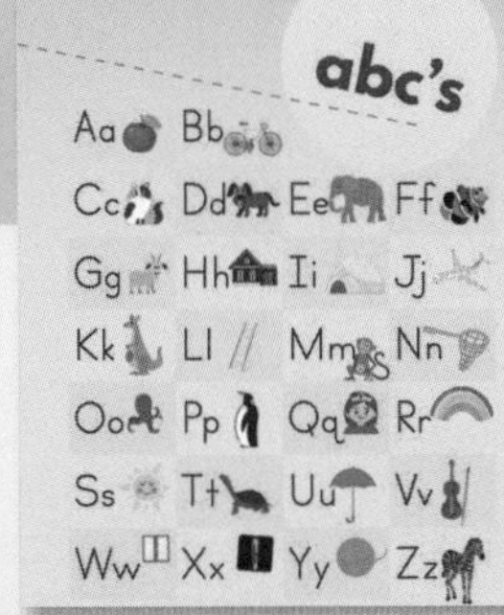

See Teacher Resource Page.

Chant the ABC chart.

Sing the ABC song.

"Let's review how to write our Gg's again.

Point to the capital G. Point to the lowercase g.

"This is the capital G and this is the lowercase g. Let's write them!

Practice writing Gg's.

"G: (over around, in)
Start a little below the top line, and go over around like a C (over around).
When you get to the middle line, you make a line in (in).

"g: (over around, up, down and curve)
Starting at the middle line, just like you make a lowercase a, go over around (over around) back up to the middle line (up).
And then down but keep going below the bottom line and curve (down and curve).

Trace the Gg's below.

Using the tracing ABC page in the back of the book, review writing letters A-F.

MINI-BOOK G:

Read the letter book again.

Advanced K — see if your child can read the book to you. Read the letter mini book.

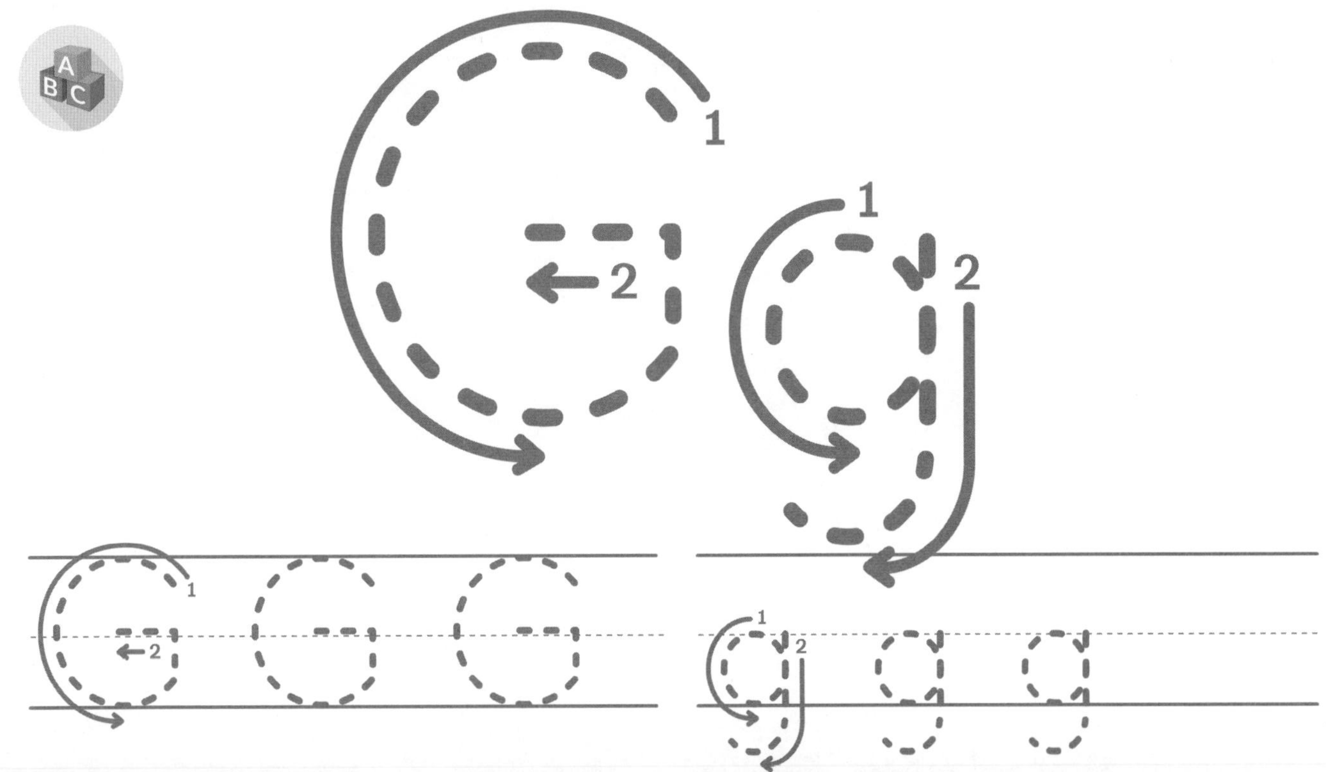

LESSON 8
Prep Page

Supply List

- ☐ Foil pan (day 1, Bible)
- ☐ Yarn (day 1, Bible)
- ☐ Rose (day 1, rhyme time)
- ☐ Blindfold (day 1, rhyme time), alternate game (day 2, life skills)
- ☐ Objects for hearing, alternate game (day 2, life skills)
- ☐ Area for senses walk (day 3, life skills)

Look Ahead

Watch the video for teaching sounds using the ABC chart. See Teacher Resource page for adding sounds for *Advanced K.*

Objectives

Letter of the week: Hh

Skills/Concepts: 5 senses, all about me (name/birthday)

Memory Verse

Ephesians 6:11

Put on the full armor of God, so that you can take your stand against the devil.

Extended Activities

Use an online resource for making free tracer pages of their name and birthday for practice. Using a plastic sleeve, you can use a dry-erase marker.

Have them find things that are the same each day (like shoes) and things that are different (like food).

Add sounds for chanting the ABC chart — see video.

LESSON 8
Day 1

LIFE SKILLS:

"Do you remember our five senses?

"Yes! Touch, taste, smell, sight, and hearing.

"Today, we will focus on smelling.

If you have the flower, blindfold them and read the poem as they smell the flowers. You can always switch the word "flower" for something else they can smell, and change the word in the poem.

RHYME TIME:

"Our poem this week is about smelling.

Read poem "Smelling" below.

See life skills section for optional use with a flower.

BIBLE:

Use the Armor of God page from Lesson 7.

"You are special to God. We are continuing to talk about the armor of God and how important it is for us to use the things God has given us to protect ourselves from sin. The Bible tells us in Ephesians 6:11:

Echo read the verse. Add motions.

Put on  the full armor of God 

so that you can take your stand 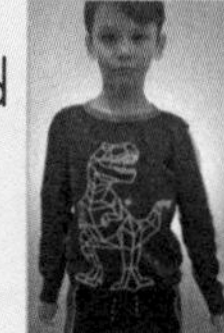

against the devil .

Smelling

There's a flower in my hand,
can you tell what it may be;
but I hope you understand,
you may smell but must not see.

If you say the proper name,
guessing by the scent alone,
you a sweet reward may claim,
for the flower shall be your own.

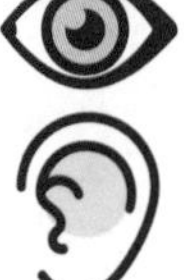

LESSON 8
Day 1

"Schemes: What does it mean to scheme? A scheme is like a plan, but in this case it is an evil plan. Satan wants to cause us to not live for God. Remember the black heart? He wants our hearts to stay that way. That is why we have to use the armor of God to protect ourselves.

"Remember the picture of our warrior? Let's read Ephesians 6:13–17 about the armor of God. There are six pieces to the armor of God.

"We will continue to discuss one piece of the armor each day. Today, we will talk about the shield of faith. Let's make a shield today. Using this foil cake pan, I will cut two slits in the middle and we will put yarn through them to tie it to make a handle for you to hold on to.

Have them hold their shield once made.

"How do you think a shield would help you? What if I threw something at you?

"What could you do with your shield? Yes! You can almost hide behind it to protect yourself from what I throw at you. That is what a warrior would have done. He would use it to protect himself from an arrow being shot at him.

"The shield of faith is what protects us spiritually. In a spiritual battle, the devil tries to hurt us. If we use our faith to protect us, then we can be safe. Faith is believing, even when we cannot see. Just like in our senses game last week. We couldn't always see the stuffed animal, but we knew it was still there. Sometimes, we can see God working, like when He heals someone or answers a prayer. Even if I cannot see Him, I know He is there. That is faith!

"Color the shield of faith.

PARENT NOTE: Children's hearts are tender and sensitive; this study would be a great way to talk to your child about salvation and what it means to really know Christ.

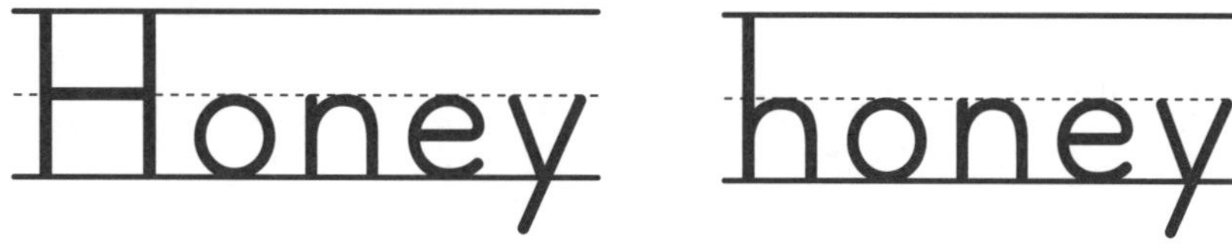

LESSON 8
Day 1

ABC'S AND MORE:

"Now, let's look at our ABC chart. Show me two capital letters. Show me two lowercase letters.

See Teacher Resource Page.

Chant the ABC chart.

Sing the ABC song.

Play the ABC's match game. Place the ABC chart on the floor. Have your child take his or her ABC cards and spread them out on the floor out of order. He or she should arrange them in the same order as the ABC chart, so when finished, the cards are like a big ABC chart in ABC order.

"Our letter this week is Hh!

"Let's point to the capital H and the lowercase h on our ABC chart.

Point to the capital H. Point to the lowercase h.

Practice writing capital H's and lowercase h's.

"H: (down, down, across in the middle)
Start at the top line, go down to the bottom line (down). Move over a little, start at the top line, go down to the bottom line (down).
Now connect them in the middle (across in the middle).

"h: (down, up and over)
Start at the top line, go down to the bottom line (down). Come back up and curve over to the bottom line (up and over).

Trace the Hh's below.

MINI-BOOK H:

See the Teacher Resource Page.

Do a picture walk.

Read the book to the student, pointing to each letter/word.

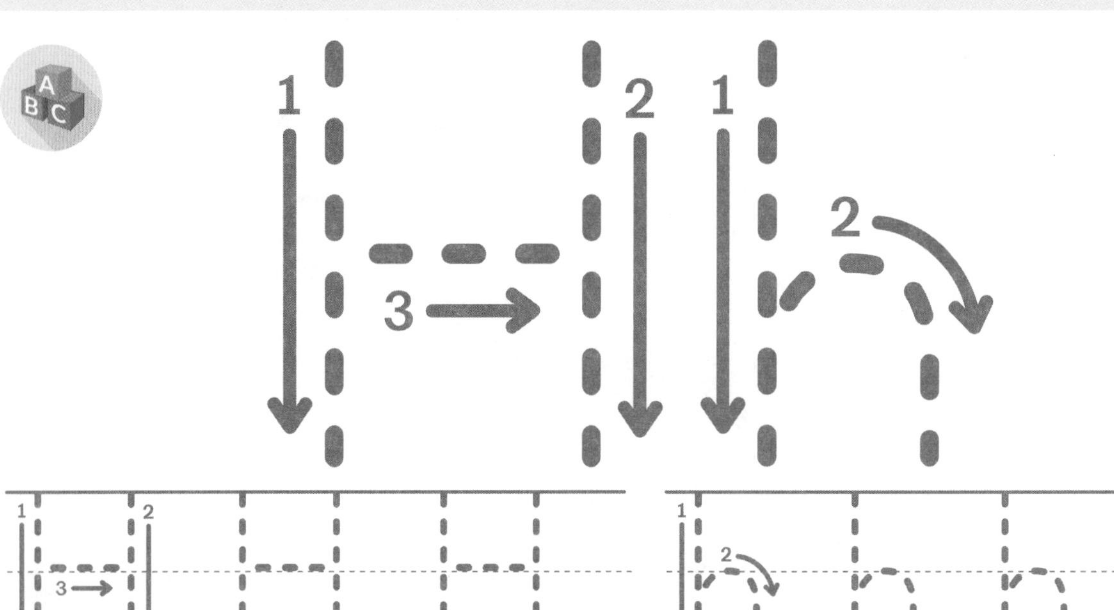

LESSON 8
Day 2

RHYME TIME:

"Do you remember our five senses?

"Yes! Touch, taste, smell, sight, and hearing. Today, we will focus on hearing.

Read poem "Hearing" below.

LIFE SKILLS:

"We will play the telephone game to see how well you hear what is said.

GAME: 3+ players. Sit in a circle. Whisper a phrase in the ear of the person to your left. Do not let anyone else hear you. Then, that person whispers the same thing you said in the ear of the person next to them. Keep going until it has been told to each person. The person on your left will say it aloud and you can verify if they heard it correctly.

Phrases: My monkey went to market.
Silly Sally ate some pickles.
Fred ran over his toe and broke it.
I hear the bells of the church ringing loudly.

Alternate game: What sound do you hear? Blindfold the child. Make different sounds like a phone ringing, pans clanging, toilet flushing, etc., and see if they can tell you what it is.

"Do you remember when your birthday is?
Yes, it is ______________________.
Let's practice writing your name.

Remember to use a highlighter for them to trace in. You could also use magnetic letters or letter tiles for them to build their name.

Hearing

Let us stand quite still and listen,
till we hear our friend strike.
What she says will be repeated,
as much as we can alike.

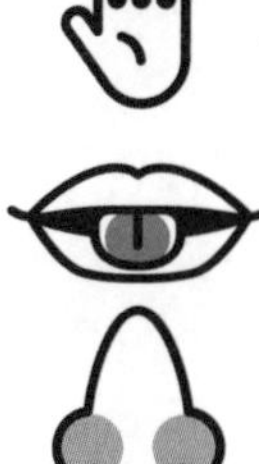

LESSON 8
Day 2

BIBLE:

Use the Armor of God page.

"We are continuing to talk about the armor of God and how important it is for us to use the things God has given us to protect ourselves from sin.

Review memory verse on page 92.

"We talked about schemes yesterday. What does it mean to scheme? Right, it means to make an evil plan.

"Now, let's see what we're going to do today.

Help them to draw pictures of the main events of your day.

Show the student the Armor of God page from Lesson 7.

"Here is our picture of our warrior. Let's read Ephesians 6:13–17 about the armor of God. There are six pieces to the armor of God.

Do you remember the pieces of armor we have talked about already? Let's name them as we point where they are located.

"Belt of truth — (hands on waist)
Breastplate of righteousness — (pat your chest)
Feet fitted with readiness of the gospel — (stomp your feet)
Shield of faith — (pretend to hold up a shield)
And today, the helmet of salvation! (pat your head)

"A helmet is a covering. It protects our thoughts or our minds. If we have a helmet of salvation, then we are covered by the blood of Jesus. We are also protecting ourselves from any evil thoughts that the devil throws our way.

"Color the helmet of salvation.

PARENT NOTE: Children's hearts are tender and sensitive; this study would be a great way to talk to your child about salvation and what it means to really know Christ.

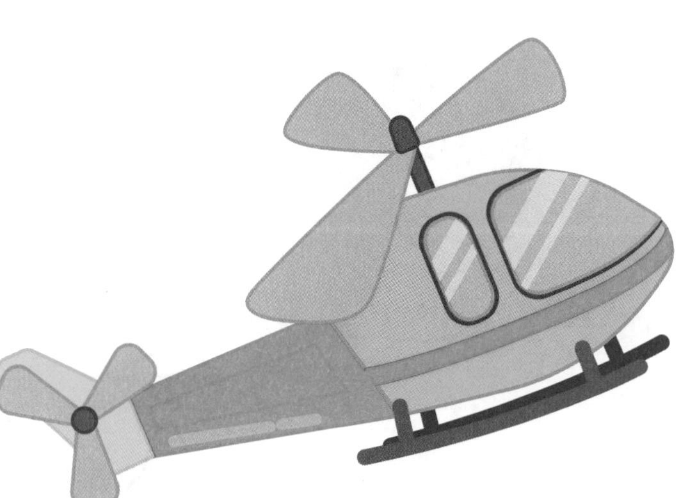

Helicopter

helicopter

LESSON 8
Day 2

ABC'S AND MORE:

"Now, let's look at our ABC chart. Show me two capital letters. Show me two lowercase letters.

Chant the ABC Chart.

Sing the ABC song.

"Our letter this week is Hh!

"Let's point to the capital H and the lowercase h on our ABC chart.

Point to the capital H. Point to the lowercase h.

Practice writing H's and h's.

"H: (down, down, across in the middle)
Start at the top line, go down to the bottom line (down).

"Move over a little, start at the top line, go down to the bottom line (down).
Now connect them in the middle (across in the middle).

"h: (down, up and over)
Start at the top line, go down to the bottom line (down).
Come back up and curve over to the bottom line (up and over).

Trace the Hh's below.

MINI-BOOK H:

Have the student highlight the capital H's and lowercase h's in the mini-book.

Read the letter book to the student.

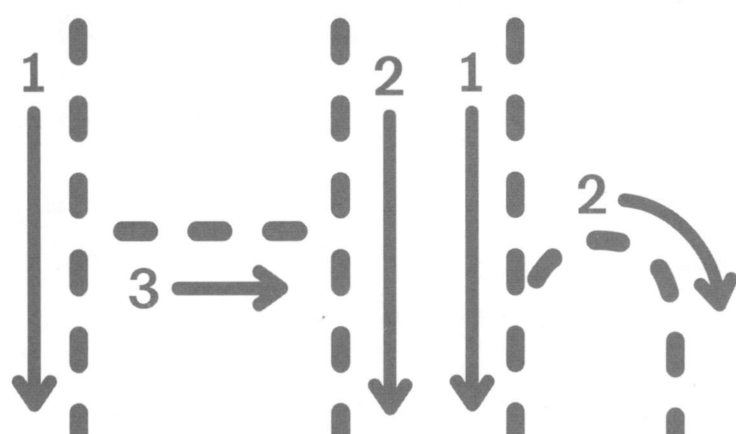

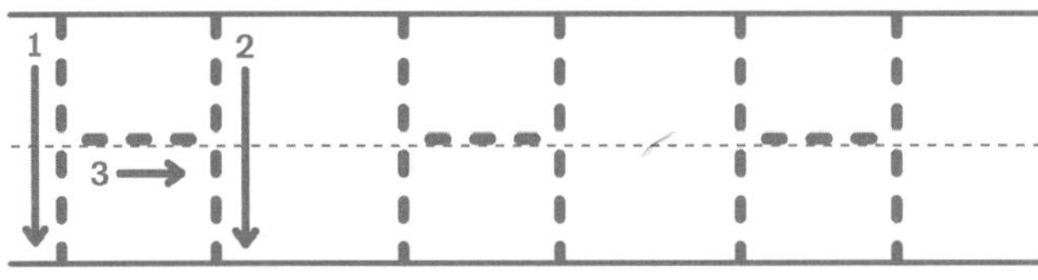

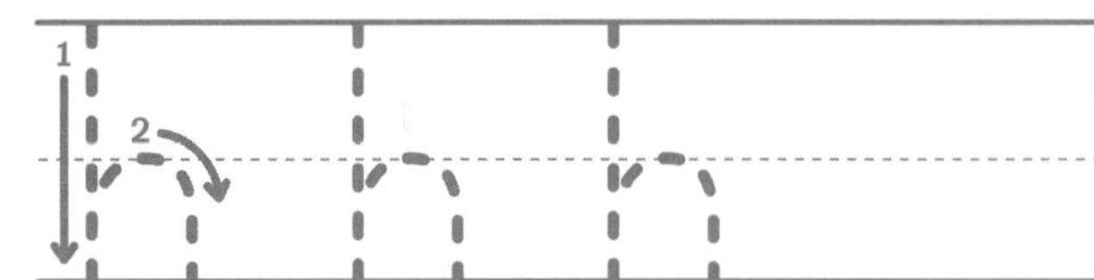

LESSON 8
Day 3

RHYME TIME:

"Our poem today is about the five senses. Let's read it now and then highlight the Hh's in the poem.

Read poem "Five Senses" below.

LIFE SKILLS:

"Today, we will go on a "senses" walk! Walk around outside to find what things you can hear, smell, see, and touch. For tasting, bring along a healthy snack to enjoy. Discuss the things that animals you see might eat.

Use caution when in nature, and discuss that we do not eat things we find (unless you have educated your child on this) and we do not touch things unless we ask an adult first (unless you have educated your child on what is safe/not safe to touch in nature).

"Do you remember when your birthday is? Yes, it is ______________________.

"Let's practice writing your name. (Remember to use a highlighter for them to trace in.)

Five Senses

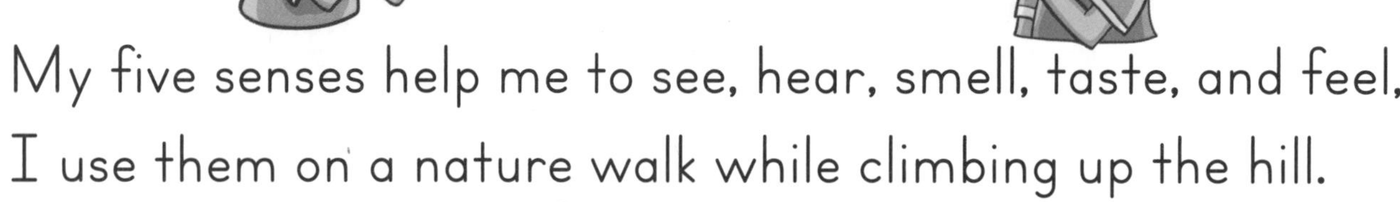

My five senses help me to see, hear, smell, taste, and feel,
I use them on a nature walk while climbing up the hill.
I can hear the sounds of animals,
and smell the fresh crisp air.
I see the trees sway and feel the wind in my hair.

LESSON 8
Day 3

BIBLE:

Use the Armor of God page.

“Here is our picture of our warrior. Let’s read Ephesians 6:13–17 about the armor of God.

“Do you remember the pieces of armor we have talked about already? Let’s name them as we point to where they are located.
Belt of truth — (hands on waist)
Breastplate of righteousness — (pat your chest)
Feet fitted with readiness of the gospel — (stomp your feet)
Shield of faith — (pretend to hold up a shield)
The helmet of salvation! — (pat your head)

“Last, we are talking about the sword of the Spirit. Our sword is the only part of the armor that we can use to fight the enemy. All of the other five pieces are for protecting us. The sword of the Spirit is our Bible, the Word of God.

“When Satan tempted Jesus, Jesus used the Word of God to speak the truth and fight the attack of Satan. We should hide God’s Word in our hearts by memorizing Scripture so we can use it to fight Satan, our enemy, when he attacks.

Review your memory verse on page 92.

“Satan will scheme, or plan, to cause us to stumble, but God’s Word says that if we have on the armor of God, we can withstand his schemes.

“Color the sword of the Spirit.

PARENT NOTE: Children’s hearts are tender and sensitive; this study would be a great way to talk to your child about salvation and what it means to really know Christ.

Harp harp

LESSON 8
Day 3

ABC'S AND MORE:

"Now, let's look at our ABC chart. Show me two capital letters. Show me two lowercase letters.

See Teacher Resource Page.

Chant the ABC chart.

Sing the ABC song.

"Let's review how to write our Hh's!

"Let's point to the capital H and the lowercase h.

Point to the capital H. Point to the lowercase h.

Practice writing H's and h's.

"H: (down, down, across in the middle)
Start at the top line, go down to the bottom line (down).
Move over a little, start at the top line, go down to the bottom line (down).
Now connect them in the middle (across in the middle).

"h: (down, up and over)
Start at the top line, go down to the bottom line (down).
Come back up and curve over to the bottom line (up and over).

Trace the Hh's below.

MINI-BOOK H:

Read the letter book again.

Advanced K — see if your child can read the book to you.

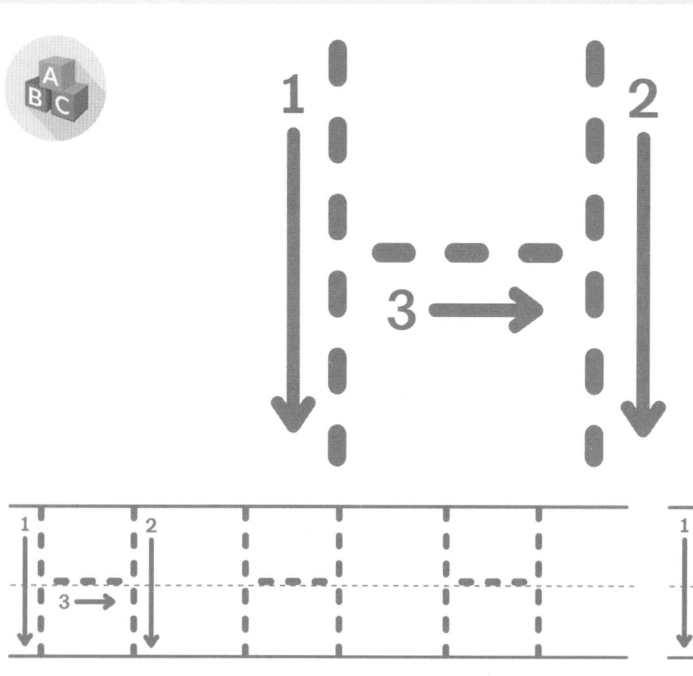

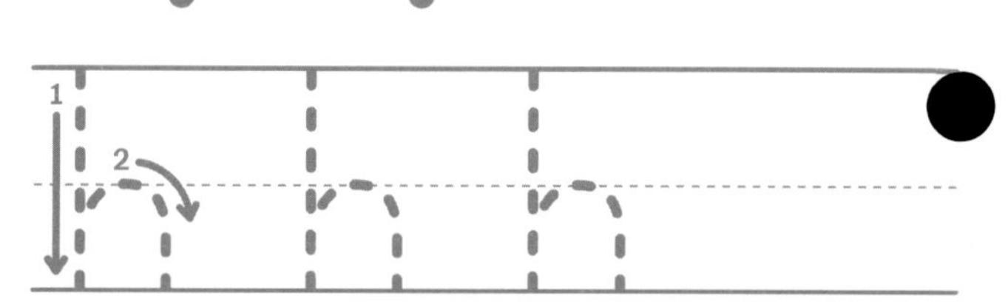

LESSON 9
Prep Page

Supply List

- ☐ Optional: cottage cheese (day 2, rhyme time)
- ☐ Paper plate (day 1, life skills)

Look Ahead

Lesson 10 has cooking, see recipes and supply list

Objectives

Letter of the week: Ii

Skills/Concepts: kinds of food, writing name

Memory Verse

Galatians 5:22-23

But the fruit of the Spirit is love, joy, peace, forbearance, kindness, goodness, faithfulness, gentleness and self-control. Against such things there is no law.

Extended Activities

Have them help you cook each day.

Teach them to use a toaster and microwave.

Stack apples to see how many you can stack.

Cut apples into slices. Put lemon juice on some and compare the length of time it takes for the apples without lemon juice to go brown versus the apples with lemon juice.

Add sounds for chanting the ABC chart — see video.

LESSON 9
Day 1

LIFE SKILLS:

"Let's practice writing your name.

Remember to use a highlighter for them to trace in, or use magnetic letters/letter tiles to build their name.

"In our poem we will cover this week, Miss Muffet was eating her curds and whey, and we will be looking at different foods this week, as well as cooking. There are four main categories or kinds of food. They are:
The milk group: milk, cheese, yogurt, and other milk-based foods
The meat group: meat, fish, poultry, and eggs, with dried legumes and nuts as alternatives
The fruits and vegetables group
The breads and cereals group

NOTE: For this age, I chose to break it into four basic groups as an introduction to food groups.

Do the maze below.

BIBLE:

"There is a story in the Bible where the disciples need to feed a large crowd of more than 5,000 people. Talk about not having enough food . . . or did they? Let's read to find out what Jesus did in Matthew 14:13–21.

"This is one of the miracles that Jesus performed. Use the maze below to help the disciples get the food from the boy to the crowd.

"The Bible says we should have fruits of the Spirit (Gal. 5:22–23):

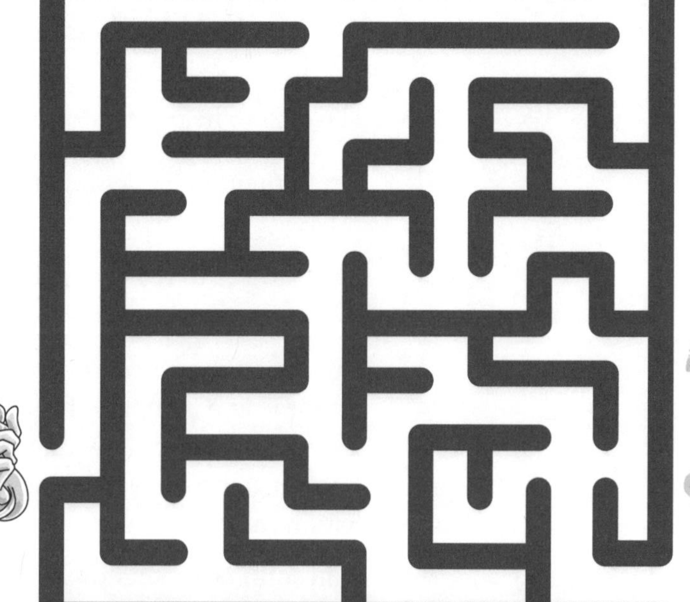

Help the disciples get the food to the crowd.

Name

Lesson 9
Day 1

Cut the pictures out and glue them where they belong on a paper plate.

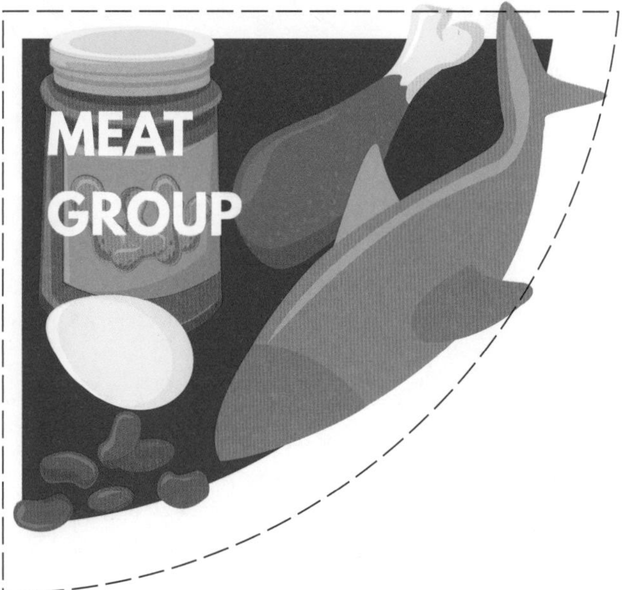

Blank Page for cutting.

LESSON 9
Day 1

Echo read the verse. Add motions.

Forbearance is patience.

But the fruit of the Spirit is love ,
joy , peace ,
forbearance , kindness, goodness ,
faithfulness, gentleness , and self-control.
Against  such things there is no law.

"We are to show these behaviors to others every day. We will focus on kindness today. To be kind means to be nice, caring, and thoughtful. How can you be kind to someone?

(Offer suggestions if needed, e.g., making a card for someone who is sick, sharing your toys, etc.)

"This week and next week we will work on memorizing this verse. We will use our Fruit of the Spirit tree to help us memorize them.

"Trace the word "kindness" on your tree, then cut out the fruit for kindness and glue it on your tree. See pages 107–109.

RHYME TIME:

"Our poem this week is "Little Miss Muffet." I will read it, then you can echo me as I read it.

Read "Little Miss Muffet" below.

"We have quite a few words that are different, like tuffet. What do you think a tuffet is? A tuffet is a footstool or low seat. We will be looking at more of those different words in our poem each day. Have you seen a tuffet before?

Little Miss Muffet

Little Miss Muffet
sat on a tuffet,
eating her curds and whey;
along came a spider,
who sat down beside her,
and frightened Miss Muffet away.

LESSON 9
Day 1

ABC'S AND MORE:

"Now, let's look at our ABC chart. Show me three capital and lowercase letters.

See Teacher Resource Page.

Chant the ABC chart.

Sing the ABC song.

"Our letter this week is Ii!

"Let's point to the capital I and the lowercase i on our ABC chart.

Point to the capital I. Point to the lowercase i.

Practice writing I's and i's.

"I: (down, across, across)
Start at the top line, go straight down to the bottom line (down).
Make a line across at the top line (across).
Make a line across at the bottom line (across).

"i: (down, dot)
Starting at the middle line, go down to the bottom line (down) and then in between the middle line and top line, place a dot (dot).

Trace the Ii's below.

MINI-BOOK I:

See Teacher Resource Page.

Do a picture walk.

Read the book to the student, point to each letter/word.

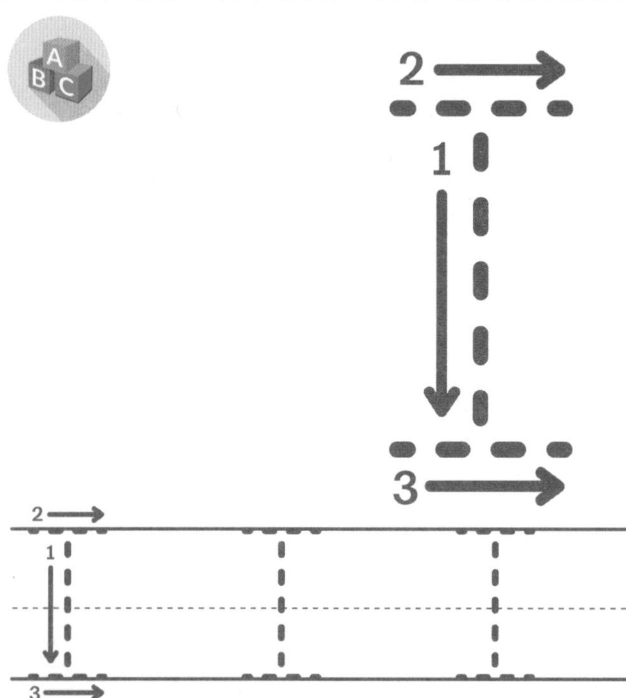

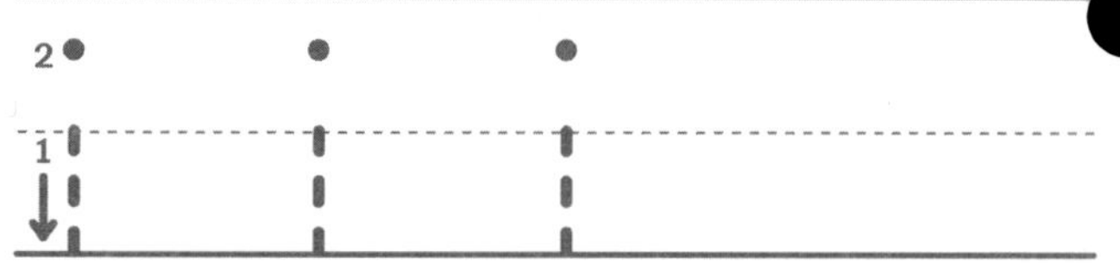

Name

Fruits of the Spirit

You will be learning about the Fruits of the Spirit through Lesson 10. As you learn about each of these Fruits of the Spirit, you will cut it out and add it to the tree on page 109 from Lesson 9, Day 1.

Save this page for future lessons.

Blank Page for cutting.

Name

Fruits of the Spirit

Keep this page for using through lesson 10.

LESSON 9
Day 2

LIFE SKILLS:

"There are four main categories or kinds of food. They are:
The milk group: milk, cheese, yogurt, and other milk-based foods
The meat group: meat, fish, poultry, and eggs, with dried legumes and nuts as alternatives
The fruits and vegetables group
The breads and cereals group

"Do you know which group the apples we have used today are in? Yes, the fruits and vegetables group.

"See if you can match the food on the next page to the correct food group.

Finish the food group activity.

BIBLE:

"The Bible says we should have the Fruit of the Spirit. Galatians 5:22–23: "But the fruit of the Spirit is love, joy, peace, forbearance, kindness, goodness, faithfulness, gentleness and self-control. Against such things there is no law."

"We are to show these behaviors to others every day.

"We have discussed joy, patience, self-control, and kindness. We will focus on love today. Love is one of the greatest gifts of all. When you love, you put others before yourself. This means that you let someone else go first, you let someone else have the treat when there is only one, you are always kind to them, and you want what is best for the other person. Jesus loved us so much that he laid down His life for us. He is the best example of love that we have.

Optional: Read 1 and 2 of the Nine Fruits of the Spirit *books from New Leaf Press if you have them. This is covered for two weeks.*

Review your memory verse on page 105.

"Trace the word "love" on your Fruit of the Spirit Tree, then cut and glue the fruit on your tree.

"Another story in the Bible is one about raining bread. Have you heard of when it rained bread?

Read Exodus 16:1–5.

"It is amazing how God provides for us. We can count our blessings every day and not complain like the Israelites did in this story.

RHYME TIME:

Read the poem "Little Miss Muffet" on page 105.

"Do you remember what a tuffet is? Yes, it is a footstool or low seat. Another different term we don't hear much is curds and whey. What are curds and whey? Curds and whey is actually cottage cheese. The lumps and the liquid in cottage cheese is curds and whey.

Optional: Try tasting cottage cheese (or eat it if they like it).

Name

Match the food to the correct group.

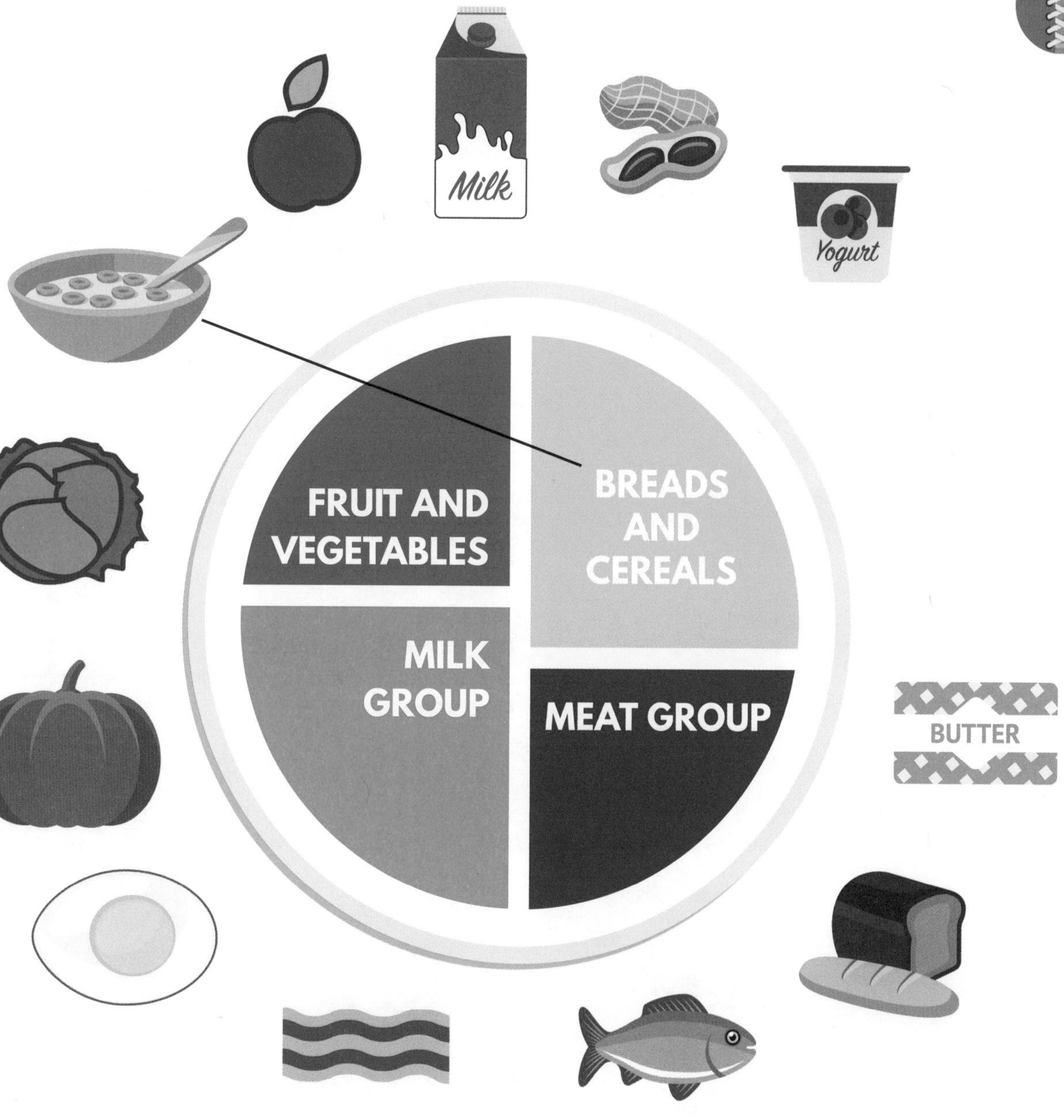

Milk

Yogurt

FRUIT AND VEGETABLES

BREADS AND CEREALS

MILK GROUP

MEAT GROUP

BUTTER

LESSON 9
Day 2

ABC'S AND MORE:

"Now, let's look at our ABC chart. Show me three capital letters. Show me three lowercase letters.

Chant the ABC chart.

Sing the ABC song.

Point to capital I.

"This the capital I.

Point to the lowercase i.

"This is the lowercase i.

"Let's review how to write our Ii's!

Practice writing I's and i's.

"I: (down, across, across)
Start at the top line, go straight down to the bottom line (down).
Make a line across at the top line (across).
Make a line across at the bottom line (across).

"i: (down, dot)
Starting at the middle line, go down to the bottom line (down) and then in between the middle line and top line, place a dot (dot).

Trace the Ii's below.

MINI-BOOK I:

Have the student highlight the capitalized and lower case letter of the week.

Read the letter Ii book to the student.

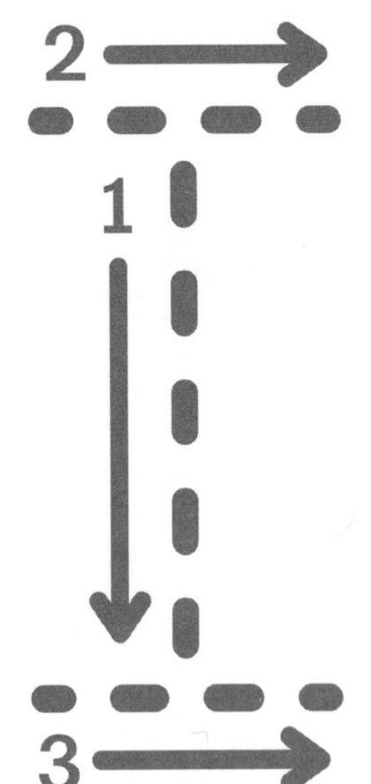

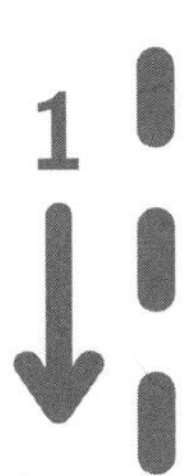

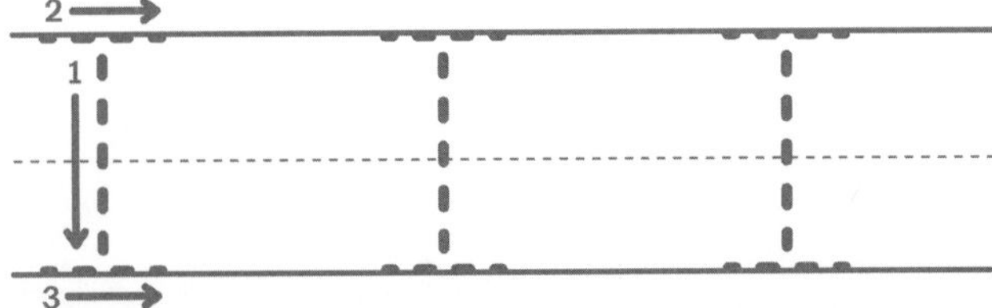

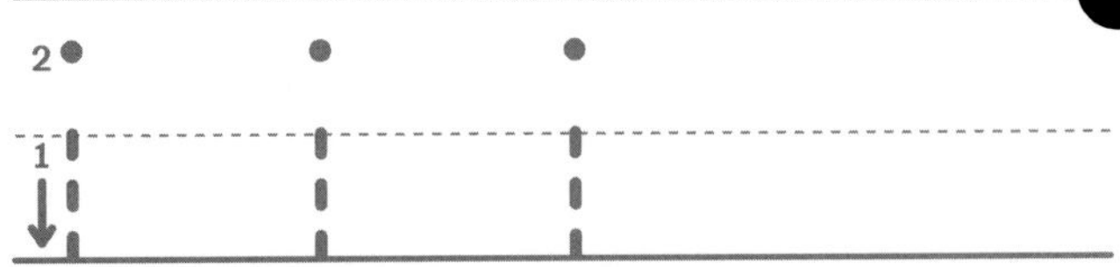

LESSON 9
Day 3

LIFE SKILLS:

"Write your name on a blank piece of paper.

"Let's play the Food Explorer Game. We will go explore our refrigerator and pantry (cabinet) to see what foods we have and sort them into our four main food groups. Remember, we have four groups, which are milk, meat, fruits and vegetables, and then breads and cereals. Let's see if we can find at least one thing for each group. A healthy meal will have something from each of these groups.

BIBLE:

"We have some food stored here, but in the Bible there were storehouses of food.

"Genesis 41, 42: Pharaoh, or the King of Egypt, was having dreams. He had Joseph, a man of God, in prison. Pharaoh was told Joseph could interpret his dreams, so he asked Joseph what his dreams meant. Joseph told him his dreams meant there would be seven years of good harvests where they would have plenty of food, but then it would be followed by seven years of bad harvests. He also told Pharaoh that he should put someone over the food so they could store food during the good harvest so they would have plenty for the years of the bad harvests. Pharaoh put Joseph over the food, and for seven years of good harvest Joseph stored extra food. Then, just as God had planned, the Egyptians came needing food, so Joseph opened up the storehouses of food to sell to them. He also had so much food he was able to feed people from other countries as well. Joseph's own brothers, who had sold him into slavery, had to come to Joseph for food, too!

"Joseph had food laid up in storehouses ready to feed others when the time came. That is how God is! He has blessings laid up for us that we don't even know about yet! He is mighty and faithful to His promises to us. We should always focus on our blessings. The Bible said Joseph had so many blessings he couldn't even measure them.

Use the Fruits of the Spirits Tree on page 109 for review.

"Let's review the fruits of the Spirit. Then, you will trace, cut, and glue peace on your tree.

"We are to show these behaviors to others every day. We have discussed joy, patience, self-control, kindness, and love. We will focus on peace today. Peace is a calm or stress-free feeling. The Bible says that God gives us peace..

Review your memory verse on page 105.

RHYME TIME:

"Can you tell me our poem this week?

(Help them if needed.) "Little Miss Muffet"

"Our word today is frightened. What does that mean? Yes, it is another word for scared or afraid. What frightens you? Would you be frightened if a spider sat down beside you?

"Highlight the I's and i's in the rhyme on page 105.

LESSON 9
Day 3

ABC'S AND MORE:

"Now, let's look at our ABC chart. Show me two capital letters. Show me two lowercase letters.

Chant the ABC chart.

Sing the ABC song.

Point to the capital I.
Point to the lowercase i.

"This is the capital I and this is the lowercase i. Let's review how to write them!

Practice writing I's and i's.

"I: (down, across, across)
Start at the top line, go straight down to the bottom line (down).
Make a line across at the top line (across).
Make a line across at the bottom line (across).

"i: (down, dot)
Starting at the middle line, go down to the bottom line (down) and then in between the middle line and top line, place a dot (dot).

Trace the Ii's below.

MINI BOOK I:

Read the letter book again.

Advanced K — see if your child can read the book to you.

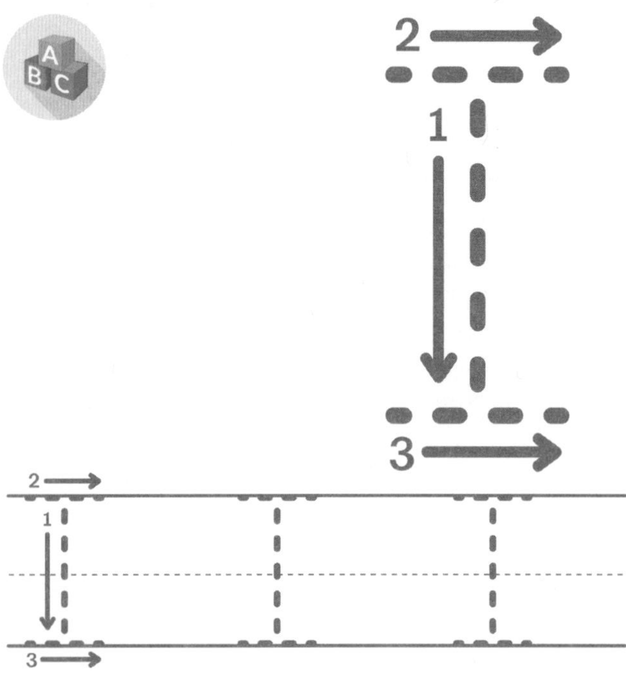

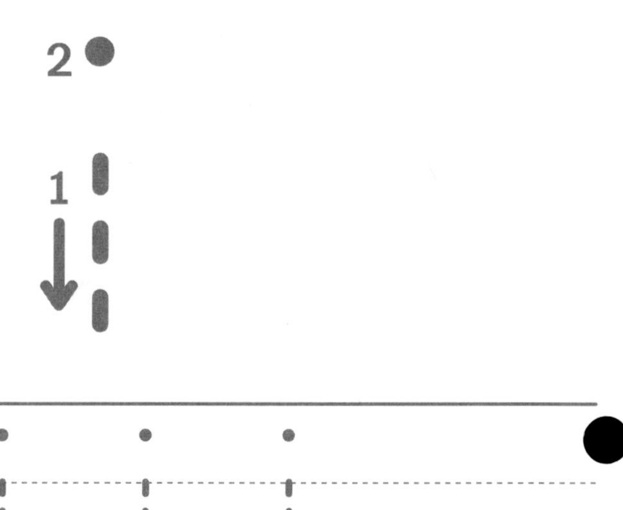

LESSON 10
Prep Page

Supply List

☐ Day 1, life skills:

Pasta with tomato meat sauce
Pasta—your favorite kind or spaghetti squash (½ pound spaghetti or 1 lb. of other pastas or 1 whole spaghetti squash)
1 lb. ground beef (optional: use onion and salt)
12 oz. can of tomato paste
28 oz. can of crushed tomatoes
1 tsp. oregano
1 tsp. garlic powder
1 tsp. onion powder
1 T parsley flakes
½ tsp. salt
½ tsp. pepper

☐ Day 3, life skills

2 grocery bags of perishable and non-perishable foods (from around your home, or go grocery shopping)

Sandwich roll-ups:
1 pkg. 8 refrigerated crescent rolls
Lunch meat of your choice
4 slices sliced cheese

Objectives

Letter of the week: Jj

Skills/Concepts: where things belong, food sorts

Memory Verse

Galatians 5:22-23

But the fruit of the Spirit is love, joy, peace, forbearance, kindness, goodness, faithfulness, gentleness and self-control. Against such things there is no law.

Extended Activities

Sort other items by type, shape, or color (shoes, clothes, toys).

Have them help you cook.

Teach them to crack an egg.

Add sounds for chanting the ABC chart — see video.

LESSON 10
Day 1

LIFE SKILLS:

"This week we will sort food for where it belongs. Some food we have to keep cold in our refrigerator or frozen in our freezer, otherwise it will ruin. Let's look at what we might need to keep cool in a refrigerator.

"Then we have food that we can store in our cabinet/pantry. Like canned goods, cereals, chips, pasta.

"We will use items from the refrigerator and pantry/cabinet to make pasta. First, make the sauce and let it simmer a while so all the flavors really mix well.

Recipe on next page.

Complete Life Skill cooking activity.

BIBLE:

"We will continue learning about the Fruits of the Spirit this week. Using your tree from last week, trace the word "goodness" and cut and paste the goodness fruit on the tree.

"We are to show these behaviors to others every day.

"We have discussed joy, patience, self-control, kindness, love, and peace. We will focus on goodness today. Goodness . . . what do you think that word might mean? Goodness means to be good. What are some of our rules in our home? *Help them come up with a few.* What are ways you can be good?

"Right — so being good or showing goodness might not always be easy, but we can do our best to show goodness to others every day.

Review your memory verse from Lesson 9 below. Echo read the verse. Add motions.

But the fruit of the Spirit is love ,

joy , peace  ,

forbearance, kindness, goodness ,

faithfulness, gentleness , and self-control.

Against  such things there is no law.

"We have talked about Joseph having storehouses of food as God had commanded him, but there was another man in the Bible who had a different attitude. He was more focused on getting more and more for himself. Read Luke 12:16–21.

"In this story, the man wasn't storing things to bless others. He was keeping it all for himself. God wants us to be cheerful givers. We should help those who are poor, but we should also share Jesus with others. If we do not tell others about Jesus, then it is also being like this man. We are just keeping Jesus to ourselves. Christ wants us to tell others about Him so they can also have eternal life.

Name

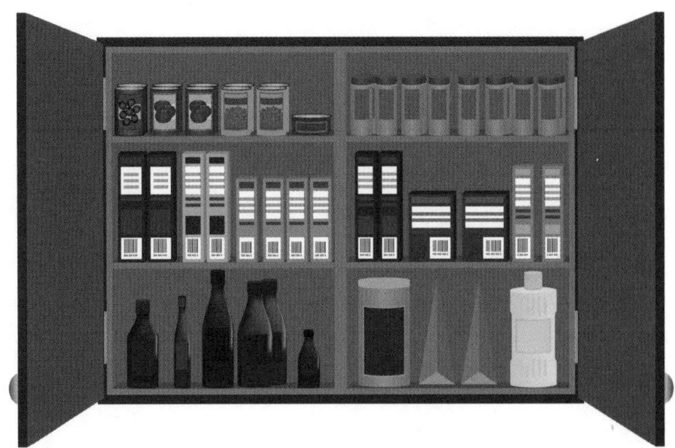

RECIPE

From the kitchen of:

Pasta—your favorite kind or even spaghetti squash is yummy! (½ lb. spaghetti or 1 lb. of other pastas or 1 whole spaghetti squash)

- ☐ 1 lb. ground beef, browned (optional: use onion and salt)
- ☐ 12 oz. can of tomato paste
- ☐ 28 oz. can of crushed tomatoes
- ☐ 1 tsp. oregano
- ☐ 1 tsp. garlic powder
- ☐ 1 tsp. onion powder
- ☐ 1 T parsley flakes
- ☐ ½ tsp. salt
- ☐ ½ tsp. pepper

In a pan, brown your meat.
In another pot, mix your crushed tomatoes, tomato paste, and all spices.
Add in the meat, mix, cover, and let it simmer, stirring occasionally, for at least 30 minutes. (an hour is preferred)
Boil your pasta for at least 10 minutes, until tender.
(Boil –means to heat the water so much that it begins to bubble up.)
Mix pasta into the sauce.

Alternate: To prepare the spaghetti squash — you can use a knife to make a cutting line around the middle horizontally. Then, microwave for 4-5 minutes. Then, use a knife to cut it in half horizontally. Drizzle olive oil, salt, and pepper and spread it over the meat of the squash. Then, in a cake pan or cookie sheet, place it face down (meat down, skin up) and bake at 400 degrees for 45 minutes. Take a fork to flip them over and rake the fork across it to make the "noodles."

LESSON 10
Day 1

RHYME TIME:

"Our poem this week is "Jack and Jill."

Read the poem below and then have them echo read with you.

ABC'S AND MORE:

"Now, let's look at our ABC chart. Show me two capital letters. Show me two lowercase letters.

See Teacher Resource Page.

Chant the ABC chart.

Sing the ABC song.

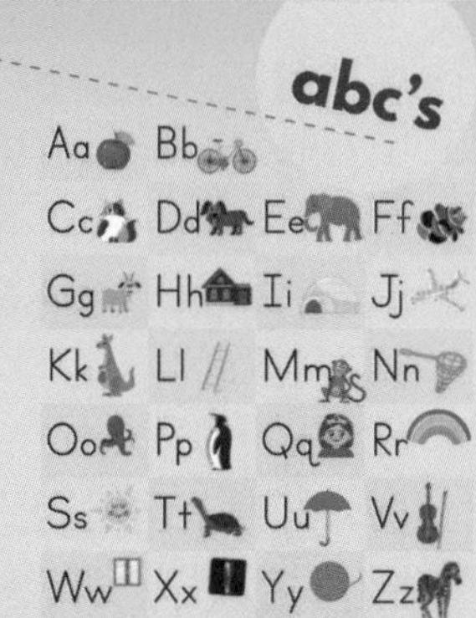

"Let's learn how to write our Jj's.

Point to the capital J. Point to the lowercase j.

"This is the capital J and this is the lowercase j. Let's write them!

Jack and Jill

Jack and Jill went up the hill
to fetch a pail of water.
Jack fell down and broke his crown
and Jill came tumbling after.

LESSON 10
Day 1

Practice writing J's and j's.

"J: (down and curve, across)
Start at the top line, go down toward the bottom line (down).
Curve back toward the middle line (curve).
Cross it at the top (across).

"j: (down, curve, dot)
Starting at the middle line, go down past the bottom line (down)
Curve up toward the bottom line and then in between the middle line and top line, place a dot (dot).

Trace the Jj's below.

MINI-BOOK J:

See the Teacher Resource Page.

Do a picture walk.

Read the book to the student, pointing to each letter/word.

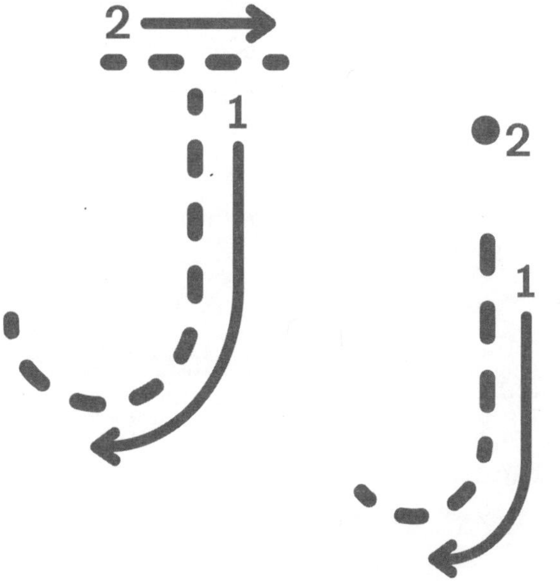

2 1 2 1

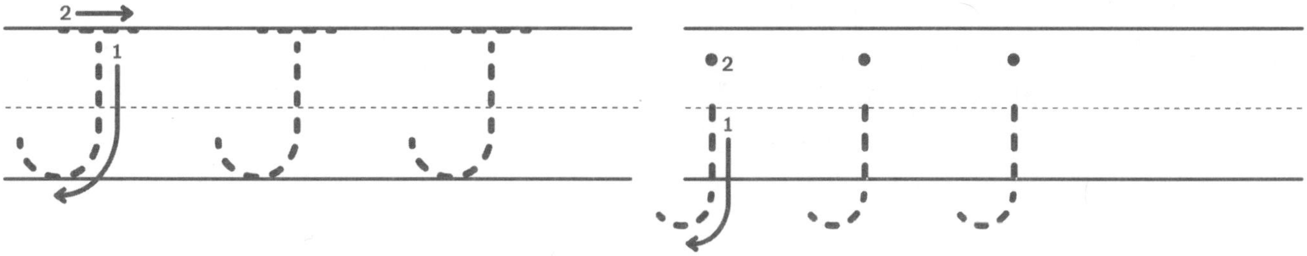

LESSON 10
Day 2

LIFE SKILLS:

"Remember, some food we have to keep cold in our refrigerator or frozen in our freezer, otherwise it will ruin. See if you can complete the activity on the following pages. And then we will do our Bible work.

Complete the Life Skills sorting activity on the next page.

BIBLE:

"We will continue learning the Fruits of the Spirit.

Review the fruits of the spirit on your tree.

"Trace and add the fruit for "faithfulness."

Complete this Bible activity.

"We are to show these behaviors to others every day.

"We have discussed joy, patience, self-control, kindness, love, peace, and goodness. We will focus on faithfulness today. Faithfulness or being faithful means to be constant and devoted, and here we mean faithful to God. Those words are still big words, so let's break them down. Constant would be to always follow God . . . constantly. Like our word we had a few weeks back on persistence. That meant never giving up even when it was hard. So, being constant means to also be persistent in our walk with God. Devoted means to be committed. This means you will not let anything get in your way of following God. God is also faithful to us.

Review your memory verse on page 116.

"There is a story in the Bible about a woman named Ruth who showed great faithfulness.

Read Ruth 1:6–22.

"Ruth 1:16 says:
But Ruth replied, "Don't urge me to leave you or to turn back from you. Where you go I will go, and where you stay I will stay. Your people will be my people and your God my God."

"Ruth was faithful to God and the family He had given her even when it seemed she had no reason to stay. God provided for Ruth and her mother-in-law, Naomi. When we are faithful to God, He will provide for us.

RHYME TIME:

"Let's read our poem this week again.

Read the poem below and then have them echo read with you.

Jack and Jill

Jack and Jill went up the hill
to fetch a pail of water.
Jack fell down and broke his crown
and Jill came tumbling after.

Name

Cut the items out and sort them into either the cabinet on this page or the refrigerator on page 123. Glue the items into place.

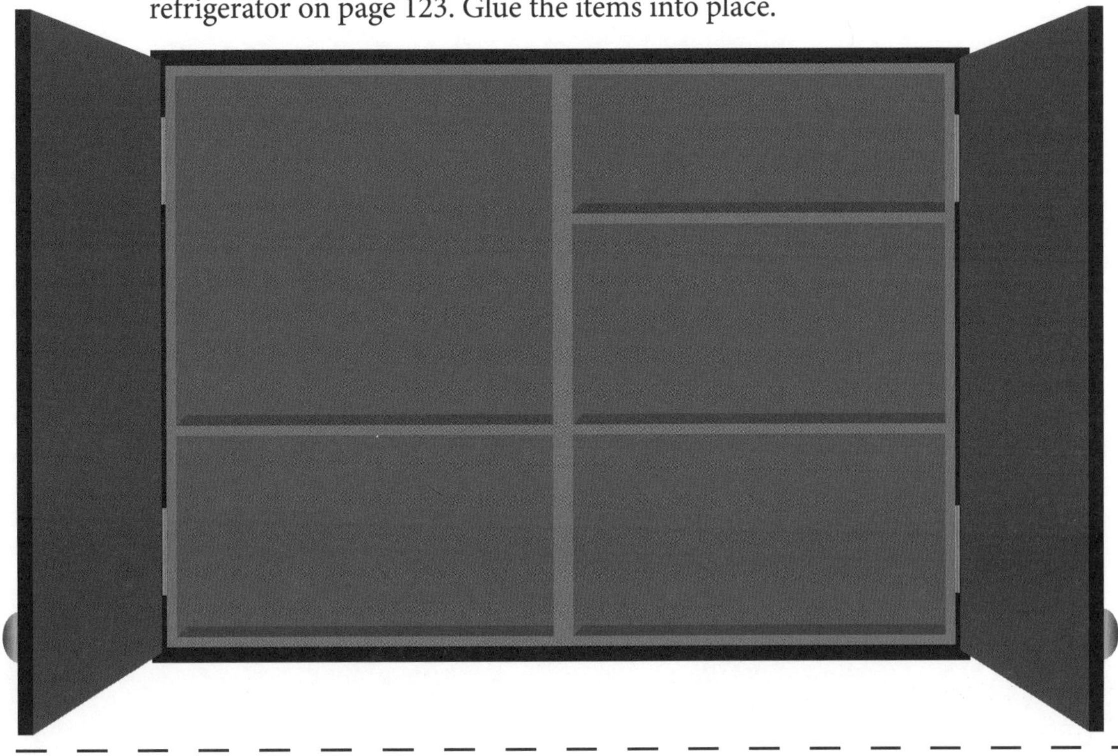

Cut page at line above.

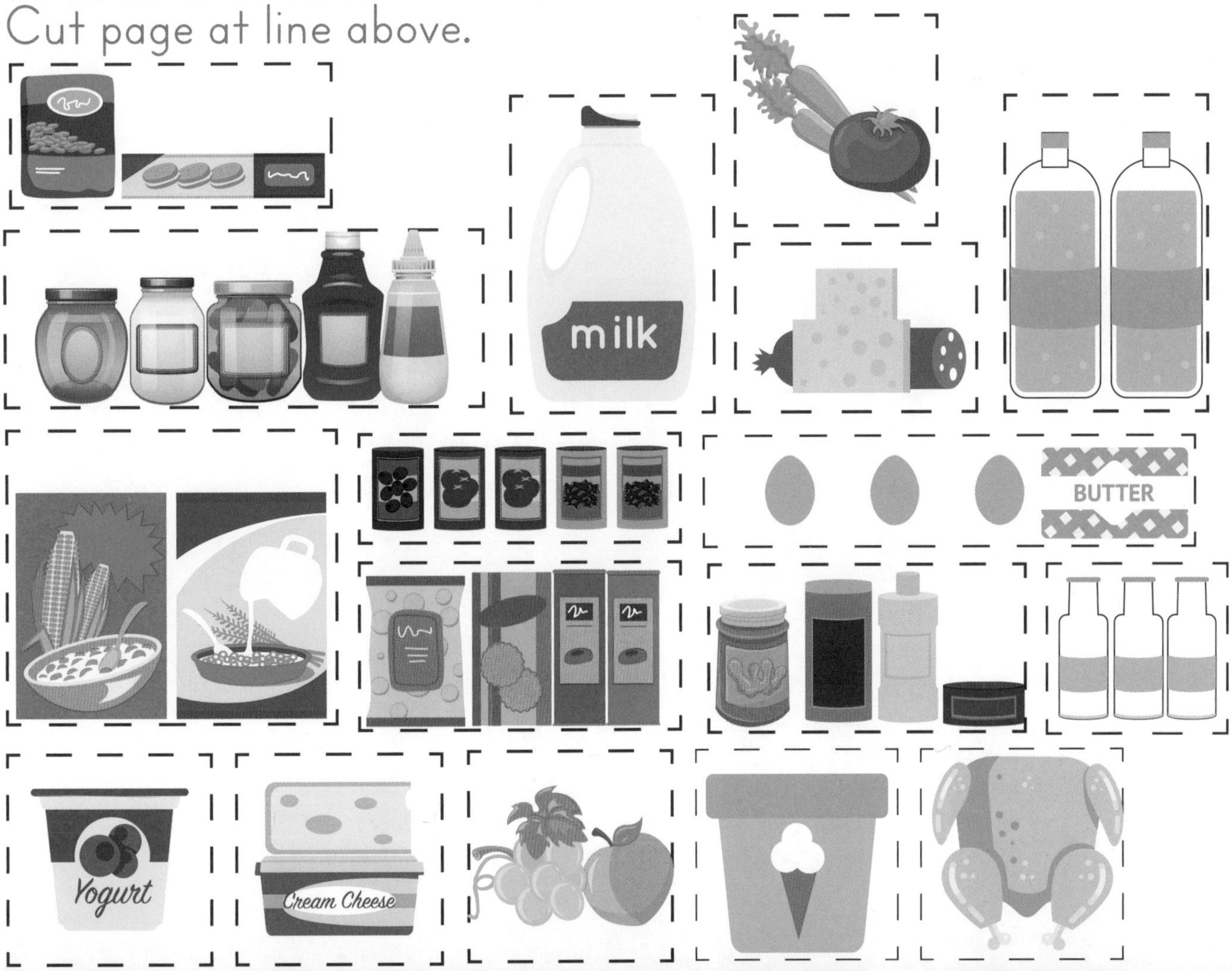

Blank Page for cutting.

Name

LESSON 10
Day 2

ABC'S AND MORE:

"Now, let's look at our ABC chart. I will say a letter, and you tell me the picture on the ABC chart *(either randomly pick some or: A, K, S, V, Z, R, H).*

Chant the ABC chart.

Sing the ABC song.

"Let's write our Jj's again today!

Practice writing J's and j's.

"J: (down and curve, across)
Start at the top line, go down toward the bottom line (down). Curve back toward the middle line (curve). Cross it at the top (across).

"j: (down, curve dot)
Starting at the middle line, go down past the bottom line (down).
Curve up toward the bottom line and then in between the middle line and top line, place a dot (dot).

Trace the Jj's below.

MINI-BOOK J:

Read the letter book to the student.

Highlight the J's and j's in the book.

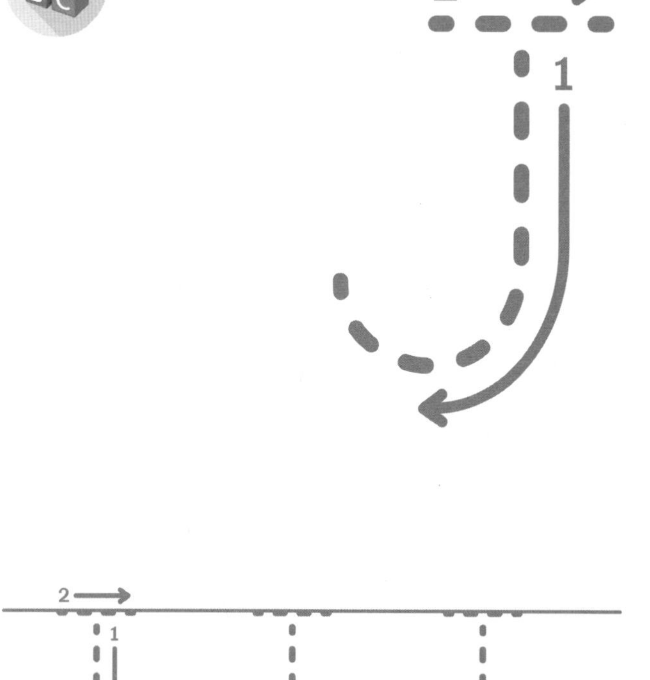

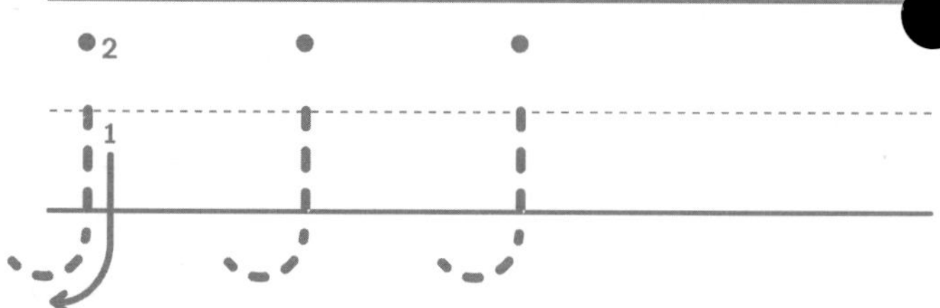

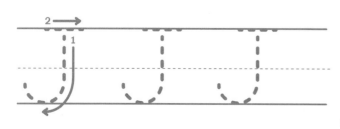

LESSON 10
Day 3

LIFE SKILLS:

"Today, I have some bags of food for you to put away where they belong.

Bag and use groceries from your home if you can. Optional extension: Go grocery shopping and have them help you put it away.

"Let's make Sandwich Roll Ups! First, we need to preheat oven to 400°.
Preheat means to heat the oven to the temperature we need to bake at before we begin baking our food.

"On a lightly greased baking sheet: Unroll your crescent rolls. Take a piece of cheese, fold it in half to form two triangles. Place one triangle on the wide end of the crescent matching up the width/length. Place a few slices of turkey on the cheese and roll up the crescent roll around it. Repeat until all crescent rolls are used. Bake for 11 minutes, or until golden brown. Enjoy!

BIBLE:

"Our poem this week reminds me of a story in the Bible where a woman went to a well to fetch water. Read from John 4:5–15. Jesus is the Living Water. That means if we have Him, then we will have eternal life. He is all we need. He is the one that keeps us, protects us, and saves us from our sin.

"Let's review the Fruits of the Spirit on your tree and any others you have left. Trace and add the fruit for gentleness to your tree.

"We are to show these behaviors to others every day.

"We have discussed all of the fruits of the spirit except one. We have talked about joy, patience, self-control, kindness, love, peace, goodness, and faithfulness. Last, we will focus on gentleness. Gentleness is another word for being kind. We can show kindness in a lot of ways. We can be kind to others in the way we speak to them, or by sharing things with them, or even taking care of a sick neighbor.

Review your memory verse from Lesson 9 on page 116.

RHYME TIME:.

"Let's read our poem for this week again.

Read the poem "Jack and Jill" and then have them echo read with you.

"Highlight the Jj's in the rhyme.

Jack and Jill

Jack and Jill went up the hill
to fetch a pail of water.
Jack fell down and broke his crown
and Jill came tumbling after.

LESSON 10
Day 3

ABC'S AND MORE:

"Now, let's look at our ABC chart. I will say a picture, and you tell me the letter on the ABC chart *(either randomly pick some or: N, I, C, Q, B, L).*

See Teacher Resource Page.

Chant the ABC chart.

Sing the ABC song.

"Let's review how to write our Jj's.

Point to capital J. Point to lowercase j.

"Remember, there are capital J's and lowercase j's.

Practice writing J's and j's.

"J: (down and curve, across)
Start at the top line, go down toward the bottom line (down).
Curve back toward the middle line (curve).
Cross it at the top (across).

"j: (down, curve dot)
Starting at the middle line, go down past the bottom line (down).
Curve up toward the bottom line and then in between the middle line and top line, place a dot (dot).

Trace the Jj's below.

MINI-BOOK J:

Read the letter book again to the student.

Advanced K — see if your child can read the book to you.

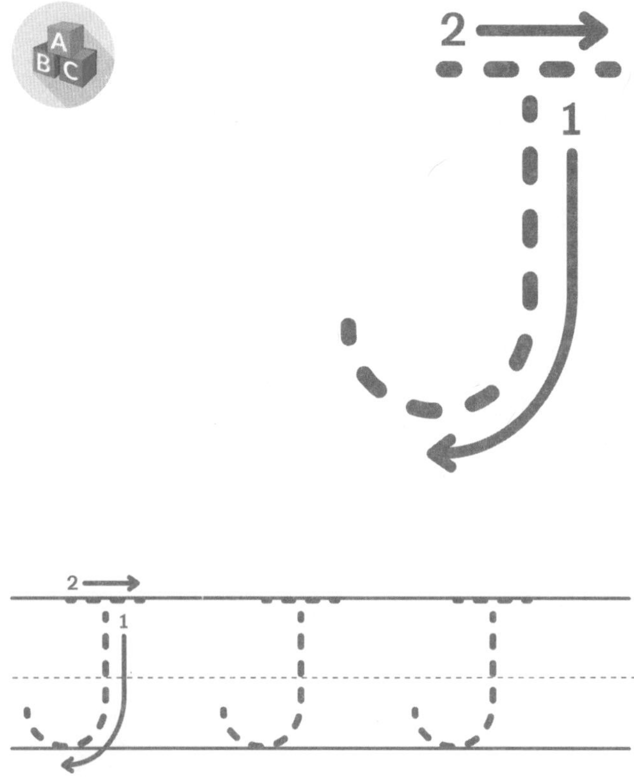

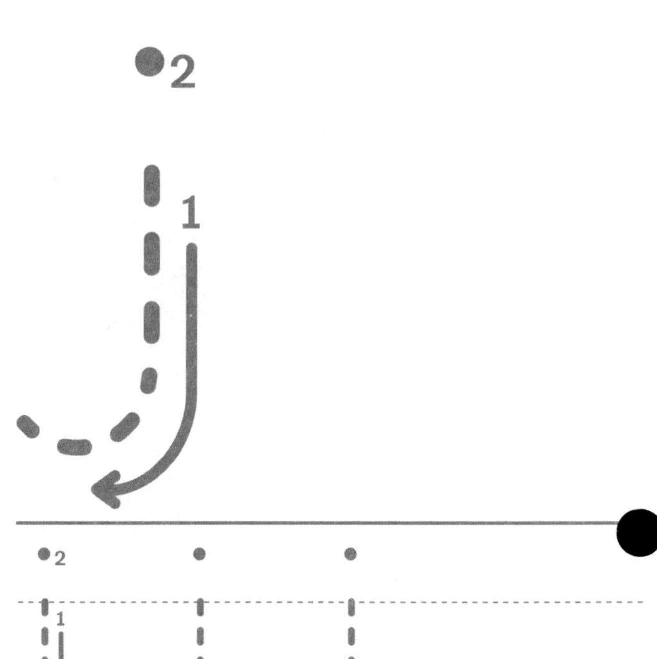

LESSON 11
Prep Page

Supply List

- ☐ Laundry (daily, life skills)
- ☐ Battery-operated candle (day 1, Bible)
- ☐ Dark room (day 1, Bible)
- ☐ Grassy area/hay/straw/tall carpet (day 1, Bible)
- ☐ Dime

Look Ahead

Day 1 has you hiding a dime in grassy area/high pile carpet before the Bible section.

See Lesson 12 for supplies for an experiment on day 3. You will need to prep things.

Objectives

Letter of the week: Kk

Skills/Concepts: sorting laundry

Memory Verse

Luke 19:10

For the Son of Man came to seek and to save the lost.

Extended Activities

Review practicing writing their name.

Add sounds for chanting the ABC chart — see video.

LESSON 11
Day 1

LIFE SKILLS:

"This week we will focus on being a good helper. What does it mean to help someone? To help someone means you make it easier for them to do something they need to do.

"A good helper does what they are asked quickly and with a good attitude. If you are asked to help with chores or other tasks, you should do it quickly and with a good attitude. One thing I will have you help me with is laundry. Last week we sorted food. This week we will sort laundry.

Have them help you sort laundry.
NOTE: This varies by family. Please teach your student(s) how you want your laundry sorted. Remember, show them first (model), then have them focus on sorting (dish towels, washcloths, bath towels).

BIBLE:

Start in a dark place with only some candlelight. Hide a dime in the grass or in hay or even high pile carpet.

"I want to tell a Bible story about a woman's coin.

Read the story in Luke 15:8–10.

"Have you ever lost something? Can you tell me about what you lost? Did you ever find it?

"When we lose something, we often search and search until we find it. This woman lost one of her coins. This was very precious as it was kind of like a wedding ring, as it showed her faithfulness to her husband. Back in Bible times, they would have had dirt, sand, or clay floors covered in hay, and they would have been dusty.

LESSON 11
Day 1

“She was in a dimly lit room, much like we are. Is it easy to find something in here? No, it isn’t. She had to use a candle to give her some light, and sweep away the hay and dust.

“Let’s go look for a silver coin in the _____ (grass/hay/carpet). Here we have good light, but think if we were looking with only candlelight. Would it be hard to find the coin?

“Yes, it would! Was the woman happy once she found her coin? Yes, she was! This is just how Jesus is happy when one sinner comes to Him and repents. The angels rejoice and I bet they sing forth His praise!

Allow the student to look for coin.

“Our memory verse is in Luke 19:10, and it says:

Echo read the verse. Add motions.

Optional: You might try the whole verse.

For the Son of Man  came

to seek 

and to save the lost. 

RHYME TIME:

“Just like the woman lost her coin, our poem is about a little girl named Lucy Locket, and she lost something, too.

Read the poem “Lucy Locket” below and then have them echo read with you.

Lucy Locket **By James Orchard Halliwell**

Lucy Locket lost her pocket,
Kitty Fisher found it;
not a penny was there in it,
only ribbon round it.

LESSON 11
Day 1

ABC'S AND MORE:

"Now, let's look at our ABC chart. Let's see if you can be the teacher and I will echo you as you say the letters and the pictures.

See Teacher Resource Page.

Chant the ABC chart.

Sing the ABC song.

"Today, we are learning how to write our Kk's.

Point to the capital K. Point to the lowercase k.

"This is a capital K. This is a lowercase k.

Practice writing K's and k's.

"K: (down, slant in, slant out)
Start at the top line, make a line down to the bottom line (down). Start at the top line, a little over from where you have your line.
Slant in at the middle line (slant in), then slant back out to the bottom line (slant out).

"k: (down, slant in, slant out)
Start at the top line, make a line down to the bottom line (down.) Start between the middle lines, a little over from where you have your line.
Slant in at the middle line (slant in), then slant back out to the bottom line (slant out).

Trace the Kk's below.

MINI-BOOK K:

See the Teacher Resource Page.

Do a picture walk.

Read the book to the student, pointing to each letter/word.

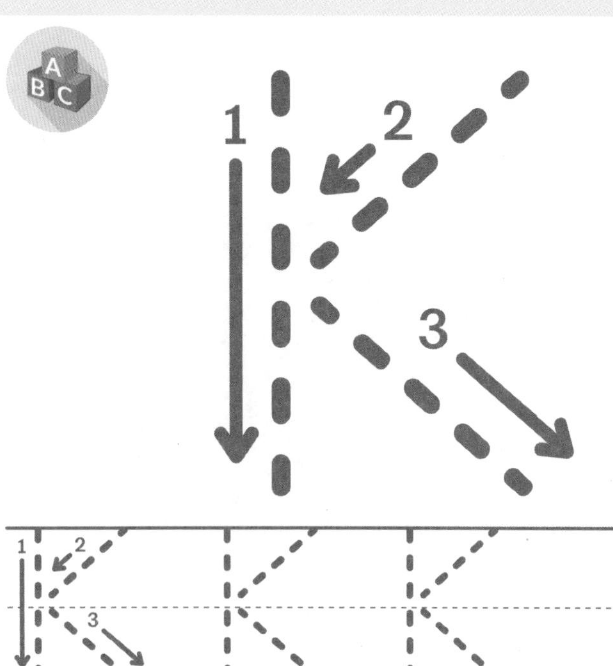

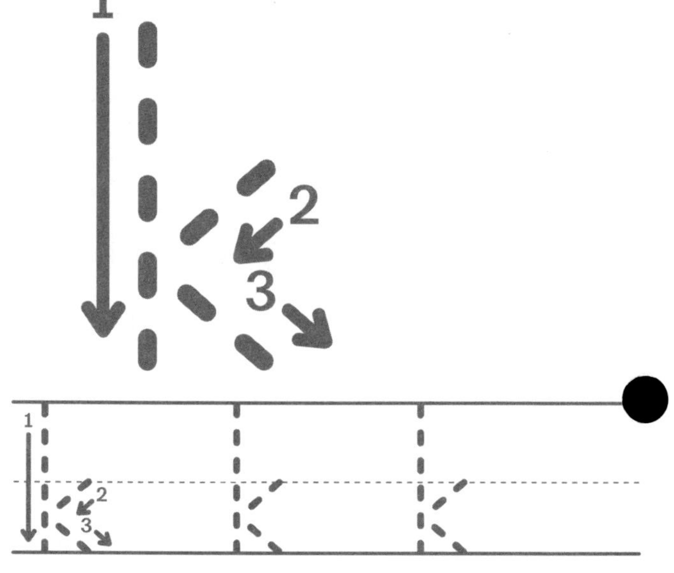

LESSON 11
Day 2

LIFE SKILLS:

"This week we are focusing on being a good helper. Do you remember what it means to help someone? Yes, to help someone means you make it easier for them to do something they need to do. You have been helping me and being a good helper with the laundry.

"A good helper does what they are asked quickly and with a good attitude. We will continue to sort laundry.

Have them help you sort laundry.

BIBLE:

"I want to tell another Bible story, but this one is about a lost sheep. Read Luke 15:3–7. Just like the woman was excited and happy to find her lost coin, the shepherd was also excited and rejoiced over finding his lost sheep. Both the woman and the shepherd called for their friends to come rejoice with them. This is how it is when someone asks for Jesus to forgive them and they become a Christian.

"We all rejoice. Rejoice means to show great joy. Heaven rejoices each time a sinner gives his or her life to Christ. We should call our friends and have them rejoice with us over every person that comes to Christ because it is such a wonderful thing! We can also rejoice in singing praise together.

Optional: Sing or play the hymn called "I Have Decided to Follow Jesus" if you have it or look up the lyrics.

Review your memory verse on page 129.

RHYME TIME:

"Remember the shepherd lost one of his sheep? Well, Lucy Locket lost her ___________. What did she lose? *(Her pocket!)*

Read the poem on the next page.

"On the next page, help Lucy find her pocket. Then we will practice writing again!

Complete the "Lucy Locket" activity on the next page.

Kangaroo

kangaroo

Lesson 11
Day 2

Name

Lucy lost her pocket and needs your help! See if you can help her get through the maze to find her pocket.

Lucy Locket

Lucy Locket lost her pocket,
Kitty Fisher found it;
not a penny was there in it,
only ribbon round it.

LESSON 11
Day 2

ABC'S AND MORE:

"Now, let's look at our ABC chart. Let's see if you can be the teacher and I will echo you as you say the letters and the pictures.

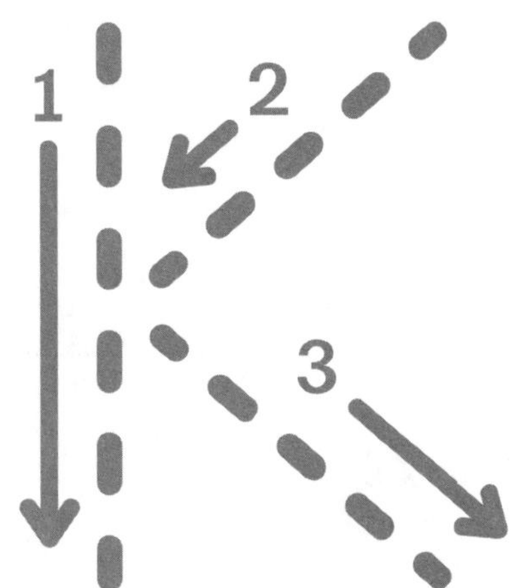

Chant the ABC chart.

Sing the ABC song.

"Let's practice writing our Kk's!

Practice writing K's and k's.

"K: (down, slant in, slant out)
Start at the top line, make a line down to the bottom line (down). Start at the top line, a little over from where you have your line.
Slant in at the middle line (slant in), then slant back out to the bottom line (slant out).

"k: (down, slant in, slant out)
Start at the top line, make a line down to the bottom line (down). Start between the middle lines, a little over from where you have your line. Slant in at the middle line (slant in), then slant back out to the bottom line (slant out).

Trace the Kk's below.

MINI-BOOK K:

Read the letter book to the student.

Have the student highlight the capital and lowercase letter of the week.

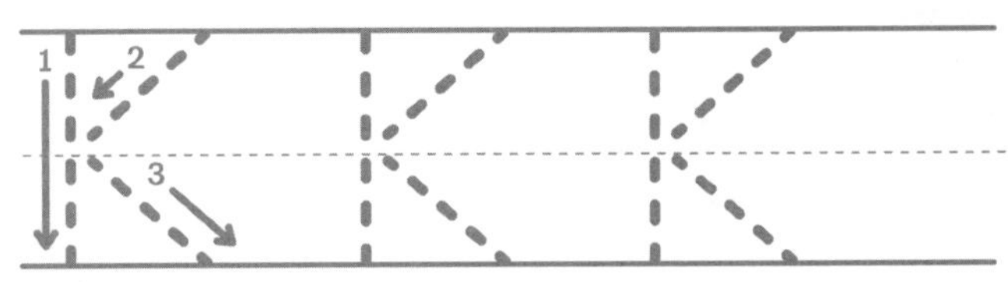

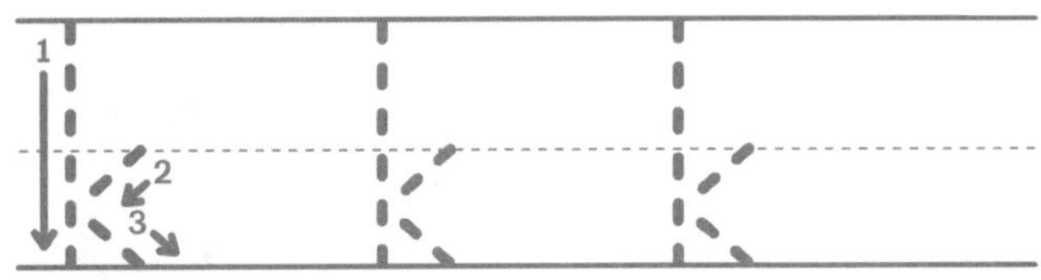

LESSON 11
Day 3

LIFE SKILLS:

"Remember, we are focusing on being a good helper. Do you remember what it means to help someone? Yes, to help someone means you make it easier for them to do something they need to do. You have been helping me and being a good helper with the laundry this week.

"How does a good helper do what they are asked? Do you remember? Quickly and with a good attitude!

Continue to sort laundry.

BIBLE:

"I want to start with a Bible story about a prodigal son. Prodigal means wasteful. That means the son wasted the money he had by spending it on things he didn't need.
Let's read the story in Luke 15:11–32.

"You see, again, when someone who was lost comes back, there is rejoicing! Remember, when we sin, it separates us from God.

"God doesn't stop loving us, and when we do come back to Him, He and all of heaven rejoice!

"We have a choice whether or not we follow Christ. He offers us salvation like a free gift. We have to accept the gift He has given.

Review your memory verse on page 129.

"Jesus wants to save everyone and that is why He came to earth. He died on the Cross so we could be saved and live forever with Him.

RHYME TIME:

Read "Lucy Locket" on the next page.

"In our Bible story, the father lost his son for a time, just like Lucy Locket lost her pocket, but it was found again.

"Highlight the K's and k's in the rhyme.

Kayak kayak

Name

Color the pocket.

Lucy Locket By James Orchard Halliwell

Lucy Locket lost her pocket,
Kitty Fisher found it;
not a penny was there in it,
only ribbon round it.

LESSON 11
Day 3

ABC'S AND MORE:

"Now, let's look at our ABC chart. Let's see if you can be the teacher and I will echo you as you say the letters and the pictures.

See Teacher Resource Page.

Chant the ABC chart.

Sing the ABC song.

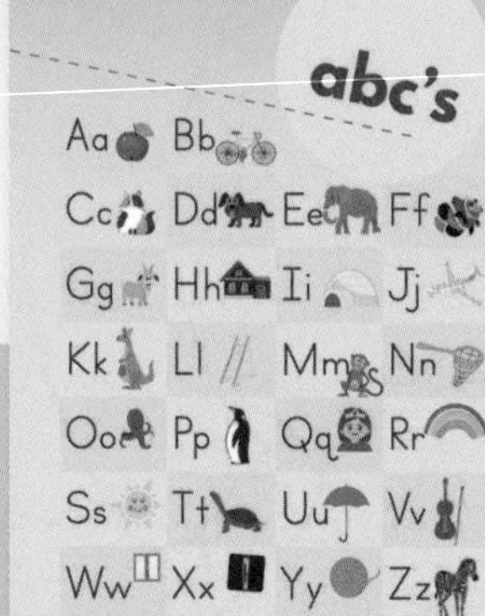

"Let's review how to write Kk's. Remember, there are capital and lowercase Kk's.

Practice writing K's and k's.

"K: (down, slant in, slant out)
Start at the top line, make a line down to the bottom line (down).
Start at the top line, a little over from where you have your line.
Slant in at the middle line (slant in), then slant back out to the bottom line (slant out).

"k: (down, slant in, slant out)
Start at the top line, make a line down to the bottom line (down).
Start between the middle lines, a little over from where you have your line.
Slant in at the middle line (slant in), then slant back out to the bottom line (slant out).

Trace the Kk's below.

MINI-BOOK K:

Read the letter book again.

Advanced K — see if your child can read the book to you.

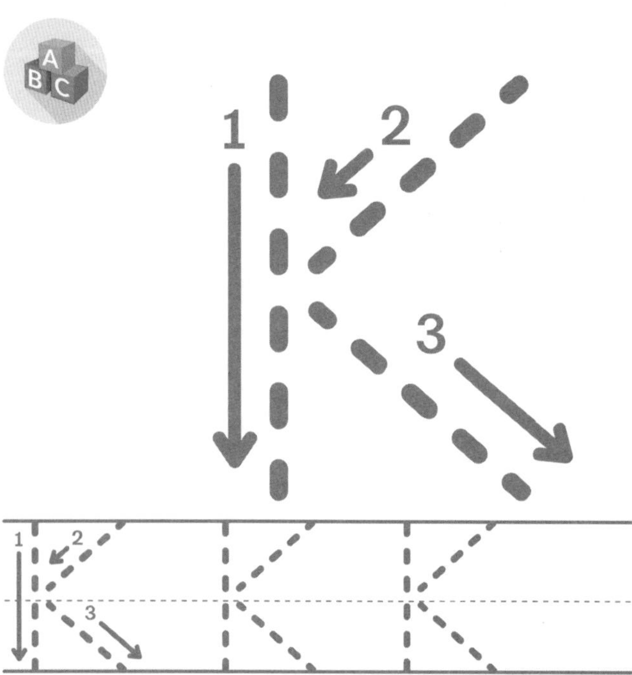

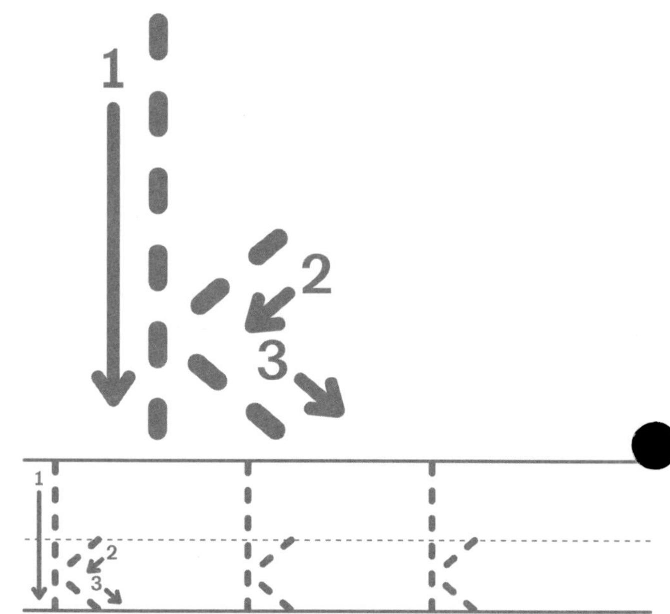

LESSON 12
Prep Page

Supply List

- ☐ Glass for sipping (day 3, rhyme time)
- ☐ 3 clear jars; iodine; bleach; water for jars (day 3, Bible)
- ☐ 3 post-its/note cards labeled Jesus, Us, Sin (day 3, Bible)
- ☐ Pairs of socks to sort
- ☐ Dry erase board/plastic sleeve (day 2, Bible)

Look Ahead

Next week you will need a basic place setting and ingredients for recipes.

Objectives

Letter of the week: Ll

Skills Concepts: matching & mating socks

Memory Verse

2 Corinthians 5:17

Therefore, if anyone is in Christ, the new creation has come: The old has gone, the new is here!

Extended Activities

Play a matching game, UNO, or Go Fish.

Add sounds for chanting the ABC chart — see video

LESSON 12
Day 1

LIFE SKILLS:

"We will focus on matching items this week. If two things match, they look exactly alike. Like this dog matches this dog.

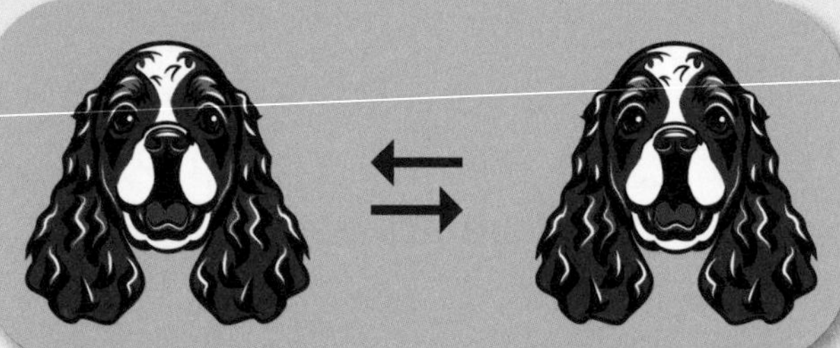

"We can also match our socks! Most socks have a mate or a match — meaning there are two that are exactly alike. Let's look at our clean socks and see how many matches we can find.

Have them help you sort laundry.

"Today we will put our little finger up and pretend that it is a worm!

"Then, we will also make a butterfly with our fingers!

Read poem through first, then, let them move their index finger as a worm. When you get to the butterfly, show them how to hook thumbs and move fingers to be like a butterfly.

"The word dazzling means stunning or amazing. The line says, "It spreads its wings so dazzling bright," so that means it spreads its wings and is amazingly bright. Let's add some color to the butterfly on the next page to make it dazzling bright.

RHYME TIME:

"We will talk about our rhyme before we do our Bible because our Bible is about our rhyme.

Little Worm

A little worm is on the ground,
it creeps, and creeps, and creeps around;
'tis spinning now a little nest,
that it may find a place to rest.
Dear little worm, we'll say "goodbye,"
'till you come out a butterfly,

Oh! There it is, oh! See it fly,
a lovely, lovely butterfly.
It spreads its wings so dazzling bright,
and seeks the joyous air and light.
'Tis sipping honey from the flowers,
dear little butterfly, you're ours.

LESSON 12
Day 1

BIBLE:

"Just like the butterfly in our poem is a new creation, we are also a new creation in Christ! Our memory verse is 2 Corinthians 5:17.

"Now we will echo read our verse. Remember, you repeat what I say like an echo.

Echo read the verse. Add motions.

Therefore, if anyone 

is in Christ  ,

the new creation has come:

The old has gone,

the new is here!

"This week we will focus on being a "new creation" and what that means.

"Let's look at the life cycle of a butterfly. At first, it starts out as a worm or caterpillar.

"Then, it eats and eats and eats until it is ready to make its chrysalis or special nest.

"Last, while in the chrysalis, it changes from a worm or caterpillar into a beautiful butterfly!

"The "old" would be the worm or caterpillar. When the butterfly comes out of the chrysalis, it is no longer a caterpillar. It is a new creation! Just like when we are saved, and we give our hearts to Christ. He takes the "old us" with our sins and He washes us clean and makes us new! We get a fresh start!

"Let's help this caterpillar find its way to the nice leaf it needs to eat so it will have energy to become a beautiful butterfly!

LESSON 12
Day 1

ABC'S AND MORE:

"Now, let's look at our ABC chart. Let's see if you can be the teacher and I will echo you as you say the letters and the pictures.

See Teacher Resource Page.

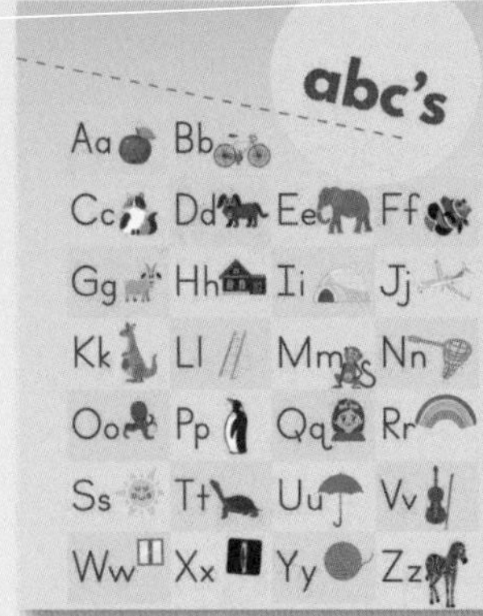

Chant the ABC chart.

Sing the ABC song.

Letter Run: Lay out your letter cards on the floor. Call out the following letters as the child races to find the letters: F, N, Q, X, C, G, R, E, T

"Let's learn to write our Ll's today!

Practice writing L's and l's.

"L: (down, over)
Start at the top line, go down the bottom line (down), then over to the right (over).

"l: (down)
Start at the top line, go down to the bottom line (down).

Trace the Ll's below.

MINI-BOOK L:

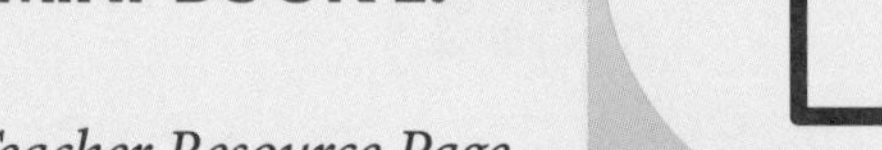

See the Teacher Resource Page.

Do a picture walk.

Read the book to the student, pointing to each letter/word.

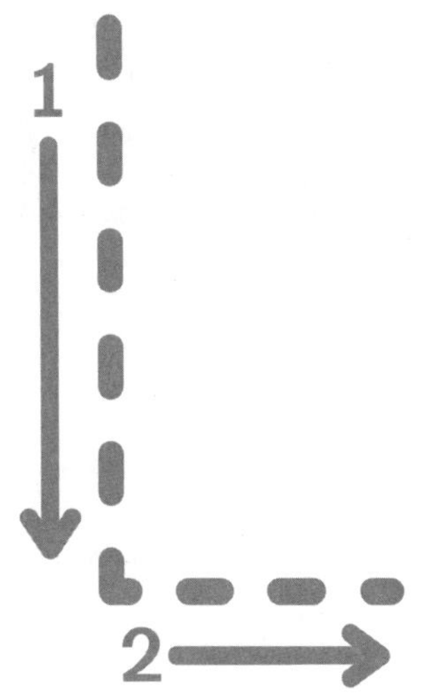

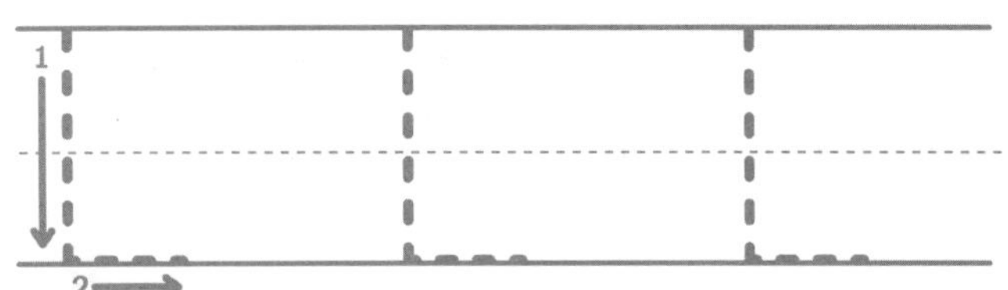

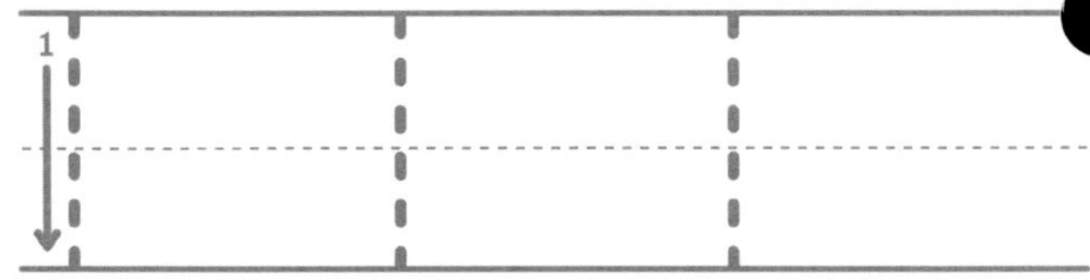

LESSON 12
Day 2

LIFE SKILLS:

"We will focus on matching items this week. If two things match, they look exactly alike. Yesterday, you matched socks from the laundry. Were you able to see how things that match look alike?

"See if you can match the pictures on the bottom of this page.

BIBLE:

"This week we are focusing on being a new creation and what that means. If we are a new creation, it means that the old is gone . . . it is no more.

On the dry erase board or plastic sleeve, write OLD.

"Just like this says OLD, when we accept Jesus Christ as our Savior, He comes in and makes us new.

Wipe away the words so the board is clean again.

"Just like this eraser removed the OLD and now it looks clean, Jesus is who helps us to change and be a new creation!

Review your memory verse on page 139.

RHYME TIME:

Read "Little Worm" on page 138.

"The word creeps means to crawl around slowly or sneak. I bet you can show me how you would creep around.

Match the pictures.

LESSON 12
Day 2

ABC'S AND MORE:

"Now, let's look at our ABC chart. Let's see if you can be the teacher and I will echo you as you say the letters and the pictures.

Chant the ABC chart.

Sing the ABC song.

Letter Run: Lay out your letter cards on the floor. Call out the following letters as the child races to find the letters: F, N, Q, X, C, G, R, E, T

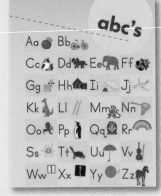

"Let's practice writing our Ll's today. Remember, there are both capital and lowercase Ll's!

Practice writing L's and l's.

"L: (down, over)
Start at the top line, go down the bottom line (down), then over to the right (over).

"l: (down)
Start at the top line, go down to the bottom line (down).

Trace the Ll's below.

MINI-BOOK L:

Read the letter book to the student.

Have the student highlight the capital and lowercase letter of the week.

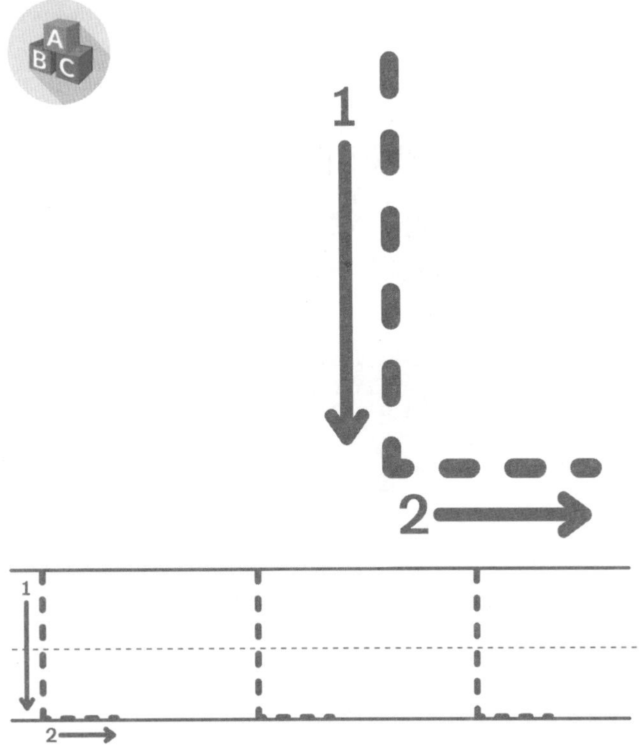

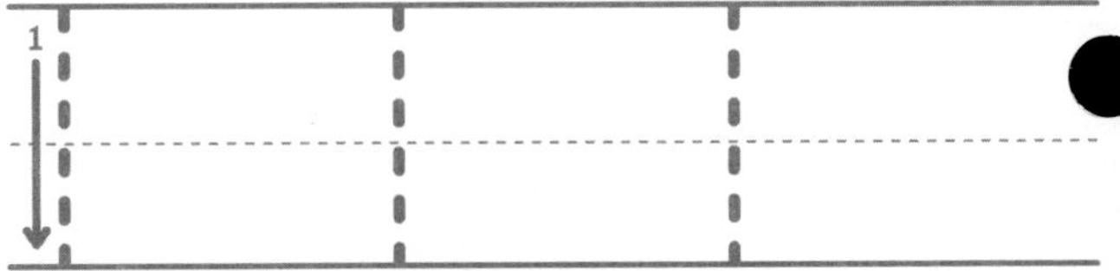

LESSON 12
Day 3

BIBLE:

Review your memory verse on page 139.

Set up prior to the lesson: 3 jars labeled Jesus, Us, and Sin; one filled ½ full with water and labeled Us; one filled ½ full with iodine and labeled Sin; one filled with bleach and labeled Jesus.

"We will do our Bible lesson first today. This week we have been talking about a NEW CREATION and how believing in Jesus and being saved is how we become new creations. Well, I want to show you how this works.

"This glass of water is like us. Then, we have this jar that is yucky and it is sin. Last, we have a jar that represents Jesus. We have that sin nature and we all sin, but Jesus never sinned and cannot sin because He is God. Why don't you try this with me?

"Let's pour some sin into our jar. What happened? Yes, we became yucky, too. Now, remember, Jesus cannot sin . . . so pour some sin into His jar. What happened? Yes, it disappears, because He cannot sin. Sin cannot enter into Christ. But it did enter into us. When we sin, we repent or ask God to forgive us, right? Who do we need to get rid of our sin? Jesus! Let's pour some JESUS into our jar. What happened? Yes! Jesus made us clean again! He is who saves us if we just ask!

"The Bible says if we ask for help, Jesus will help us. Always remember that He is our help! (John 14:13–14 and Psalm 121:2).

RHYME TIME:

Read poem through first, then, let them move their index finger as a worm. When you get to the butterfly, show them how to hook thumbs and move fingers to be like a butterfly.

"The word sipping means to drink small, quick amounts at a time. Let's see if you can show me how you can sip water.

"Highlight the L's and l's in the poem.

Little Worm

A little worm is on the ground,
it creeps, and creeps, and creeps around;
'tis spinning now a little nest,
that it may find a place to rest.
Dear little worm, we'll say "goodbye,"
'till you come out a butterfly,

Oh! There it is, oh! See it fly,
a lovely lovely butterfly.
It spreads its wings so dazzling bright,
and seeks the joyous air and light.
'Tis sipping honey from the flowers,
dear little butterfly, you're ours.

LIFE SKIL

"We will finish
the week. The n
try to trick you
and the type c

Finish the ma

Practice ma

Lesson 12
Day 3

Name

Find the match.

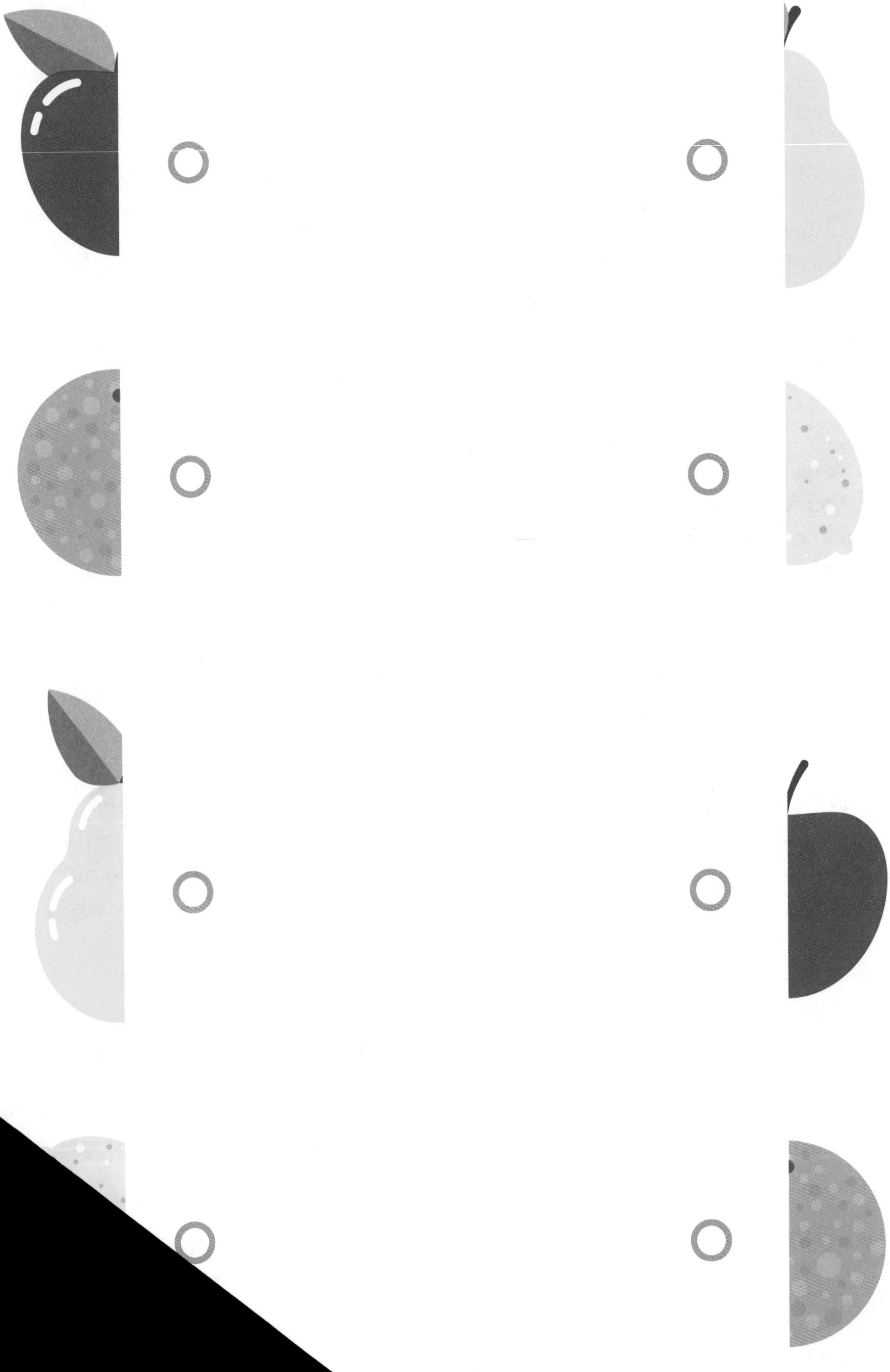

LESSON 12
Day 3

ABC'S AND MORE:

"Now, let's look at our ABC chart. Today, you will be matching capital letters and lowercase letters.

See Teacher Resource Page.

Chant the ABC chart.

Sing the ABC song.

Letter Run: Lay out your letter cards on the floor. Call out the following letters as the child races to find the letters: F, N, Q, X, C, G, R, E, T

"Let's review how we write Ll's!

Practice writing L's and l's.

"L: (down, over)
Start at the top line, go down the bottom line (down), then over to the right (over).

"l: (down)
Start at the top line, go down to the bottom line (down).

Trace the Ll's below.

MINI-BOOK L:

Read the letter book again.

Advanced K — see if your child can read the book to you.

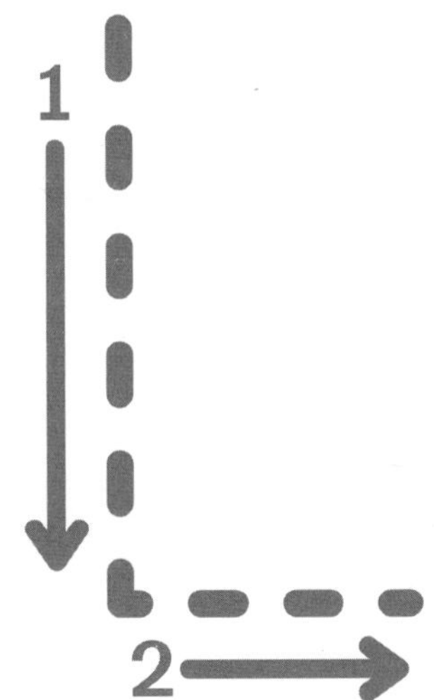

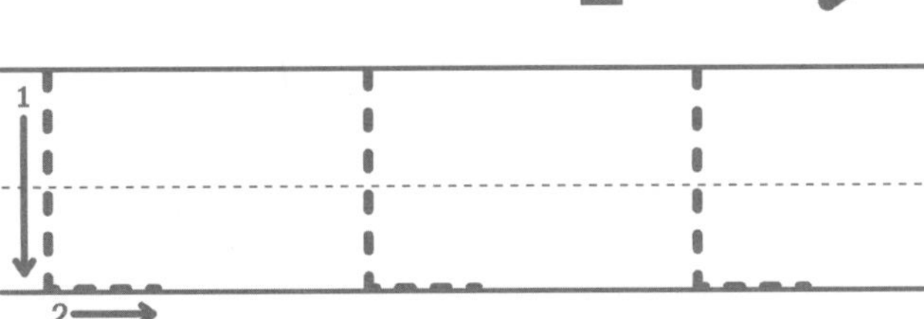

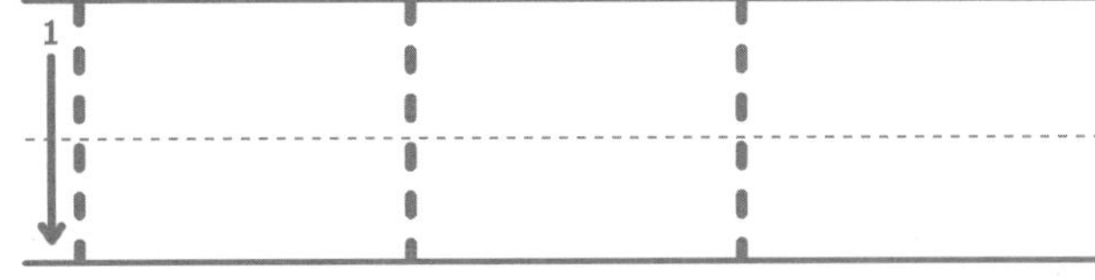

LESSON 13
Prep Page

Supply List

- ☐ Place setting (day 2, life skills; see page 218)
- ☐ See Banana Pancake recipe, Lesson 13, Day 1
- ☐ See Chili recipe, Lesson 13, Day 2
- ☐ Butter on a dish and bread on a plate (day 2, life skills)

Look Ahead

You will need an American flag for Lesson 14 (any size).

Objectives

Letter of the week: Mm

Skills/Concepts: manners (setting table, please, thank you, yes/no sir, yes/no ma'am, may I)

Memory Verse

1 Chronicles 29:13

Now, our God, we give you thanks, and praise Your glorious name.

Extended Activities

Have them help you cook daily and measure items.

Use rice bins for measuring and comparing.

Practice or teach how to use a microwave, toaster, and can opener.

Let them play dress up and pretend tea time, modeling good manners.

If you go to a restaurant, let them order their meal using correct sentences and manners. They should practice with you before telling the server. Teach them the proper way to request more to drink from the server.

LESSON 13
Day 1

LIFE SKILLS:

"We will practice good manners at each meal this week. We will also be learning how to set the table. You can help me with this each evening.

NOTE: This is a concept they will need to practice often and may not master in a week. If you do not prefer this method, please teach your child your preference. We will only be doing a casual setting. If you want to do a formal setting, please do so.

"Let's practice some manners at the table. We call these "table manners." Table manners include responding using yes ma'am, no ma'am, yes sir, no sir, thank you, and asking for things using the words "please" and "may I " instead of "can I." Let's practice asking for more to drink. You would say "May I have more milk please?"

"Will you say that now please? Then, I will get you more milk. What should you say when I give you your milk?

"Yes, you should say "Thank you."

Begin by using their thumbs for estimating one inch (or use a ruler). The utensils should be placed 1" in from the edge of the table. Explain that you work from the outside in when using utensils.

"Some restaurants will give you more utensils than we use at home.

The next time you are at a restaurant, explain what foods the extra utensils on the table are used for to eat; for example, appetizers (a small sample of food or a snack before the main meal) which could be a salad, soup, or other foods.

"The teaspoon, knife, and fork for the main course should be placed beside the plate.

"Let's set our table using the diagram below. You will do this for each person in the family for dinner (supper).

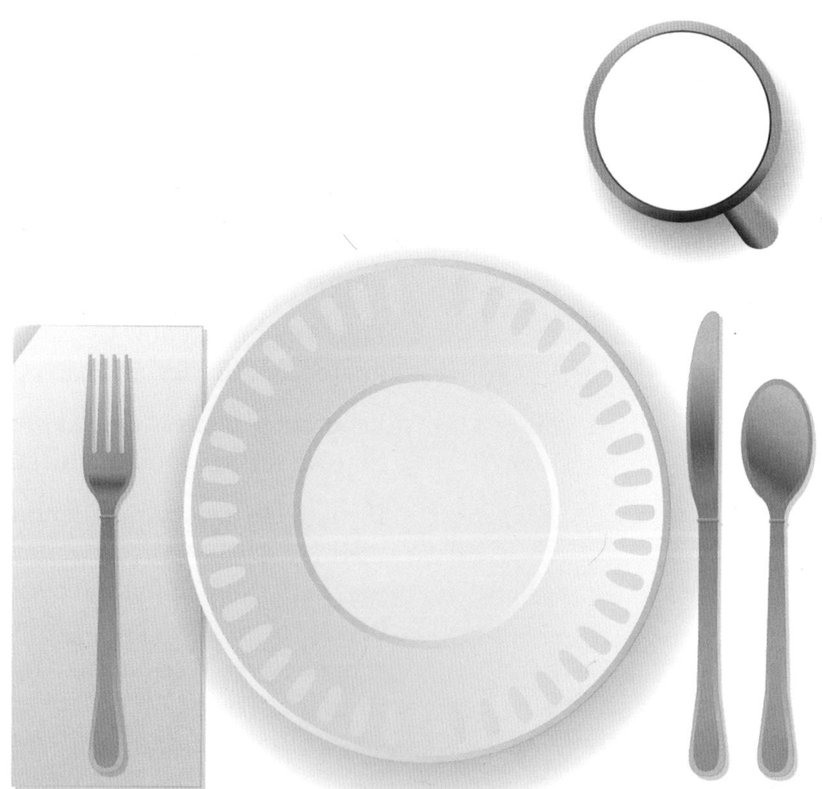

LESSON 13
Day 1

"Now, you can help me cook, too! We will be making banana pancakes. You can help me mix the pancake batter.

TIPS: a THIN spatula/turner is best. Setting the middle is best, which means it will be jiggly.

Complete the recipe activity below.

"Noah, Jonah, Daniel, Paul, or us — we all have a reason to be thankful. What is something you can be thankful about? One way I show gratitude or thankfulness is by praying to God. We can ask God to bless our meal before we eat. Do you say a prayer before you eat your food?

BIBLE:

"Our memory verse is also on being thankful. It is found in 1 Chronicles 29:13, and it says:

Echo read the verse. Add motions. ------→

Now, our God  we give

Your glorious name.

"I can think of a time in the Bible that I think Noah was thankful to God. If I were Noah, I would have been most thankful for God's promise and saving me and my family.

Recipe: Banana Pancakes

INGREDIENTS:	DIRECTIONS:
1 ripe banana, mashed or pureed with mixer	Beat the eggs and mix in banana in a bowl, like you would scrambled eggs. Add in *vanilla.
2 large eggs, lightly beaten	Spray or coat skillet with oil (we prefer a spray olive oil) and heat on medium heat until ready.
OPT — 1/2 tsp. vanilla	Pour 2 tbsp. of the mixture out into small pancakes, leaving approximately 2" between.
oil, for cooking	*They will be liquidy, so give them time to "set."
maple syrup, jam, powdered sugar, or any other toppings, for serving	When pancakes are golden brown on edges, but middle is "set" and not runny, gently slide the turner under and flip it. Some liquid may escape, and that's okay.
	If needed, you can flip it again to set the middle more.
	Top with favorite toppings and enjoy! Servings: 8 small pancakes

LESSON 13
Day 1

RHYME TIME:

"Our poem this week talks about a teapot. Let's read it now and do motions with it.

Read "I'm a Little Teapot" below.

"I'm a little teapot, short and stout, Here is my handle.

(hand on hip)

"Here is my spout.

(arm curved out to the side curving hand down)

"When I get all steamed up, hear me shout, "Tip me over and pour me out!"

(tip over sideways)

I'm a Little Teapot

I'm a little teapot, short and stout,
here is my handle,
here is my spout.
When I get all steamed up, hear me shout,
"Tip me over and pour me out!"

LESSON 13
Day 1

ABC'S AND MORE:

"Now, let's look at our ABC chart. Today, you will be matching capital letters and lowercase letters.

TIPS: See instructional video for this and the instructions in the beginning of the book. See Teacher Resource Section for pertinent information.

See Teacher Resource Page.

Chant the ABC chart.

Sing the ABC song.

Match the capitals with the lowercase letters on the next page.

"Let's learn to write Mm's today!

Practice writing M's and m's.

"M: (up, slant down, slant up, down)
Start at the bottom line, go up to the top line (up). Slant down to the bottom line (slant down). Slant up to the top line (slant up) then straight back down to the bottom line (down).

"m: (down, up and over, up and over)
Start at the middle line, go down to the bottom line (down) then back up the line you just drew and over, like it's hopping to the bottom line (up and over), then back up and over again (up and over) — now it looks like it made two hops!

Trace the Mm's below.

MINI-BOOK M:

See the Teacher Resource Page.

Do a picture walk.

Read the book to the student, pointing to each letter/word.

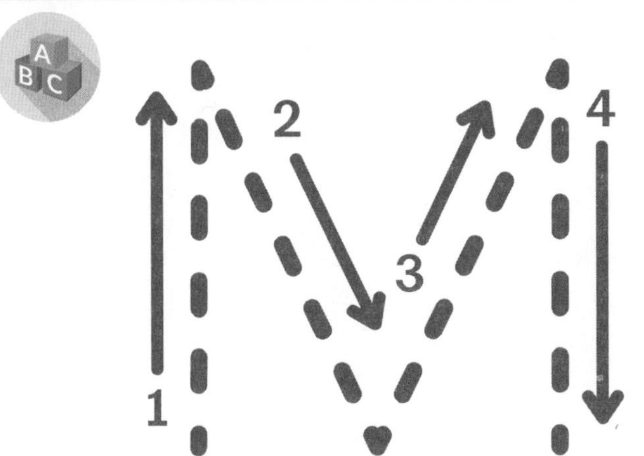

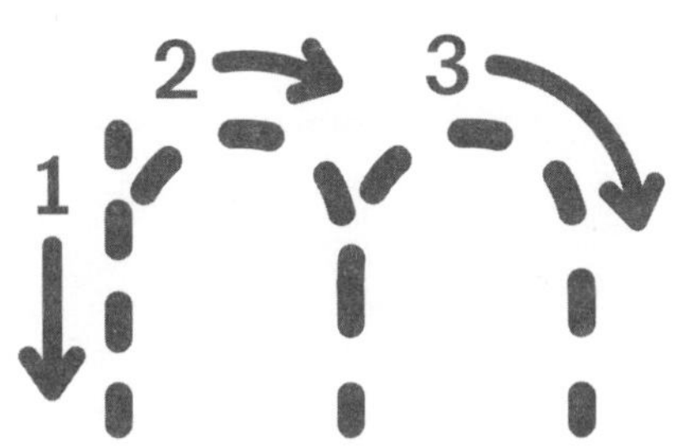

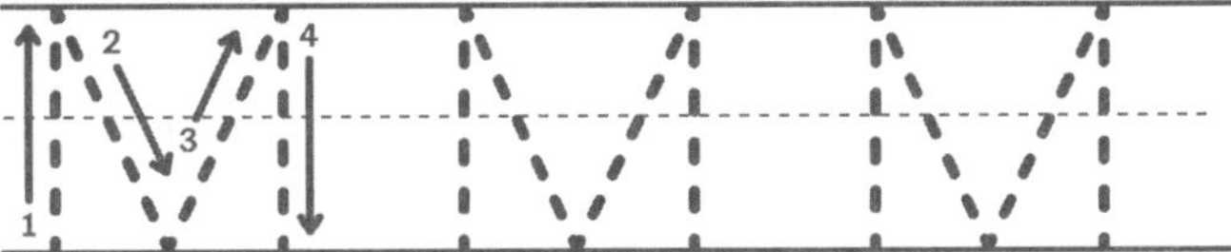

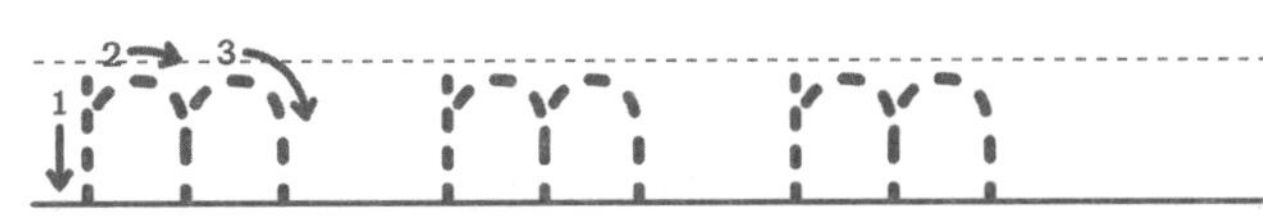

Lesson 13
Day 1

Name

Draw a line from the capital letter to its lowercase letter. A is already done for you.

A	b
B	d
C	f
D	h
E	a
F	g
G	e
H	c

LESSON 13
Day 2

LIFE SKILLS:

Practice setting two places at the table. Have them place a piece of bread on each plate. Have a seat at the table. Place the butter dish near you and away from the student.

"Let's practice our table manners. Let's pretend we are at the table and there is food in a dish or basket in front of you that you need. For example, if you were served bread, but there is a butter dish on the table near me, then you would need to ask me for it. It would be bad table manners for you to reach across me or the table to get it. So you would say, "Will you please pass the butter?" Let's practice this now. Make sure you say "Thank you" after the butter is given to you.

"Now, you can help me cook more. We will be making chili. You can help me measure out the seasonings for our chili.

Complete the Life Skills cooking activity.

Recipe: Chili

INGREDIENTS:	DIRECTIONS:
1 can chili beans	Begin browning meat. Sprinkle in soy sauce as meat is browning as well as 2 squeezes of lemon juice.
1 can tomato sauce (15 oz.)	Mix all spices in a small bowl and set aside.
lemon juice (2 squeezes)	Once meat is *browned, add in spices and ¼ cup of water (*Drain meat prior if needed.)
soy sauce (sprinkled in meat)	Add in the tomato sauce and chili beans.
1 lb. ground beef	Let simmer for 30 minutes or longer, stirring occasionally.
1 onion, chopped fine	
SEASONING: 1 tsp. salt	
1 tbsp. chili powder	
1 tsp. garlic powder	
¼ tsp. black pepper	
dash paprika, dash of cumin	
pinch of ground mustard	

LESSON 13
Day 2

BIBLE:

"Our memory verse is also on being thankful.

Review your memory verse on page 149.

"We can always have an ATTITUDE OF GRATITUDE.

Read Luke 17:11–19.

"In this story, ten men were healed, but only one came back to give praise to God and thank Him. It is important that we always have an attitude of gratitude and give thanks to God for all the blessings and gifts He has given us. Let's pray now, giving God thanks.

Say a prayer of thanksgiving or let your child pray.

RHYME TIME:

Read "I'm a Little Teapot."

I'm a Little Teapot

I'm a little teapot, short and stout,
here is my handle,
here is my spout.
When I get all steamed up, hear me shout,
"Tip me over and pour me out!"

"Some people also have a tea time. This is a special time during the day where hot tea is served with a small cookie or pastry. Tea is served in a teapot and each person has a small saucer with a teacup. A saucer is a small plate, typically that has decorations on it, like flowers. A teacup is a small cup with a handle that also has decorations on it.

Motorcycle

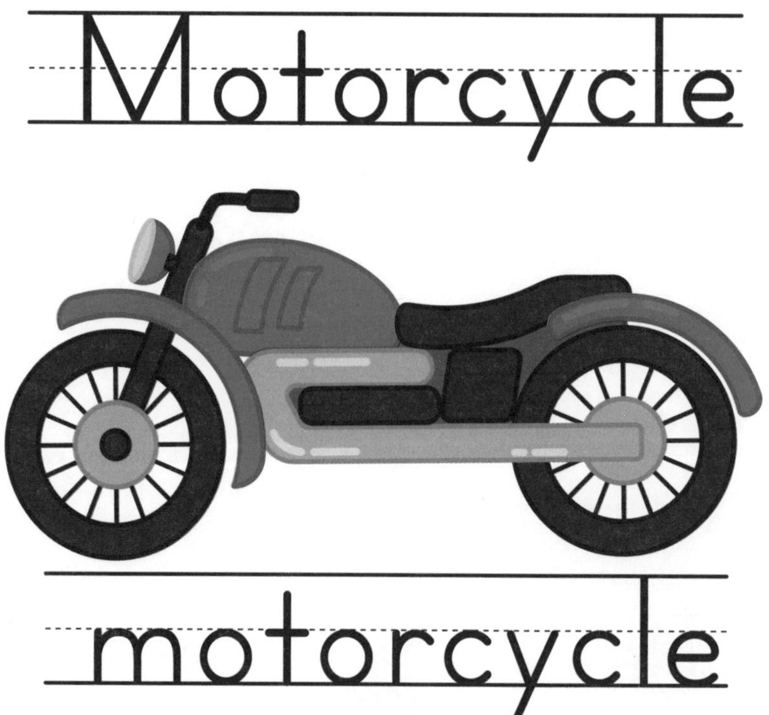

motorcycle

LESSON 13
Day 2

ABC'S AND MORE:

"Now, I will hide our ABC chart and see if you can tell me which picture goes with the letter. Which letter goes with . . . (point to ladder, umbrella, yo-yo, octopus)

See Teacher Resource Page.

Chant the ABC chart.

Sing the ABC song.

"Let's practice writing our Mm's today!

Practice writing M's and m's.

"M: (up, slant down, slant up, down) Start at the bottom line, go up to the top line (up). Slant down to the bottom line (slant down). Slant up to the top line (slant up) then straight back down to the bottom line (down).

"m: (down, up and over, up and over) Start at the middle line, go down to the bottom line (down) then back up the line you just drew and over, like it's hopping to the bottom line (up and over), then back up and over again (up and over) — now it looks like it made two hops!

Trace the Mm's below.

MINI-BOOK M:

Read the letter book to the student.

Have the student highlight the capital and lowercase letter of the week.

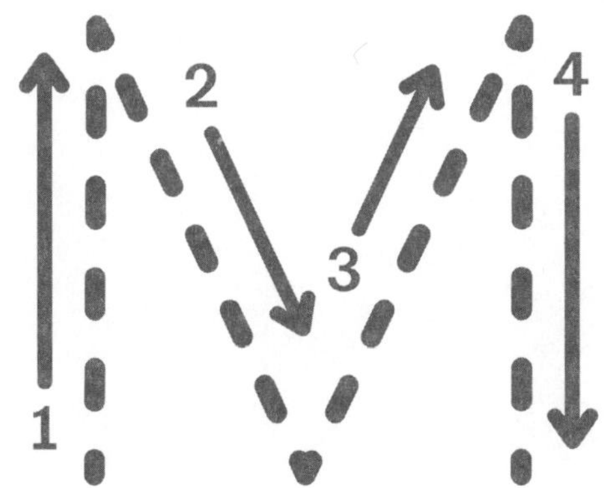

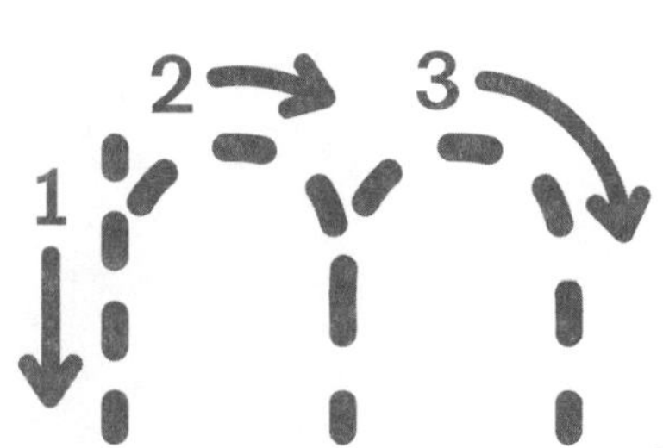

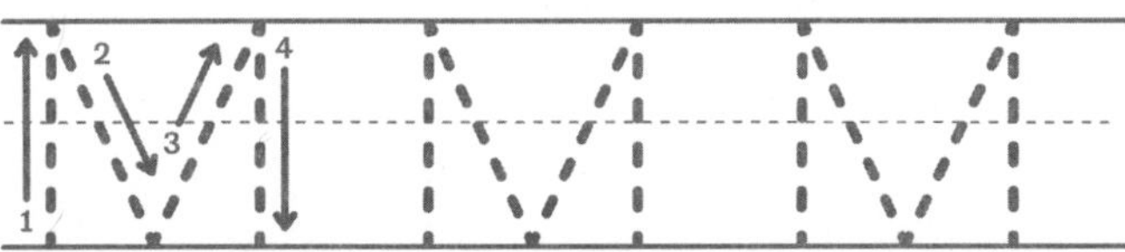

LESSON 13
Day 3

LIFE SKILLS:

"See if you remember how to do a place setting on the table below. Draw a line from the spoon, knife, fork and cup to their proper place.

Practice matching more socks.

"Now, you can help me cook more. Today, we will be making your favorite recipe.

Have the child gather the items and cooking supplies.

BIBLE:

Review your memory verse on page 149.

"We can always have an ATTITUDE OF GRATITUDE. What are some things we can be thankful for?

"How can you show thankfulness to God?

"Second Chronicles 7:6 says: The priests took their positions, as did the Levites with the LORD's musical instruments, which King David had made for praising the LORD and which were used when he gave thanks, saying,

LESSON 13
Day 3

"His love endures forever." Opposite the Levites, the priests blew their trumpets, and all the Israelites were standing.

"See, we can give God thanks in song as well. The Bible talks a lot about them blowing trumpets and using instruments as a means of praise and thanksgiving.

RHYME TIME:

Read "I'm a Little Teapot" with motions on page 150.

"Our rhyme says short and stout. Stout means to be plump or chunky. Can you see how a teapot might be short and chunky?

"Highlight the M's and m's in the rhyme.

I'm a Little Teapot

I'm a little teapot, short and stout,
here is my handle,
here is my spout.
When I get all steamed up, hear me shout,
"Tip me over and pour me out!"

"Help the teapot find the cup below.

Trace the line from the teapot to the cup.

LESSON 13
Day 3

ABC'S AND MORE:

"Now, I will hide our ABC chart and see if you can tell me which picture goes with the letter. Which letter goes with . . . (cat, penguin, fish, net, house)

See Teacher Resource Page.

Chant the ABC chart.

Sing the ABC song.

"Let's practice writing our Mm's!

Practice writing M's and m's.

"M: (up, slant down, slant up, down)
Start at the bottom line, go up to the top line (up). Slant down to the bottom line (slant down). Slant up to the top line (slant up) then straight back down to the bottom line (down).

"m: (down, up and over, up and over)
Start at the middle line, go down to the bottom line (down) then back up the line you just drew and over, like it's hopping to the bottom line (up and over), then back up and over again (up and over) — now it looks like it made two hops!

Trace the Mm's below.

MINI-BOOK M:

Read the letter book again.

Advanced K — see if your child can read the book to you.

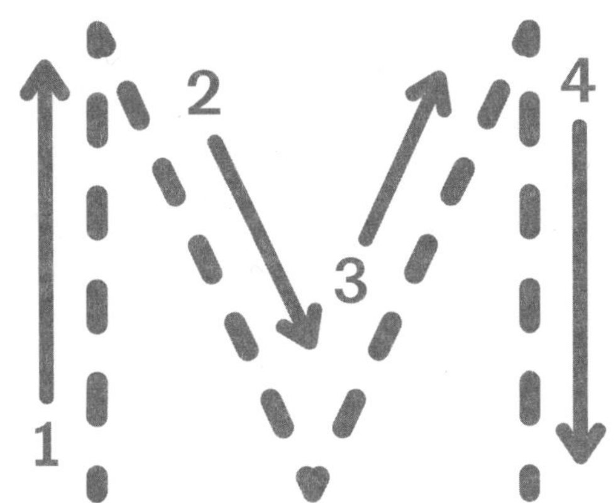

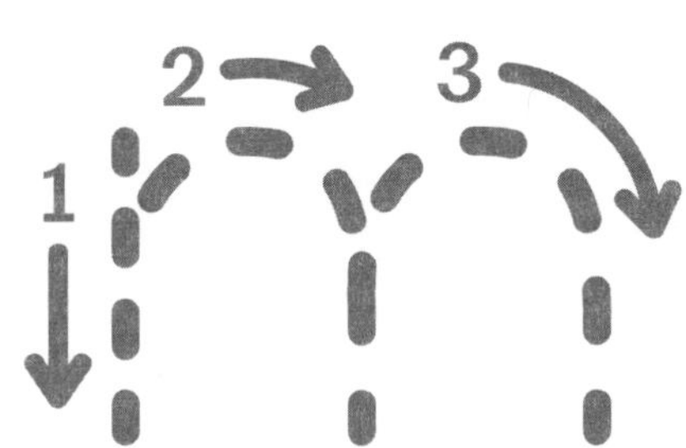

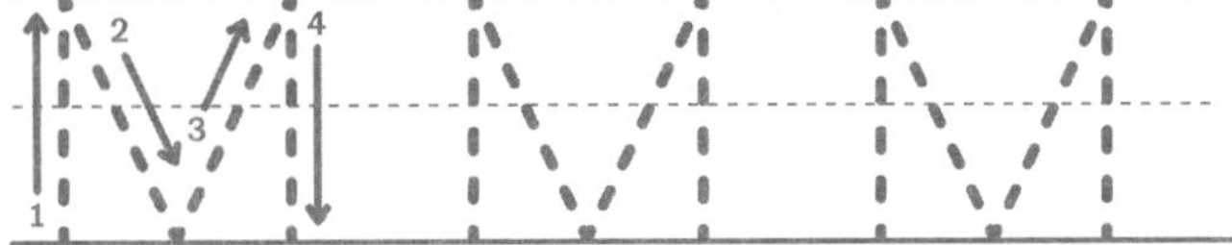

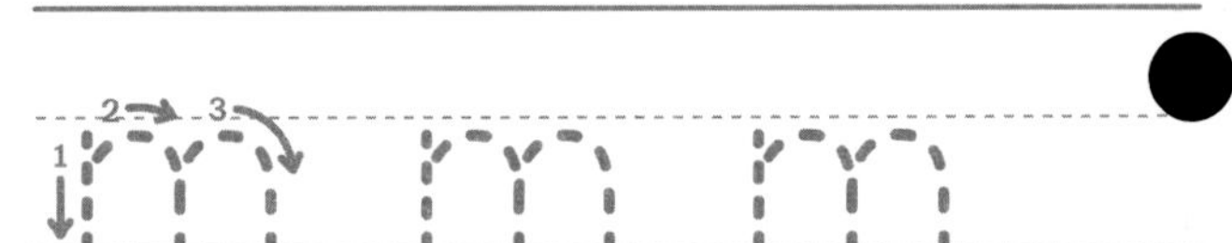

LESSON 14
Prep Page

Supply List

- ☐ U.S. flag
- ☐ Red and blue markers or crayons
- ☐ Liquid glue, black construction paper, and glitter (day 3, life skills)

Objectives

Letter of the week: Nn

Skills/Concepts: manners in social settings – patriotism, opening doors, elevators

Memory Verse

Philippians 4:13

I can do all this through Him who gives me strength.

Extended Activities

Learn more about our flag. Make a flag using construction paper and star stickers.

Look at different flags of the world. (***Passport to the World*** or ***Children's Atlas of the World*** by Master Books is great for this!) Make a family flag, using colors and symbols.

LESSON 14
Day 1

LIFE SKILLS:

"This week we will be focusing more on manners in different settings as well as learning some about patriotism. Patriotism is showing a love for our country. The United States of America is a special place to live because we have freedom of religion. That means we can worship God how we want. There are places in our world that do not allow people to be Christians. We should be thankful for the freedoms we have in America. One way we can show patriotism is by saying the Pledge of Allegiance to the American Flag. When we say the Pledge of Allegiance, there are manners and things you do as you say it.

Show the child the U.S. flag.

"Here is the flag for the United States of America. When we say the pledge, we stand and we place our right hands over our hearts, like this:

Help child do this.

"If you are wearing a hat, you remove it and hold it at your side. If you are in the military, they hold a salute like this, while saying the pledge.

Show them a salute.

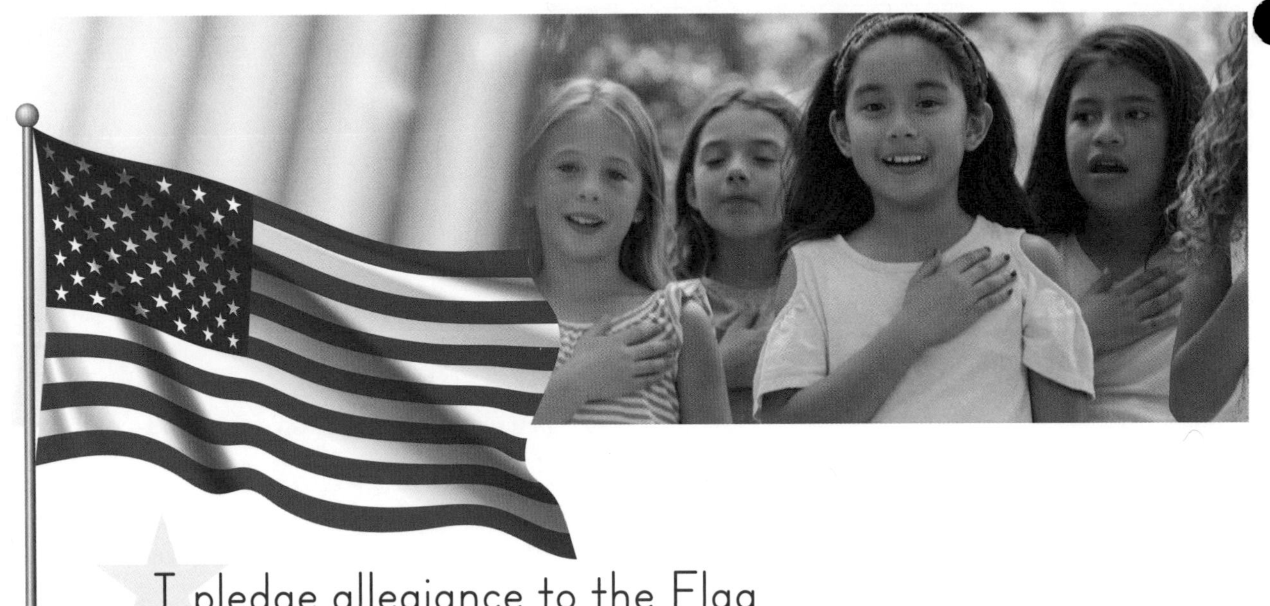

I pledge allegiance to the Flag
of the United States of America,
and to the Republic
for which it stands,
one Nation under God, indivisible,
with liberty and justice for all.

LESSON 14
Day 1

"Let's practice how we stand, place our hands on our hearts, and look at the flag as we say the Pledge of Allegiance. You repeat or echo me as I say it.

Break it down in lines. Do this daily for practicing and memorizing.

"There is a song called "The National Anthem" or "The Star Spangled Banner" by Francis Scott Key. We also should stand, face the flag, and put our hands over our hearts as we sing this song.

Sing or find a recording of "The Star Spangled Banner."

BIBLE:

"We have talked a lot about patriotism today and how blessed our nation, the United States of America, really is. In Psalms 33:12–22, it talks about how we can be a blessed nation.

Read Psalms 33:12–22 from your Bible.

"We have people who fight for our freedoms here in America, but God is the One who gives us true freedom. If we put our focus on Him, we will be blessed.

"Our memory verse, Philippians 4:13, says, "I can do all this through Him who gives me strength." When a soldier goes to fight for our freedom, he can use these words to help him rely on God in difficult times. What is something that is hard for you to do?

Echo read the verse. Add motions.

I  can do all this

through Him 

who gives me strength.

"You can rely on God and His Word to comfort you and give you the strength you need to succeed.

Nest nest

LESSON 14
Day 1

RHYME TIME:

Read "Yankee Doodle."

"Our poem this week is a patriotic poem. It is called "Yankee Doodle" and it is actually part of a song that was written years ago around the time of the Revolutionary War. Let's read it now.

ABC'S AND MORE:

"Now, let's look at our ABC chart.

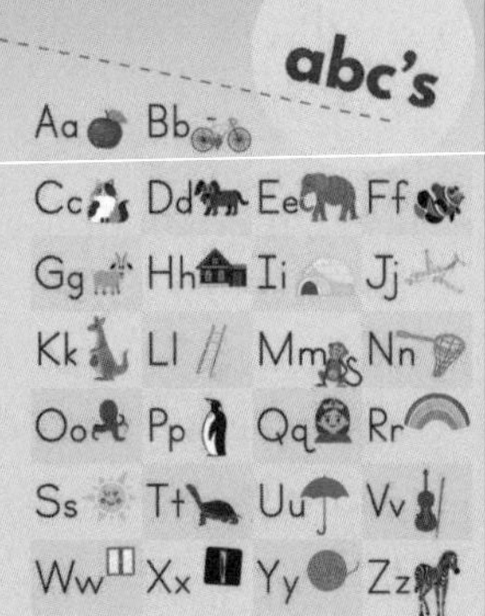

See Teacher Resource Page.

Chant the ABC chart.

Sing the ABC song.

Yankee Doodle

Dr. Richard Shuckburgh

Yankee Doodle went to town,
a-riding on a pony.
He stuck a feather in his hat
and called it macaroni.

Yankee Doodle, keep it up,
Yankee Doodle dandy.
Mind the music and the step,
and with the girls be handy!

LESSON 14
Day 1

"Let's learn to write Nn's! Remember there are capital and lowercase Nn's.

Point to the capital N. Point to the lowercase n.

"This is the capital N. This is the lowercase n.

Practice writing N's and n's.

"N: (up, slant down, up)
Start at the bottom line, go up to the top line (up). Slant down to the bottom line (slant down) then straight back up to the bottom line (up).

"n: (down, up and over)
Start at the middle line, go down to the bottom line (down) then back up the line you just drew and over, like it's hopping to the bottom line (up and over).

Trace the Nn's below.

See the Teacher Resource Page.

Do a picture walk.

Read the book to the student, pointing to each letter/word.

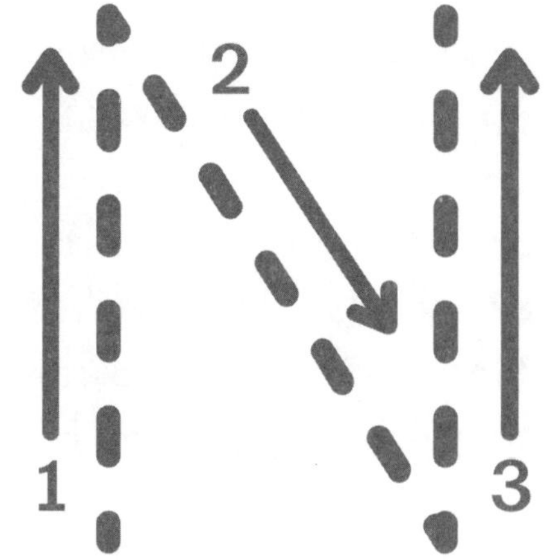

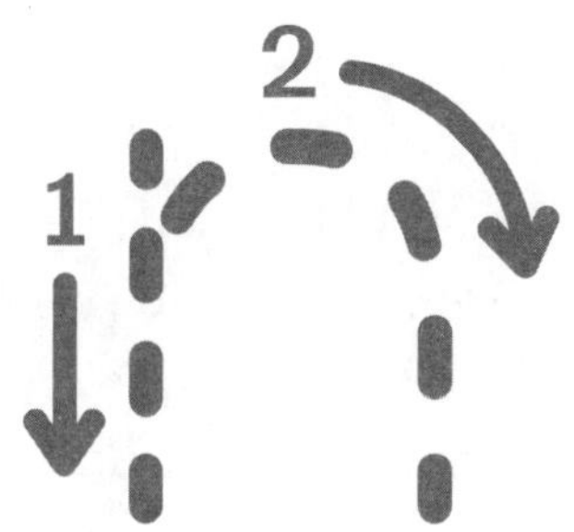

LESSON 14
Day 2

LIFE SKILLS:

"Manners are important in our everyday lives. Sometimes we have manners that are social manners. One way we can show social manners when we are out in other places is to open doors for others, or if we are waiting on an elevator, we let those on the elevator get off before we try to get on. Let's pretend that our door is an elevator and you are inside.

Use a small room or closet to be the elevator.

"You go inside, and I will pretend to push the button on the elevator. As the door opens, I will stand to the side so you can come out. Then, I will go into the elevator.

Role play this and switch roles so they know what to do.

"Do you remember what patriotism is? Yes, showing a love for our country.

Say the Pledge of Allegiance on page 160 and sing the "National Anthem," reminding the student what to do.

BIBLE:

"Honor is a word often used in the Bible or even for heroes today. We "honor" them or we "honor" God. Honor means to give respect or reverence. We can honor our president because he is the President of the United States and his position brings respect, but we honor God by how we live our lives. In 1 Peter 2:17 it says: "Show proper respect to everyone, love the family of believers, fear God, honor the emperor."

"We can give honor to others, but we also honor God by loving others, fearing God, and giving respect to those over us, like a president or a boss.

Review your memory verse on page 161.

RHYME TIME:

"Let's read our poem again now and then highlight the N's and n's we find.

Yankee Doodle

Yankee Doodle went to town,
a-riding on a pony.
He stuck a feather in his hat
and called it macaroni.

Yankee Doodle, keep it up,
Yankee Doodle dandy.
Mind the music and the step,
and with the girls be handy!

"Let's count the Nn's! How many did you find?

LESSON 14
Day 2

ABC'S AND MORE:

"Now, let's look at our ABC chart.

Chant the ABC chart.

Sing the ABC song.

Do the uppercase and lowercase activity on the following page.

"Remember there are capital and lowercase Nn's! Let's practice writing Nn's.

Point to the capital N. Point to the lowercase n.

"This is the capital N. This is the lowercase n.

Practice writing N's and n's.

"N: (up, slant down, up)
Start at the bottom line, go up to the top line (up). Slant down to the bottom line (slant down) then straight back up to the bottom line (up).

"n: (down, up and over)
Start at the middle line, go down to the bottom line (down) then back up the line you just drew and over, like it's hopping to the bottom line (up and over).

Trace the Nn's below.

MINI-BOOK N:

Read the letter book to the student.

Have the student highlight the capital and lowercase letter of the week.

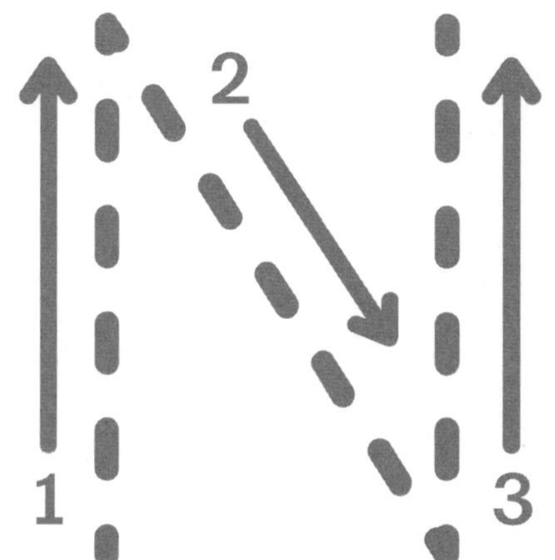

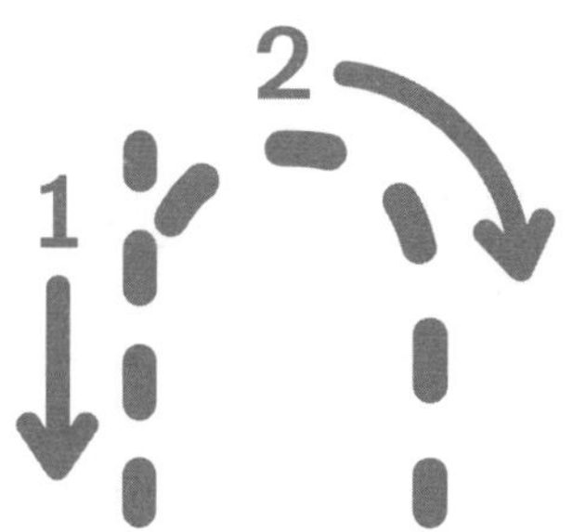

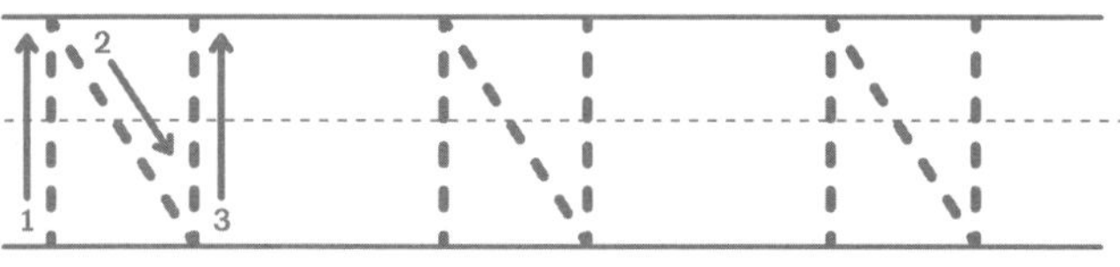

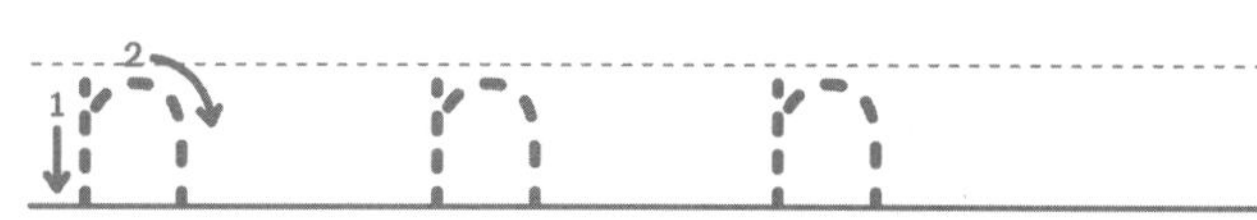

Lesson 14
Day 2

Name

Draw a line from the capital letter to its lowercase letter. H is already done for you.

H	f
D	d
E	a
F	g
G	e
A	h

LESSON 14
Day 3

LIFE SKILLS:

"Let's practice opening a door for someone. If we are entering a store or business, and we are coming to the door around the same time as someone else, or if someone is coming out, we should open the door and hold it for them until they are through. We will role play this today.

NOTE: If you can go to a store or a place with doors and elevators to practice these concepts, it would help them fully understand.

"Do you remember what patriotism is? Yes, showing a love for our country.

Say the Pledge of Allegiance and sing the "National Anthem," reminding the student what to do.

"Color the flag below.

"We will use our glue and glitter to make fireworks on black construction paper.

NOTE: This is best done outside, as glitter can be messy.

Using the glue, make firework type shapes one at a time (curved lines blossoming out). Have them sprinkle one color of glitter over the firework and shake the paper so the glue is fully covered. Do this two more times using two different colors of glitter.

BIBLE:

"You know, we can be encouraged that no matter what happens in our world, God is with us. In Joshua 1:9 it says: "Have I not commanded you? Be strong and courageous. Do not be afraid; do not be discouraged, for the Lord your God will be with you wherever you go." I know that I can be strong and courageous, and I do not have to be afraid. Courageous means to show that you are brave. I know that God is with me wherever I go. He is always there. I cannot see Him, but I can see Him working in my life. I know that no matter what, He will never leave me alone.

"Just like we can be strong and courageous, we can do ALL things through Christ because He gives us strength!

Review your memory verse on page 161.

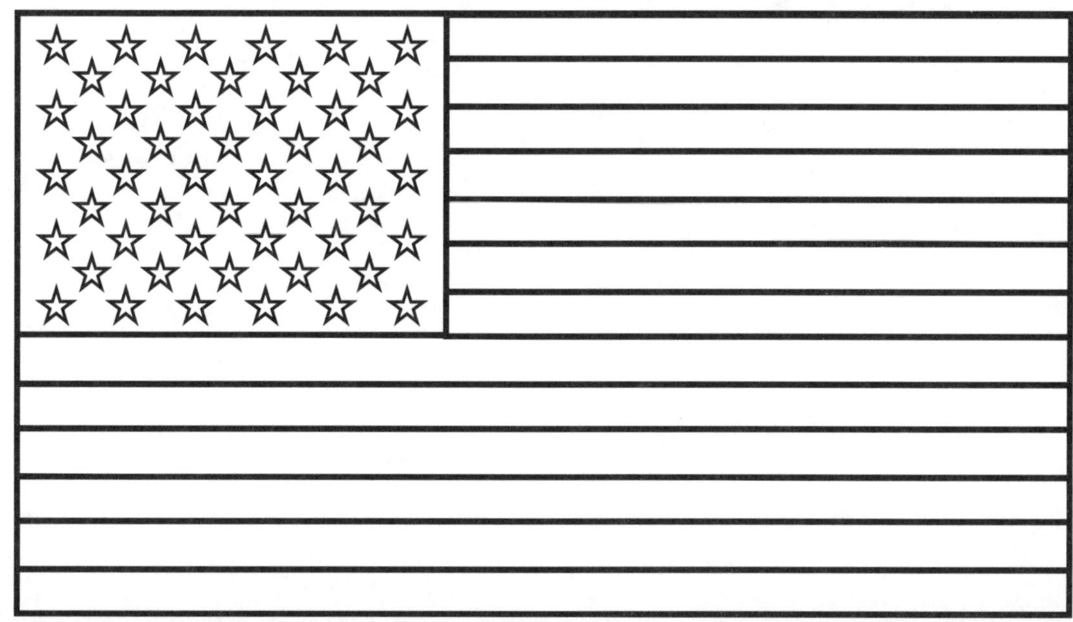

LESSON 14
Day 3

RHYME TIME:

Read "Yankee Doodle" on page 164.

ABC'S AND MORE:

"Now, let's look at our ABC chart. Find the lowercase p, h, v, n. Find the capital Q, U, Y, O.

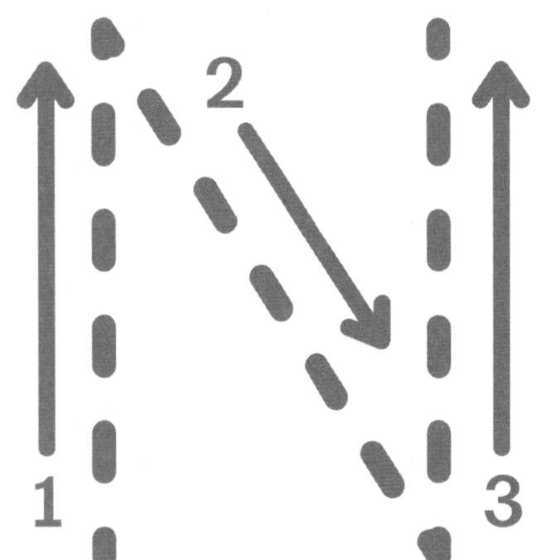

See Teacher Resource Page.

Chant the ABC chart.

Sing the ABC song.

"Let's practice writing Nn's!

Practice writing N's and n's.

"N: (up, slant down, up)
Start at the bottom line, go up to the top line (up). Slant down to the bottom line (slant down) then straight back up to the bottom line (up).

"n: (down, up and over)
Start at the middle line, go down to the bottom line (down) then back up the line you just drew and over, like it's hopping to the bottom line (up and over).

Trace the Nn's below.

MINI-BOOK N:

Read the letter book again.

Advanced K — see if your child can read the book to you.

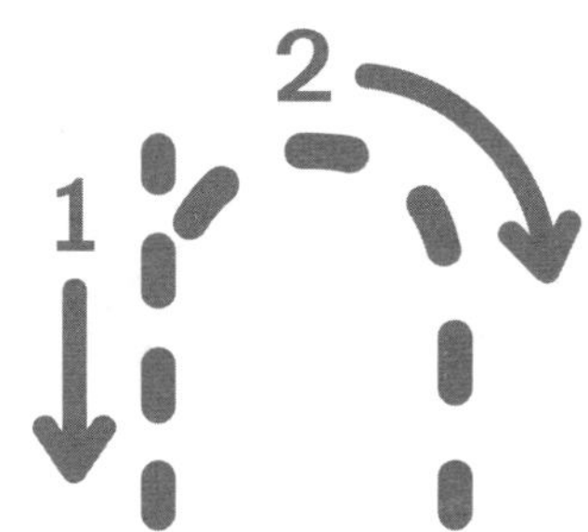

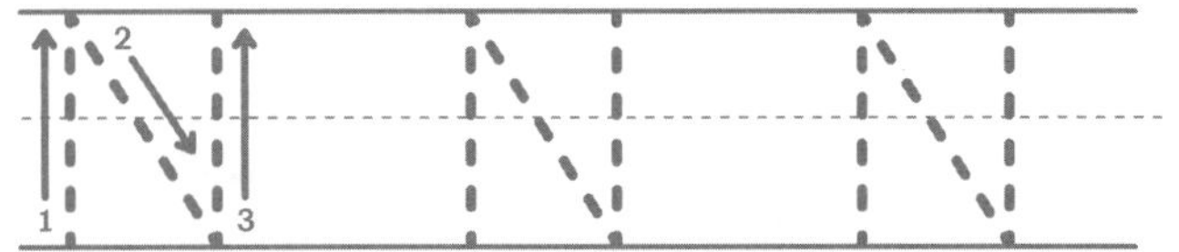

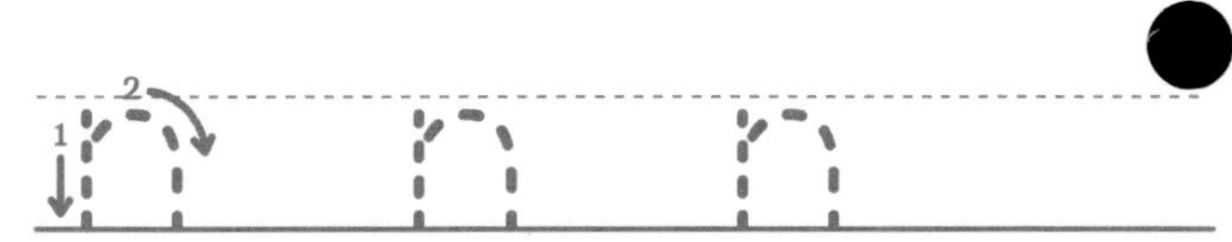

LESSON 15
Prep Page

Supply List

- ☐ Faucet (daily, life skills)
- ☐ Soap (daily, life skills)
- ☐ Hand towel (daily, life skills)

Look Ahead

Lesson 16 has a service project. Please take time to look at this.

Objectives

Letter of the week: Oo

Skills/Concepts: health – basic hygiene

Memory Verse

Psalms 139:14

I praise you because I am fearfully and wonderfully made; your works are wonderful, I know that full well.

Extended Activities

Play Operation™ game

Play I Spy to review colors

Name that body part game: Call out a body part and have them show you where it is (head, wrist, ankles, knees, elbows, chest, stomach, back, shin, thigh, fingertip, hands, eyes, ears, lips, chin, etc.).

LESSON 15
Day 1

LIFE SKILLS:

“We should care for our bodies, and one way we can do that is by what we call hygiene. Hygiene means being clean or caring for our body. We will focus on three things this week to help you have better hygiene. One of the best things we can do to not be sick is to wash our hands. Look at the picture below that shows you the steps for washing your hands.

“First, you will turn on the water and wet your hands. Next, add soap and scrub “backs, bottoms, in between.”

Do the backs of your hands, palms (bottoms), and in between their fingers by locking fingers.

You can teach them to sing a song while they wash, like “Wash, wash, wash your hands, wash the germs away, we want to be healthy so wash the germs away” to the tune of “Row, Row, Row Your Boat.”

“Rinse all the soap bubbles off.

“Dry hands with a towel.

“Use a towel or napkin to turn off the water.

This step is especially important in public places.

“Practice, practice, practice!

“Another way we can show good hygiene is to get clean in the shower/bath. I will teach you how to wash your hair and body.

“The third thing we will focus on is sleep hygiene. This is a different type of hygiene, but is very important. Sleep hygiene focuses on you setting a mood for sleep and getting good rest.

1

2

3

4

5

6

LESSON 15
Day 1

"Our bodies need rest. We will talk more on this tomorrow, but tonight, I will help you set a "mood for sleep" by turning down the lights, talking quieter, and doing slower activities.

NOTE: Remind the student at bedtime of the ways to set a mood for sleep.

BIBLE:

"Did you know that you are fearfully and wonderfully made? Fearfully and wonderfully made means that we are extremely brilliantly made. We are so special to God. The Bible says in Psalms 139:14:

Echo read the verse. Add motions. ---->

"In Jeremiah 1:5, it also states that before we were born, while we were still in the womb, God knew us and had a plan for us. We are made so detailed and in His image. Each of us is unique! The way everything in our body works together is amazing! God is really an amazing Creator!

I praise  you because I  am fearfully and wonderfully made; your works are wonderful, I know  that full well.

Nachos nachos

LESSON 15
Day 1

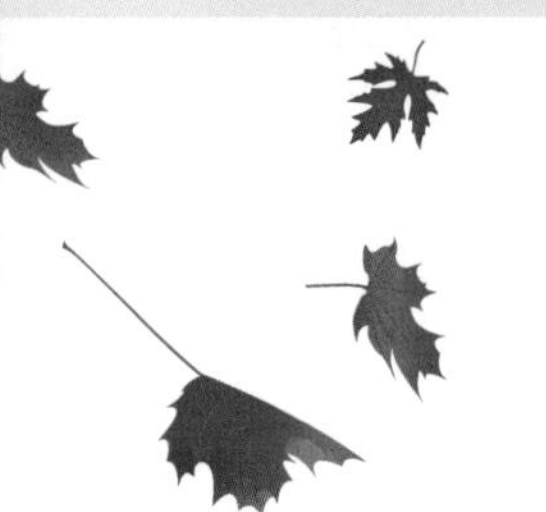

RHYME TIME:

"Our poem this week will be about leaves, and it is called "Come, Little Leaves."

Read "Come, Little Leaves" below.

"Can you imagine the leaves as they changed colors?

"What about when they fluttered over the fields? Do you remember our seasons? We have four, and they are winter, spring, summer, and fall (or autumn). Which season does this poem make you think of? Yes, fall, because the leaves are falling!

Come, Little Leaves

Come little leaves, said the wind one day,
come o'er the meadows with me and play.
Put on your dresses of red and gold,
for summer is gone, and the days grow cold.

Soon as the leaves heard the wind's loud call,
down they came fluttering one and all.
Over the brown fields they danced and flew,
singing the soft little songs they knew.

Dancing and whirling the little leaves went,
winter had called them and they were content.
Soon fast asleep in their earthy beds,
the snow laid a cover-lid o'er their heads.

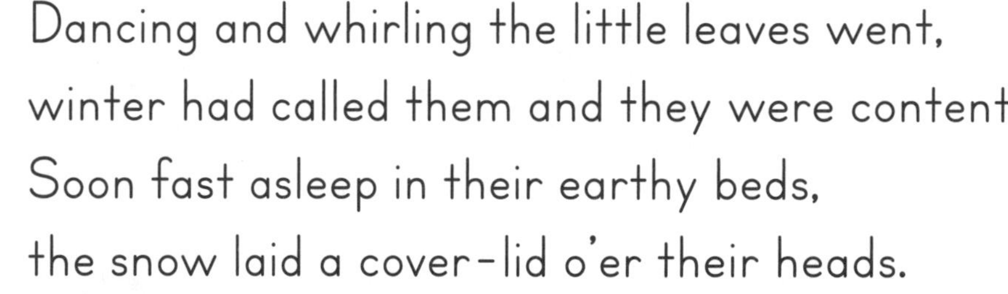

LESSON 15
Day 1

ABC'S AND MORE:

"Now, let's look at our ABC chart.

See Teacher Resource Page.

Chant the ABC chart.

Sing the ABC song.

"Let's learn to write Oo's today!

Point to the capital O. Point to the lowercase o.

"This is the capital O and this is the lowercase o. Let's write them!

Practice writing O's and o's.

"O: (over, around, and close)
Start at the top line, go over, around, and close like a circle.

"o: (over, around, and close)
Start at the middle line, go over, around, and close, like a circle.

Trace the Oo's below.

MINI-BOOK O:

See the Teacher Resource Page.

Do a picture walk.

Read the book to the student, pointing to each letter/word.

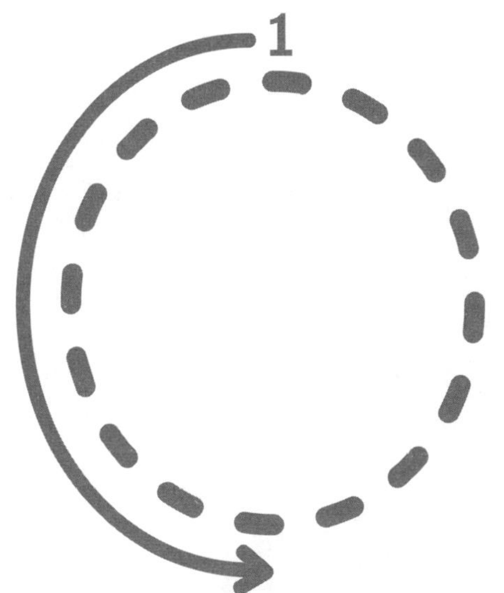

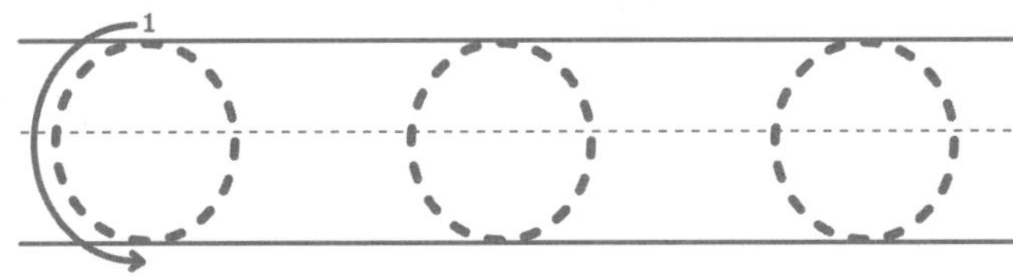

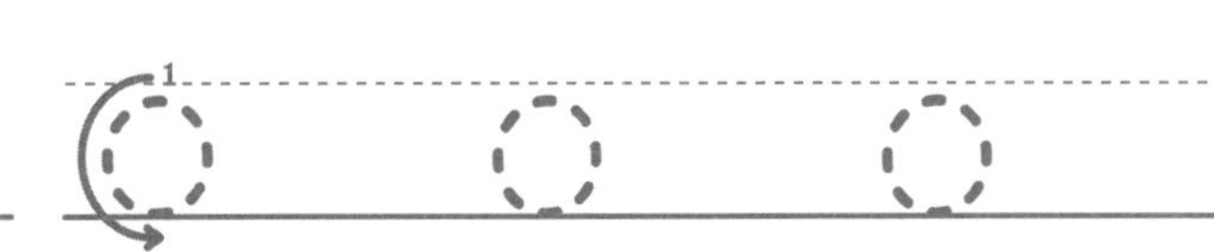

LESSON 15
Day 2

BIBLE:

"We are doing the Bible first today. Remember how special you are to God? How He said you were "fearfully and wonderfully made"?

Review memory verse on page 171.

"Remember "hygiene" means caring for our body. This reminds me of a story when Jesus cleansed a leper. Leprosy was an awful skin disease and you were not allowed to be near anyone if you had it. It was awful and there was no cure. But Jesus performs miracles.

Read Mark 1:40–45.

"Isn't that an amazing miracle that Jesus performed? Just in the same way Jesus healed the leper by cleansing him, He can also cleanse us of any sin we may have. We just have to ask.

LIFE SKILLS:

"The three things we are looking at this week on hygiene are hand washing, getting clean in the shower/bath, and sleep hygiene. Do you remember what we can do to help us not get sick? Yes, wash our hands.

"Continue to practice the steps for washing your hands, washing in the shower/bath, and sleep hygiene.

NOTE: Remind the student at bedtime of the ways to set a mood for sleep.

RHYME TIME:

"Let's review our poem for this week.

Read "Come, Little Leaves" on page 172.

Octopus octopus

LESSON 15
Day 2

ABC'S AND MORE:

"Now, let's look at our ABC chart.

See Teacher Resource Page.

Chant the ABC chart.

Sing the ABC song.

"Let's practice writing our Oo's today!

Practice writing O's and o's.

"O: (over, around, and close)
Start at the top line, go over, around, and close like a circle.

"o: (over, around, and close)
Start at the middle line, go over, around, and close like a circle.

Trace the Oo's below.

MINI-BOOK O:

Read the letter book to the student.

Have the student highlight the capital and lowercase letter of the week.

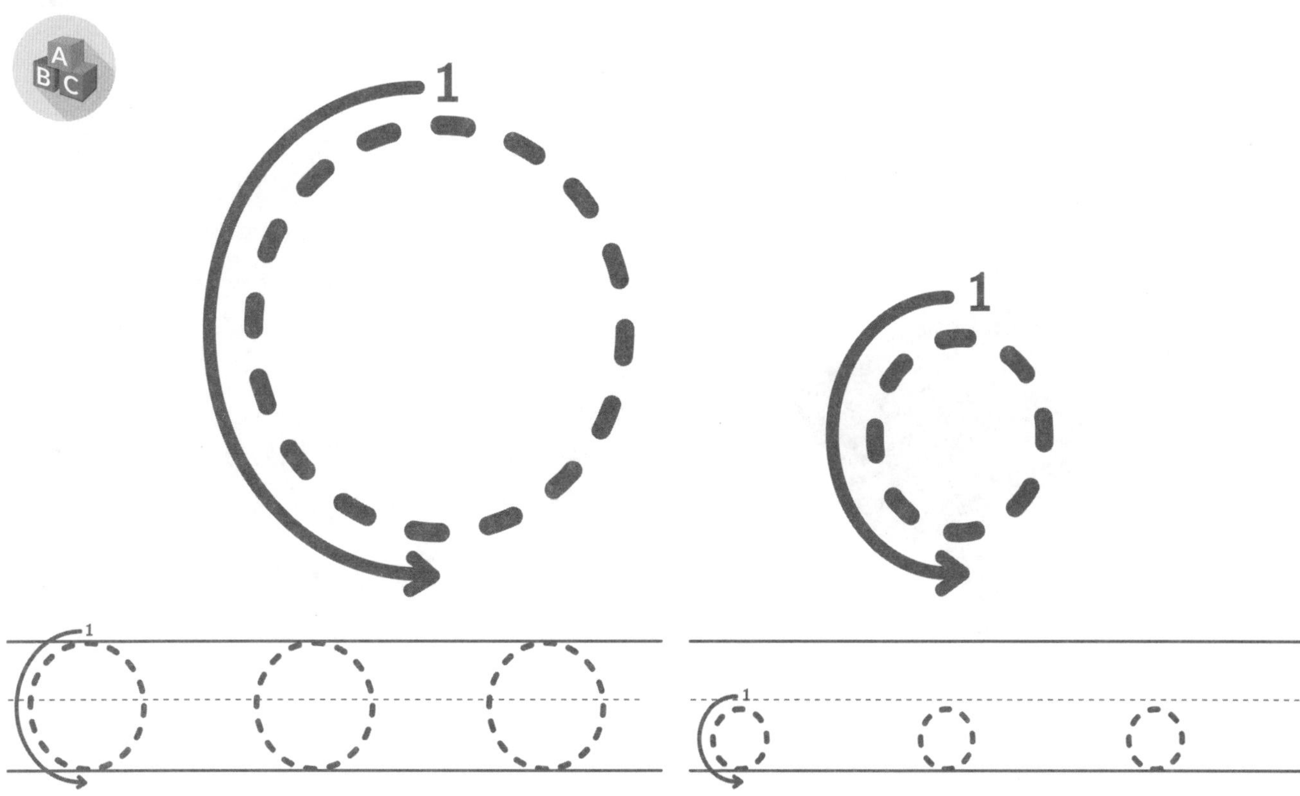

LESSON 15
Day 3

BIBLE:

"Remember how special you are to God and how he said you were "fearfully and wonderfully made"? The Bible says in Psalms 139:14, "I praise you because I am fearfully and wonderfully made; your works are wonderful, I know that full well."

Review your memory verse on page 171.

"Remember that hygiene means caring for our body.

"I am reminded of another story of a commander of the king's army that had leprosy, too.

Read 2 Kings 5:1–13.

"See, Naaman didn't want to go dip in the river seven times. He wanted Elisha to just say the words "be healed" so he could quickly be healed. This is a lesson that teaches us that we have to be obedient to God. If Naaman had obeyed immediately, then he would have been healed then. Instead, he made his disease last even longer and suffered more by not obeying.

RHYME TIME:

Read "Come, Little Leaves" below.

"Whirling . . . dancing and whirling the little leaves went. What does it mean that the leaves were whirling? Can you take a leaf and make it whirl?

"Highlight the letters O and o in the poem.

Come, Little Leaves

Come little leaves, said the wind one day,
come o'er the meadows with me and play.
Put on your dresses of red and gold,
for summer is gone, and the days grow cold.

Soon as the leaves heard the wind's loud call,
down they came fluttering one and all.
Over the brown fields they danced and flew,
singing the soft little songs they knew.

Dancing and whirling the little leaves went,
winter had called them and they were content.
Soon fast asleep in their earthy beds,
the snow laid a cover-lid o'er their heads.

LESSON 15
Day 3

ABC'S AND MORE:

"Now, let's look at our ABC chart.

Chant the ABC chart.

Using the tracing ABC page in the back of the book, review writing letters K-O.

Sing the ABC song.

"Let's practice writing our Oo's!

Practice writing O's and o's.

"O: (over, around, and close)
Start at the top line, go over, around, and close like a circle.

"o: (over, around, and close)
Start at the middle line, go over, around, and close like a circle.

Trace the Oo's below.

MINI-BOOK O:

Read the letter book again.

Advanced K — see if your child can read the book to you.

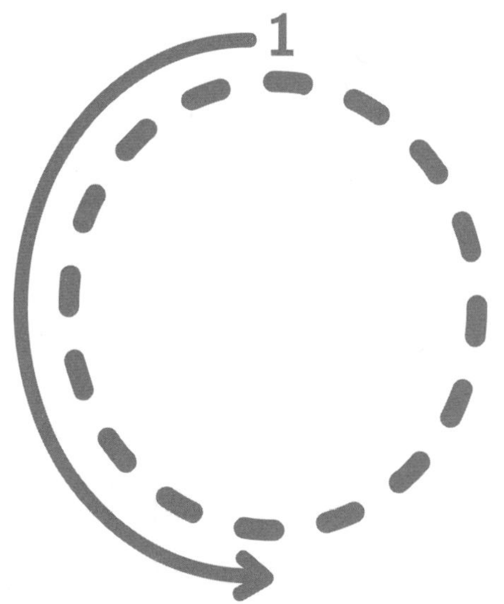

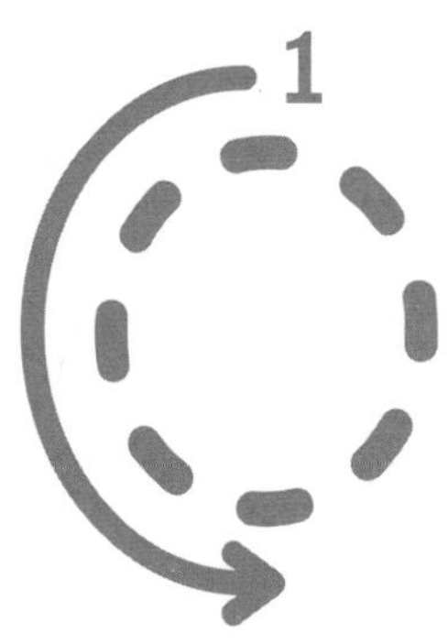

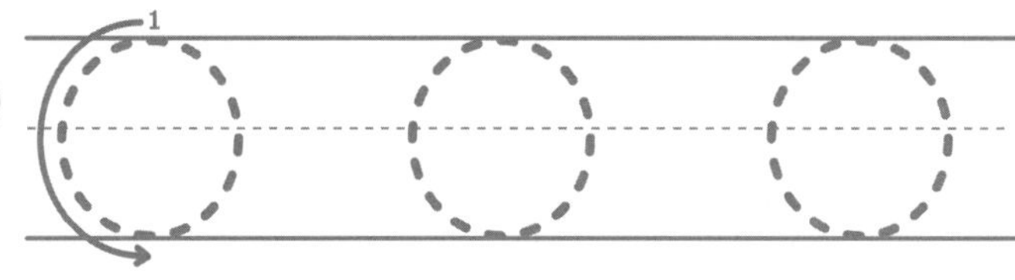

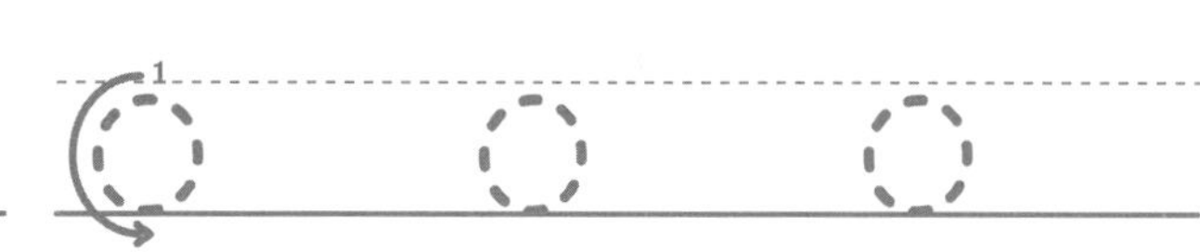

LESSON 16
Prep Page

Supply List

- ☐ SERVICE PROJECT (day 1, Bible) (have student choose a project and help get items): tube socks, toothbrushes, small toothpaste, small deodorant, non-perishable ready to open and eat food items, a tract on salvation would be an awesome addition
- ☐ Packages of cheese crackers, beef jerky sticks, nuts, etc.

Look Ahead

Next week you will need some various food items and small number stickers. Please see the supply list.

Objectives

Letter of the week: Pp

Skills/Concepts: basic hygiene

Memory Verse

Isaiah 1:17

Learn to do right; seek justice. Defend the oppressed, Take up the cause of the fatherless; Plead the case of the widow.

Extended Activities

Coughing/sneezing — teach them to cough or sneeze into a tissue or their elbows to help prevent germs from spreading.

Add sounds for chanting the ABC chart — see video.

LESSON 16
Day 1

LIFE SKILLS:

"Remember how important it is to care for our bodies? Last week we focused on three things to have good hygiene — washing our hands, washing our bodies, and sleep hygiene.

"This week, we will focus on brushing your teeth, blowing your nose, and fixing your hair.

"Today, let's go over how to brush your teeth. We will practice this each day.

Go over the chart below with your student.

BIBLE:

"We are also discussing ways to bless others. Some people do not have homes, and therefore we call them homeless, because they are less a home. The Bible tells us to care for those in need. One way we can care for the homeless is to provide things for them. Our memory verse says:

Echo read the verse. Add motions.

Learn to do right  ;

seek justice.

Defend  the oppressed,

Take up the cause of the

fatherless; Plead  the case

of the widow.

Service Project–Stocking Stuffers: Help your child be a stocking stuffer and stuff tube socks with things the homeless can use. Remind your child that most of them live in wooded places without running water, toilets, electricity, stoves, etc. Some live on the streets. Teaching our children empathy and compassion is very important in our "me" society. Be the hands and feet of Jesus. It is best to find a ministry in your area that is ministering to them already and see if you can assist. Another idea is what they call "Nighty Night" Bags for children in foster care. You can also google this and do it instead. Work on a project this week, relating it to the message on the next page.

HOW TO BRUSH YOUR TEETH

Use a small amount of toothpaste

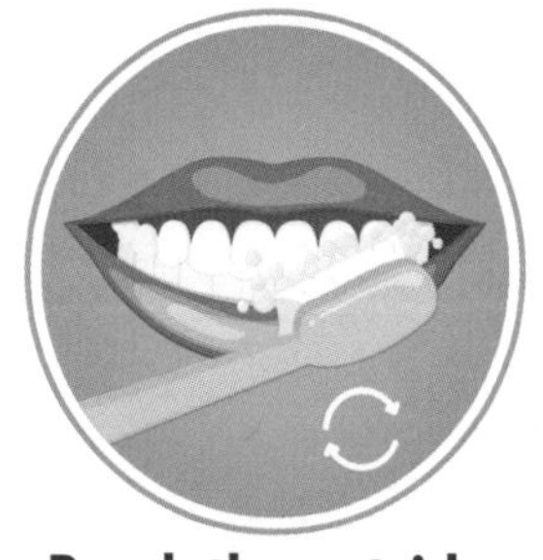

Brush the outside surface of all teeth using circular motion

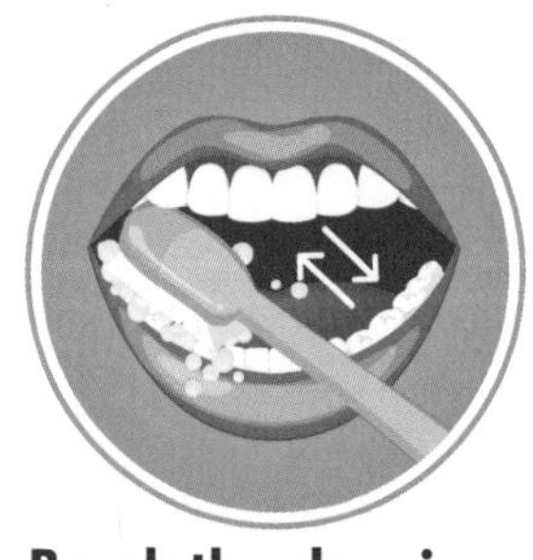

Brush the chewing surface of all teeth

Brush the tongue

LESSON 16
Day 1

"We are called to bless others. The Bible says in Luke 6:31: "Do to others as you would have them do to you." We are to care for the poor. One way we can do this is to help them have good health and hygiene. They can always use socks, and sometimes they even use them as gloves. They need food that is easy to eat out of the package because they do not have silverware, stoves, or even plates. We want to do our best to provide foods that will give them some form of nutrition, like nuts, cheese and crackers, and even meat.

"We are to have compassion and empathy for others. Compassion is kindness and concern for others.

"Empathy is when we think of how we would feel if we were that person and we care about their feelings. These are wonderful traits. Let's get started on gathering items for our project. We will work on it this week.

RHYME TIME:

"Our poem is called "Apples Ripe."

Read "Apples Ripe" below.

"What does it mean for an apple to be ripe? Ripe means that it is developed and ready to be eaten. If an apple is ripe, it will come off the tree easily.

Apples Ripe

Apples ripe, apples ripe,
who will buy my apples ripe?
Apples ripe, apples ripe,
I will buy your apples ripe.

LESSON 16
Day 1

ABC'S AND MORE:

"Now, let's look at our ABC chart.

See Teacher Resource Page.

Chant the ABC chart.

Sing the ABC song.

Letter Run: Lay out your letter cards on the floor. Call out the pictures as the child races to find the letter: S, L, H, O, Y

"Today we will learn to write Pp's.

Point to the capital P. Point to the lowercase p.

"This is the capital P and this is the lowercase p. Let's write them!

Practice writing P's and p's.

"P: (down, up, around)
Start at the top line, go down to the baseline (down), go back up your line to the top (up) and around toward the middle line and stop at your straight line (around).

"p: (down, up, around)
Start at the middle line, go down below the baseline (down), go back up your line to the middle line (up) and around toward the bottom line and stop at your straight line (around).

Trace the Pp's below.

MINI-BOOK P:

See the Teacher Resource Page.

Do a picture walk.

Read the book to the student, pointing to each letter/word.

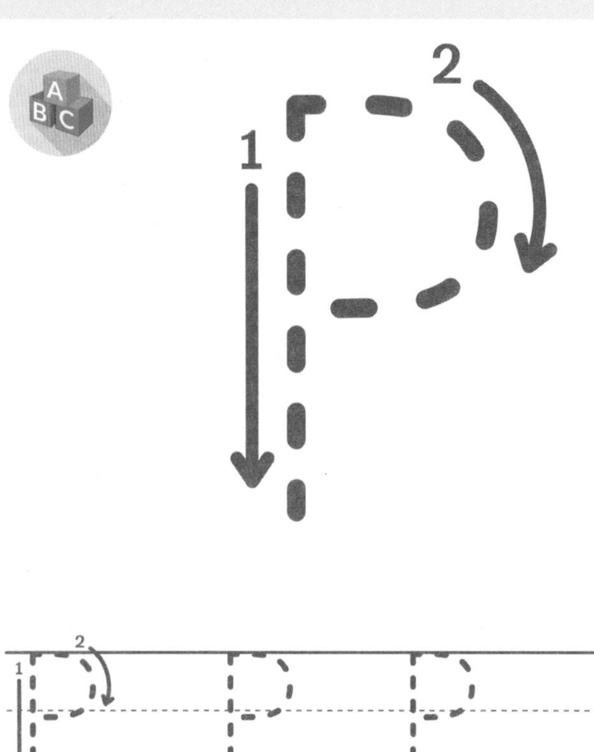

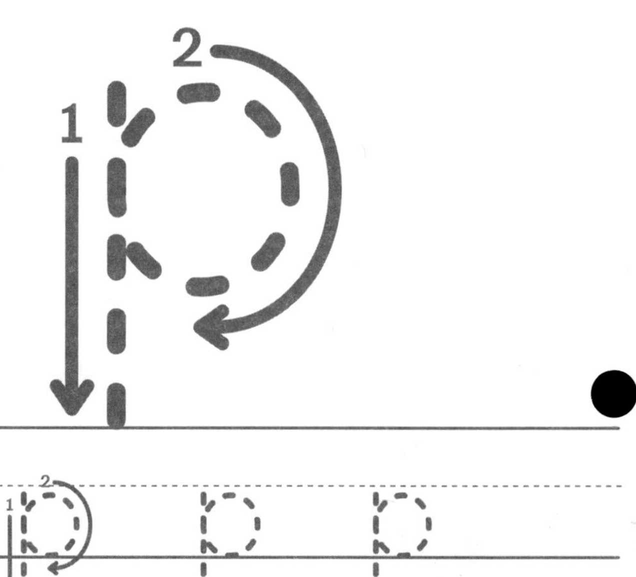

LESSON 16
Day 2

LIFE SKILLS:

"This week, we are focusing on brushing your teeth, blowing your nose, and fixing your hair. Today, I will teach you the proper hygiene for blowing your nose.

Use the image below to teach the steps.

"We will practice this each day.

"Practice brushing your teeth and using the graphic on Day 1 of this lesson for cues.

BIBLE:

"Do you remember a way we can bless others?

Review your memory verse on page 180.

Service Project–Stocking Stuffers: Work on this project this week, relating it to the following message:

"We are called to bless others. The Bible says in Luke 6:31: "Do to others as you would have them do to you." We are to care for the poor. One way we can do this is to help them have good health and hygiene.

"They can always use socks, and sometimes they even use them as gloves. They need food that is easy to eat out of the package because they do not have silverware, stoves, or even plates. We want to do our best to provide foods that will give them some form of nutrition, like nuts, cheese and crackers, and even meat.

"We are to have compassion and empathy for others. Compassion is kindness and concern for others. Empathy is when we think of how we would feel if we were that person. We care about their feelings.

RHYME TIME:

Read "Apples Ripe" below.

Apples Ripe

Apples ripe, apples ripe,
who will buy my apples ripe?
Apples ripe, apples ripe,
I will buy your apples ripe.

get tissue | blow nose | wipe nose | put in trash | get hand sanitizer

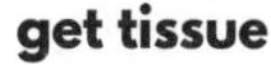

LESSON 16
Day 2

ABC'S AND MORE:

"Now, let's look at our ABC chart.

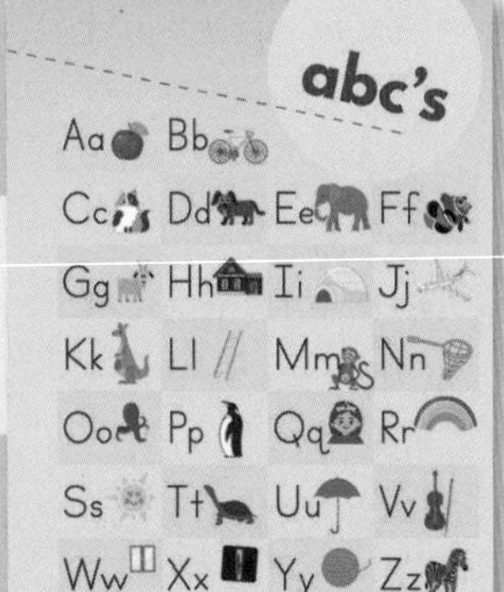

Chant the ABC chart.

Sing the ABC song.

"Let's practice writing Pp's today!

Practice writing P's and p's.

"P: (down, up, around)
Start at the top line, go down to the baseline (down), go back up your line to the top (up) and around toward the middle line and stop at your straight line (around).

"p: (down, up, around)
Start at the middle line, go down below the baseline (down), go back up your line to the middle line (up) and around toward the bottom line and stop at your straight line (around).

Trace the Pp's below.

Read the letter book to the student.

Have the student highlight the capital and lowercase letter of the week.

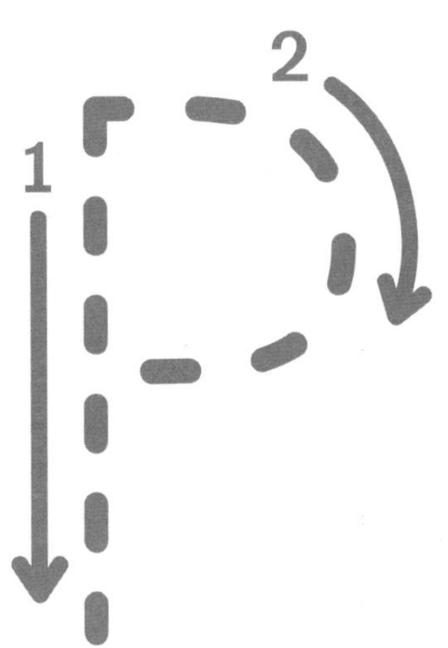

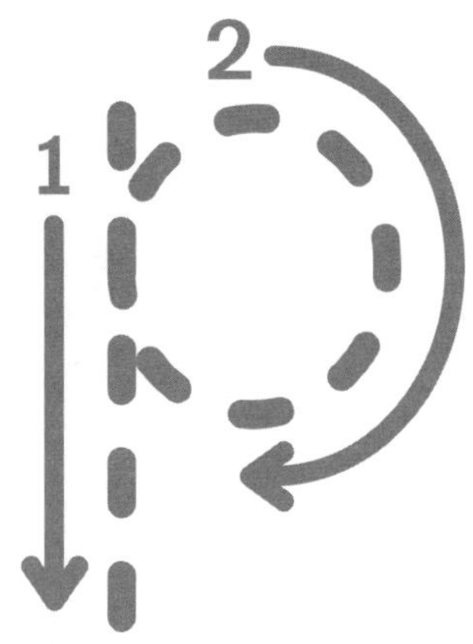

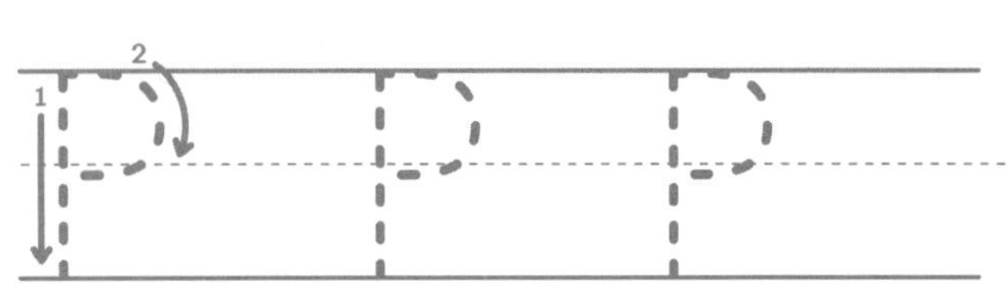

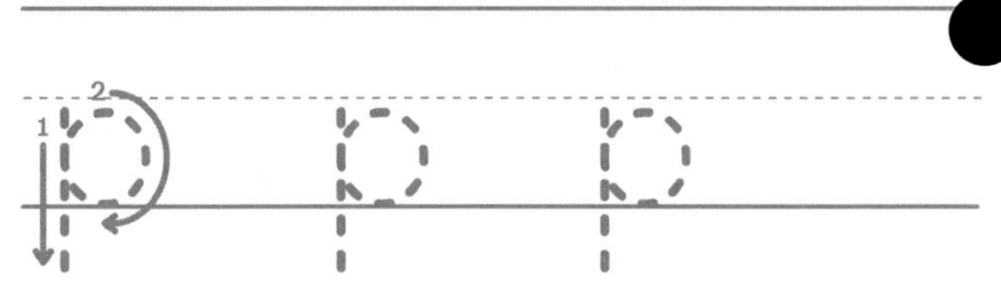

LESSON 16
Day 3

LIFE SKILLS:

"This week, we are focusing on brushing your teeth, blowing your nose, and fixing your hair. Today, I will teach you the proper hygiene for combing/brushing your hair.

In a step-by-step process, show your child how to comb or brush their hair. Model first, then work together, then let them try it alone.

"Practice brushing your teeth and blowing your nose using the graphics shown this week on Days 1 and 2 for cues. We will practice this each day.

These are found on pages 180 and 183.

BIBLE:

Review your memory verse on page 180.

Service Project–Stocking Stuffers

"Complete your project today if you haven't already.

"We have been focusing on helping those in need this week. Why do you think we should help others in need? What are some ways we can do this each day?

"When we treat others like we want to be treated, it helps us to be better Christians and show good character. We should always show compassion and empathy toward others. We can be a blessing to others, but a lot of times we are blessed the most when we help others.

"You know, in Acts 19:11–12, it says that God did extraordinary miracles through Paul, so that even handkerchiefs and aprons that had touched him were taken to the sick, and their illnesses were cured, and the evil spirits left them. Just like people brought handkerchiefs to Paul and people's lives were changed, we can also pray over each one of these socks, that those who receive this will be touched by God. Let's finish our project as we pray for those in need.

RHYME TIME:

Read "Apples Ripe."

"Our poem this week is "Apples Ripe." Let's read it again. Highlight the P's and p's in the poem below.

Apples Ripe

Apples ripe, apples ripe,
who will buy my apples ripe?
Apples ripe, apples ripe,
I will buy your apples ripe.

LESSON 16
Day 3

ABC'S AND MORE:

"Now, let's look at our ABC chart.

See Teacher Resource Page.

Chant the ABC chart.

Sing the ABC song.

"P: (down, up, around)
Start at the top line, go down to the baseline (down), go back up your line to the top (up) and around toward the middle line and stop at your straight line (around)

"p: (down, up, around)
Start at the middle line, go down below the baseline (down), go back up your line to the middle line (up) and around toward the bottom line and stop at your straight line (around).

Trace the Pp's below.

"See what you remember about capital letters and lowercase letters. See if you can match them on the following page. When done, be sure to do your mini-book work as well!

Complete the matching page of apples, matching lowercase with capital letter on the following page.

MINI-BOOK P:

Read the letter book again.

Advanced K — see if your child can read the book to you.

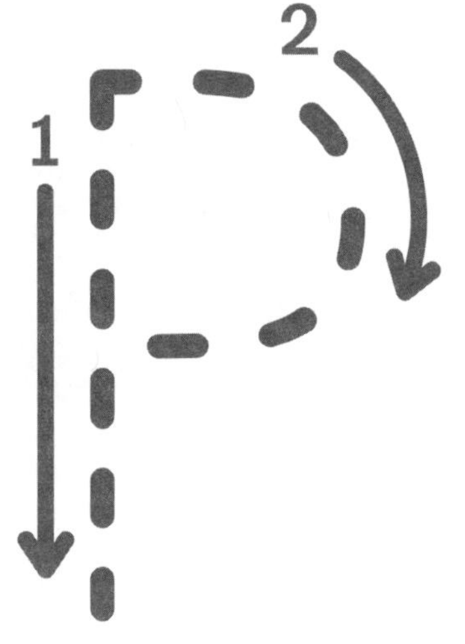

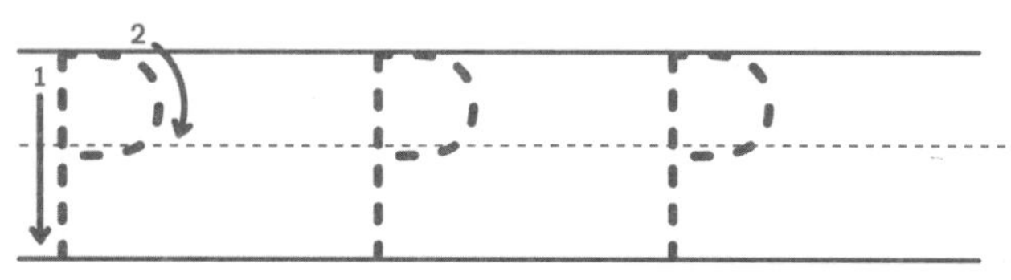

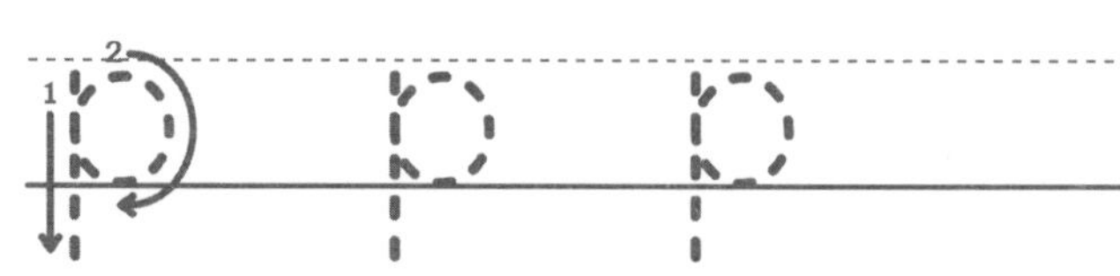

Name

Match each capital letter to its lowercase letter.

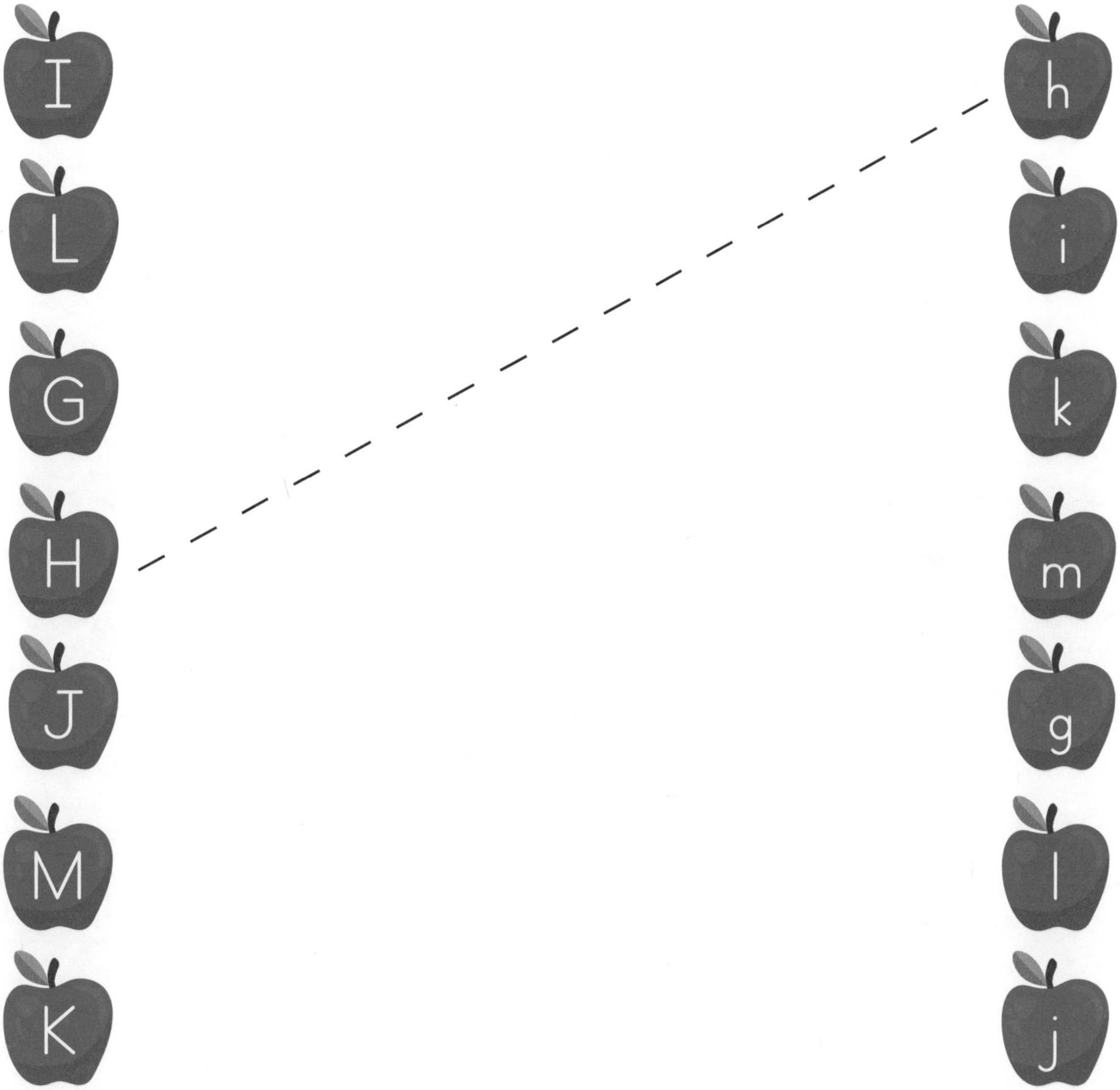

I	h
L	i
G	k
H	m
J	g
M	l
K	j

LESSON 17
Prep Page

Supply List

- ☐ Slice of an apple, peanut butter, teddy grahams, a grape, graham crackers, pretzel sticks, animal crackers, a yellow fruit snack (or equivalent for a star) (day 1, Bible)
- ☐ Small number stickers (see space for size of stickers) (day 3, life skills)
- ☐ Piece of paper (day 3, life skills)

Look Ahead

Play phone dial pad: Using an 18 count empty egg carton, cut off all but 7 slots to make a "phone pattern" using the bottom of each carton for a number (1-3, 4-6, 7-9, 0). Practice having them dial the number (or you can use an old phone or toy phone).

OPTIONAL: Using a highlighter and plain paper or an index card, write your address and phone number. Have the child trace it and say it each day. You can laminate it or put it in a plastic sleeve so they can use a dry-erase marker.

Objectives

Letter of the week: Qq

Skills/Concepts: learning address and phone number

Memory Verse

Luke 2:14

Glory to God in the highest heaven, and on earth peace to those on whom his favor rests.

LESSON 17
Day 1

LIFE SKILLS:

"This week you will learn our address and our phone number. Our phone number is: ______________

Say, repeat, say together.

TIP: Here you will say your phone number/ address aloud, then have them echo you, then say it together. Continue to do this throughout the week several times a day. Another tip is to make up a funny story. Example: Pickens Chapel Rd. I would say "no picken your nose in the chapel" to help them recall that. Or Campbell Dr. I ring my camp bell when I camp to keep the raccoons away.

"Our address is: ______________

Say, repeat, say together.

BIBLE:

"The next few weeks we will focus on Jesus, from His birth to His death on the Cross. Our memory verse says in Luke 2:14:

Echo read the verse. Add motions.

Glory  to God

in the highest heaven,

and on earth  peace

 to those on whom

his favor rests.

Read Luke 2:1–7.

NOTE: You may choose to read about the birth of Jesus from a children's Bible instead, or from Matthew.

"We will make a manger scene, and you can retell the story of baby Jesus being born in a manger. Do you know what a manger is? It is a feeding box for farm animals.

Use a slice of an apple, peanut butter, teddy grahams, graham crackers, pretzel sticks, animal crackers, and a yellow fruit snack (or equivalent, for a star).

Place the pretzel sticks on the plate (hay), use a little peanut butter as your glue to secure the graham crackers (halved) to make a triangle "stable." Place an apple slice on the hay as the manger, and put peanut butter on it and add a grape for baby Jesus. Place the graham crackers there for Mary and Joseph. Add a yellow fruit snack for the star over the stable and secure it with peanut butter. Use the animal crackers to put animals around the stable. (You can opt to modify this.)

Have your child tell you the story of baby Jesus being born. Enjoy!

RHYME TIME:

"Our poem this week is "Quack Quack Little Duck." Let's read it now.

Read "Quack Quack Little Duck" on the next page.

Quack Quack Little Duck by Carrie Bailey

"Quack, quack," said the little duck,
for he was stuck in the muck.
"Quack, quack," said Mother duck,
as she saw he was stuck in the muck.
Mother gave a loud quack as she pulled on his snout,
little duck could not quack as she pulled him out.
With a quack, quack, little duck flew loose,
then landed on his caboose.

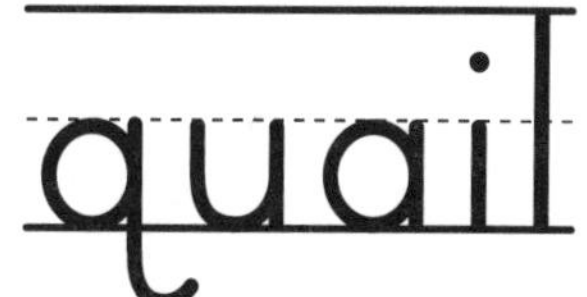

LESSON 17
Day 1

ABC'S AND MORE:

"Now, let's look at our ABC chart.

See Teacher Resource Page.

Chant the ABC chart.

Sing the ABC song.

"This week we will be learning how to write the letter Qq.

Point to capital Q.

"This the capital Q.

Point to the lowercase q.

"This is the lowercase q.

"Now, let's write our Qq's!

Practice writing Q's and q's.

"Q: (over, around and close, slant out)
Start at the top line, go over, around and close it, like a circle (over, around and close), then give it a leg by slanting out from below the middle line to the bottom line so it doesn't roll away! (slant out).

"q: (over, around, up, down, curve)
Start at the middle line, go over, around and up to the middle line (over, around, up) then straight down below the bottom line with a slight curve back (down, curve).

Trace the Qq's below.

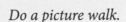

MINI-BOOK Q:

See the Teacher Resource Page.

Do a picture walk.

Read the book to the student, pointing to each letter/word.

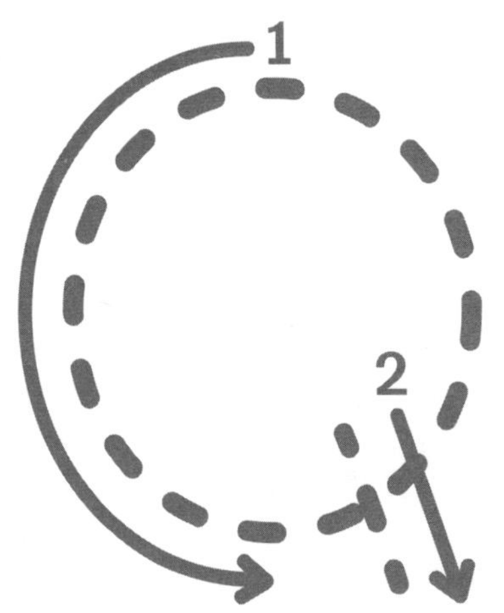

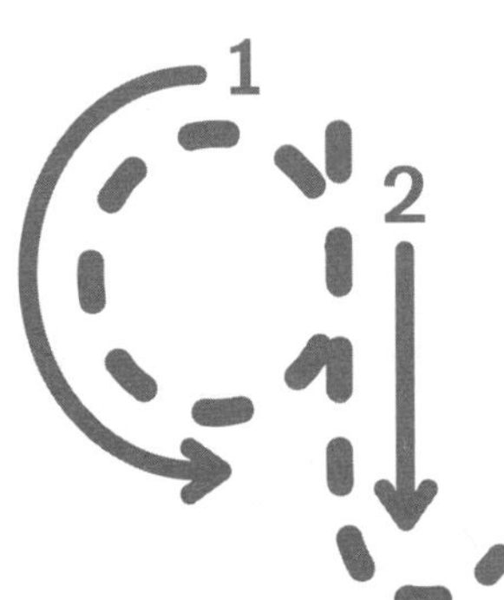

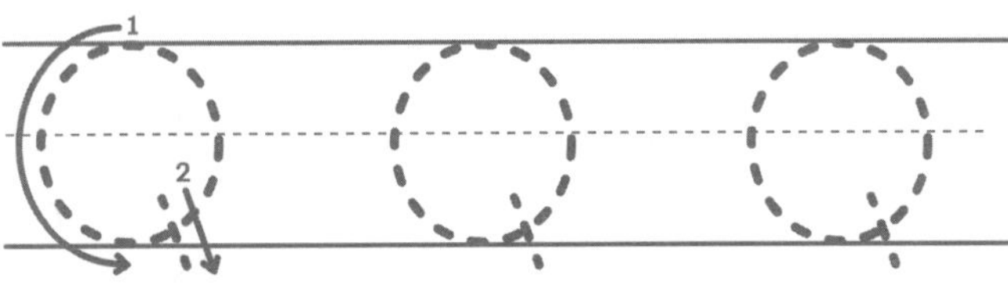

LESSON 17
Day 2

LIFE SKILLS:

"Let's work on our address and phone number some more. Our phone number is: ______________

Say, repeat, say together. Practice dialing.

"Our address is: ______________

Say, repeat, say together.

Take them to the mailbox or out to the front of your house so they can see where your house number is and show them the street sign (if you have one) where you live, even a highway sign as you are driving. Point out special landmarks around your house to help them notice their surroundings and make observations.

BIBLE:

Practice memory verse on page 190.

We are continuing the life of Jesus. We talked about His birth already, and now we will discuss a time when Jesus was a young boy at 12 years old.

Read Luke 2:41–52.

"Jesus really scared His parents, didn't He? They were looking for Him and couldn't find Him. Have you ever hid from your parents in a store or somewhere? Tell me about that time.

"When you are a parent, it is scary when you cannot find a child. Then, when Mary and Joseph found Jesus, they were astonished. Astonished means surprised or amazed. They couldn't believe that Jesus was answering the questions and that He had stayed behind. Notice, it says that after that, Jesus went with His parents and was obedient to them. Then, He grew in wisdom and stature, meaning He grew wiser, but also grew bigger. By doing this, He had favor with God and man. This should be an example of the importance of obeying our parents. Even Jesus obeyed His parents.

"Let's play a game of hide and seek!

You might discuss the appropriate time to play this game versus not appropriate — like in a store or crowded area is not an appropriate time to play hide and seek.

RHYME TIME:

"Let's review our poem "Quack Quack Little Duck"!

Read "Quack Quack Little Duck."

Quack Quack Little Duck

"Quack, quack," said the little duck,
for he was stuck in the muck.
"Quack, quack," said Mother duck,
as she saw he was stuck in the muck.
Mother gave a loud quack as she pulled on his snout,
little duck could not quack as she pulled him out.
With a quack, quack, little duck flew loose
then landed on his caboose.

LESSON 17
Day 2

ABC'S AND MORE:

"Now, let's look at our ABC chart.

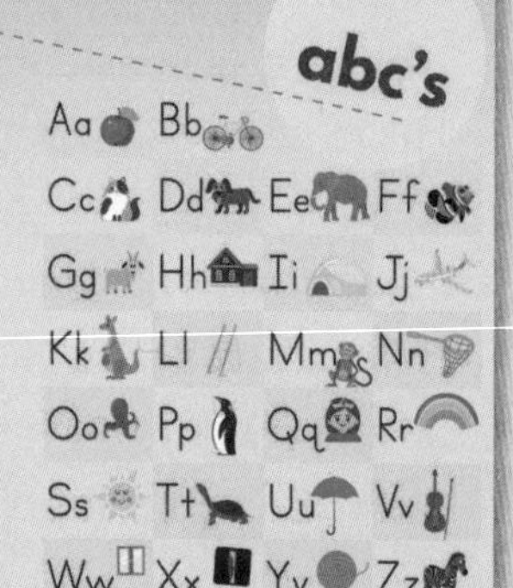

Chant the ABC chart.

Sing the ABC song.

"Let's practice making our Qq's today!

Point to the capital Q. Point to the lowercase q.

"This is the capital Q and this is the lowercase q. Let's write them!

Practice writing Q's and q's.

"Q: (over, around and close, slant out)
Start at the top line, go over, around and close it, like a circle (over, around and close), then give it a leg by slanting out from below the middle line to the bottom line so it doesn't roll away! (slant out).

"q: (over, around, up, down, curve)
Start at the middle line, go over, around and up to the middle line (over, around, up) then straight down below the bottom line with a slight curve back (down, curve).

Trace the Qq's below.

MINI-BOOK Q:

Read the letter book to the student.

Have the student highlight the capital and lowercase letter of the week.

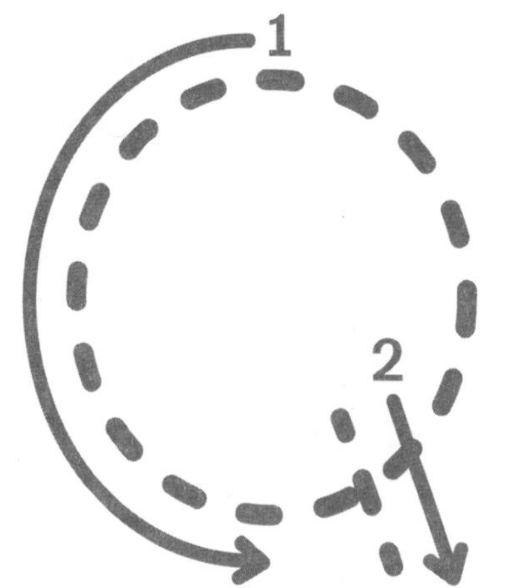

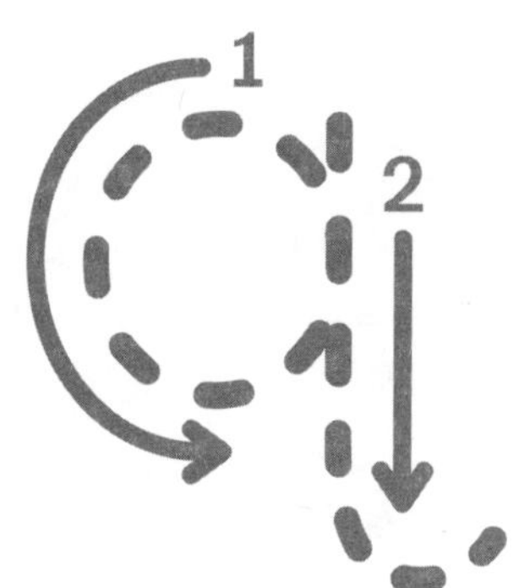

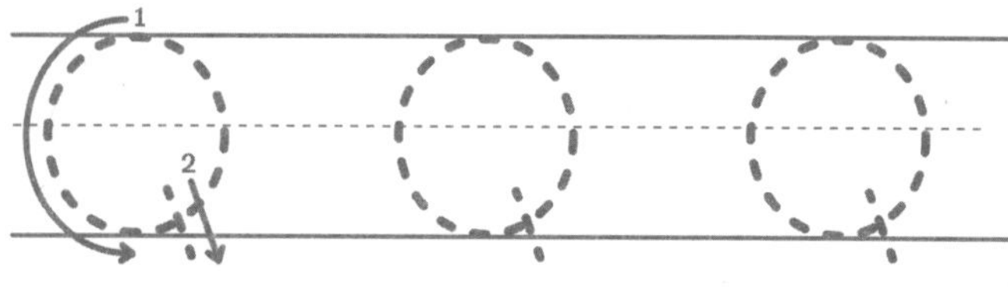

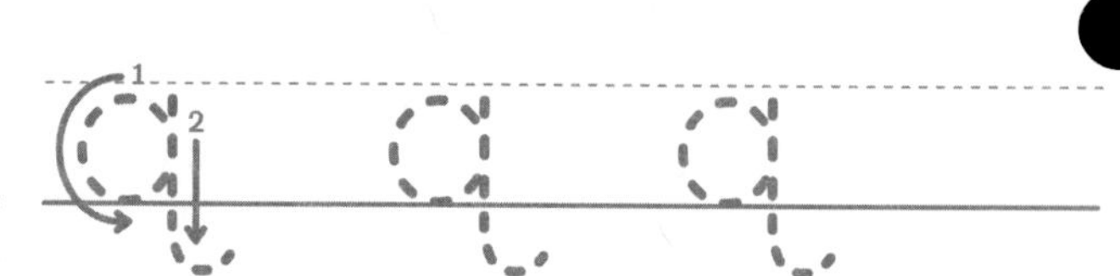

LESSON 17
Day 3

LIFE SKILLS:

"Let's work on our address and phone number some more. Our phone number is: ______________________

Say, repeat, say together. Practice dialing.

"Use the number stickers to put on the blank phone below. Help write the phone number on the top of the phone.

"Our address is: ______________________

Say, repeat, say together.

"On a piece of paper, draw a picture of your house. Have your parent help you put your house number on the house in order.

BIBLE:

Review memory verse on page 190.

"We are continuing the life of Jesus.

"You know Jesus was a King. He could have come into this world in a fancy way, but instead He chose to come in what we call a humble way. Being humble means meek or not bringing attention to yourself so you get the glory. Jesus definitely did not take attention away from the ultimate plan God had. He came in a humble way. He showed humility. We can also be humble and show humility. Here is another time He showed humility.

"We have discussed Jesus' birth, then Him as a boy, and now we will talk about Jesus and His ministry while on earth. While Jesus was on earth, he performed many miracles. There are seven great miracles of Jesus Christ recorded in the Gospel of John. John 20:31 says the reason the miracles were performed was "that you may believe that Jesus is the Messiah, the Son of God, and that by believing you may have life in his name." The first miracle He performed was turning water into wine. Let's read about this in John 2:1–11.

"WOW! So, pretend you are at a wedding. Someone forgot the punch, the crowd is thirsty, and everyone is beginning to complain. Then, this guy sets out six jars and the wedding servants put water in them, but when you look inside, it is not water, but rather punch. That is amazing, right? What Jesus did immediately made the disciples believe that He really was Jesus, the Messiah.

LESSON 17
Day 3

"We might not get to see Jesus come before us and perform a miracle, but some people believe miracles still happen. The Bible says the same power that was in Jesus is in us, too! (Ephesians 1:19). We just have to have faith and trust that God is doing what is best for us.

RHYME TIME:

"Our poem this week is "Quack Quack Little Duck." Let's read it now.

Read "Quack Quack Little Duck."

"Highlight the Q's and q's in the poem.

Quack Quack Little Duck

"Quack, quack," said the little duck,
for he was stuck in the muck.
"Quack, quack," said Mother duck,
as she saw he was stuck in the muck.
Mother gave a loud quack as she pulled on his snout,
little duck could not quack as she pulled him out.
With a quack, quack, little duck flew loose
then landed on his caboose.

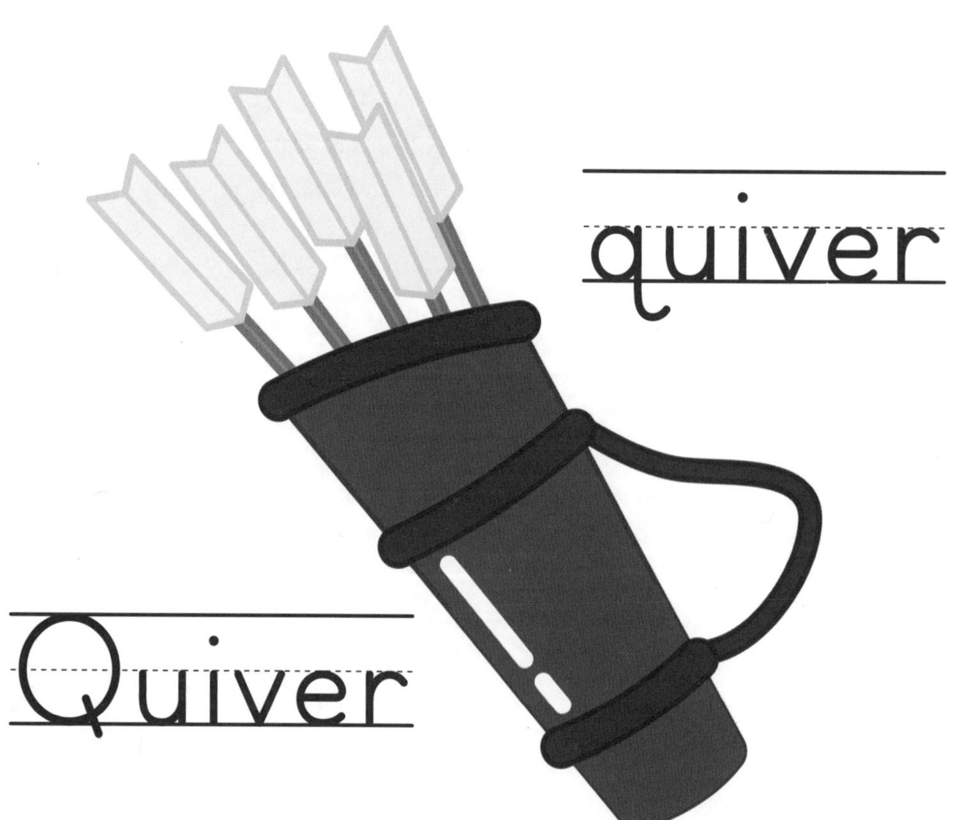

LESSON 17
Day 3

ABC'S AND MORE:

"Now, let's look at our ABC chart.

See Teacher Resource Page.

Chant the ABC chart.

Sing the ABC song.

"Let's practice making our Qq's!

Practice writing Q's and q's.

"Q: (over, around and close, slant out)
Start at the top line, go over, around and close it, like a circle (over, around and close), then give it a leg by slanting out from below the middle line to the bottom line so it doesn't roll away! (slant out).

"q: (over, around, up, down, curve)
Start at the middle line, go over, around and up to the middle line (over, around, up) then straight down below the bottom line with a slight curve back (down, curve).

Trace the Qq's below.

MINI-BOOK Q:

Read the letter book again.

Advanced K — see if your child can read the book to you.

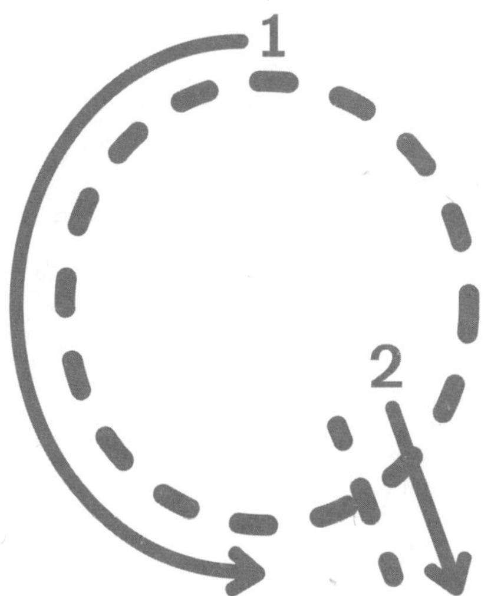

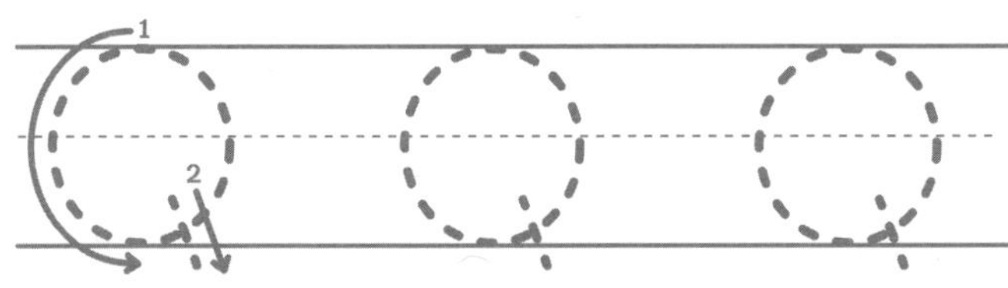

LESSON 18
Prep Page

Supply List

- ☐ 12 dominoes (day 1, Bible)
- ☐ Boiled egg (cooled), butter knife (day 3, Bible)
- ☐ Playdough (day 3, Bible)

Objectives

Letter of the week: Rr

Skills/Concepts: safety – natural disasters, emergencies, seat belts/car seats

Memory Verse

John 12:32

And I, when I am lifted up from the earth, will draw all people to myself.

Extended Activities

Designate them to be the "Safety Check Engineer" and have them double check that each person is wearing a seat belt in the car. Give them a small notebook for them to "check off" or make a sheet and laminate or place in a plastic sleeve with a dry erase marker. Also have them be in charge of family plans in emergencies and post the plan (pictures drawn by them), etc.

There are more resources and information at www.nfpa.org. Please make sure you have working smoke detectors in your home.

It would be very impactful if your child could visit the fire station and have the firemen discuss fire safety. Kids are often scared of a fireman in all his gear, and it is great for them to see them in their gear.

LESSON 18
Day 1

LIFE SKILLS:

"We will be discussing safety today. What do you think it means to be safe? Safety is when we use protection or care that will keep us from getting hurt or being harmed. An example is when it is storming. We do not go outside and play in the rain if we hear thunder or see lightning. Why do you think we would not play in the rain during that time? If you hear thunder, most likely there is lightning. If you see lightning, then you definitely know it is not safe to be in the rain. Lightning could strike you and cause harm to you. We need to be safe.

"Natural disasters happen all over the world. In the United States, we experience several types of natural disasters, which include flooding, fires, tornadoes, hurricanes, and earthquakes. There are things we can do to be safe from a natural disaster. We talked earlier this year about what to do in a tornado, hurricane, earthquake, and thunderstorm. Let's review the chart on page 52.

"One of the best ways to be safe is to be prepared and know what to do if you are in that situation. I want to teach you about fire safety. We are going to make a fire plan. A fire plan is what you study and practice so you know what to do if there is a fire in your house. Let's decide on a designated spot outside where we all will meet.

TIP: This will be covered over two days.

Create and practice a home fire escape plan with two ways out of every room in case of a fire.

"Do not try to get anything when there is a fire. Just get out and go to your meeting place. Let's use a stopwatch and time how fast our family can escape.

"Do you remember how a smoke alarm sounds? When a room fills with smoke, we need to get low to the ground. Smoke will rise, so the air near the floor is safer to breathe. It is also good to use a damp rag or even a piece of clothing to put over your mouth and nose to breathe into.

Share your family's plan for what to do and how to get out when they hear a smoke alarm.

"If in a closed room during a fire, never open the door without checking it first. Use the backside of your hand to feel the door to see if it is hot. This will prevent your more sensitive palm from getting burned. If it is hot, use your other escape route to get out of the room.

"If you catch on fire, STOP, DROP, ROLL. This will extinguish the fire. Fire has to have oxygen to keep burning, so by rolling you remove its oxygen and it will stop. Let's practice this.

"Often, kids try to hide from the fire and go into closets or under beds. NEVER do this. If a fireman is coming to save you, you make it more difficult for them if you are hiding. Stay low to the ground, and in an open area if you cannot get out.

Review this again by using the next page.

Name

❶ Fire Escape Plan

❷ Stay low to the ground

❸ Check the door for heat

❹ Stop Drop Roll

❺ Don't hide!

LESSON 18
Day 1

BIBLE:

"This week our memory verse is from John 12:32, that says:

Echo read the verse. Add motions.

And I , when I

am lifted 

up from the earth ,

will draw  all people

to myself.

"Last week we discussed Jesus' birth, a time from His childhood, and His first miracle. Let's look at how Jesus called the first disciples. A disciple is a student or follower. Once a disciple has learned what they need to know, they share what they learned with someone.

Set up up a row of 12 dominoes close enough in a line so that if you knock one down, it creates a chain reaction that sends each one falling down — don't knock it over yet.

Read Luke 5:1–11 from your Bible.

"Jesus eventually asked 12 specific men to be His disciples. He also gave us instructions that we are to disciple others or win others to Christ. See, when we share the good news of the gospel with others, it spreads from one person to the next to the next. Watch what happens . . . *(knock the first domino over)*. See, when we share the good news, then the next person shares it, then the next one shares it, and it just keeps going. This is why it is so important to tell others about Christ. We want everyone to be able to have eternal life and live with Jesus forever. We want to share the good news of Jesus. See if you can find someone this week to share the good news of Jesus with.

RHYME TIME:

"Let's read our poem for the week. It's "Row, Row, Row Your Boat."

Have the student echo you. You may also choose to sing it as you pretend to row a boat.

Row, Row, Row Your Boat

Row, row, row your boat
gently down the stream.
Merrily, merrily, merrily, merrily,
life is but a dream.

LESSON 18
Day 1

ABC'S AND MORE:

"Now, let's look at our ABC chart.

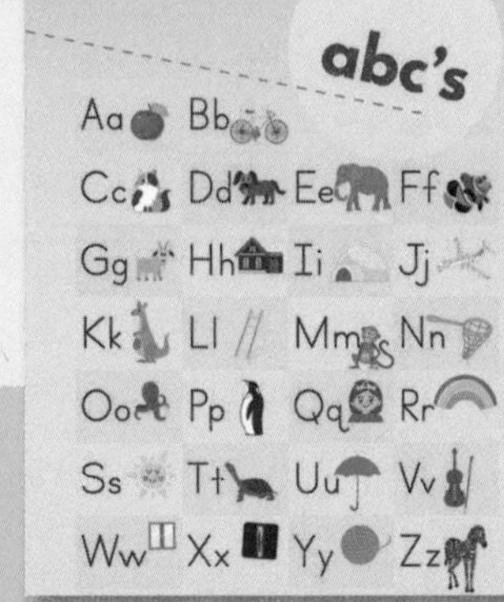

See Teacher Resource Page.

Chant the ABC chart.

Sing the ABC song.

"We will be learning how to write our Rr's this week.

Point to capital R.

"This the capital R.

Point to the lowercase r.

"This is the lowercase r.

Practice writing R's and r's.

"R: (down, up, around, slant out)
Start at the top line, go down to the bottom line (down), go back up your line to the top (up) then around toward the middle line (around) then slant out to the bottom line (slant out).

"r: (down, up, and over)
Start at the middle line and go down to the bottom line (down), go back up the line and curve over a little past the middle line (up and over).

Trace the Rr's below.

MINI-BOOK R:

See the Teacher Resource Page.

Do a picture walk.

Read the book to the student, pointing to each letter/word.

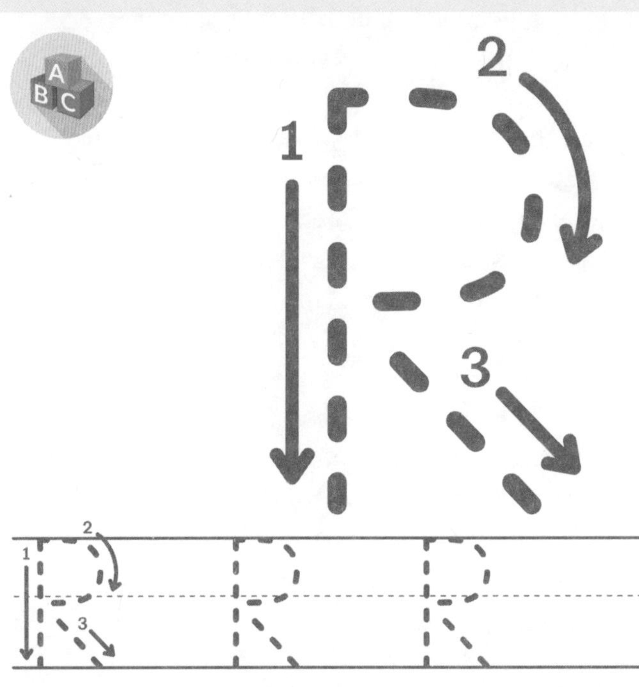

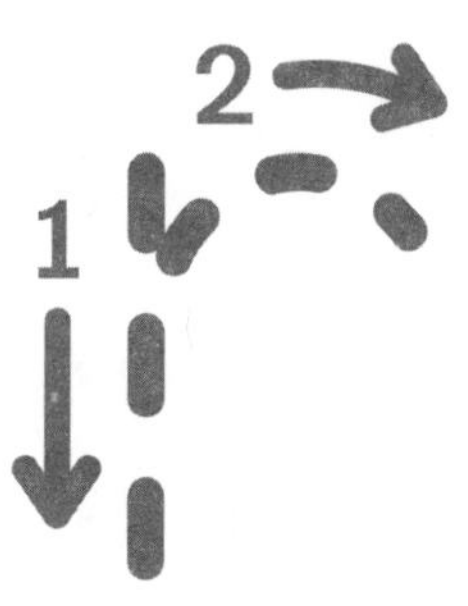

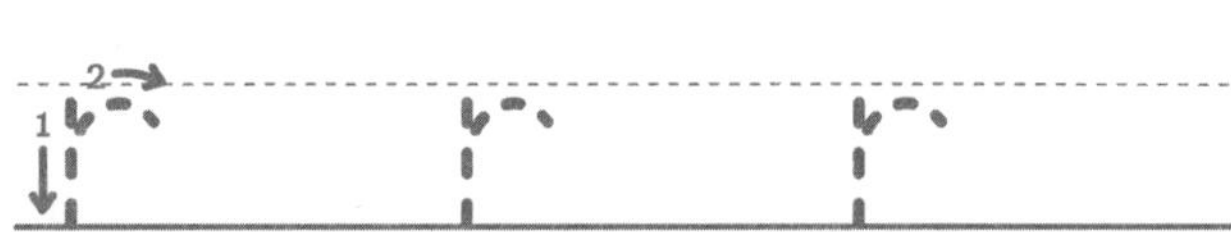

LESSON 18
Day 2

LIFE SKILLS:

"We will continue discussing fire safety and go over our steps and our fire plan for our home.

Complete fire plan and continue practicing your evacuation plan.

"Do you know what an emergency is? An emergency is when something is happening that can cause something bad to happen to someone, property, or the environment. Examples of an emergency are a house fire, a car wreck, or someone who needs medical help.

"In these situations, you should call 911.

"We NEVER call 911 for fun. If we do that, then the people talking to you cannot help someone with a real emergency. Let's use this diagram to practice dialing 911.

BIBLE:

Practice your memory verse on page 202.

"We are continuing the life of Jesus. Jesus' life was an example for us to follow. He showed compassion, He reached out to those who needed to be saved no matter where they were from or how much money they had, and He showed love to others. Jesus changed lives, and He is still changing lives today. Jesus was around 30 years old when he died on the Cross for our sins.

"One of his own 12 disciples, Judas, betrayed him. Betray means that Judas turned Jesus over to His enemies. Jesus had warned His disciples that one of them would betray Him. Before Jesus went to the Cross, He was in the Garden of Gethsemane. He had Peter, John, and James with Him. He asked the three disciples with Him to stay awake and pray. Jesus also moved away a little from them, and He began to pray. He prayed for God's will to be done, not His own. Jesus knew what was coming. He knew He was about to face an angry crowd that wanted Him to be crucified or killed. The disciples were so tired they kept falling asleep. Then, Judas and a crew of soldiers gathered near the garden. They had come after Jesus. The soldiers took Jesus to Pontius Pilate, the leader of that time. The people were so confused and believed that Jesus was a bad person. They actually begged for a criminal to be set free and for Jesus to take his place on the Cross. That is really what Jesus did. He took our place on the Cross so we could be free. He died for our sins, but Jesus did not stay on the Cross. They put His body in a tomb. A tomb is kind of like a cave. They put a huge stone in front of the opening with guards at the sides so no one could enter. We will finish the story tomorrow about how Jesus rose again.

LESSON 18
Day 2

“We will make artwork today of a cross. The cross is a sign to us that we have eternal life because of what Jesus did in dying on the Cross. Draw a hill in green on the paper.

Cut painter’s tape (1”) in half down the middle to make it more narrow. Using the cut painter’s tape, make a cross on top of the hill, with two smaller crosses on each side. Don’t press down really hard, but just barely secure the tape to the paper.

“Paint the sky and ground using watercolors. Remove the painter’s tape to reveal the three crosses.

RHYME TIME:

“Let’s read our poem again.

Read/sing “Row, Row, Row your Boat” on page 202.

ABC’S AND MORE:

“Now, let’s look at our ABC chart.

Chant the ABC chart.

Sing the ABC song.

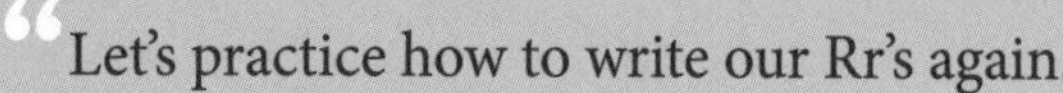

“Let’s practice how to write our Rr’s again.

Point to the capital R. Point to the lowercase r.

“This is the capital R and this is the lowercase r. Let’s write them!

Practice writing R’s and r’s.

“R: (down, up, around, slant out)
Start at the top line, go down to the bottom line (down), go back up your line to the top (up) then around toward the middle line (around) then slant out to the bottom line (slant out).

“r: (down, up, and over)
Start at the middle line and go down to the bottom line (down), go back up the line and curve over a little past the middle line (up and over).

Trace the Rr’s below.

MINI-BOOK R:

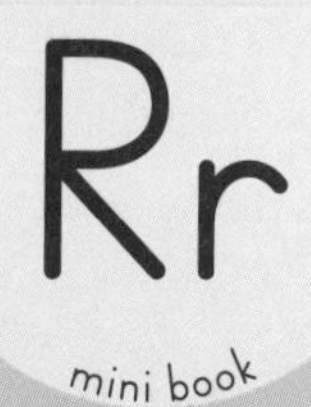

Read the letter book to the student.

Have the student highlight the capital and lowercase letter of the week.

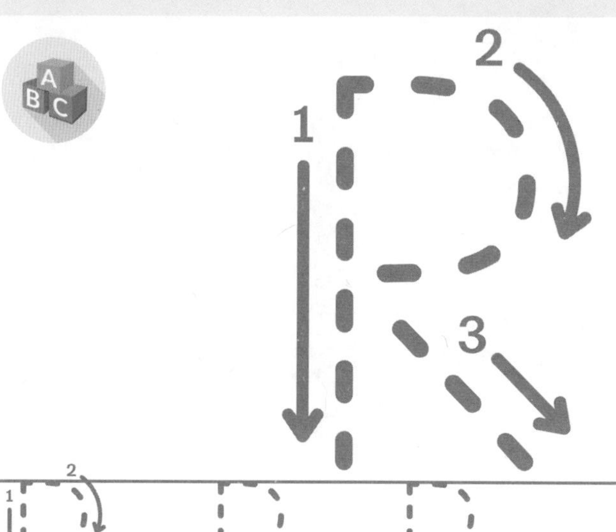

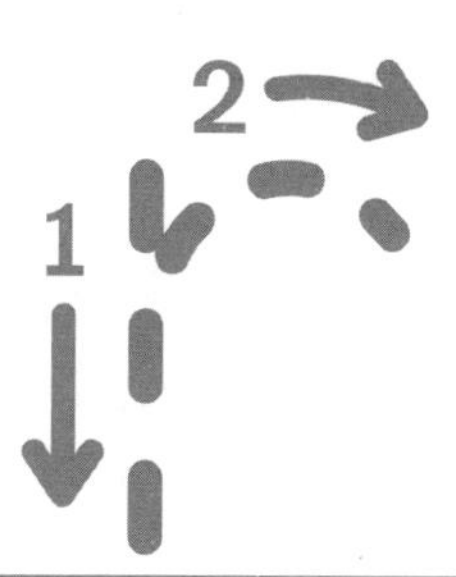

LESSON 18
Day 3

LIFE SKILLS:

Review the 911 rules/steps on page 204.

"We NEVER call 911 for fun. If we do that, then the people talking to you cannot help someone with a real emergency. Let's use this diagram to practice dialing 911.

"Another way we can be safe is by using our seat belts and car seats to stay safe in a car. Let's look at your car seat/seat belt and make sure you are in the safest position.

Some fire departments, police departments, and hospitals will do free car seat safety checks and even install them for you. Check car seat laws in your state.

BIBLE:

Review your memory verse on page 202.

"Let's think about our story of Jesus on the Cross. Jesus was placed in a tomb, but He didn't stay there. The soldiers put a stone over the entry, and they put guards at the door. The prophets had stated that after three days, Jesus would rise from the dead. The angels of the Lord came and rolled away the stone. The ground shook like an earthquake as Jesus rose from the dead. He is risen! Praise God!

Read Matthew 28.

"Jesus told them the Holy Spirit would be sent as our supporter. In Acts 2, 50 days after Jesus' Resurrection, 11 of Jesus' disciples and a few others were in an upper room praying. He baptized each of them with the Holy Spirit. He told them that the Holy Spirit will give them power.

"We have that power today. The Holy Spirit is what gives us power over sin and helps us to live a holy life. Let's look at this egg. This helps us understand God better. We have a shell *(crack the egg and peel away the shell)*. Then, we have the part of the egg we call egg white. Last, we have the middle part *(cut it open)* called the yolk. This is how God, Jesus, and the Holy Spirit are. There is one God, but Jesus is God in flesh like we are, and the Holy Spirit is the spirit of God. There are three parts of an egg, but it's still one egg, just like there are three parts, but only one God.

"Use your playdough to make a tomb and a stone that you can roll away just like the angels rolled away the stone at the tomb of Jesus.

RHYME TIME:

"Let's review our poem for the week.

Read/sing the rhyme "Row, Row, Row your Boat."

"Now, highlight the R's and r's in the rhyme on the following page.

Name

Row, Row, Row Your Boat

Row, row, row your boat
gently down the stream.
Merrily, merrily, merrily, merrily,
life is but a dream.

LESSON 18
Day 3

ABC'S AND MORE:

"Now, let's look at our ABC chart.

See Teacher Resource Page.

Chant the ABC chart.

Sing the ABC song.

Play this Memory Challenge game.

Using your letter cards, lay them out in ABC order like the ABC chart. Then, flip over the letters G, J, E, U, P, C. See if they can figure out which letters are flipped over and then have them flip it to check their memory.

"That was fun! Now, let's review writing our Rr's.

Point to the capital R. Point to the lowercase r.

"This is the capital R and this is the lowercase r. Let's write them!

Practice writing R's and r's.

"R: (down, up, around, slant out)
Start at the top line, go down to the bottom line (down), go back up your line to the top (up) then around toward the middle line (around) then slant out to the bottom line (slant out).

"r: (down, up, and over)
Start at the middle line and go down to the bottom line (down), go back up the line and curve over a little past the middle line (up and over).

Trace the Rr's below.

MINI-BOOK R:

Read the letter book again.

Advanced K — see if your child can read the book to you.

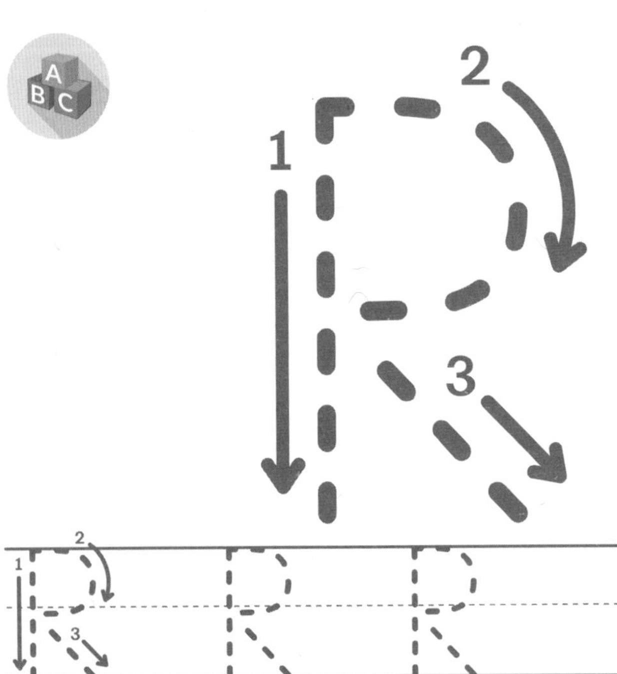

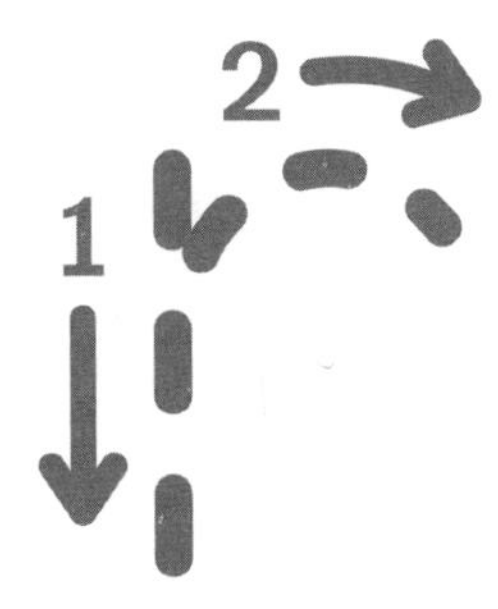

LESSON 19
Prep Page

Look Ahead

- ☐ Next week you will need 12 stones or rocks, needle and thread, as well as scrap fabric or an old shirt.

Objectives

Letter of the week: Ss

Skills/Concepts: Understanding street signs

Memory Verse

John 14:6

I am the way and the truth and the life. No one comes to the Father except through me.

Extended Activities

Game: Zipongo to Go! (matching game with stoplight)

Count the sides of a stop sign.

LESSON 19
Day 1

LIFE SKILLS:

"Last week we talked about safety. Another way we can stay safe on the road is by understanding street signs. If crossing a street, we should always hold the hand of an adult. We are known as pedestrians, which means walkers. When crossing a street, we also need to find the crosswalk. A crosswalk is a designated place for pedestrians or walkers to cross a street.

"Here is a picture of a crosswalk.

"If we are crossing a street, we may see a sign like this. This one means it is okay to walk across the street using the crosswalk, but we still should check both ways to make sure the cars are stopping.

"This sign means it is NOT safe to cross and we should wait to cross the street.

BIBLE:

"There is something so special about coming to Jesus. Jesus is all we need. If we start our day with time with God, then our whole day will go better.

"Our memory verse says in John 14:6:

Echo read the verse. Add motions.

I am the way  and the truth  and the life . No one  comes to the Father except through me .

"Jesus is the way. We will learn what it means for someone to be "the way." Jesus' disciples had been following Him for a few years and Jesus was telling them about His death and how He was going to prepare a place for them. Jesus told them in John 14:4 that they knew the way to the place where He was going. They were confused. Thomas, one of the disciples, asked Jesus how they could know the way if they didn't know where He was going. Jesus told them He was the way. A "way" is a path or direction to go. You see, Jesus' disciples knew Him.

LESSON 19
Day 1

"They just did not realize that THE WAY to heaven is through Jesus Christ! The only way to go to heaven is through Jesus. He has left us instructions to live by in the Word of God. All we have to do is believe on and follow Him. Just like Acts 4:12 states: "Salvation is found in no one else, for there is no other name under heaven given to mankind by which we must be saved." We are not saved by our neighbor, or our parents, or our friends. The only way we are saved is through Jesus Christ. He offers us salvation and eternal life with Him.

"Let's follow THE WAY to get to Jesus.

Complete Bible maze activity below.

RHYME TIME:

"Our poem this week is "Do You Know How Many Stars?"

Read "Do You Know How Many Stars?" on page 212.

"You know, if we look at God's creation we can appreciate all that He has made. Appreciation or to appreciate means to show our thankfulness for something. Our poem says that God in heaven counted all the stars and clouds and He would miss one, or know, if one fell. I think it is amazing to find things like stars and clouds that we can appreciate.

Help the boy find the way to Jesus.

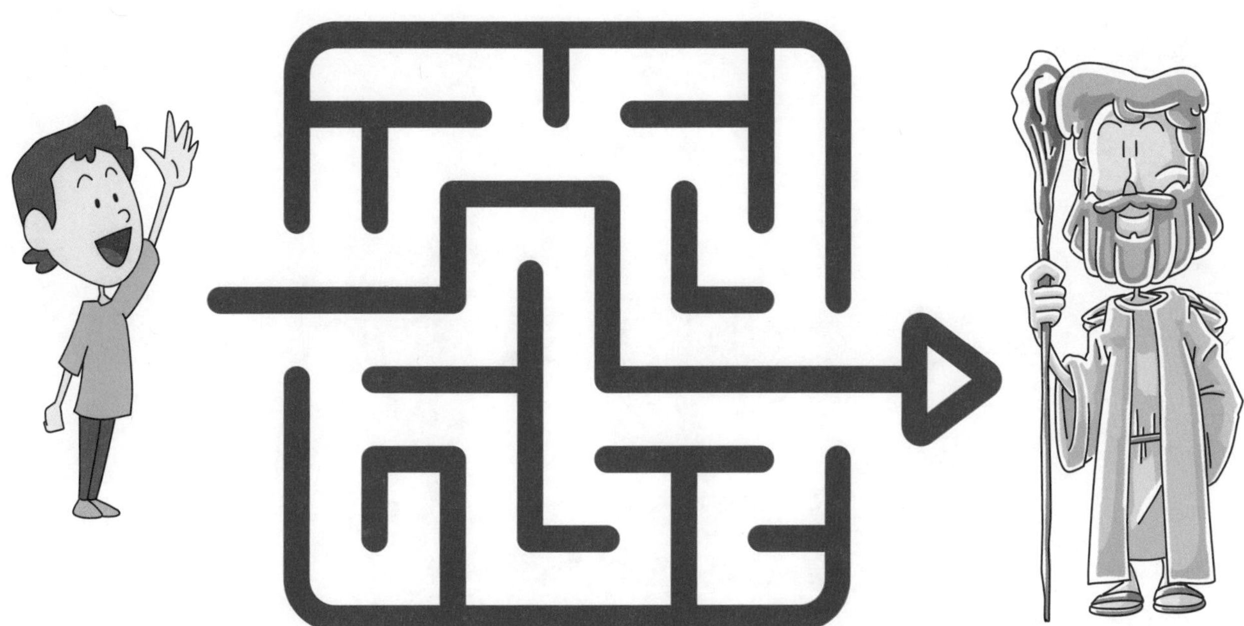

Do You Know How Many Stars?

Do you know how many stars
there are shining in the sky?
Do you know how many clouds
every day go floating by?
God in heaven has counted all,
He would miss one should it fall.

Do you know how many children
go to little beds at night?
And without a care or sorrow
wake up in the morning light?
God in heaven each name can tell,
knows you too, knows you well.

LESSON 19
Day 1

ABC'S AND MORE:

"Now, let's look at our ABC chart.

See Teacher Resource Page.

Chant the ABC chart.

Sing the ABC song.

Practice writing the letters Aa-Ff.

On the next page, they will match upper and lowercase letters.

"Today we will learn how to write Ss's! Don't forget that there is a capital letter and a lowercase letter.

Point to capital S.

"This the capital S.

Point to the lowercase s.

"This is the lowercase s. It's time to write your Ss's!

Practice writing S's and s's.

"S: (curve back, curve forward)
Start at the top line, curve back toward the middle line, then curve forward toward the bottom line (curve back, curve forward).

"s: (curve back, curve forward)
Start at the middle line, curve back between the middle line and bottom line, then curve forward toward the bottom line (curve back, curve forward).

Trace the Ss's below.

MINI-BOOK S:

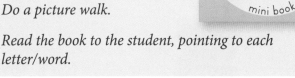

See the Teacher Resource Page.

Do a picture walk.

Read the book to the student, pointing to each letter/word.

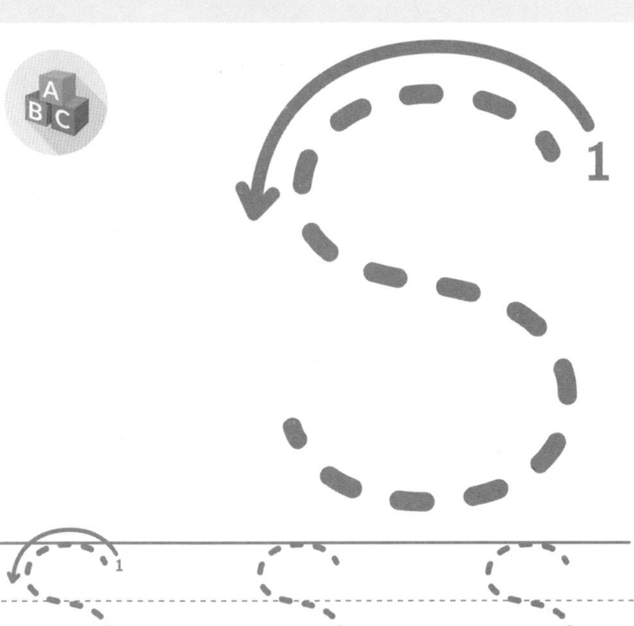

Lesson 19
Day 1

Name

Draw a line from the capital letter to its lowercase letter. C is already done for you.

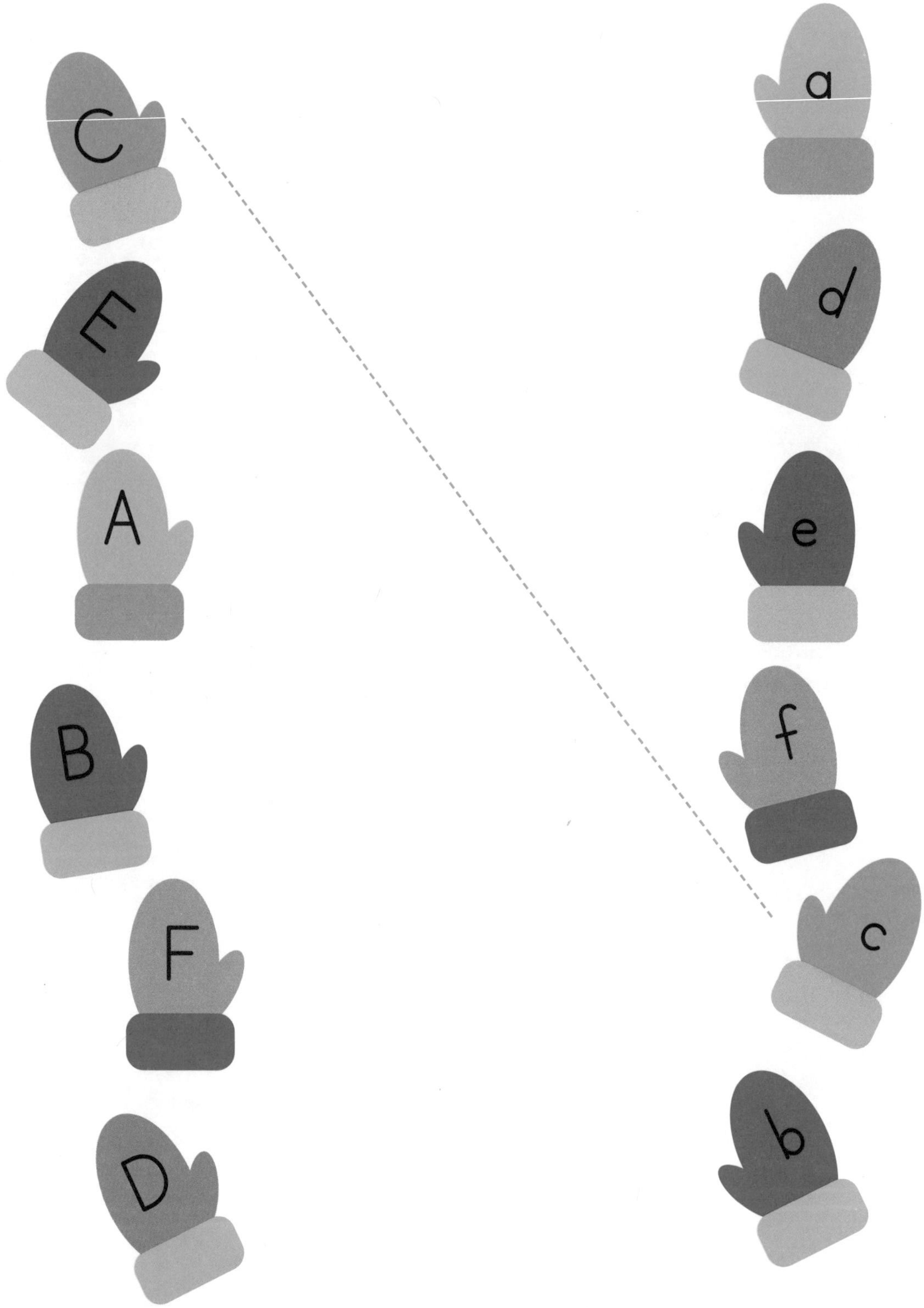

C
E
A
B
F
D

a
d
e
f
c
b

LESSON 19
Day 2

LIFE SKILLS:

Review graphic of crosswalk from day 1 on page 210.

"Do you remember what this is called?

"Does this sign mean to walk or do not walk?

NOTE: If you have crosswalks, it would be ideal to go practice using them this week. Even some stores will have areas specifically for pedestrians to walk.

"STOP! This is a stop sign.

"When you see this sign, it means you stop. Cars are supposed to stop at the stop sign.

"This is a stoplight. Green means go, yellow means caution and red means stop.

"Let's play the stoplight game.

Directions: Find a place to be the starting line with enough space to run/stop/go slow. This would be best outside. Make a finish line or a stopping place. You will call out a color of the stoplight and the student(s) will walk quickly for green, stop for red, and walk for yellow, carefully looking both ways.

BIBLE:

"Remember, if we start our day with God and appreciating all that He has done, our whole day will go better.

Review your memory verse on page 210.

"Yesterday, we discussed Jesus and how He is the Way. Today, we will talk about how Jesus is the Truth and what that means. What does it mean to tell the truth? Truth means that it is a fact or real. So, if Jesus is the Truth, that means that Jesus is factual or real. The Bible says in John 8:32 that you will know the truth and the truth will set you free. Once again, we have Jesus, or the truth, setting us free. So, who sets us free? Jesus! We know that Jesus cannot lie. He is God and God cannot sin. Remember our demonstration with the jars where we poured sin into Jesus. What happened? Sin disappeared because it cannot be in Jesus because He is without sin. He is truth. He is pure. The goal of Jesus is to seek and save the lost. We should be like Jesus and try to help others be saved. What are some ways you can help someone be saved?

Pray for them, witness to them, invite them to church, be kind. . . .

"Let's learn to be seekers of those who need to hear the Word of God so we can share it with them.

Seek and Find: Find the hidden objects on the next page.

LESSON 19
Day 2

RHYME TIME:

Read "Do You Know How Many Stars?"

Highlight the S's and s's in the poem below.

Do You Know How Many Stars?

Do you know how many stars
there are shining in the sky?
Do you know how many clouds
every day go floating by?
God in heaven has counted all,
He would miss one should it fall.

Do you know how many children
go to little beds at night?
And without a care or sorrow
wake up in the morning light?
God in heaven each name can tell,
knows you too, knows you well.

Find and circle these hidden objects in the picture.

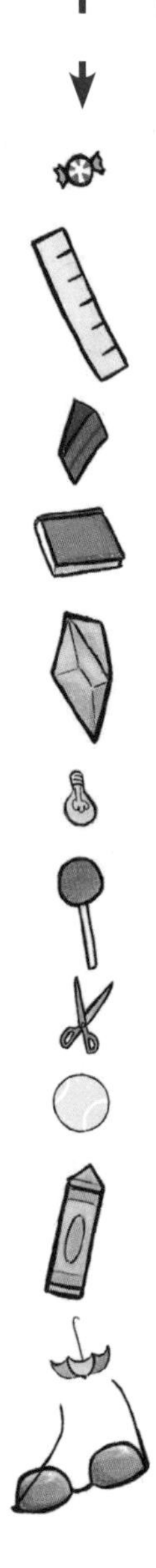

LESSON 19
Day 2

ABC'S AND MORE:

"Now, let's look at our ABC chart.

Chant the ABC chart.

Sing the ABC song.

Practice writing Gg through Ll.

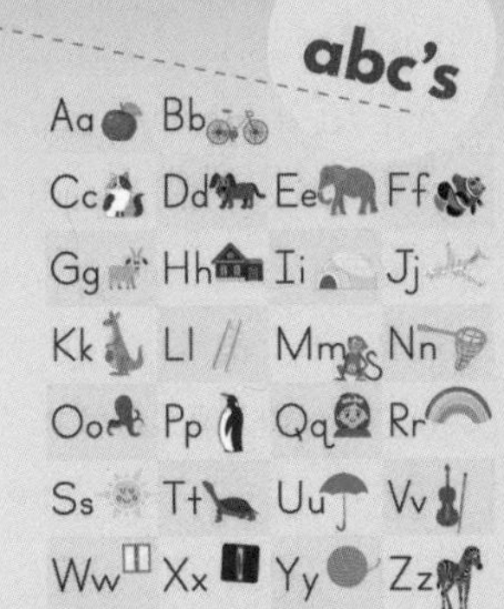

"Let's practice writing our Ss's today!

Point to the capital S. Point to the lowercase s.

"This is the capital S and this is the lowercase s. Let's write them!

Practice writing S's and s's.

"S: (curve back, curve forward)
Start at the top line, curve back toward the middle line, then curve forward toward the bottom line (curve back, curve forward).

"s: (curve back, curve forward)
Start at the middle line, curve back between the middle line and bottom line, then curve forward toward the bottom line (curve back, curve forward).

Trace the Ss's below.

MINI-BOOK S:

Read the letter book to the student.

Have the student highlight the capital and lowercase letter of the week.

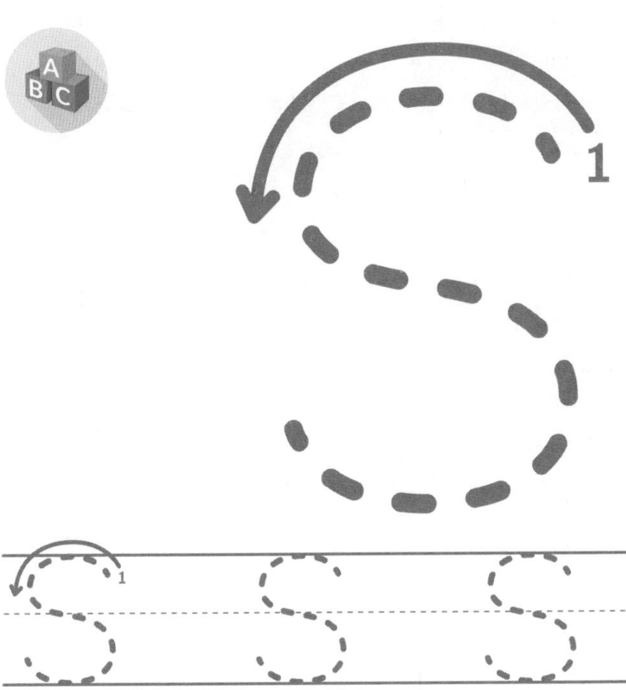

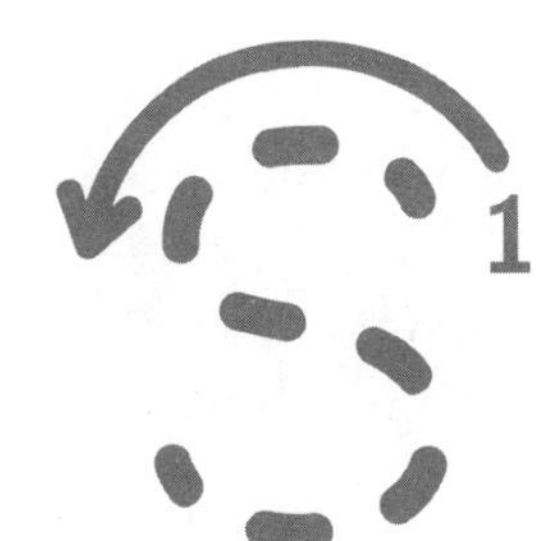

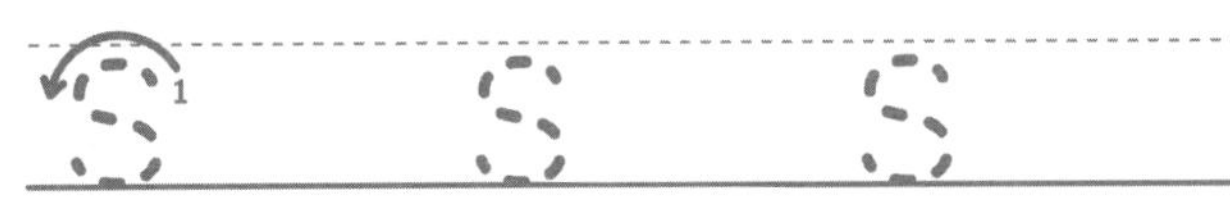

LESSON 19
Day 3

LIFE SKILLS:

"Write your name on a blank piece of paper.

Review from graphic of crosswalk from day 1 on page 210.

"Do you remember what this is called?

"Does this sign mean to walk or do not walk?

Review from graphic of stop sign and stop light from day 2 on page 215.

"What does this sign mean? What do the colors on this mean?

Play the stoplight game and add in the alternate movements below.

Directions: Find a place to be the starting line with enough space to run/stop/go slow. This would be best outside. Make a finish line or a stopping place. You will call out a color of the stoplight and the student(s) will walk quickly for green, stop for red, and walk for yellow, carefully looking both ways.

ALTERNATE: Have them use giant steps for green, fast walking for yellow, and freezing on red.

BIBLE:

"Remember, if we start our day with God and appreciating all that He has done, our whole day will go better.

Review your memory verse on page 210.

"We have discussed Jesus and how He is the Way and the Truth. Today, we will talk about how Jesus is the Life and what that means. Jesus says in John 10:10, "I have come that they may have life, and have it to the full." Jesus wants us to have eternal life with Him. Eternal means forever, or that it never ends. We should all want to have eternal life with Jesus. Do you want to live with Jesus? I know I do!

"Jesus came to earth as a baby, lived and taught a holy life, died on the Cross for our sins, and rose again on the third day. Then, God gave us the Holy Spirit to give us power to overcome sin. We will sin, or make mistakes, but it is by the blood of Jesus that we can be forgiven of our sins. All we have to do is ask Him to forgive us and He will.

"Jesus' death and Resurrection was so that we could have life. John 3:16 says, "For God so loved the world that he gave his one and only Son, that whoever believes in him shall not perish but have eternal life." When we follow and believe in Jesus, who is the way, the truth, and the life, then we can have eternal life.

"We often use a tree as a symbol of life. Jesus even said he is the vine and we are the branches (John 15:5). I love looking at how the center of a tree or a vine is the main part like a trunk, then the part that spreads out is the branches. This is much like our lives. Jesus is the center, and our job is to be the branches, or to spread the message of Christ to others.

Color the tree on the next page.

Name

Color the tree.

LESSON 19
Day 3

RHYME TIME:

Read "Do You Know How Many Stars?" on page 212.

"Do you remember what it means to appreciate something or show appreciation? Yes, appreciation means to show our thankfulness for something.

ABC'S AND MORE:

"Now, let's look at our ABC chart.

See Teacher Resource Page.

Chant the ABC chart.

Sing the ABC song.

Match the capital and lowercase letters on the next page.

Practice writing letters Mm-Rr.

"Let's review how to write our Ss's again.

Practice writing S's and s's.

"S: (curve back, curve forward)
Start at the top line, curve back toward the middle line, then curve forward toward the bottom line (curve back, curve forward).

"s: (curve back, curve forward)
Start at the middle line, curve back between the middle line and bottom line, then curve forward toward the bottom line (curve back, curve forward).

Trace the Ss's below.

MINI-BOOK S:

Read the letter book again.

Advanced K — see if your child can read the book to you.

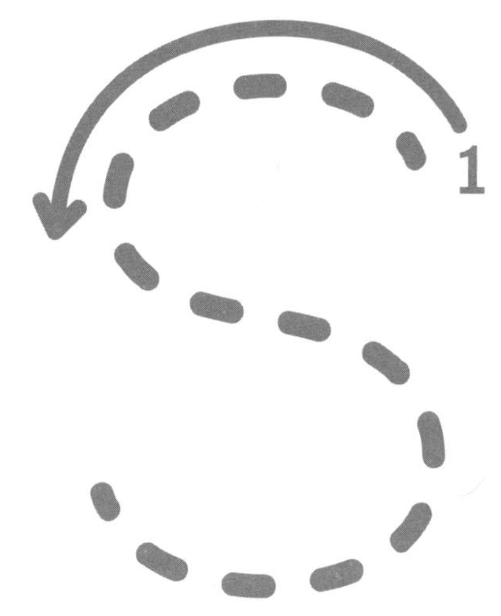

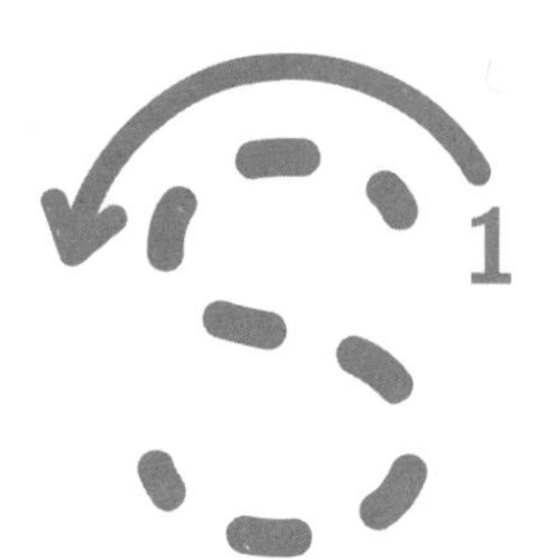

Name

Lesson 19
Day 3

Match the capital letters and the lowercase letters.

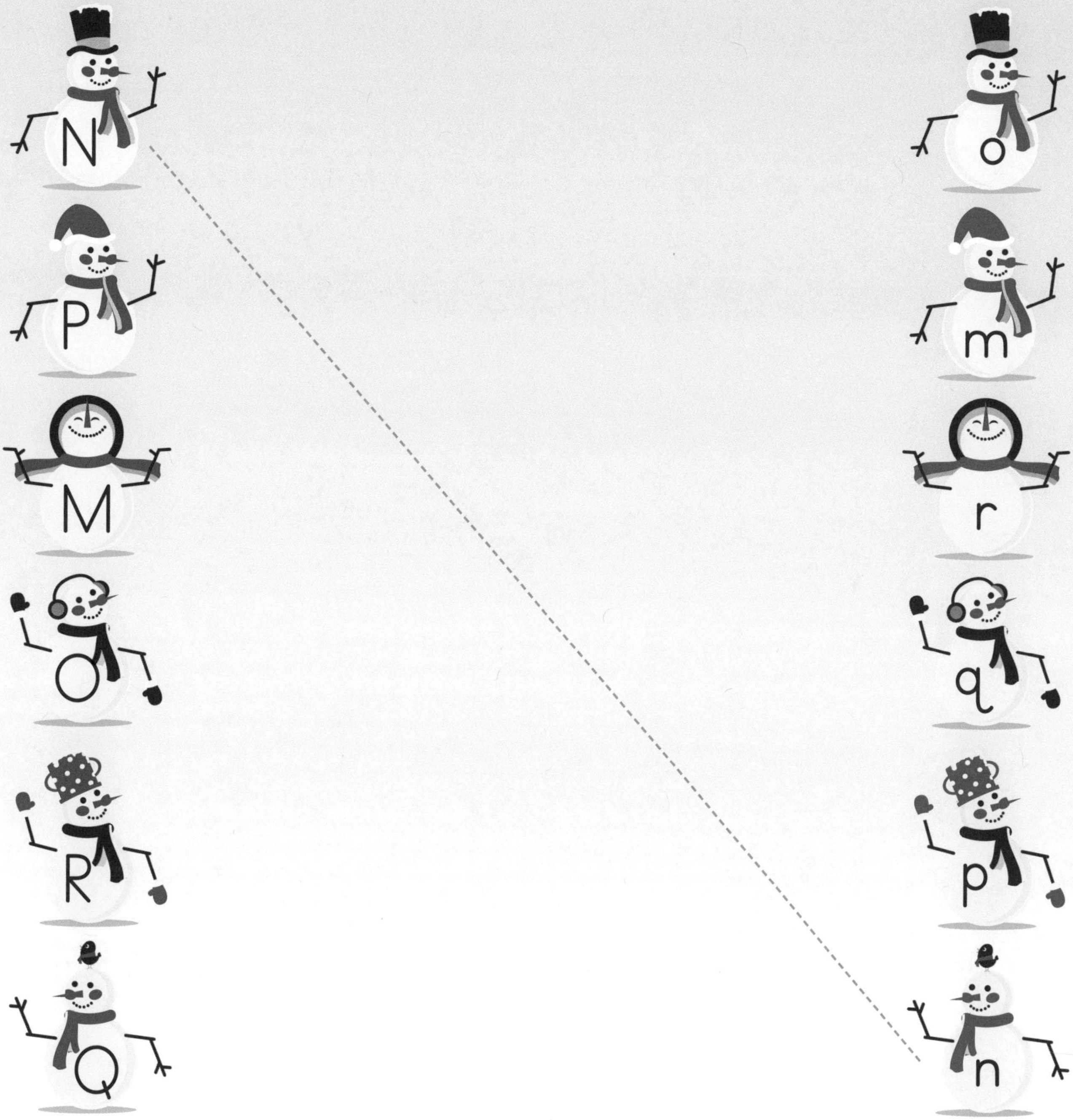

N o

P m

M r

O q

R p

Q n

LESSON 20
Prep Page

Supply List

- ☐ Shoe with laces (daily, life skills)
- ☐ 12 stones (day 2, Bible)
- ☐ Buttons (at least 7) (day 1, life skills)
- ☐ Needle, thread, scrap fabric or old shirt (daily, life skills)

Objectives

Letter of the week: Tt

Skills/Concepts: Tying shoes, sewing a button

Memory Verse

Ephesians 6:1

Children obey your parents in the Lord, for this is right.

Extended Activities

Teach how to sew scrap fabrics together by hand or machine.

Teach how to slip stitch to sew scrap fabric together.

Practice sewing a button.

Practice address, phone number, birthday, and writing name.

LESSON 20
Day 1

LIFE SKILLS:

Tying Shoes: Get a shoe with laces.

Teach your child, using this method or another method if you prefer, the easy bunny ears method of tying laces. Two bunny ears help the child tie a square knot, one of the easiest knots to learn. Try teaching this:

“Fold each end of the lace into a single “bunny ear.” You can hold the “ears” in place between your thumb and pointer finger on each hand.

“Cross the bunny ears so that they form an “X” in the air.

“Loop the bottom bunny ear over and through the top bunny ear. This will create a second knot.

“Pull the bunny ears out to the side away from the shoe. This will create a square knot that will not easily come undone and will hold the shoe in place.

“We will be learning how to sew on a button. One word you will hear me say is thread. Thread means to put your thread in the hole of the needle. There are also other meanings of this word. Like this is a spool of thread. Or I have a loose thread on my shirt. So it depends on how this word is used as to what it means.

Bunny Ears

❶

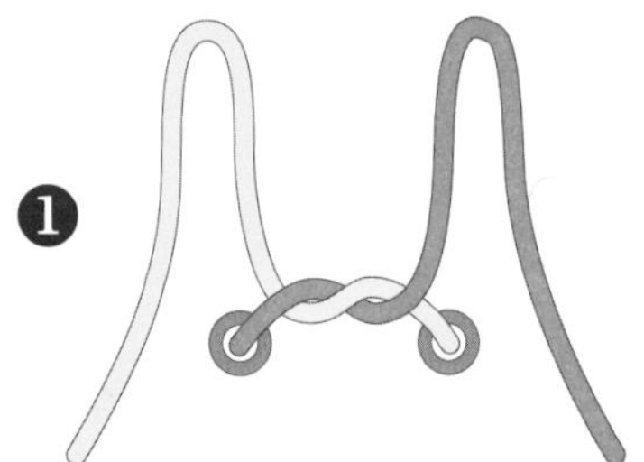

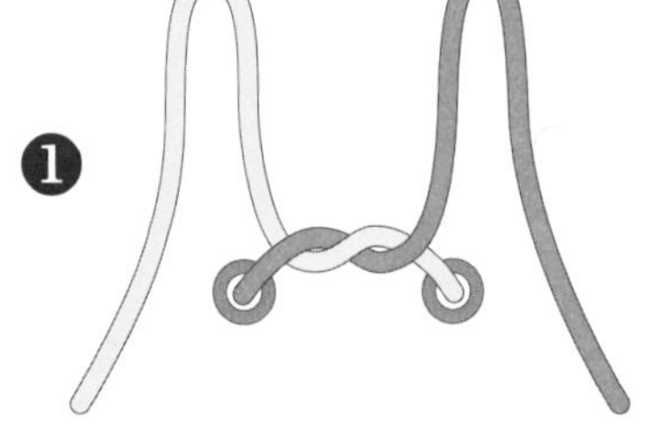

❷

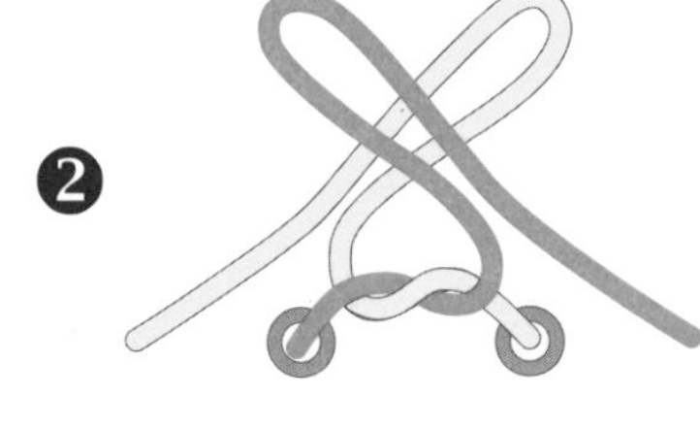

❸

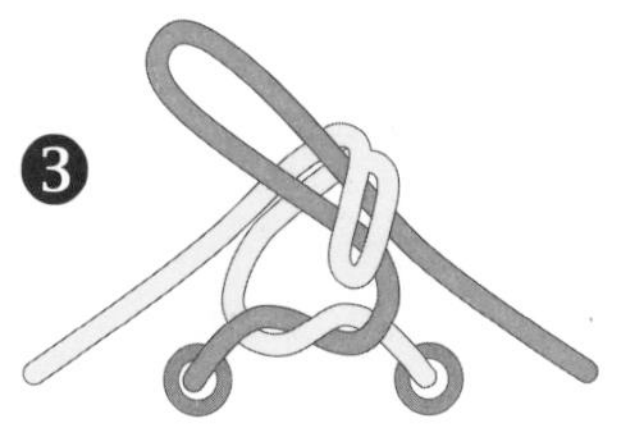

❹

❺

❻

LESSON 20
Day 1

"Just like there are seven days in a week, count and show me 7 buttons.

Teach your child these steps to sew on a button.

1. Thread the needle.
2. Tie a knot at the end of the thread.
3. Position the button on the fabric.
4. Push the threaded needle up through the back of the fabric and through one hole in the button.
5. Push the needle down through the opposite hole and through the fabric.
6. Continue doing this and alternate the holes each time.
7. When finished, knot off the end of the thread by slipping your needle into the underside of the fabric (not the button side) and do not pull your thread all the way through, but slip your needle through the hole, then pull the thread. Do this 3 times to secure it well.

BIBLE:

"Do you know what it means to obey? When we obey, that means that we follow what we have been told or asked to do. This is called obedience.

"Our Memory Verse is on obedience. In Ephesians 6:1 it says:

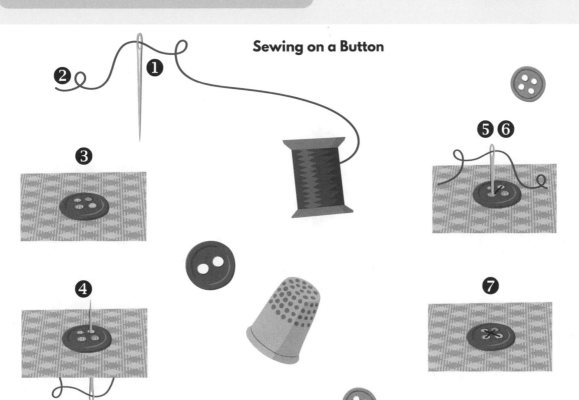

Echo read the verse. Add motions.

Children, obey 

your parents in the Lord ,

for this is right.

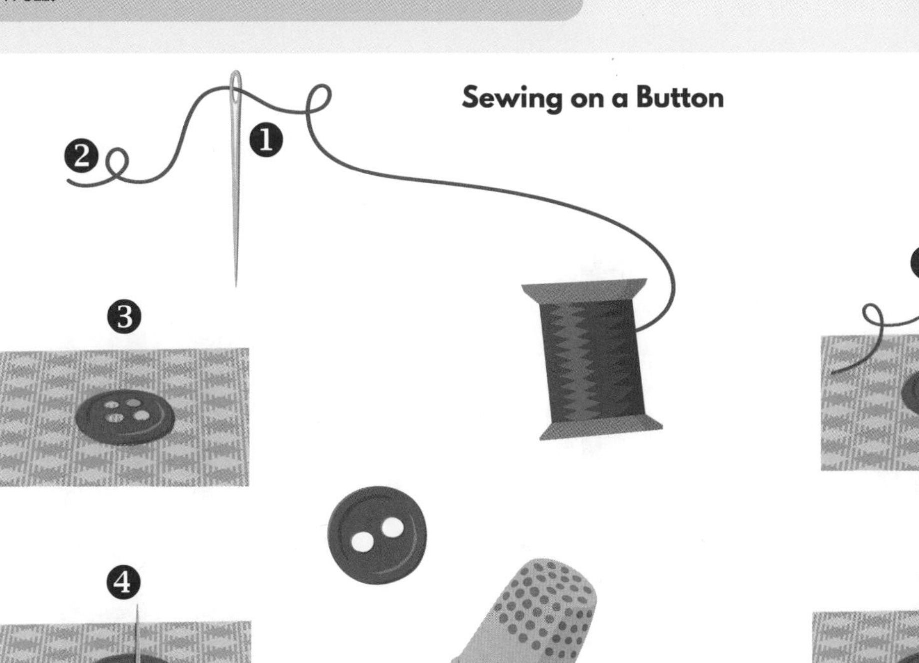

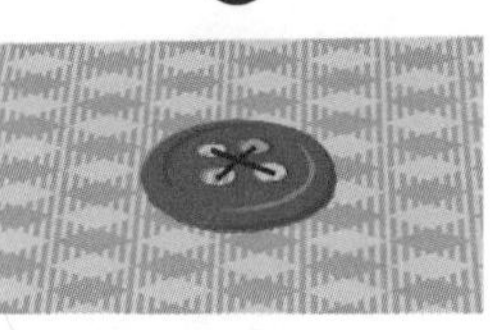

LESSON 20
Day 1

“Noah showed obedience. Noah knew that by obeying God’s commands that he and his family would be saved. We can look at the story of Noah in Genesis chapters 6–7. We see that Noah was told to build the Ark and given exact instructions on how to do it. Noah trusted God and obeyed what He said to do. Then, Noah and his family and all the animals entered the Ark. God closed the door. The rains came for 40 days and 40 nights, yet Noah and his family were saved because of Noah’s obedience. What do you think would have happened if Noah had not obeyed God and did not build the Ark? Yes, he and his family would have been destroyed. Because of Noah’s obedience to God, he and his family were saved. It is the same way for us. If we obey God and His Word, we can be saved. The Bible says, “Believe in the Lord Jesus, and you will be saved — you and your household” (Acts 16:31).

“Just like Noah’s household was saved, we can have salvation too!

“Let’s see if you can complete our activity for today. Help Noah and the animals get off the Ark after the Flood.

Complete Bible maze activity below.

RHYME TIME:

“Our poem for this week is “Star Light, Star Bright.” Let’s read it now!

Optional: Sing “Twinkle, Twinkle, Little Star” or find a recording and play it.

“Now see if you can trace the stars on the next page!

Help Noah and the animals get off the Ark.

Star Light, Star Bright

Star light, star bright,
first star I see tonight.
I wish I may, I wish I might,
have this wish I wish tonight.

Trace the stars.

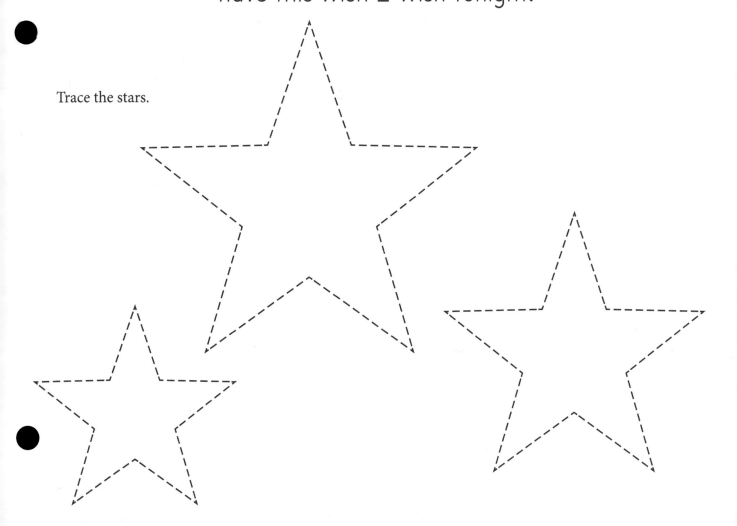

LESSON 20
Day 1

ABC'S AND MORE:

Memory Challenge: Lay out your letter cards in ABC order like the ABC chart is. Then, flip over the letters Q, A, H, L, P, V. See if they can figure out which letters are flipped over and then have them flip the cards to check their memory.

Letter Run: Lay out your letter cards on the floor. Call out the following letters as the child races to find the letters: B, P, Q, D, K, Z

See Teacher Resource Page.

Chant the ABC chart.

Sing the ABC song.

> "Today we will learn how to write Tt's! Don't forget that there is a capital letter and a lowercase letter.

Point to capital T. Point to the lowercase t.

> "This is the capital T. This is the lowercase t. It's time to write your Tt's!

Practice writing Tt's.

> "T: (down, across)
> Start at the top line, go down to the bottom line (down)
> Cross it at the top along the top line (across).

> "t: (down, across)
> Start at the top line, go down to the bottom line (down)
> Cross it at the middle line (across).

Trace the Tt's below.

MINI-BOOK T:

See the Teacher Resource Page.

Do a picture walk.

Read the book to the student, pointing to each letter/word.

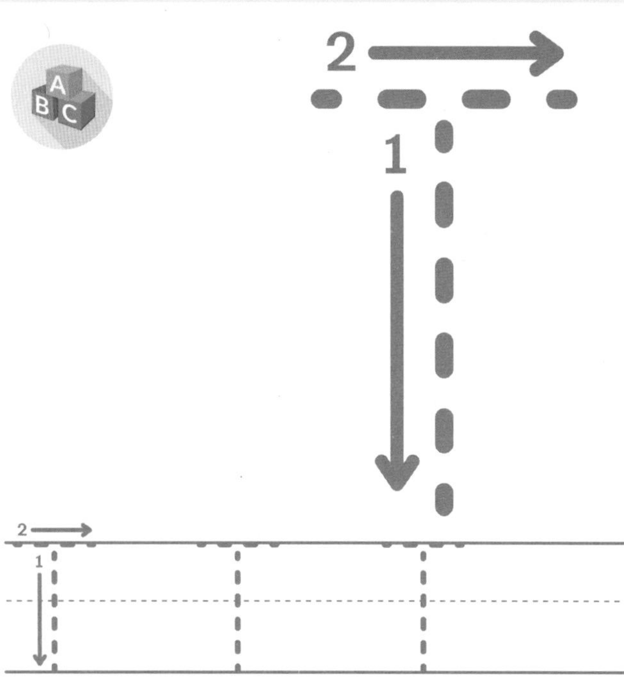

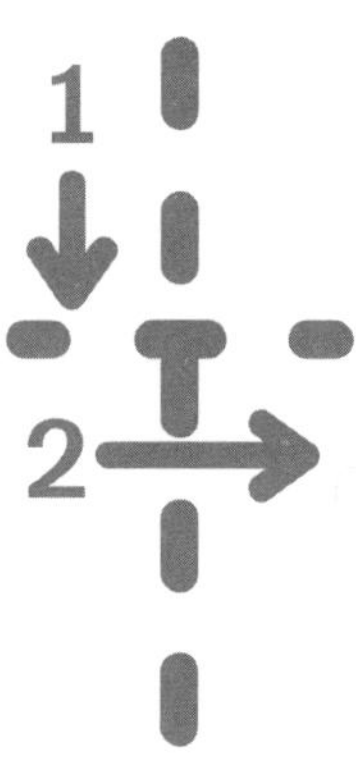

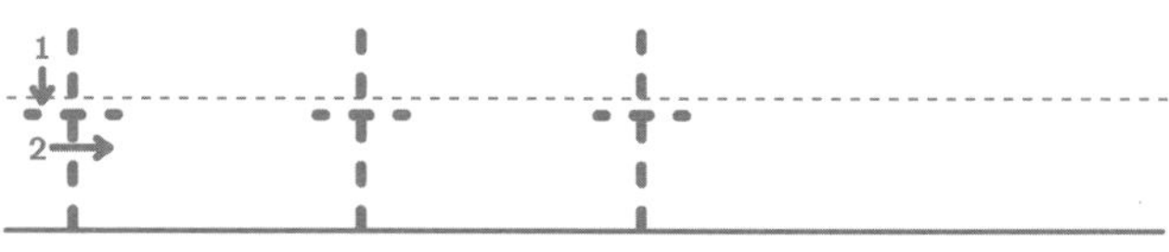

LESSON 20
Day 2

LIFE SKILLS:

Tying Shoes: Practice tying shoes with the method you chose. Practice sewing on buttons.

BIBLE:

"Do you remember what it means to obey? When we obey, that means that we follow what we have been told or asked to do. This is called obedience.

Review memory verse on page 225.

"There was a man named Joshua. He also showed obedience to God. Joshua was a leader of the Israelites after Moses died. Let's read to find out what miracle God did before the Israelites entered the Promised Land.

Read Joshua 3–4.

"Can you imagine being able to stop a large river from flowing? Every time God told Joshua to do something, He commanded the Israelites to do it. He obeyed God, and the Israelites obeyed God. When we obey God, like Joshua did, then He will perform miracles in our lives. We have to be obedient to God and our parents. God blessed the children of Israel with a land of promise. Do you think they would have still received the land of promise if they did not obey what God said?

"The 12 stones in the story are for each tribe of Israel. They made a monument, or a special memorial, so that it could be a testimony to future generations of what God had done. Let's use 12 stones to make a monument like you think theirs might have looked like.

RHYME TIME:

"Let's read our poem for this week, "Star Light, Star Bright" again.

Star Light, Star Bright

Star light, star bright,
first star I see tonight.
I wish I may, I wish I might,
have this wish I wish tonight.

"Our poem says, "I wish I may, I wish I might." The word *wish* means request or be hopeful about something you want. We can wish for a gift for our birthday, but it does not mean we will get it. A wish just means we are requesting something we want. A star might remind us of something that we are wishing for, but it is just a star. It can't give us what we wish for. We can ask our parents or even pray about the things we want and trust our parents and God to know what is best for us. Can you think of something you might wish for?

LESSON 20
Day 2

ABC'S AND MORE:

Memory Challenge: Lay out your letter cards in ABC order like the ABC chart. Then, flip over the letters K, Z, S, U, E, P. See if they can figure out which letters are flipped over and then have them flip the card to check their memory.

Chant the ABC Chart.

Sing the ABC song.

"Let's practice writing our Tt's today!

Point to the capital T. Point to the lowercase t.

"This is the capital T and this is the lowercase t. Let's write them!

Practice writing Tt's.

"T: (down, across)
Start at the top line, go down to the bottom line (down)
Cross it at the top along the top line (across).

"t: (down, across)
Start at the top line, go down to the bottom line (down)
Cross it at the middle line (across).

Trace the Tt's below.

MINI-BOOK T:

Read the letter book to the student.

Have the student highlight the capital and lowercase letter of the week.

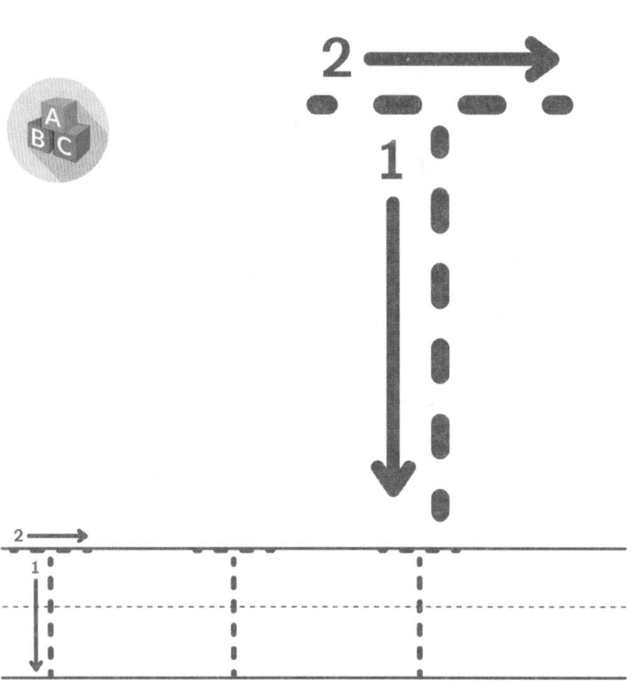

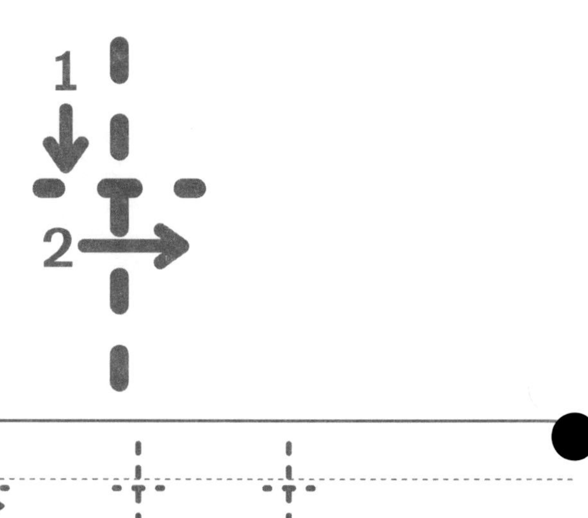

LESSON 20
Day 3

LIFE SKILLS:

Tying Shoes: Practice tying shoes with the method you chose. Practice sewing on a button.

BIBLE:

"Do you remember what it means to obey? When we obey, that means that we follow what we have been told or asked to do. This is called obedience.

Review memory verse on page 225.

"Our memory verse is the beginning of chapter 6 in Ephesians. Let's take a look at the rest of that thought. "Children, obey your parents in the Lord, for this is right. 'Honor your father and mother' — which is the first commandment with a promise — 'so that it may go well with you and that you may enjoy long life on the earth' " (Ephesians 6:1–3). In Ephesians we can see that the Bible says for children to obey their parents and honor their father and mother. Last, it tells you the promise you receive if you are obedient — "So that it may go well with you and that you may enjoy long life on the earth." This statement is so important. This promise God made is given if you obey your parents and honor them. This is why it is so important to obey your parents. I want you to have a long, good life and to be blessed by God. When you obey your parents, this promise is attached to that obedience. Don't you want to enjoy a long life and be blessed by God? I know I do!

RHYME TIME:

Read "Star Light, Star Bright" on page 232.

"Highlight the T's and t's on the next page.

"How many T's and t's did you find?

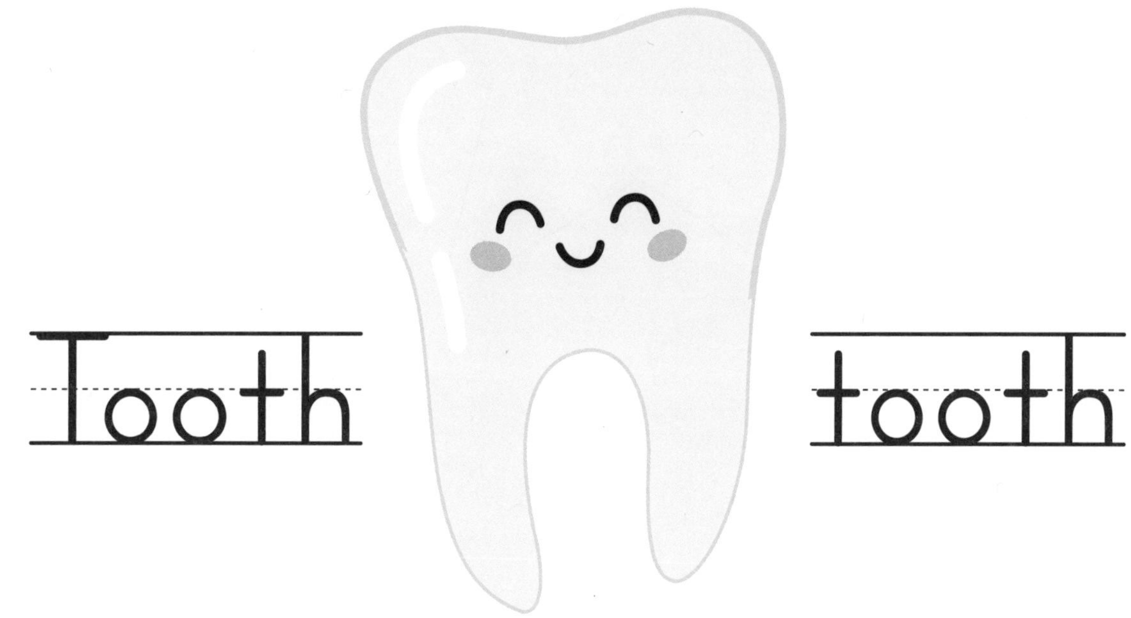

Lesson 20
Day 3

Name ______________________

Star Light, Star Bright

Star light, star bright,
first star I see tonight.
I wish I may, I wish I might,
have this wish I wish tonight.

How many t's did you find? ____

Color the stars.

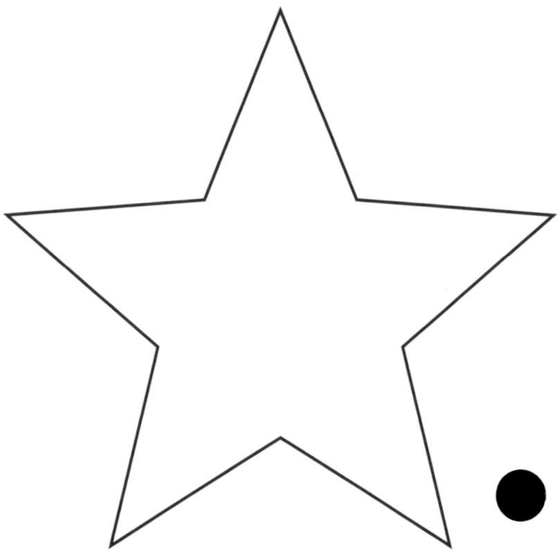

LESSON 20
Day 3

ABC'S AND MORE:

Memory Challenge: Lay out your letter cards in ABC order like the ABC chart is. Then, flip over the letters S, J, N, U, I, W. See if they can figure out which letters are flipped over and then have them flip those cards to check their memory.

Letter Run: Lay out your letter cards on the floor. Call out the pictures as the child races to find the letters: G, D, F, X, M

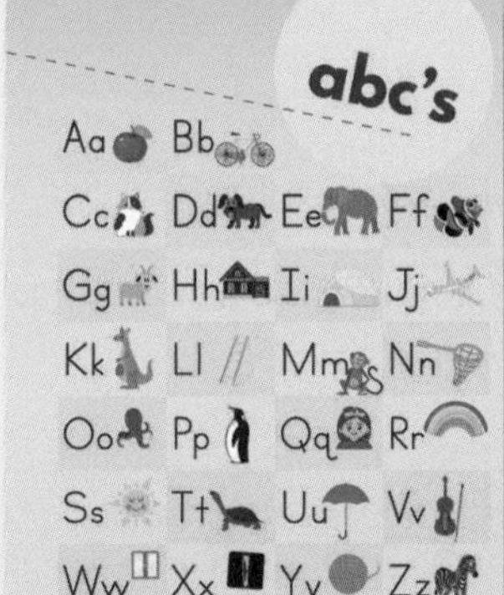

See Teacher Resource Page.

Chant the ABC chart.

Sing the ABC song.

"Let's review how to write our Tt's again.

Practice writing Tt's.

"T: (down, across)
Start at the top line, go down to the bottom line (down)
Cross it at the top along the top line (across).

"t: (down, across)
Start at the top line, go down to the bottom line (down)
Cross it at the middle line (across).

Trace the Tt's below.

MINI-BOOK T:

Read the letter book again.

Advanced K — see if your child can read the book to you.

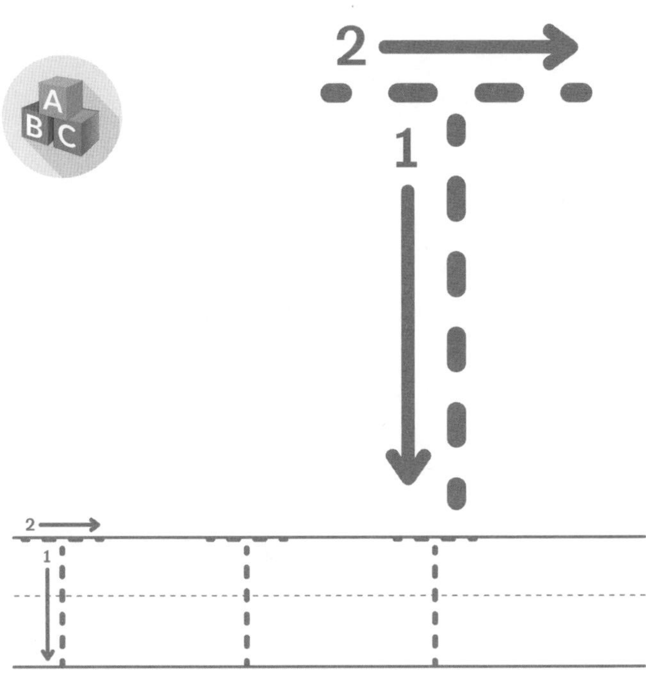

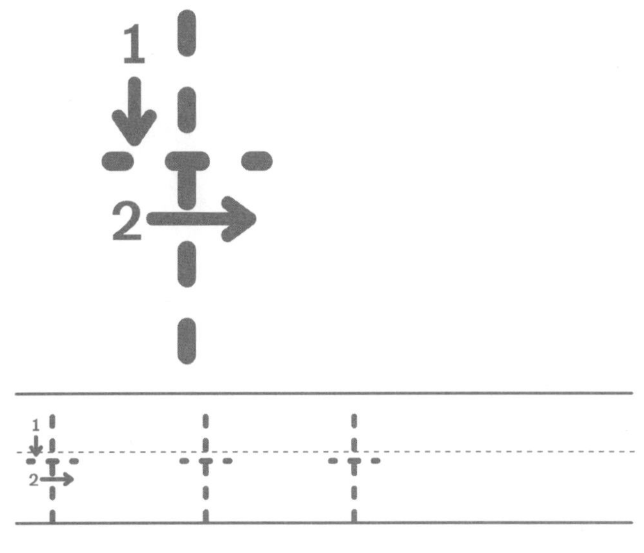

LESSON 21
Prep Page

Supply List

- ☐ Cleaning supplies for dusting (daily, life skills)
- ☐ Cleaning supplies for sweeping (daily, life skills)
- ☐ Cleaning supplies for wiping spills/messes (daily, life skills)
- ☐ Cotton balls (day 1, rhyme)
- ☐ Scissors (day 1, rhyme)

Objectives

Letter of the week: Uu

Skills/Concepts: cleaning – sweeping, dusting, and wiping spills/messes

Memory Verse

Psalm 51:10

Create in me a pure heart, O God, and renew a steadfast spirit within me.

Extended Activities

Teach how to clean counters and wipe down the refrigerator.

LESSON 21
Day 1

BIBLE:

"Today, we will begin with the Bible. Do you know how much God loves you? He loves you so much!

Read Mark 10:13–16 from your Bibles.

"Verse 14 says Jesus was indignant. Indignant means to be outraged or very angry. Jesus did not like that people thought that the children should not come to Him. He even told them the kingdom of God belongs to them. He also said that if we do not receive the kingdom of God as a child does, we will never enter it. Jesus also blessed the children just like He has blessed us!

"Let's say a thankful prayer today, thanking God for His blessings on us.

"The disciples thought that Jesus would be bothered by the young children, and so they sent them away. A lot of times things happen that do not go how we think they should. We can either adapt or show adaptability by saying to ourselves, "You know, that is not how I thought this should have happened," or, "This is not how we planned this." Then we tend to throw a fit because it is not our way. We can replace that thought with one like this: "I am going to adapt and adjust myself so I can still show self-control and find something to be happy about right now." When we adapt, that means that we have to adjust our thoughts and actions. We have to show that we can still be in control of our thoughts and actions even when things do not go our way. We will practice being adaptable this week.

"Our memory verse is Psalm 51:10.

Echo read the verse. Add motions.

Create in me a pure heart ,

O God, and renew a steadfast spirit

within me .

"Do you remember our other lesson where the heart was all dirty and black and then it became clean and healthy? This Scripture also is a reference to that. God will take our hearts and make them clean, and He renews our spirit or makes our spirits new and strong.

LIFE SKILLS:

NOTE: Prior to doing this part, spill a small amount of water on the floor or table so they can clean it up.

"Just like God cleans our hearts, you can learn to clean things in your home. We will gather some cleaning supplies for dusting, sweeping, and cleaning up spills/messes.

"Now that you have your supplies, I will show you how to clean up a spill or mess.

"Next, I will show you things to dust and how to dust.

"Then, I will show you how to sweep a floor.

(Teach child how to hold a broom and sweep using the dust pan.)

"We will do these tasks each day so you can practice.

LESSON 21
Day 1

RHYME TIME:

"Our poem for this week is "Mary Had a Little Lamb." After we read it, you will make your own little lamb!

Read "Mary Had a Little Lamb."

Complete lamb/wool activity on page 239.

ABC'S AND MORE:

TIPS: See instructional video for this and the instructions in the beginning of the book. See Teacher Resource Section for pertinent information.

See Teacher Resource Page.

Chant the ABC chart.

Sing the ABC song.

Point to the capital U. Point to the lowercase u.

"Now, let's learn how to write Uu's! Remember that there is a capital U and a lowercase u.

"It's time to write your Uu's!

Practice writing U's and u's.

"U: (down, curve up)
Start at the top line, go down toward the bottom line (down)
Curve back up to the top line (curve up).

"u: (down, curve up, down)
Start at the middle line, go down toward the bottom line (down)
Curve back up to the middle line (curve up) and back down to the bottom line (down).

Trace the Uu's below.

MINI-BOOK U:

See the Teacher Resource Page.

Do a picture walk.

Read the book to the student, pointing to each letter/word.

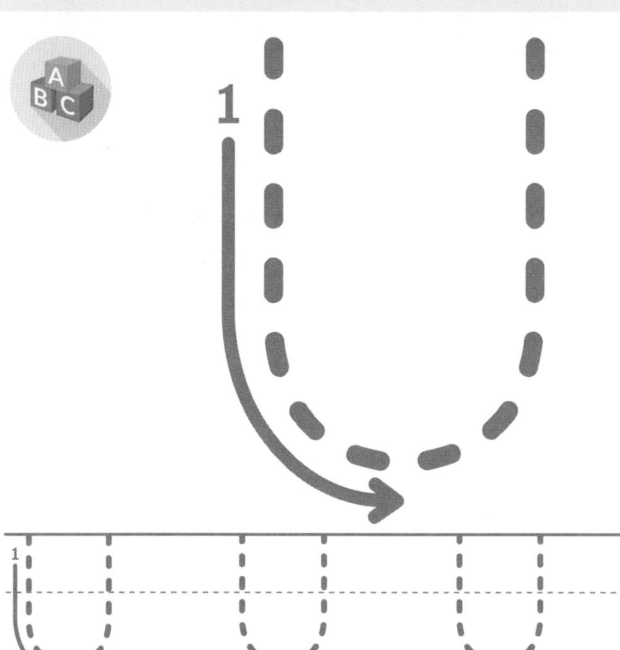

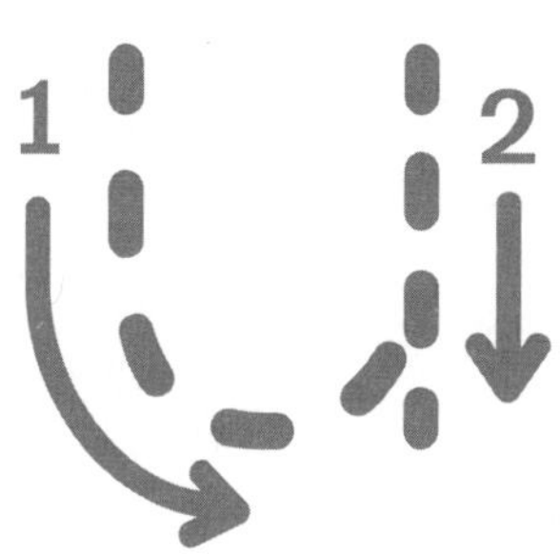

Mary Had a Little Lamb By: Sarah Josepha Hale

Mary had a little lamb,
little lamb, little lamb.
Mary had a little lamb,
whose fleece was white as snow.

And everywhere that Mary went,
Mary went, Mary went,
everywhere that Mary went,
the lamb was sure to go.

He followed her to school one day,
school one day, school one day.
He followed her to school one day,
which was against the rules.

It made the children laugh and play,
laugh and play, laugh and play,
It made the children laugh and play,
to see a lamb at school.

Name

Cut out the lamb and glue it to black construction paper. Add cotton to the lamb to give it wool.

Blank Page for cutting.

LESSON 21
Day 2

LIFE SKILLS:

"Gather your cleaning supplies for dusting, sweeping, and cleaning up spills/messes.

Practice dusting, cleaning up spills/messes, and sweeping. Offer praise for their efforts, and give constructive feedback when needed.

BIBLE:

Review memory verse on page 236.

"Cleaning reminds me of a story in the Bible when Jesus and His disciples were coming to visit. Jesus was coming to town, and a woman named Martha opened her home to Him and the disciples. What happens when you are having company over? We usually clean and make sure everything is nice and neat. Do you serve food for others when they come over? Sometimes we do, but sometimes we just play and enjoy spending time together, right? Well, Martha was busy, because she was so worried about everything being perfect. I bet if Jesus was coming to my house for dinner, I would also want to make sure the food was good and the house was clean! Once Jesus arrived, Martha was still running around cleaning and getting the food ready. She was so worried about being prepared that she missed the most important thing! Martha had a sister named Mary. Mary was not worried about the preparations. Instead, she sat at the feet of Jesus just listening to His every word. Mary was spending time with Jesus instead of cleaning and making food. Martha was so upset that she went to Jesus and complained about Mary just sitting when she was up doing all the work!

You may choose to read this in Luke 10:40–42.

"This doesn't mean that cleaning or working is not a good thing, but we can be so busy and worried about things that we miss spending time with Jesus. It is so important that we make time to be with Jesus. Jesus said only one thing was needed, and Mary chose the best part. I know that we can allow things like electronics, sports, or even other people to come in the way of us having time to be at the feet of Jesus and spending time with Him each day. What are some ways we can spend time with Him? Praying, reading the Word, worship, serving others, etc. Each day, let's let our focus be on Him and not forget that Jesus is here with us just like He was with Mary and Martha. I don't want to be so busy like Martha was that I miss spending time with Jesus.

"Do you remember what it means to be adaptable? A lot of times things happen that do not go how we think they should. We can either adapt or lose control and throw a fit. Do you think Martha adapted to what was going on in her home? Did she become upset and even whine to Jesus because her sister was not doing what she thought was important? Yes, she did. We can learn from Martha though. Jesus told her Mary had chosen the good part. Not only did Mary choose to be with Jesus, but she also didn't let the preparations ruin her day. We can choose to allow ourselves to be all worked up and lose control, or we can stop, choose to be happy, and adapt our thinking.

LESSON 21
Day 2

RHYME TIME:

"Let's read our poem this week, "Mary Had a Little Lamb."

You may choose to have them color the image below while reading and discussing the poem, or after.

Mary Had a Little Lamb

Mary had a little lamb,
little lamb, little lamb.
Mary had a little lamb,
whose fleece was white as snow.

And everywhere that Mary went,
Mary went, Mary went,
everywhere that Mary went
the lamb was sure to go.

He followed her to school one day,
school one day, school one day.
He followed her to school one day,
which was against the rules.

It made the children laugh and play,
laugh and play, laugh and play,
it made the children laugh and play,
to see a lamb at school.

"The poem says the lamb's fleece was white as snow. The word fleece in the poem means its fur or wool. It uses a phrase to help you make a picture in your mind of how white the fleece on the lamb was. It states that it was "white as snow." That means it is pure white without any color, right? It helps us know that this lamb's fleece, or fur, was very white and clean.

Color this picture.

LESSON 21
Day 2

ABC'S AND MORE:

Chant the ABC Chart.

Sing the ABC song.

"Let's practice writing our Uu's today!

Point to the capital U.
Point to the lowercase u.

"This is the capital U and this is the lowercase u. Let's write them!

Practice writing U's and u's.

"U: (down, curve up)
Start at the top line, go down toward the bottom line (down)
Curve back up to the top line (curve up)

"u: (down, curve up, down)
Start at the middle line, go down to toward the bottom line (down).
Curve back up to the middle line (curve up) and back down to the bottom line (down).

Trace the Uu's below.

Read the letter book to the student.

Have the student highlight the capital and lowercase letter of the week.

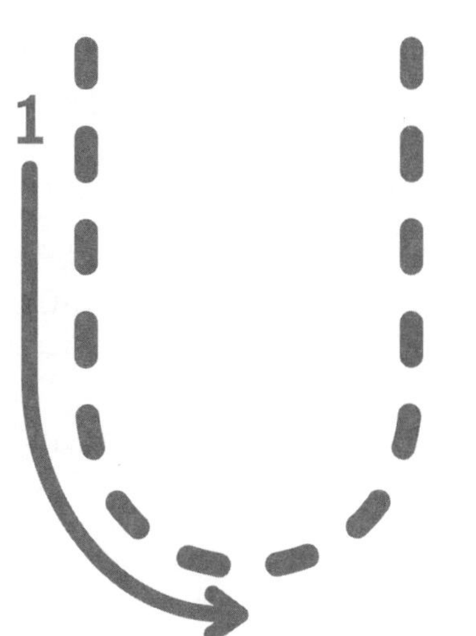

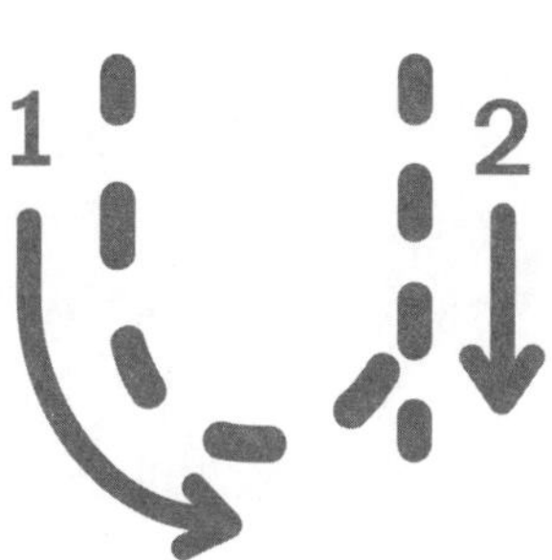

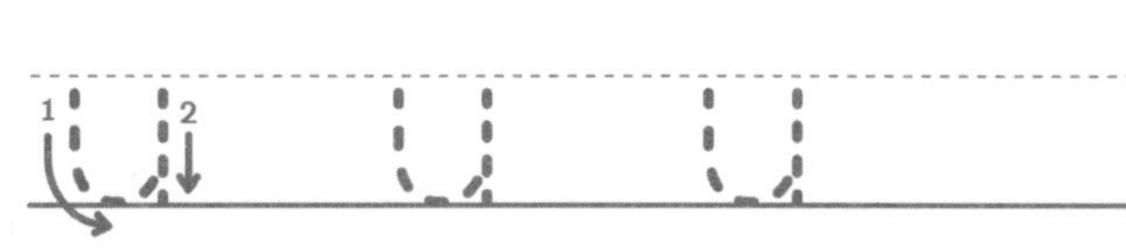

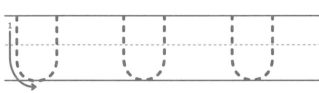

LESSON 21
Day 3

LIFE SKILLS:

Gather your cleaning supplies for dusting, sweeping, and cleaning up spills/messes.

Practice the skills of dusting, cleaning up spills/ messes, and sweeping.

BIBLE:

Review memory verse on page 236.

In 1 Timothy 4:12 it says, "Don't let anyone look down on you because you are young, but set an example for the believers in speech, in conduct, in love, in faith and in purity."

Even though you may be young, you can still be an example for others. Paul was talking to Timothy, who was young at the time. He wanted Timothy to know that even though he was young, he could still set a godly example. You can be an example in the way you speak. Speak kindly toward others and do not speak things that would provoke or stir up anger in someone. If we provoke or aggravate someone with our words or actions, then we are wrong. Paul told him to also be an example in conduct. Conduct is how we act or behave. If we are losing our ability to be adaptable, then we are not showing good conduct. We should be loving and kind toward others. He also said to be an example in love, faith, and purity. Love is not always easy, because love has a lot of qualities like patience, kindness, not keeping up with who did something wrong, and a lot more.

Faith is believing, even when we cannot see, and purity means to guard our hearts and minds from evil. This is easy to read, but a lot harder to do. You have to pray for God's help so you can be adaptable and live a godly example even though you are young. If you follow God and put your faith in Him, then He will help you be an example to others.

RHYME TIME:

Read "Mary Had a Little Lamb."

Highlight the U's and u's in the poem. How many did you find?

Mary Had a Little Lamb

Mary had a little lamb,
little lamb, little lamb.
Mary had a little lamb
whose fleece was white as snow.

And everywhere that Mary went,
Mary went, Mary went,
everywhere that Mary went,
the lamb was sure to go.

He followed her to school one day,
school one day, school one day.
He followed her to school one day,
which was against the rules.

It made the children laugh and play,
laugh and play, laugh and play,
it made the children laugh and play,
to see a lamb at school.

LESSON 21
Day 3

ABC'S AND MORE:

See Teacher Resource Page.

Chant the ABC chart.

Sing the ABC song.

"Let's review how to write our Uu's again.

Practice writing U's and u's.

"U: (down, curve up)
Start at the top line, go down toward the bottom line (down).
Curve back up to the top line (curve up).

"u: (down, curve up, down)
Start at the middle line, go down to toward the bottom line (down).
Curve back up to the middle line (curve up) and back down to the bottom line (down).

Trace the Uu's below.

Complete the umbrella tracing/coloring activity on the next page.

MINI-BOOK U:

Read the letter book again.

Advanced K — see if your child can read the book to you.

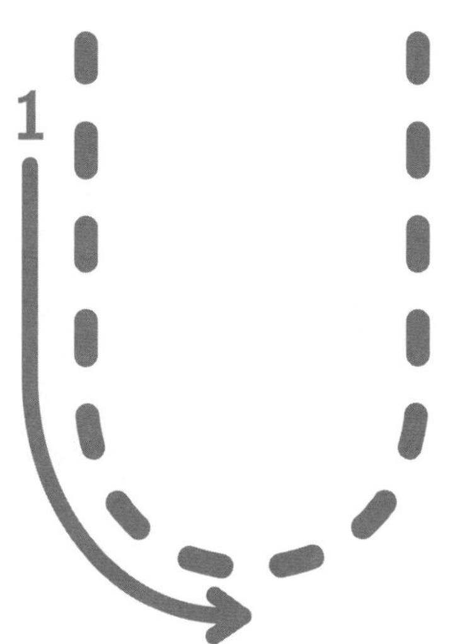

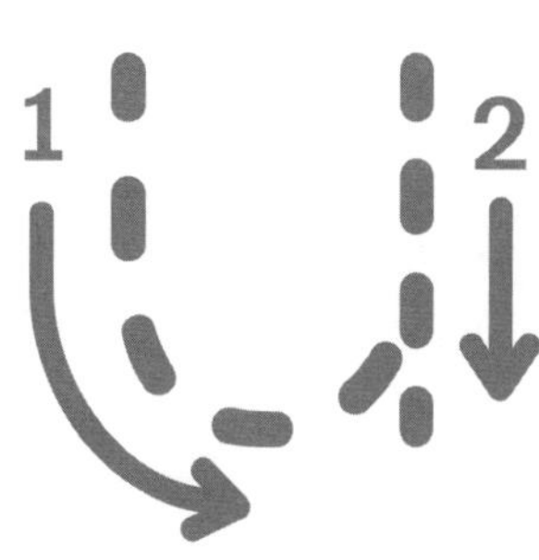

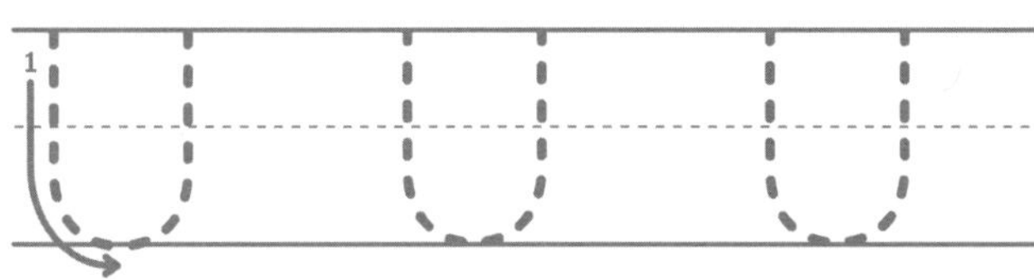

Lesson 21
Day 3

Name

Trace the umbrella and the raindrops. Then color the umbrella.

LESSON 22
Prep Page

Supply List

- ☐ Blocks for building

Objectives

Letter of the week: Vv

Skills/Concepts: Making a bed

Memory Verse

Psalm 41:3

The LORD sustains them on their sickbed and restores them from their bed of illness.

Extended Activities

Use egg cartons for sorting small objects.

Practice tying shoes.

LESSON 22
Day 1

LIFE SKILLS:

Sing or play a recording of "Five Little Monkeys Jumping on the Bed."
NOTE: Use your fingers to count down from 5.

"The five little monkeys jumped on their bed, but I will show you how to make your bed.

NOTE: Please use steps to teach your child a basic way for them to make their bed.

"Each day, you will have to be motivated to make your bed and show initiative. Motivation is having a drive or inspiration to do something. Showing initiative means you are taking action to do something without being told or asked. Let's see if you can be motivated and show initiative this week and make your bed each day.

BIBLE:

"Our memory verse is Psalm 41:3:

Echo read the verse. Add motions.

The Lord  sustains them on their sickbed  and restores  them from their bed of illness.

"The word *sustains* means strengthens or supports them on their sickbed.

Van van

LESSON 22
Day 1

"There is a story about a man who could not walk for 38 years, but Jesus healed him! We will read about it in our Bibles from John 5:1–9.

"In this story, Jesus restored the man from his sickbed just like our memory verse stated. This man had been laying at the pool of Bethesda. From time to time an angel of the Lord would come down and stir up the waters. The first one into the pool after each such disturbance would be healed. This man had been laying there a long time. Can you imagine laying by a pool of water, knowing if you could just get in the water when the angel came that you would be healed, yet you could not even move to get in the water?

"Yet this man laid there still hoping that one day he too could get into the water. He didn't know that Jesus would walk by and heal him, but that is exactly what happened. Jesus told him to take up his mat and walk, and that is exactly what he did! It was a miracle!

RHYME TIME:

"Let's read our poem this week, "I Should Like to Build Today."

Help your child build a cube (box) using blocks.

I Should Like to Build Today

I should like to build today,
please give me my box of bricks.
I will open it and say,
one, two, three, four, five, and six.
Now a cube before me stands,
and I with joy will clap my hands.

LESSON 22
Day 1

ABC'S AND MORE:

See Teacher Resource Page.

Chant the ABC chart.

Sing the ABC song.

"Today we will learn how to write Vv's! Don't forget that there is a capital letter and a lowercase letter.

Point to capital V.

"This the capital V.

Point to the lowercase v.

"This is the lowercase v. It's time to write your Vv's!

Practice writing V's and v's.

"V: (slant down, slant up)
Start at the top line, slant down to the right (slant down).
Slant back up to the top line (slant up).

"v: (slant down, slant up)
Start at the middle line, slant down to the bottom line (slant down).
Slant up to the middle line (slant up).

Trace the Vv's below.

Match the capital and lowercase letters on the next page.

MINI-BOOK V:

See the Teacher Resource Page.

Do a picture walk.

Read the book to the student, pointing to each letter/word.

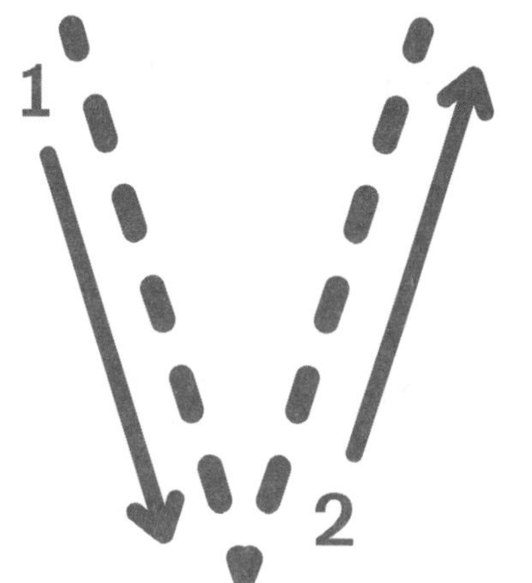

Name

Match each capital letter to its lowercase letter. A is already done for you.

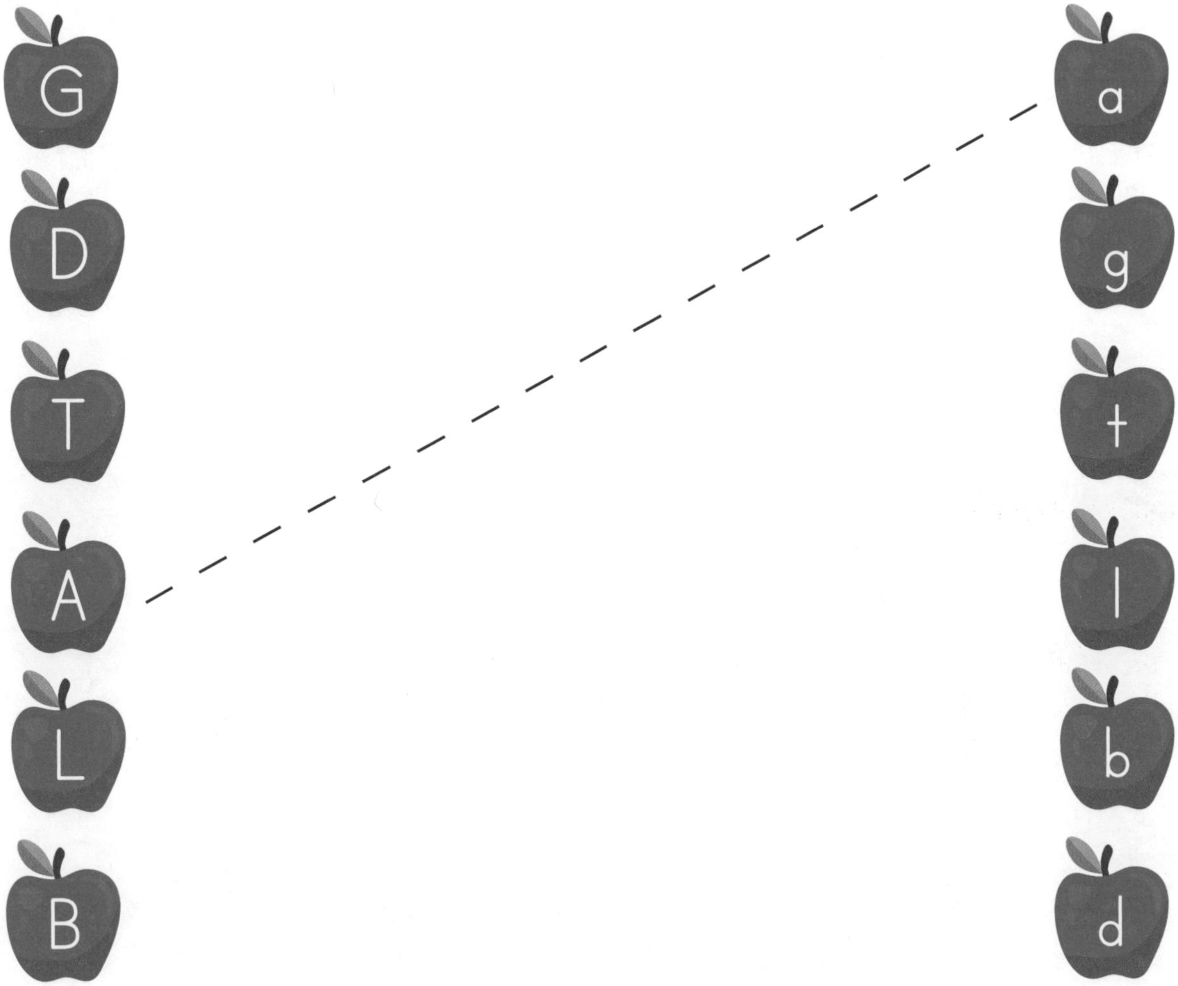

G	a
D	g
T	t
A	l
L	b
B	d

LESSON 22
Day 2

LIFE SKILLS:

"I wonder if the five little monkeys made their beds. Show me how you showed motivation and initiative and made your bed today.

"Remember, motivation is having a drive or inspiration to do something. Showing initiative means you are taking action to do something without being told or asked. Did you remember to do this and make your bed?

"Help the monkeys find their bed below.

Complete the tracing activity below.

BIBLE:

Review memory verse on page 248.

"I remember another story about a little girl who was sick. She even died, but Jesus brought her back to life. Listen to this story as it shows how Jesus doesn't just sustain this girl on her sickbed, but He raises her from the dead. This story is found in Mark 5:21–43.

Read Mark 5:21–43.

"Wow, how amazing that Jesus healed this girl! When we are touched by Jesus, we are not just healed, but we are completely restored or brought back to full health.

RHYME TIME:

"Let's read our poem again this week.

Read poem on page 249.

"Build whatever you want with blocks.

Help the monkeys find their bed.

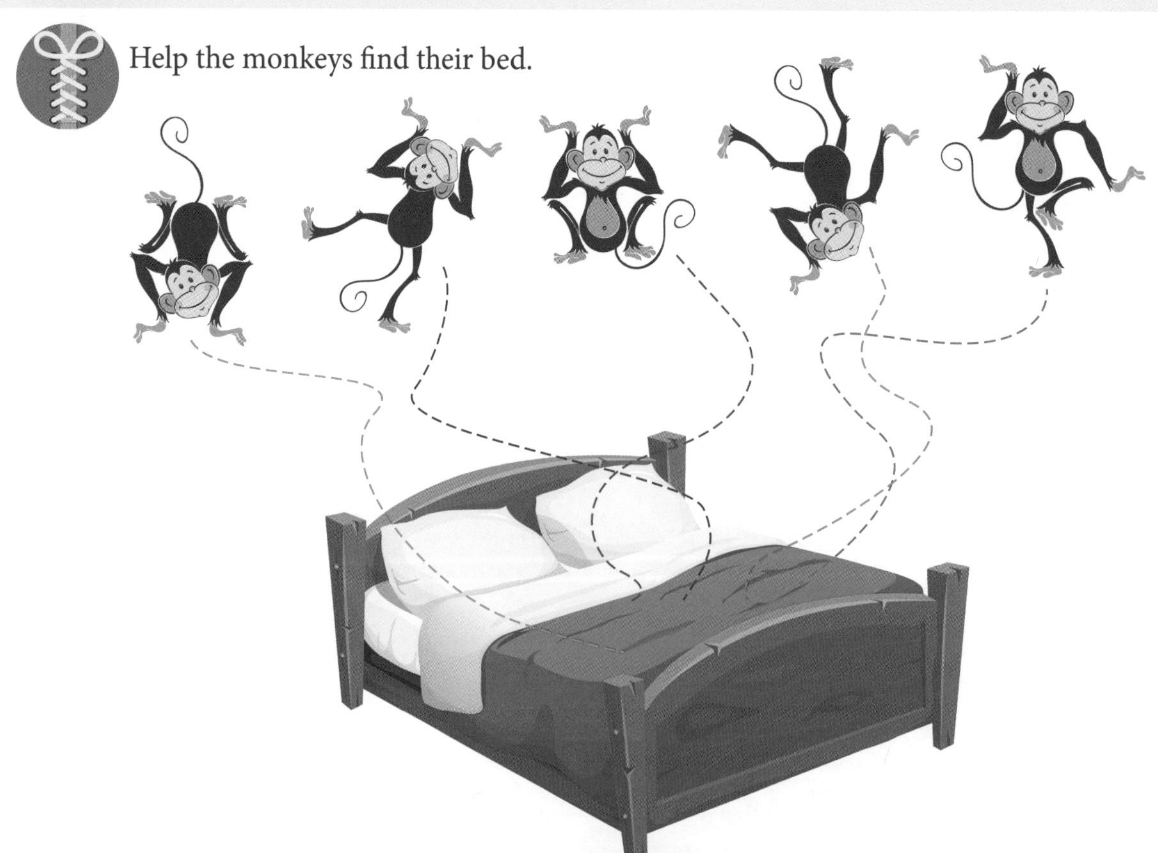

LESSON 22
Day 2

ABC'S AND MORE:

"Cut the capital letters out and glue them to their matching lowercase letter.

Chant the ABC Chart.

Sing the ABC song.

"Let's practice writing our Vv's today!

Point to the capital V.
Point to the lowercase v.

"This is the capital V and this is the lowercase v. Now, let's write them!

Practice writing V's and v's.

"V: (slant down, slant up)
Start at the top line, slant down to the right (slant down).
Slant back up to the top line (slant up).

"v: (slant down, slant up)
Start at the middle line, slant down to the bottom line (slant down).
Slant up to the middle line (slant up).

Trace the Vv's below.

MINI-BOOK V:

Read the letter book to the student.

Have the student highlight the capital and lowercase letter of the week.

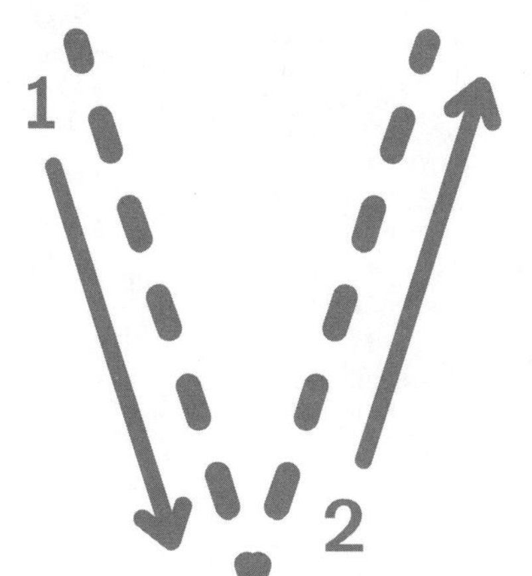

LESSON 22
Day 3

LIFE SKILLS:

"Do you remember what motivation and initiative are? Motivation is having a drive or inspiration to do something. Showing initiative means you are taking action to do something without being told or asked. Did you remember to do this and make your bed?

RHYME TIME:

"We will be reading our poem and building more with blocks before we do our Bible story today.

Read "I Should Like to Build Today" below.

"Highlight the capital letters in the poem.

"Can you build a tower using blocks?

BIBLE:

Practice your memory verse on page 248.

"The Tower of Babel may have been a type of Babylonian temple, called a ziggurat. Ziggurats were pyramid-shaped and some may have been over 300 feet high! They had steps on the outside and a temple at the top." Genesis 11:1–9 tells us about the Tower of Babel. (*Illustrated Family Bible Stories*, page 20)

Read Genesis 11:1–9.

"Because the people were prideful, made a tower for themselves, and were not honoring God, He chose to scatter them out. This was so God would be glorified and not man or a building.

"Now, let's see if you can trace from the bottom of the ziggurat to the top!

I Should Like to Build Today

I should like to build today,
please give me my box of bricks.
I will open it and say,
one, two, three, four, five, and six.
Now a cube before me stands,
and I with joy will clap my hands.

Trace your way from the bottom of the ziggurat to the top. Stay as close to the dotted line as you can.

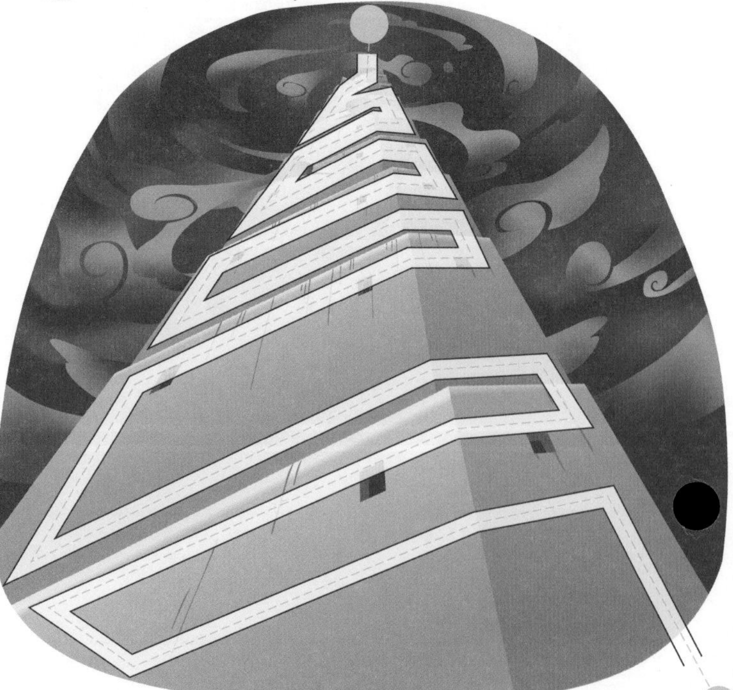

LESSON 22
Day 3

ABC'S AND MORE:

See Teacher Resource Page.

Chant the ABC chart.

Sing the ABC song.

"Let's review how to write our Vv's again.

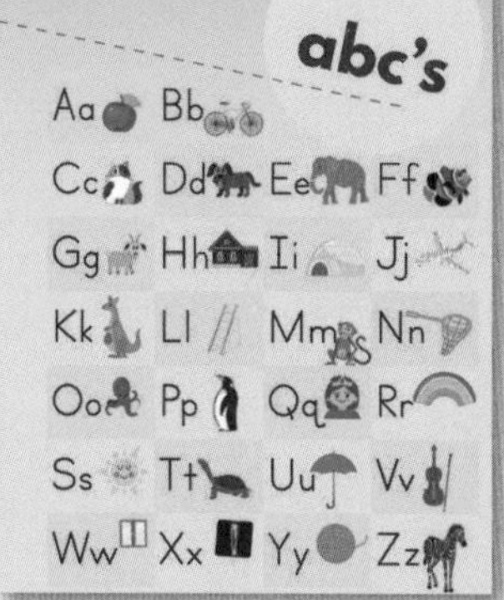

MINI-BOOK U:

Read the letter book again.

Advanced K — see if your child can read the book to you.

Practice writing V's and v's.

"V: (slant down, slant up)
Start at the top line, slant down to the right (slant down).
Slant back up to the top line (slant up).

"v: (slant down, slant up)
Start at the middle line, slant down to the bottom line (slant down).
Slant up to the middle line (slant up).

Trace the Vv's below.

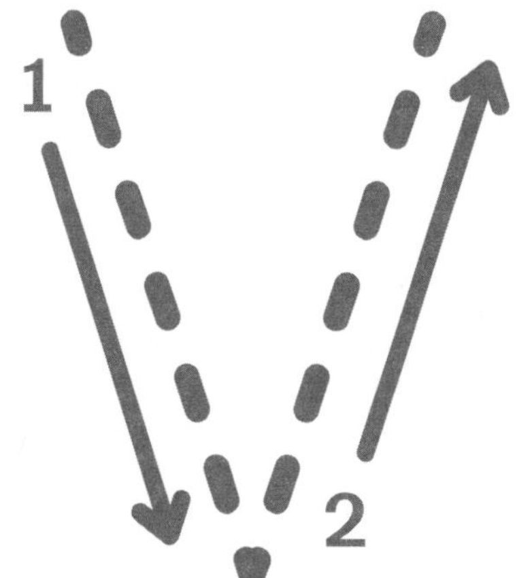

LESSON 23
Prep Page

Supply List

- ☐ Toilet paper tubes (or paper towel tubes) (day 3, Rhyme Time)
- ☐ Bird seed (day 3, Rhyme Time)
- ☐ Peanut butter (day 3, Rhyme Time)
- ☐ Yarn (day 3, Rhyme Time)
- ☐ Paper plate (day 3, Rhyme Time)
- ☐ Items to make a bird's nest and feathers (day 1, Rhyme Time)
- ☐ Items for sorting (toys, buttons, silverware, clothes)
- ☐ Journal (daily, Bible)
- ☐ Pen/pencil (daily, Bible)

Look Ahead

Label 6–10 objects with the word SIN on one side and FORGIVEN on the other side. See Lesson 24 Day 2.

Bake a cake/tea time/hot cocoa (optional) for week 24.

Objectives

Letter of the week: Ww

Skills/Concepts: sorting – toys, clothes

Memory Verse

Matthew 28:18–19

Then Jesus came to them and said, "All authority in heaven and on earth has been given to me. Therefore go and make disciples of all nations, baptizing them in the name of the Father and of the Son and of the Holy Spirit."

Extended Activities

Bird hunt — birds in your area. Journal/draw

Research their favorite bird.

Look into the Audubon society in your area for a field trip.

Check the Great Backyard Bird Hunt dates (http://gbbc.birdcount.org/) to see if you can help keep a count for science.

LESSON 23
Day 1

LIFE SKILLS:

Gather items for sorting.

"We have some items we will be sorting into piles. Let's look at these items and see how we can sort them. We could sort things by color, size, or what kind they are. How would you like to sort these items?

Help them pick a way to sort and place the items in groups.

BIBLE:

"We are going to play a game today called Go! You will stand at the wall (or a spot in the yard) and when I say "Go!" you will either crawl, run, walk, zigzag walk, or hop to the other side. I will tell you each time how you will get to the other side.

1. Walk
2. Crawl (belly crawl or normal crawl)
3. Hop
4. Run
5. Zigzag to the other side

You might need to show them how to zigzag.

"Which way did you prefer? Some ways are quicker than other ways, aren't they?

"In the Bible, Jesus told his disciples to "Go!" He had equipped or prepared and armed them to do what He wanted them to do. Our verse this week says "GO and make disciples." Let's read it now.

"Our memory verse this week is Matthew 28:18–19.

Echo read the verse. Add motions.

"We are like the 12 disciples. We are to GO and make disciples. How can we do that? We simply share the message of the Bible with others and help them in being a follower of Christ. We can pray for them, give them godly advice, and even just live a Christian life in front of them. Jesus taught the disciples, then they taught others, then those taught others. It was a great plan to help the Kingdom of God grow.

"Do you remember how many disciples Jesus had? Just like the 12 disciples, we can show love to others and share about Jesus.

"Disciples had discipline. This is not only discipline like when you are corrected for something you did wrong, but discipline also means they had self-control and focus. They were disciplined or focused on what God called them to do. Sometimes we get distracted by things and forget what our goal is. I want to focus on prayer this week and showing discipline in prayer. We will come together and pray each day. I will help you to write down some prayers and you can illustrate them. This will be your prayer journal.

Help them make a prayer journal. This can be a spiral notebook, blank papers stapled together, or an actual journal. You can write their prayer, as basic as it may be, at the top, and then they can illustrate using colors, pencils, or even watercolors. Let this be a time for helping them and setting an example through prayer.

Name

Matthew 28:18-19

Then Jesus  came to them

and said, "All authority  in heaven and

on earth  has been given to me  .

Therefore go  and make disciples of all

nations, baptizing them in the name of the

Father  and of the Son and of the

Holy Spirit.

LESSON 23
Day 1

RHYME TIME:

"Let's read our poem this week, "A Little Bird Made a Nest."

Try having your child make a bird's nest. Look for feathers outside. You can laminate the feather onto paper or even do a crayon rubbing.

"Remember to not touch dead birds and wash your hands after touching a feather.

"Do you know how much God cares for you? Matthew 6:25–26 says, "Therefore I tell you, do not worry about your life, what you will eat or drink; or about your body, what you will wear. Is not life more than food, and the body more than clothes? Look at the birds of the air; they do not sow or reap or store away in barns, and yet your heavenly Father feeds them. Are you not much more valuable than they?"

"God values you so much! He created the birds and cares for them, and He created you and cares for you too!

A Little Bird Made a Nest

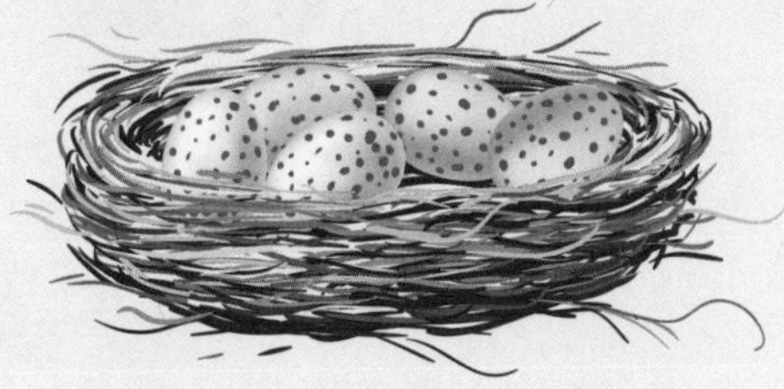

A little bird once made a nest,
of moss, and hay, and hair.

And there she laid five speckled eggs,
and covered them with care.

Five little birds were hatched in time,
so small, and bare, and weak,

The father fed them every day,
with insects from his beak.

At last the little birds were fledged,
and strong enough to fly,

And then they spread their tiny wings,
and bade the nest "goodbye."

LESSON 23
Day 1

ABC'S AND MORE:

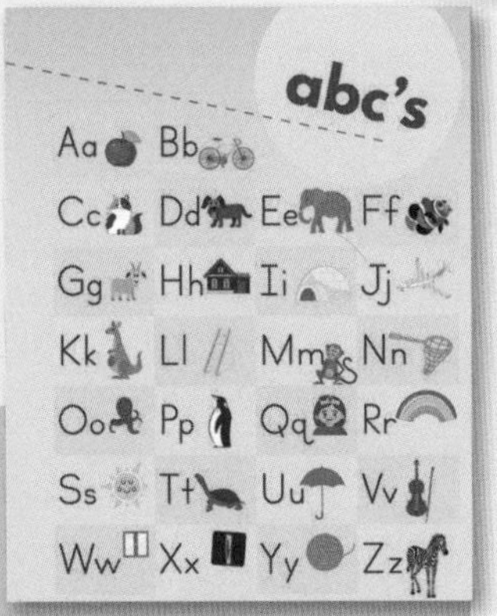

See Teacher Resource Page.

Chant the ABC chart.

Sing the ABC song.

"Let's learn to write Ww's today. Don't forget that there is a capital letter and a lowercase letter.

Point to the capital W. Point to the lowercase w.

"This is the capital W and this is the lowercase w. Let's write them!

Practice writing W's and w's.

"W: (slant down, slant up, slant down, slant up)
Start at the top line, slant down to the right (slant down).
Slant back up to the top line (slant up).
Slant down to the right (slant down).
Slant back up to the top line (slant up).

"w: (slant down, slant up, slant down, slant up) Start at the middle line, slant down to the bottom line (slant down).
Slant up to the middle line (slant up).
Slant down to the bottom line (slant down).
Slant up to the middle line (slant up).

Trace the Ww's below.

"Now see if you can match letters A-H!

Complete the matching activity on the next page.

MINI-BOOK W:

See the Teacher Resource Page.

Do a picture walk.

Read the book to the student pointing to each letter/word.

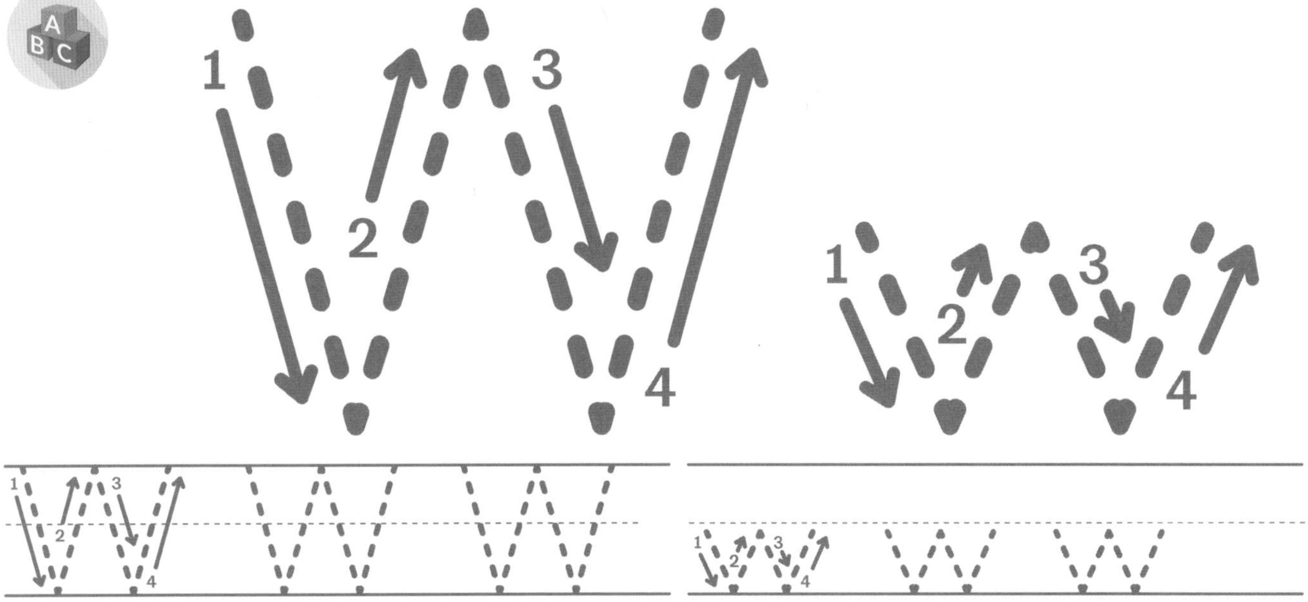

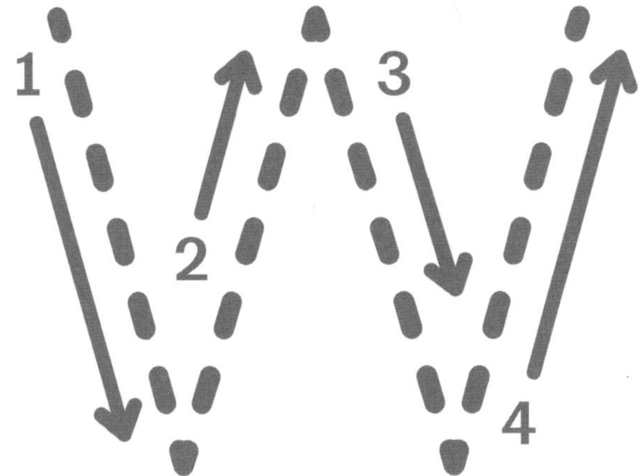

Lesson 23
Day 1

Name

See if you can match the uppercase and lowercase letters!

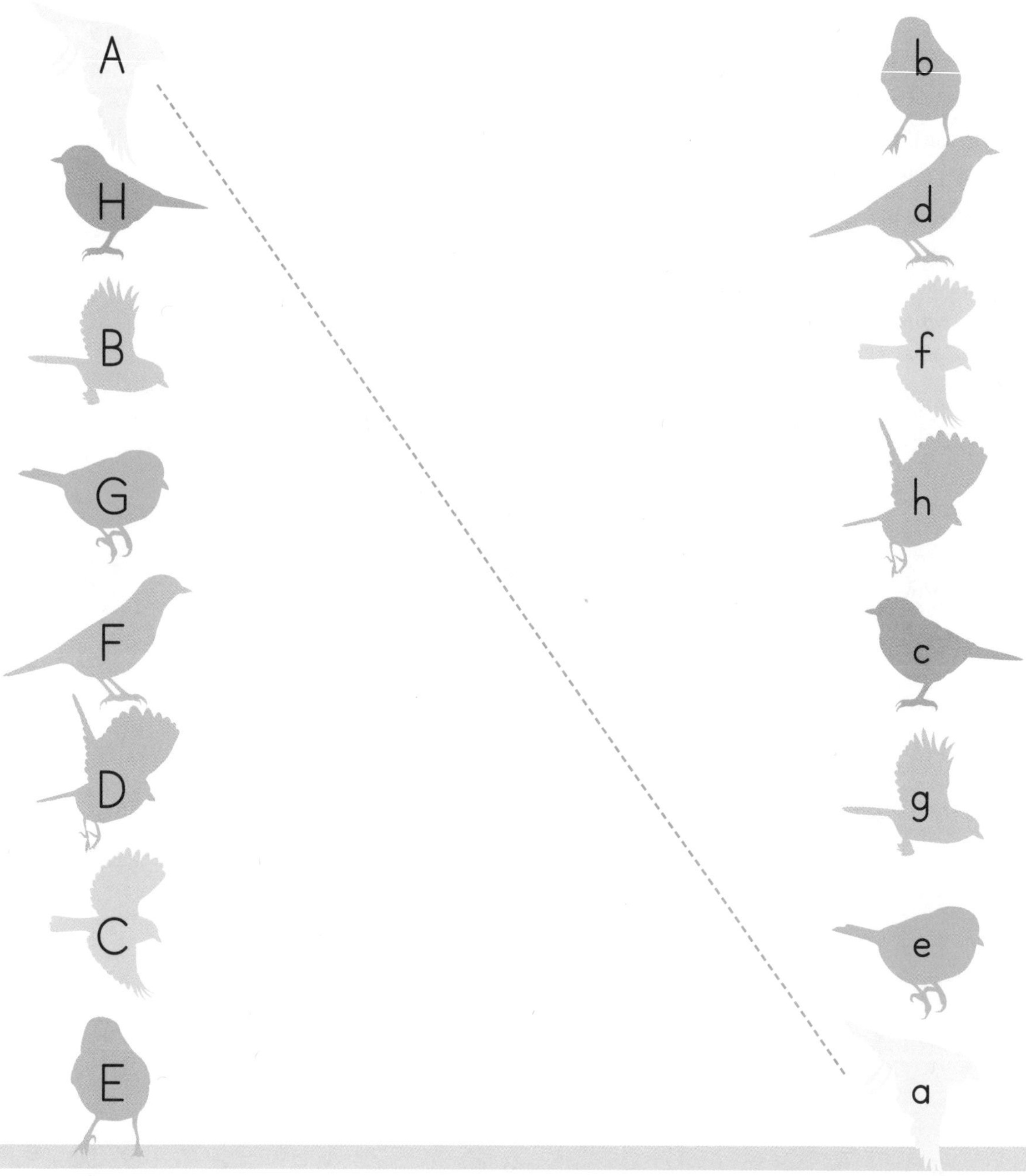

A	b
H	d
B	f
G	h
F	c
D	g
C	e
E	a

LESSON 23
Day 2

LIFE SKILLS:

Gather toys or have them pick up toys by sorting (cars, Legos®, dolls, dress up clothes . . .).

"When I walk into a room with toys all over, I have to pick something that I can sort out in order to get it all picked up. If I look at the toys, and I see a lot of ____________ then I can sort those out by only focusing on collecting those items. Let's practice this method of sorting.

Help them pick a way to sort and place the items in groups or bins where they belong.

BIBLE:

"A disciple follows someone else or is like a student. The 12 disciples followed Jesus. He taught them daily. They were on a journey with Jesus. The Bible tells us of Jesus walking on the water in Matthew 14:22–36.

Read Matthew 14:22–36.

"My favorite part of the story is when Peter had enough faith to step out of the boat and begin to walk on the water to Jesus. I also noticed that when Peter stopped looking at Jesus and put his focus back on the wind and waves, he began to sink. We can also apply this to our lives. If we keep our focus on Jesus, we can do mighty things, but if we take our focus off of Him, then we will fall. My second favorite part is afterward when people brought all their sick to Him and that even when they touched the edge of His cloak, or His robe, they were healed! Can you imagine how much power is in Jesus that just touching His hem like this we could be healed?

(show them a hem)

"That is some awesome power. Do you know that we have that same power? We do! Remember how the disciples were disciplined or focused on what God called them to do? We are showing discipline in prayer by using a prayer journal.

NOTE: Help them with their prayer journal.

Review your memory verse on page 259.

RHYME TIME:

"Let's read our poem again this week.

Read "A Little Bird Made a Nest" below.

Go bird watching! See how many birds you can find and try to name the kinds.

"Just like Jesus cares for the birds, oh, how He cares for you! He loves you so much!

A Little Bird Made a Nest

A little bird once made a nest,
of moss, and hay, and hair.

And there she laid five speckled eggs,
and covered them with care.

Five little birds were hatched in time,
so small, and bare, and weak,

The father fed them every day,
with insects from his beak.

At last the little birds were fledged,
and strong enough to fly,

And then they spread their tiny wings,
and bade the nest "good-bye."

LESSON 23
Day 2

ABC'S AND MORE:

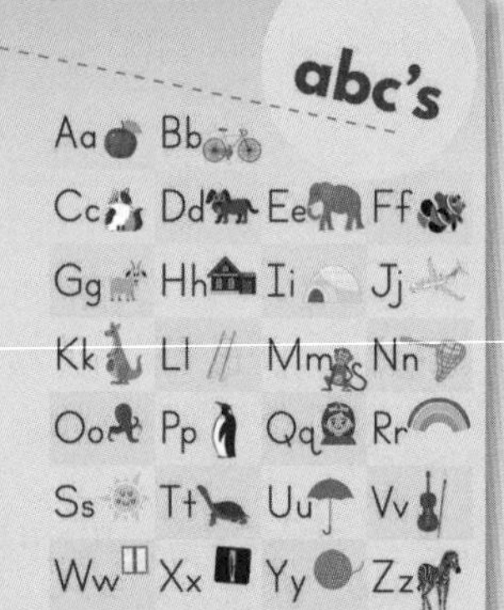

See Teacher Resource Page.

Chant the ABC chart.

Sing the ABC song.

Review writing letters I–P.

"Let's learn to write our Ww's today!

Point to the capital W. Point to the lowercase w.

"This is the capital W and this is the lowercase w. Now, let's write them!

Practice writing W's and w's.

"W: (slant down, slant up, slant down, slant up)
Slant up start at the top line, slant down to the right (slant down).
Slant back up to the top line (slant up).
Slant down to the right (slant down).
Slant back up to the top line (slant up).

"w: (slant down, slant up, slant down, slant up)
Slant up start at the middle line, slant down to the bottom line (slant down).
Slant up to the middle line (slant up).
Slant down to the bottom line (slant down).
Slant up to the middle line (slant up).

Trace the Ww's below.

Complete matching activity on the next page.

Read the letter book to the student.

Have the student highlight the capital and lowercase letter of the week.

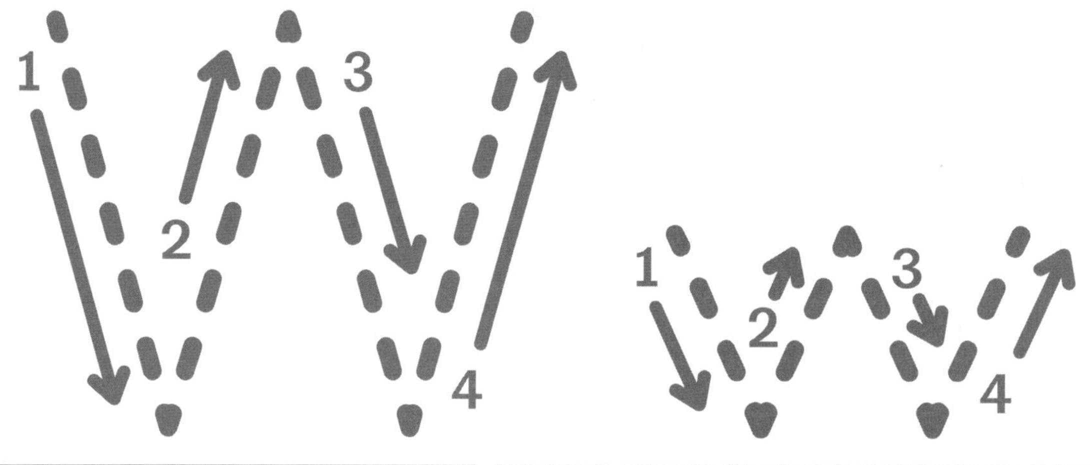

Name

Lesson 23
Day 2

See if you can match the uppercase and lowercase letters!

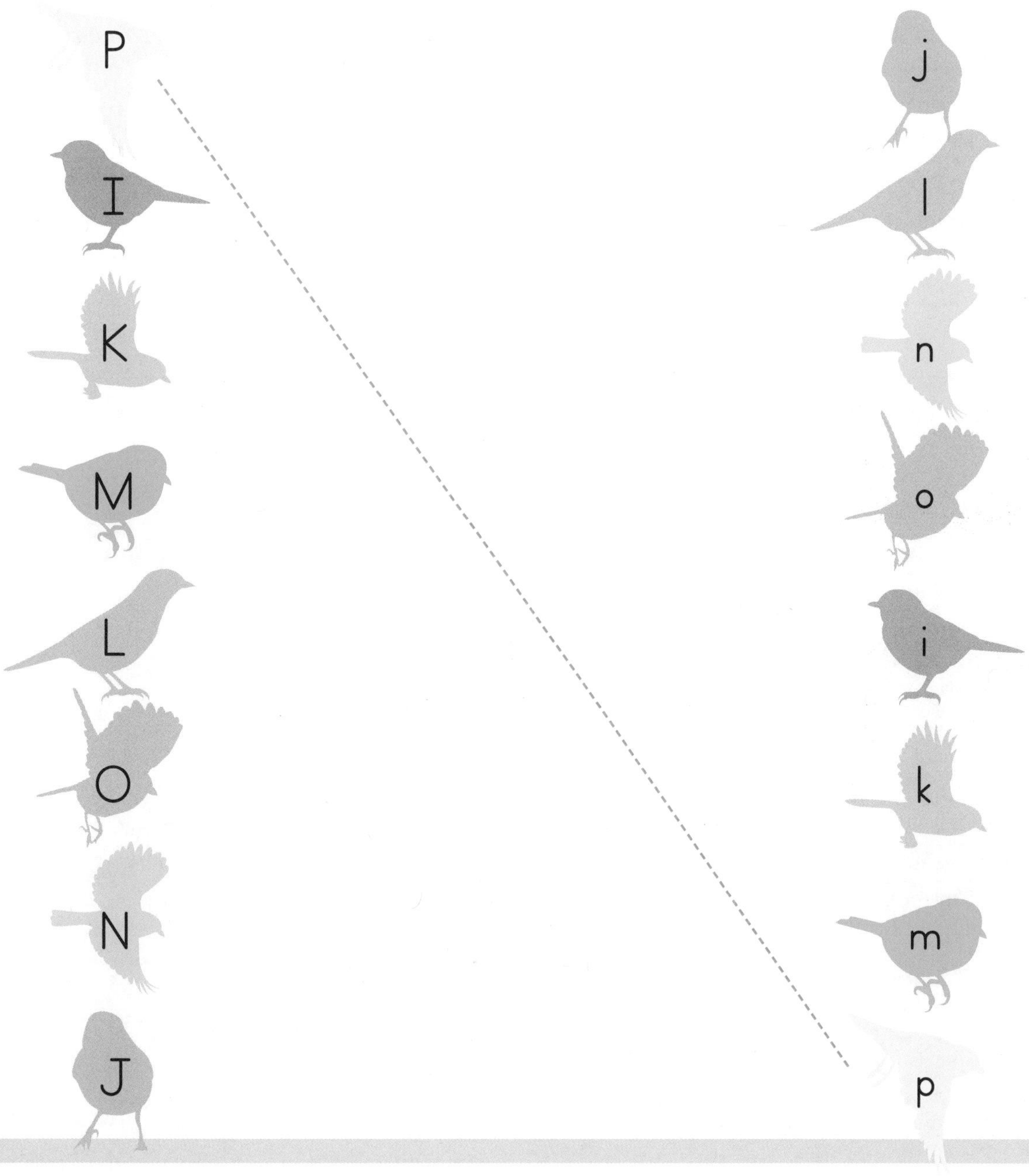

P	j
I	l
K	n
M	o
L	i
O	k
N	m
J	p

LESSON 23
Day 3

LIFE SKILLS:

"When I do laundry, I can sort things by color like all dark colors together and all whites or light colors together. I can sort things by type, like all towels together or all clothes together. I can sort by to whom it belongs. I want you to help me sort by ___________ as we load the washing machine.

Help them pick a way to sort and place the items in groups.

BIBLE:

Review your memory verse on page 259.

"Do you know what unity is? Unity means to be in agreement or harmony, to work together as one. That is how God is. He is what we call triune. Triune means three as one — just like our memory verse lists the Father, Son, and Holy Spirit. This is kind of like three jobs of God. He is a father, a son, and a Spirit all in one. There is one God who became flesh and came to live among us (John 1:14). He sent the Holy Spirit to give us His power. This is what helps us to be better disciples. The Holy Spirit is what also helps us to fight sin. It is the working of the Spirit in our lives that helps lead and guide us. Let's give God thanks for the Holy Spirit working in our lives.

"Remember how the disciples were disciplined or focused on what God called them to do? We are showing discipline in prayer by using a prayer journal.

RHYME TIME:

"Let's read our poem for this week.

Read "A Little Bird Made a Nest."

"Highlight the W's and w's in the poem.

A Little Bird Made a Nest

A little bird once made a nest,
of moss, and hay, and hair.

And there she laid five speckled eggs,
and covered them with care.

Five little birds were hatched in time,
so small, and bare, and weak,

The father fed them every day,
with insects from his beak.

At last the little birds were fledged,
and strong enough to fly,

And then they spread their tiny wings,
and bade the nest "good-bye."

"Jesus loves His creation so much! He loves you too! Let's help take of the birds by making a bird feeder.

Bird Feeders:

Coat toilet paper or paper towel tubes with peanut butter.

Pour some bird seed into a paper plate and roll the tube to coat it entirely.

Use yarn to tie it to a tree.

LESSON 23
Day 3

ABC'S AND MORE:

See Teacher Resource Page.

Chant the ABC chart.

Sing the ABC song.

Review writing letters Q-X.

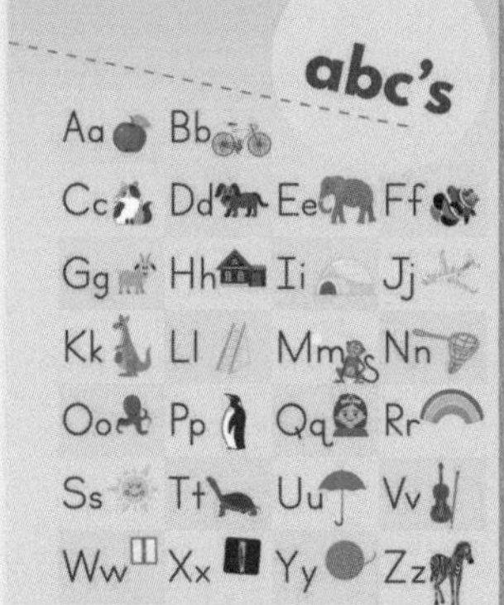

"Let's review how to write our Ww's again.

Practice writing W's and w's.

"W: (slant down, slant up, slant down, slant up)
Start at the top line, slant down to the right (slant down).
Slant back up to the top line (slant up).
Slant down to the right (slant down).
Slant back up to the top line (slant up).

"w: (slant down, slant up, slant down, slant up)
Start at the middle line, slant down to the bottom line (slant down).
Slant up to the middle line (slant up).
Slant down to the bottom line (slant down).
Slant up to the middle line (slant up).

Trace the Ww's below.

Complete the letter matching on the next page.

Read the letter book again.

Advanced K — see if your child can read the book to you.

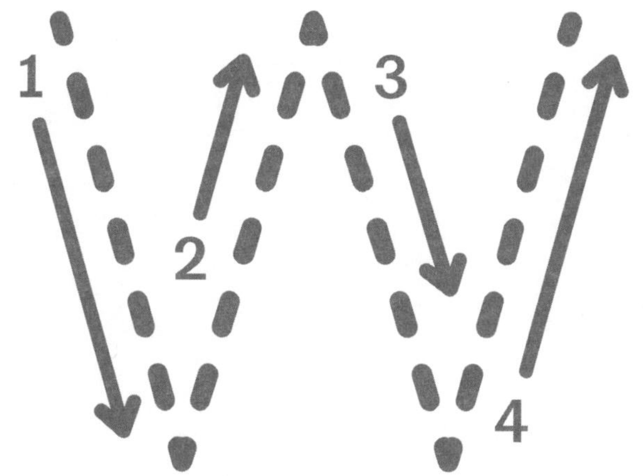

Lesson 23
Day 3

Name

See if you can match the uppercase and lowercase letters!

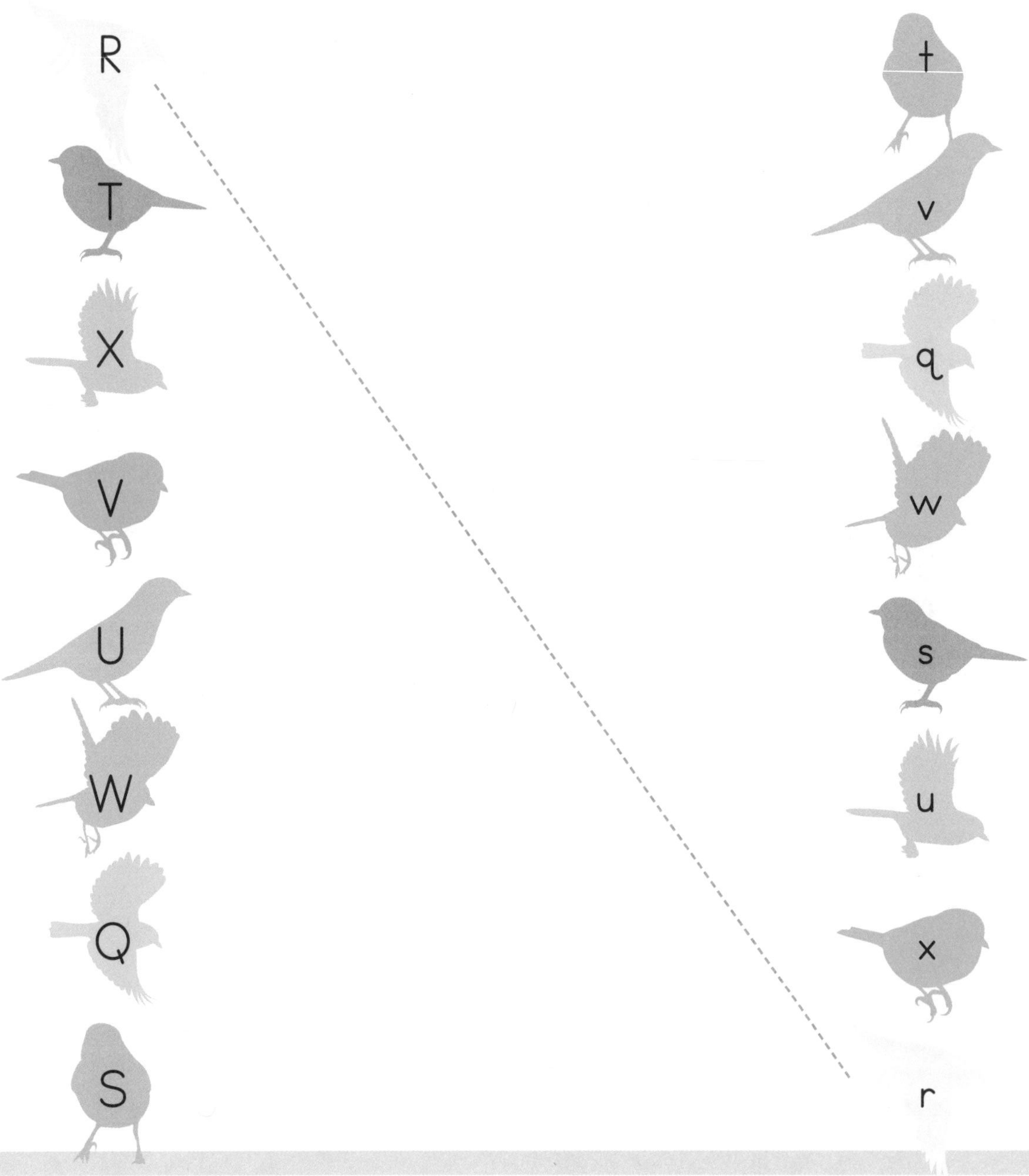

R	t
T	v
X	q
V	w
U	s
W	u
Q	x
S	r

LESSON 24
Prep Page

Supply List

- ☐ Bake a cake/tea time/hot cocoa (optional)
- ☐ 6–10 objects large enough to label with word SIN in black taped on them and FORGIVEN in red on the backside, unseen (day 2, Bible)
- ☐ Timer (day 2, Bible)
- ☐ Index cards (day 2, Bible)
- ☐ Tape (day 2, Bible)
- ☐ Marker (day 2, Bible)
- ☐ Blank paper (day 3, ABC's & More)

Objectives

Letter of the week: Xx

Skills/Concepts: cleaning the table after eating, which shoe on which foot

Memory Verse

Matthew 18:19 (KJV)

Again I say unto you, That if two of you shall agree on earth as touching any thing that they shall ask, it shall be done for them of my Father which is in heaven.

Look Ahead

Planting basil: Go ahead and have them plant over the weekend so they can draw sprouts during the week of Lesson 25.

You also need 3–4 different kinds of fruit.

LESSON 24
Day 1

LIFE SKILLS:

LEFT OR RIGHT? Work with your child to learn left and right. Here are some ideas:

- ☐ *Each time your child gets dressed, tell them which arm is their right and left.*
- ☐ *Show them how to know the difference between their left and right shoes.*
- ☐ *While eating, point out which hand is the left and which is the right.*
- ☐ *Before making a turn in your vehicle, ask them if they know which way is right or left, or point and have them point with you as you tell them which way is right/left.*

Work on this concept each day until they master it. This may take several months, or even longer. Be patient and continuously practice.

NOTE: I would not do this while writing or cutting. Children at this age may not have "chosen" which hand they will use. Please use caution at this age as this is a developmental milestone.

Clean Up Song: Sing the "Clean Up Song" as you have your child clean up after each meal. Remind them how they learned to clean up messes a few weeks back. (The "Clean Up Song" is by Barney™ and can be found online.)

BIBLE:

"Last week we made a prayer journal and were showing discipline in prayer. This week we will still focus on prayer, but on the four main kinds of prayer. Our memory verse is in Matthew 18:19 and says:

Echo read the verse. Add motions.

"A lot of times we come to God in prayer and we sit and cannot think of what to pray about. Or we get stuck and think we do not know how to pray. There are four main kinds of prayers.

"PRAISE: Praising God for how marvelous and awesome He is, praising God for all He has done

"THANKS: Showing an attitude of gratitude for the things God has done or is doing

"REPENTANCE: Asking God to forgive us for something we have done

"REQUEST: Asking God for healing, a need, guidance, or something else

"We will focus on praise and thanks today. The Bible tells us to give thanks to the Lord many times in Scriptures (almost 50 times!). We should learn to be prayerful. If we are prayerful, we are always praying, using one of the four kinds of prayer. A prayer life is a very important part of a Christian's life. Second Chronicles 31:2 tells us that King Hezekiah assigned the priests and Levites to divisions — each of them according to their duties (jobs) as priests or Levites — to offer burnt offerings and fellowship offerings, to minister, to give thanks, and to sing praises at the gates of the Lord's dwelling.

Name ______________________

Lesson 24
Day 1

 Matthew 18:19 (KJV)

Again I say unto you, That if two  of

you shall agree on earth  as

touching any thing that they shall ask  ,

it shall be done for them of my

Father  which is in heaven.

Praise

Thanks

Repentance

Request

LESSON 24
Day 1

"It was so important to give thanks and sing praises at the gates of the Lord's dwelling that King Hezekiah assigned different priests and Levites to do this. *Dwelling* is another word for house or home, so at the Lord's house the king assigned people to offer praise and thanks. A lot of times in the Old Testament the way they offered praise was with music and song. David, who wrote most of the Book of Psalms, was a musician. Psalm 150:4 even says to praise Him with tambourine and dance. We should always give God praise and thanks. Psalm 100:4 says, "Enter his gates with thanksgiving and his courts with praise; give thanks to him and praise his name." Let's add some things to our journal that we can give praise about and things we can give God thanks for.

RHYME TIME:

"Let's read our poem this week, "Pat-a-Cake."

Optional: Bake a cake this week or mini cakes/ loaves and have a tea time or cocoa and cakes.

X-ray

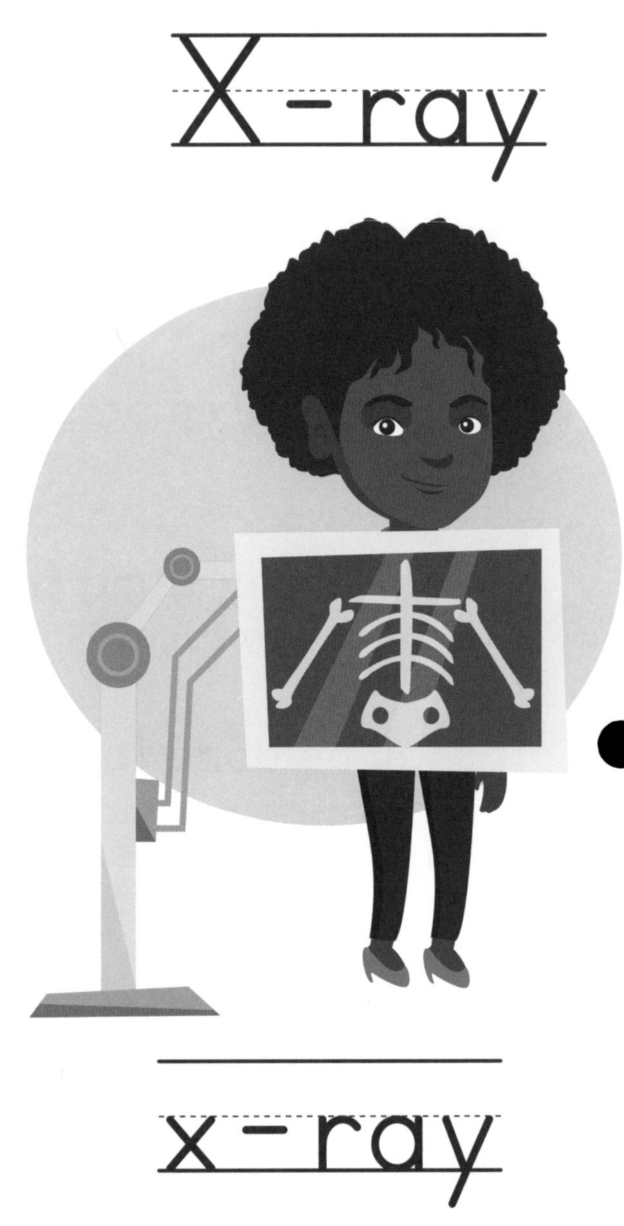

x-ray

Pat-a-cake

Pat-a-cake, pat-a-cake, baker's man,
bake me a cake, as fast as you can.
Pat it and prick it and mark it with a B,
and put it in the oven for baby and me.

LESSON 24
Day 1

ABC'S AND MORE:

See Teacher Resource Page.

Chant the ABC chart.

Sing the ABC song.

Memory Challenge: Lay out your letter cards in ABC order like the ABC chart is. Then, flip over the letters A, E, I, O, U. See if they can figure out which letters are flipped over and then have them flip it to check their memory.

Letter Run: Lay out your letter cards on the floor. Call out the following letters as the child races to find the letters: S, W, M, P, B.

"This week we will learn to write Xx's.

Practice writing X's and x's.

"X: (slant forward, slant back)
Start at the top line, slant forward to the bottom line (slant forward). Start at the top line a little over from the first line, slant back to the bottom line (slant back).

"x: (slant forward, slant back)
Start at the middle line, slant forward to the bottom line (slant forward).
Start at the middle line a little over from the first line, slant back to the bottom line (slant back.

Trace the Xx's below.

MINI-BOOK X:

See the Teacher Resource Page.

Do a picture walk.

Read the book to the student pointing to each letter/word.

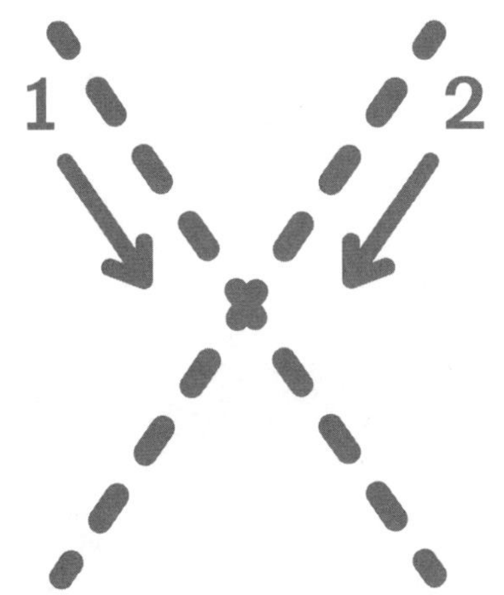

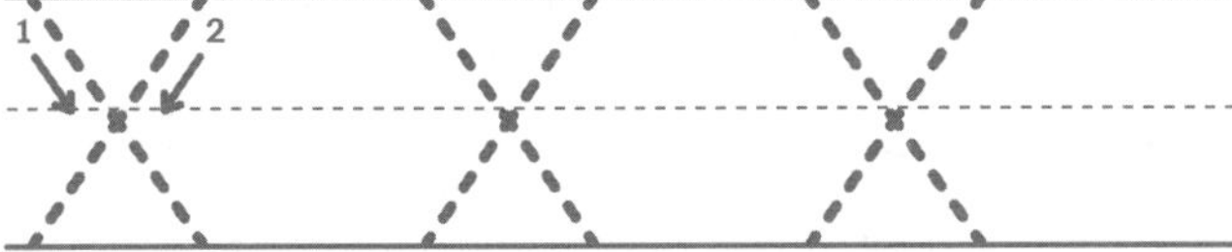

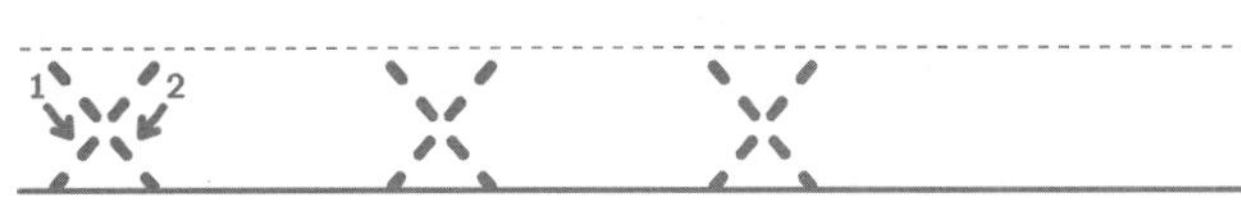

LESSON 24
Day 2

LIFE SKILLS:

LEFT OR RIGHT? Each time your child gets dressed this week, help them by telling them which arm is their right and which is left. Work on this concept each day until they master it. This may take several months, or even longer. Be patient and continuously practice.

Clean Up Song: Sing the "Clean Up Song" as you have your child clean up after each meal.

BIBLE:

"Remember, this week we are focusing on being prayerful. Do you remember what being prayerful means?

"There are four main kinds of prayer. We discussed two kinds yesterday. Do you remember them?

"Right — praise and thanksgiving.

"Today, we will focus on prayers of repentance. Repentance is not simply asking for forgiveness. Repentance requires action from us. Repentance means to turn away from.

Have objects spread apart, but visible. Sin label up.

"Let's play a little game. I am going to set out some things and you will try to collect them all before the timer sounds. On your mark, get set, GO!

Set the timer for 12 seconds and see how many things they can get.

"This says SIN. Sin is something we do that hurts or separates us from God. Can you think of something that is a SIN?

Allow time and give examples if needed.

"So, when we sin, we can ask God to forgive us and He will.

Flip one object over.

"This says FORGIVEN. Repenting is not just saying you're sorry you sinned. That would mean you are just sorry you got caught. Repentance means to turn from the sin.

Turn over about half of the objects to read FORGIVEN.

Praise

Thanks

Repentance

Request

LESSON 24
Day 2

"Let's play this again. This time, some of these will have the word FORGIVEN on them, but some will have SIN on them. If you see the SIN (in black), then you are to turn away from it and do not collect it. Only collect the ones with FORGIVEN (in red) on them.

Set the timer for 7 seconds.

"On your mark, get set, GO!

"You see, when we ask for forgiveness from God, it is more than just an "I'm sorry" — it requires us to turn away from sin.

Practice your memory verse on page 271.

Read "Pat-a-Cake."

Pat-a-Cake

Pat-a-cake, pat-a-cake, baker's man,
bake me a cake, as fast as you can.
Pat it and prick it and mark it with a B,
and put it in the oven for baby and me.

Optional: Bake a cake this week or mini cakes/ loaves and have a tea time or cocoa and cakes.

Xylophone

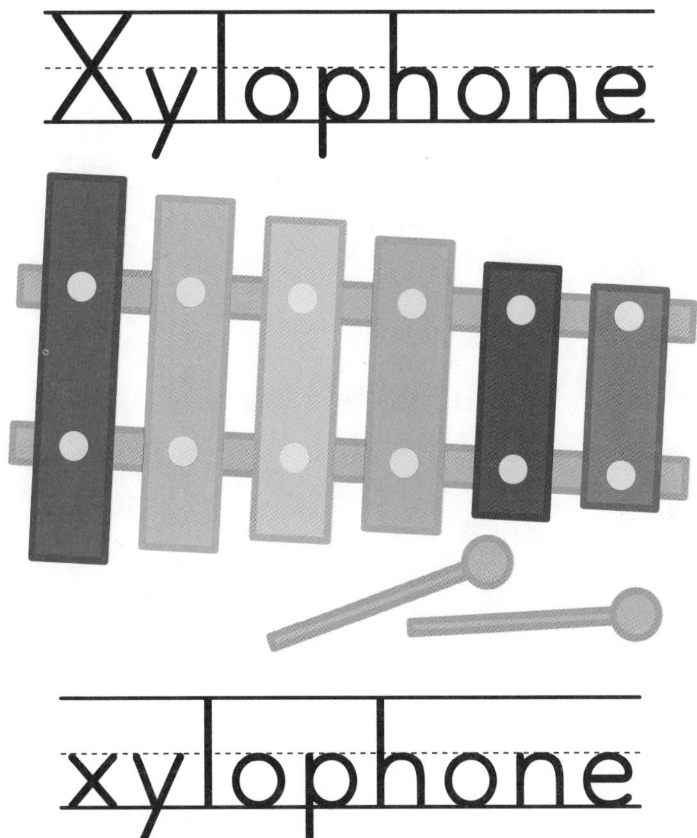

xylophone

LESSON 24
Day 2

ABC'S AND MORE:

Chant the ABC Chart.

Sing the ABC song.

"Let's practice writing our letter Xx's!

Practice writing X's and x's.

"X: (slant forward, slant back)
Start at the top line, slant forward to the bottom line (slant forward).
Start at the top line a little over from the first line, slant back to the bottom line (slant back).

"x: (slant forward, slant back)
Start at the middle line, slant forward to the bottom line (slant forward).
Start at the middle line a little over from the first line, slant back to the bottom line (slant back).

Trace the Xx's below.

MINI-BOOK X:

Read the letter book to the student.

Have the student highlight the capital and lowercase letter of the week.

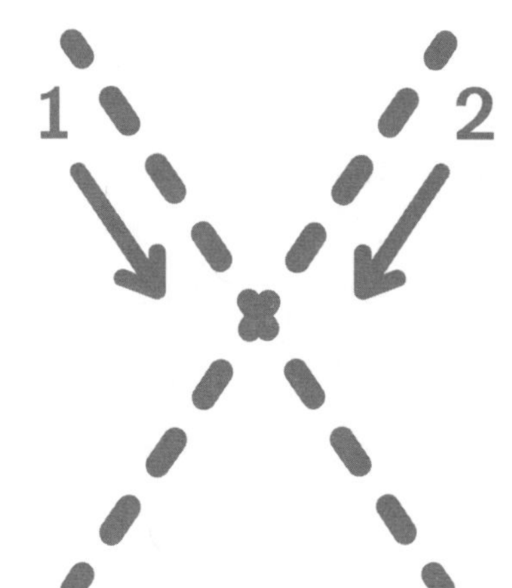

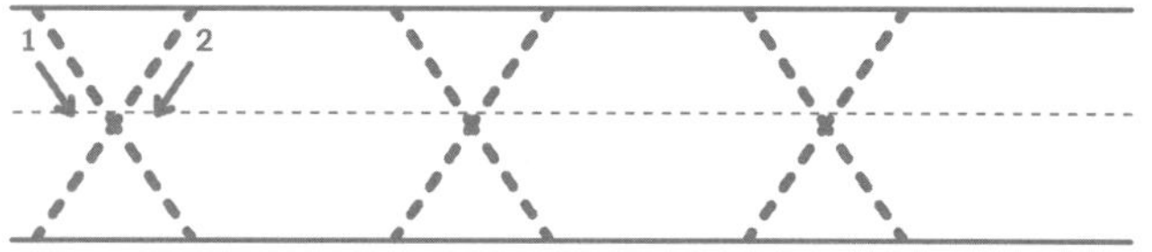

LESSON 24
Day 3

LIFE SKILLS:

Continue to practice learning left and right through daily activities.

"Let's see if you remember about right and left.

Complete the left/right activity on page 278.

Sing the "Clean Up Song" as you have your child clean up after each meal.

BIBLE:

"We are continuing our focus on being prayerful.

"There are four main kinds of prayer. We have discussed three kinds so far, do you remember them?

"Right — Praise, thanksgiving, and repentance.

Use chart on 4 types of prayer from page 270.

"Today, we will focus on prayers of request.

"Sometimes we have a need or a request. A need is something that is necessary, it is not something we just want, like a new toy. A need is essential. If we are sick with cancer, then a need we have is healing. If your parent loses their job, then a need is for God to bless them with a new job. We make requests to God based on our needs. Sometimes we come to God with our wants instead of our needs. God knows what is best for us, just like parents are also watching out for what is best for you, and He will not give you what is not His will or desire for you. Can you think of a request or a need?

"Needs can be for us or they can be for someone or something else. Maybe you want your church to grow, so you pray for God to send people your way to witness and help it grow. Maybe you are sick and need healing. Our memory verse also tells us to pray with others.

Practice your memory verse on page 271.

"Matthew 18:19 (KJV) says: "Again I say unto you, That if two of you shall agree on earth as touching any thing that they shall ask, it shall be done for them of my Father which is in heaven."

"See, when we agree and ask God, He hears us and will answer our prayers. He is faithful to care for us. When we pray, we can use this chart for helping us know which type of prayer we are focusing on. In our prayer time, we can pray through all four kinds of prayers.

"Do you have any needs today that we should pray about?

RHYME TIME:

Read "Pat-a-Cake" on page 275.

"There are not any X's in the poem, but we will have a different activity during ABC's and More time.

Lesson 24
Day 3

Name

Look at each picture below; decide if it is facing left or right. Then circle the correct arrow below each image. (Hint! Look for the front of each car or bike.)

LESSON 24
Day 3

ABC'S AND MORE:

See Teacher Resource Page.

Chant the ABC chart.

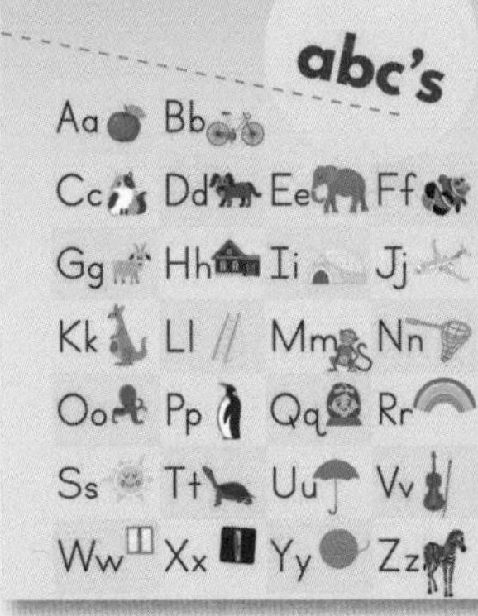

Sing the ABC song.

X marks the spot! Hide a toy and make a treasure map showing an X mark where you hid your toy. Have others see if they can use the map to locate the toy. The Bible says in Matthew 6:21, "For where your treasure is, there your heart will be also." Remember our treasure is in God!

Memory Challenge: Lay out your letter cards in ABC order like the ABC chart. Then, flip over the letters X, D, Y, T, I, L. See if they can figure out which letters are flipped over and then have them flip it to check their memory.

" Let's review how to write Xx's.

Practice writing X's and x's.

" X: (slant forward, slant back)
Start at the top line, slant forward to the bottom line (slant forward).
Start at the top line a little over from the first line, slant back to the bottom line (slant back).

" x: (slant forward, slant back)
Start at the middle line, slant forward to the bottom line (slant forward).
Start at the middle line a little over from the first line, slant back to the bottom line (slant back.

Trace the Xx's below.

MINI-BOOK X:

Read the letter book again.

Advanced K — see if your child can read the book to you.

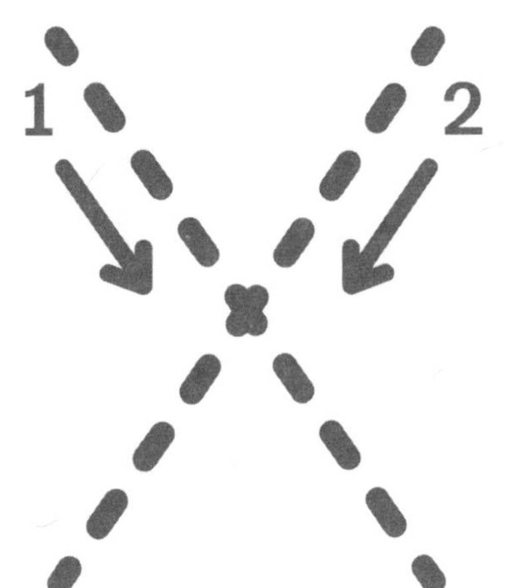

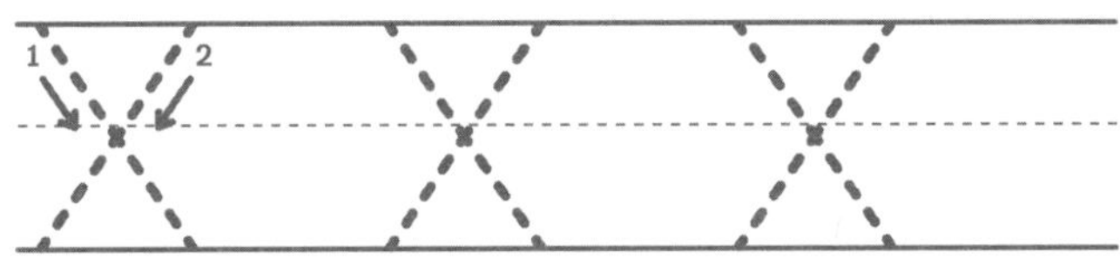

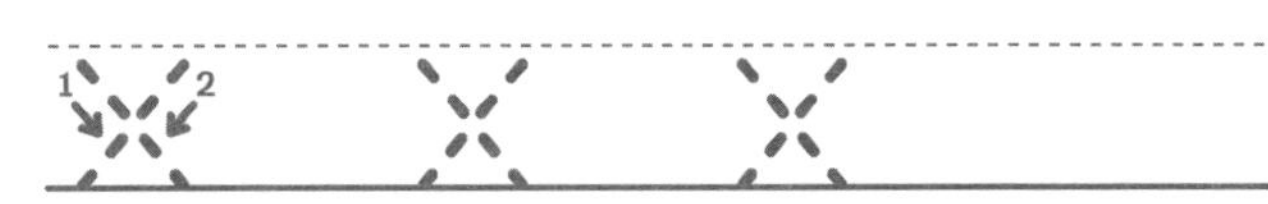

LESSON 25
Prep Page

Supply List

- ☐ Basil seeds for planting (day 1, life skills)
- ☐ Paper egg cartons (for planting) (day 1, life skills)
- ☐ 3–4 different kinds of fruit (only 1 each) (day 2, Bible)
- ☐ Crayons
- ☐ Small amount of soil for seeds (day 1, life skills)

Look Ahead

Please look at supplies for Lesson 26.

Objectives

Letter of the week: Yy

Skills/Concepts: animal/plant care

Memory Verse

Proverbs 12:10

The righteous care for the needs of their animals, but the kindest acts of the wicked are cruel.

Extended Activities

Sing “He’s Got the Whole World in His Hands” and use hand motions.

Visit an animal shelter or pet store to learn more about caring for animals.

You might volunteer to walk the dogs at the shelter.

Research spiders. Count the legs on spiders.

LESSON 25
Day 1

LIFE SKILLS:

You can do both or choose based on if you have a pet or only plants.

"If you have a pet, how you do you care for it? Are you diligent or hard-working in caring for it? Let's make sure that our pet has plenty of fresh water and food each day. We also need to make sure their home environment is clean. Animals also need exercise. Is your pet getting the correct exercise it needs?

Help your child in being diligent in caring for their animal. You might make a checklist for them to mark each day they do this and give lots of praise for their diligence each day.

"Do you have any plants or flowers? What kind of care do you have to give a plant or flower for it to grow?

"Yes, it needs water and sunlight to grow as well as good food which is its soil. We will be planting and caring for basil. Basil is an herb and we can actually add it in to our food and eat it! Typically, basil sprouts at around four days old. So, we will need to make sure we have good soil, water it a little each day, and let it get sunlight so it can grow.

Care for it all this week. We will also make drawings of what we see and do each day.

BIBLE:

Read this section and then have the student color the picture of the third day of creation.

"Remember how much God cares for you? We should also care for His world, like plants and animals.

"There are a lot of ways we can show a caring attitude and have compassion on God's creation. Our memory verse is in Proverbs 12:10. It states:

Echo read the verse. Add motions.

The righteous  care for the needs of their animals , but the kindest acts of the wicked are cruel .

"On day 3 of creation, God created all kinds of plants! There are flowers, herbs, shrubs, bushes, trees, grass. Even weeds are plants. Just because there are different kinds of plants, doesn't mean they are not all plants. Plants have different purposes, just like we all have a purpose. Herbs are for seasoning our foods and some even help us be healthy. Some plants are for nutrition and we can eat them. Plants help us get oxygen too. Some plants are great at filtering the air and making it clean. God gave us all of these plants to help us and our world be healthy. Now, Genesis 1:10–13 tells us that God created the plants after their own kind. We don't see a tree ever become a head of lettuce, do we? And poison ivy does not become a grass does it? No! Each plant is a different kind of plant producing after its own kind.

Complete the coloring activity on the next page.

RHYME TIME:

Read "Yik Yak Yam" on the following page.

Name

Color the picture of the third day of creation when God created the plants. Use at least three different colors.

Yik Yak Yam by Carrie Bailey

Yik Yak Yoshi likes to eat yam.
He sits on his feet while he eats.
Yik Yak Yoshi does not like jam,
but yam he will eat 'til he can't feel his feet.

LESSON 25
Day 1

ABC'S AND MORE:

See Teacher Resource Page.

Chant the ABC chart.

Sing the ABC song.

"Let's learn to write our Yy's!

Practice writing Y's and y's.

"Y: (slant down, slant up, down)
Start at the top line, slant forward and down to the middle line (slant down), slant out and up to the top line (slant up). Now make a line down from the middle line to the bottom line. (down).

"y: (slant back, slant in)
Start at the middle line, slant back to the left (slant back).
Move over to the left at the middle line and slant down and in to the bottom line (slant in).

Trace the Yy's below.

MINI-BOOK Y:

See the Teacher Resource Page.

Do a picture walk.

Read the book to the student pointing to each letter/word.

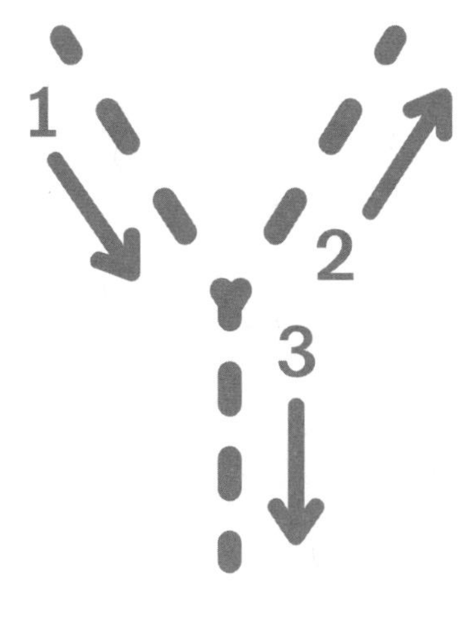

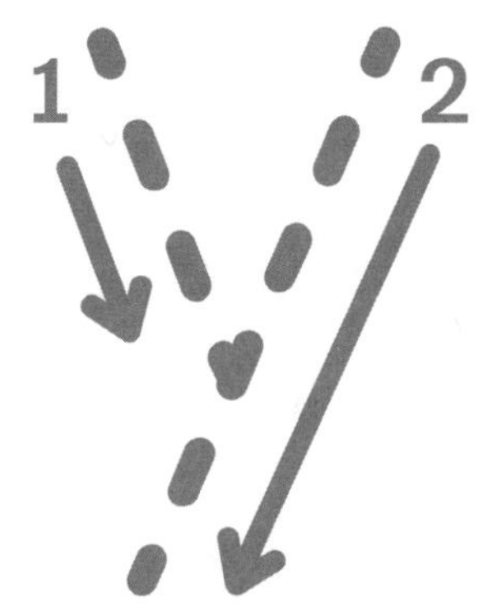

LESSON 25
Day 2

LIFE SKILLS:

You can do both or choose based on if you have a pet or only plants.

"Did you care for your animal(s) today? What did you do?

Help your child in being diligent in caring for their animal. You might make a checklist for them to mark each day they do this and give lots of praise for their diligence each day.

You could also feed the birds in your own yard, but please note that if you feed the birds, they begin to depend on you for the food. You can also create a compost pile where worms would be plentiful to feed the birds too.

"Check your basil. See if anything has changed. Give it a little water if needed. If the soil is damp, it does not need water. If the soil feels dry, then it needs water. Typically, basil sprouts at around four days, and this is day two, so you might not see a sprout yet, but draw/sketch what you did to care for it. If you show diligence in caring for this plant, it will grow and produce basil leaves.

Students will use the next page for drawing/sketching their basil.

BIBLE:

"Do you remember how you can have a caring attitude and have compassion on God's creation?

"Yes! By caring for the animals and plants.

Practice your memory verse on page 282.

"Yesterday we talked about plant kinds. Today, we will discuss animal kinds. Let's read Genesis 1:20–26.

"If you notice, it says "according to their kinds" or "according to its kind" six times in these verses. What is a kind? Well, here are some kinds of fruit. They are all fruit, but each one is a different kind. This means each one is a different type, but still the same category. Like this fruit, it is all in the fruit category, but each one is a different kind or type of fruit.

"God created all of the dogs, but there are different kinds of dogs. He created all of the cats, which could be a lion or a house cat, but they are both still a kind of cat. Then, God created mankind. We are not an animal. We were created in a unique way in the image of God. We are created in His image. We are not of an animal kind, we are mankind, and that is special!

RHYME TIME:

"Let's read our poem, "Yik Yak Yam."

Yik Yak Yam

Yik Yak Yoshi likes to eat yam.
He sits on his feet while he eats.
Yik Yak Yoshi does not like jam,
but yam he will eat 'til he can't feel his feet.

Lesson 25, Day 2

Name

LESSON 25
Day 2

ABC'S AND MORE:

Chant the ABC Chart.

Sing the ABC song.

"Practice writing your Yy's this week!

Practice writing Y's and y's.

"Y: (slant down, slant up, down)
Start at the top line, slant forward and down to the middle line (slant down), slant out and up to the top line (slant up). Now make a line down from the middle line to the bottom line. (down).

"y: (slant back, slant in)
Start at the middle line, slant back to the left (slant back).
Move over to the left at the middle line and slant down and in to the bottom line (slant in).

Trace the Yy's below.

MINI-BOOK Y:

Read the letter book to the student.

Have the student highlight the capital and lowercase letter of the week.

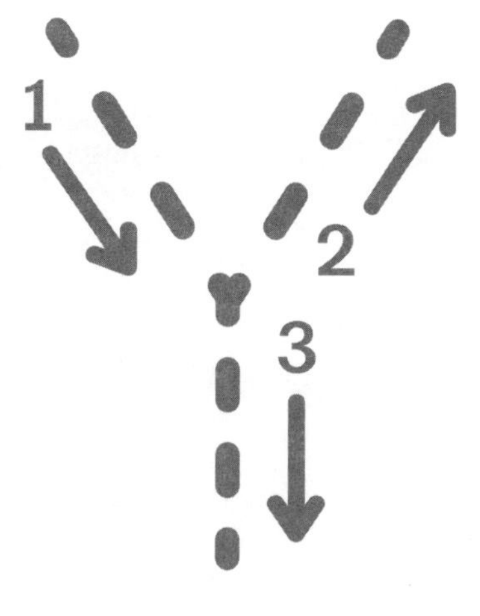

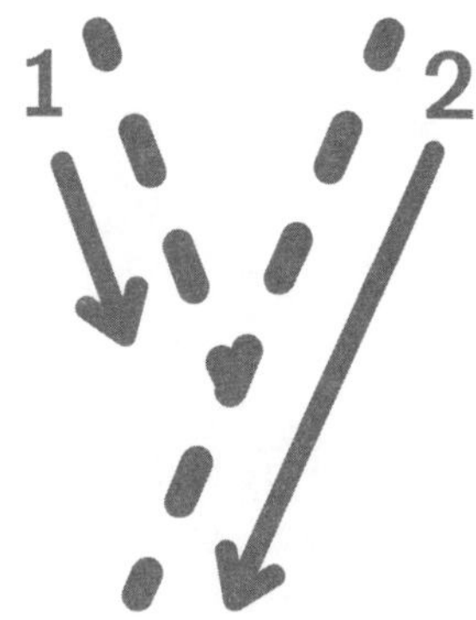

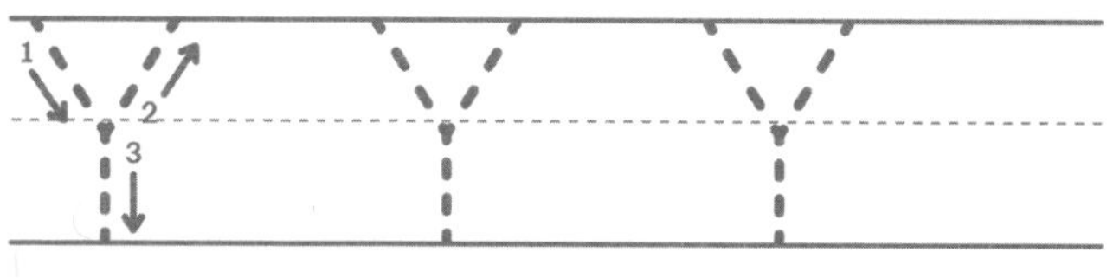

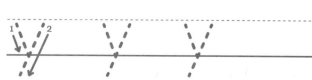

LESSON 25
Day 3

LIFE SKILLS:

You can do both or choose based on if you have a pet or only plants.

"Did you care for your animal(s) today? What did you do?

You can make an animal habitat for frogs by using about a 3' section of 1.25" diameter PVC pipe in the ground. The frogs will make a home in it. It should be perpendicular (vertical) in the ground. You can even decorate the outside. Make sure it is a PVC pipe with thin walls. The best places for this are shaded moist areas near bushes/shrubs, around trees, or even the end of gutters. If a frog has not come after a week, you might consider trying a different location in your yard.

If you do not have a pet: Check your basil for water/sunlight, and draw/sketch any changes. Keep doing this until you have leaves. If you show diligence in caring for this plant, it will grow and produce basil leaves, then you can use it in a recipe!

Students will use the next page for their drawings/sketches.

If your child has really taken an interest in gardening, I recommend they plant sunflowers and cabbage. Cabbage needs a good-sized area, as they can grow quite large. This helps your child's self-esteem, patience, and many other great qualities.

BIBLE:

"God cares for YOU! Matthew 6:26 says, "Look at the birds of the air; they do not sow or reap or store away in barns, and yet your heavenly Father feeds them. Are you not much more valuable than they?"

Review the memory verse on page 282.

"This verse tells us about how much God cares for you! We know that God cares for us. He created us in His image, and we are unique! He created us as a triune being, just like He is triune! We have a body, soul, and spirit, and we are valued by God. The Bible says that He knew us before we were born. He knows the number of hairs on our heads! Isn't that amazing?! If He cares how many hairs on our heads, then He really cares about every single part of us. He "knit" us together (Ps. 139:13). When you knit something, you interlock the yarn or unite it together. Remember that we talked about unity. Well, our bodies are made by God, interlocking and uniting each part of us. We are so detailed and wonderfully made! Our bodies are amazing! You are so special!

You might look up finger knitting and do this activity for fun.

RHYME TIME:

"Let's read our poem again this week.

Read "Yik Yak Yam."

"Highlight the Y's and y's in the poem.

Yik Yak Yam

Yik-yak Yoshi likes to eat yam.
He sits on his feet while he eats.
Yik-yak Yoshi does not like jam,
but yam he will eat 'til he can't feel his feet.

Name

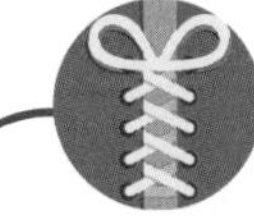

LESSON 25
Day 3

ABC'S AND MORE:

See Teacher Resource Page.

Chant the ABC chart.

Sing the ABC song.

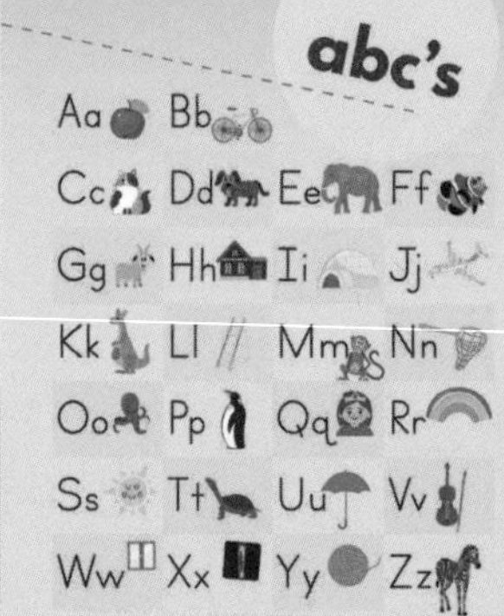

"Let's review how we write our Yy's.

Practice writing Y's and y's.

"Y: (slant down, slant up, down)
Start at the top line, slant forward and down to the middle line (slant down), slant out and up to the top line (slant up). Now make a line down from the middle line to the bottom line. (down).

"y: (slant back, slant in)
Start at the middle line, slant back to the left (slant back).
Move over to the left at the middle line and slant down and in to the bottom line (slant in).

Trace the Yy's below.

MINI-BOOK Y:

Read the letter book again.

Advanced K — see if your child can read the book to you.

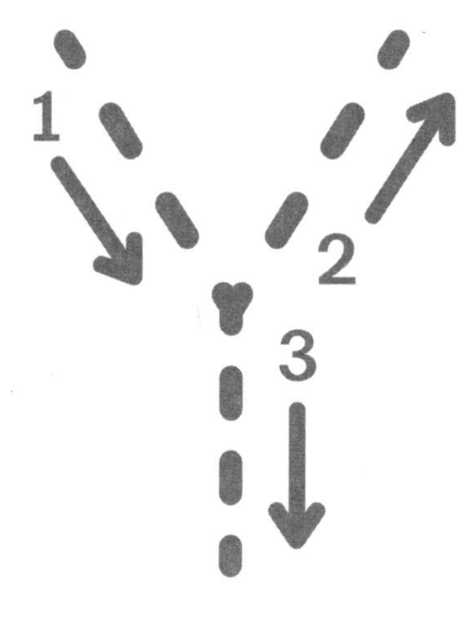

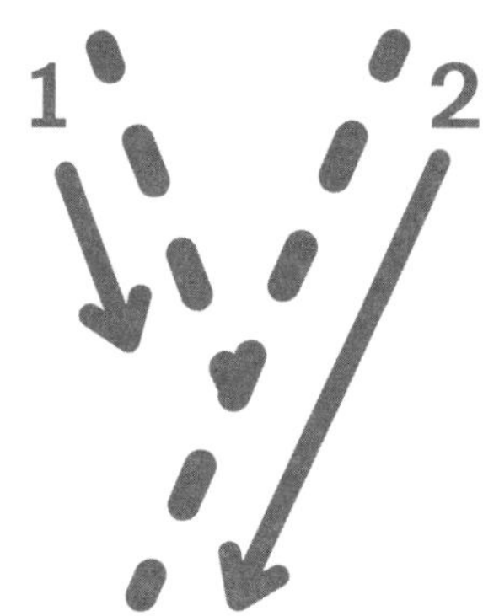

LESSON 26
Prep Page

Supply List

- ☐ Googly eyes (day 1, Rhyme Time)
- ☐ White washable paint (day 1, Rhyme Time)
- ☐ White liquid glue (day 1, Rhyme Time)
- ☐ Salt (day 1, Rhyme Time)
- ☐ Yellow ink pad or washable paint (day 2, Rhyme Time)
- ☐ Fine tip black marker (day 2, Rhyme Time)
- ☐ Box (shoebox or other small box) (day 3, Bible)
- ☐ Stickers/markers (things to decorate box) (day 3, Bible)
- ☐ Post-it notes (day 3, Bible)
- ☐ Things with zippers, buttons, and snaps (daily, life skills)
- ☐ A belt (daily, life skills)
- ☐ Parent's shirt (day 3, Bible)
- ☐ Plastic cup and small ball (day 2, Bible)

Look Ahead

Check supplies for Week 27.

Objectives

Letter of the week: Zz

Skills/Concepts: snaps, zippers, buttons, and belts

Memory Verse

1 Samuel 17:45

You come against me with sword and spear and javelin, but I come against you in the name of the Lord Almighty, the God of the armies of Israel, whom you have defied.

Extended Activities

Go to the post office/shipping store to mail something and weigh it. If they will do a brief demonstration for you, it will help your student learn more about weight with shipping.

Put a jacket and/or a belt around a chair and have them practice zipping/fastening it.

LESSON 26
Day 1

LIFE SKILLS:

Zippers, Snaps, Buttons, and Belts: This week focuses on teaching your child how to zip things up, snap a snap, button a button in a hole, and buckle and unbuckle a belt.

Here are some tips.

Buttons in a hole — it it easier to start with half through the hole, then push through.

Zippers — holding the bottom with one hand helps get you started, then pulling down as you zip up with the other hand.

Snaps — line it up, place a thumb behind and fingers on top, then squeeze.

Buckles — this might be learned best using a stuffed toy first before trying it on themselves.

BIBLE:

“1 Samuel 17:45 says:

Echo read the verse. Add motions.

You come against me with

sword  and spear

and javelin, but I 

come against you in the name

of the LORD 

Almighty, the God of the armies

of Israel, whom you have defied.

“This Scripture is about David. We are going to look at the life of David this week. The Bible tells us that David was a man after God’s own heart (Acts 13:22).

“There was a king of Israel that God rejected, named Saul. God sent His prophet, Samuel, to pick a new king for Israel. God had Samuel go to the house of Jesse. Jesse had eight sons.

Read 1 Samuel 16:6–13 that tells the story as Samuel arrives at the house of Jesse.

“Notice that God told Samuel he didn’t look at the outward appearance like we do, but that He looks at our hearts. I want to have a heart like David — one that is pleasing to the Lord. David’s own father didn’t even choose him to come in from the fields to be seen by the prophet Samuel. Most people saw David as a young boy, too young and not equipped to fight — after all, he was only a shepherd boy. We know he was full of faith and we will focus more on that as we learn more about David. Faith is believing and having hope in something even if we cannot see or touch it. We see proof of God, but we cannot see Him. We see proof of God working, like when He heals someone, but we cannot see Him. Faith is knowing that God is God and that He is able to do anything! Even the impossible!

LESSON 26
Day 1

RHYME TIME:

"Let's read our poem this week, "I Am a Busy Bee."

Read "I Am a Busy Bee."

"Springtime is time that shows us how the dead leaves and trees can come to life again. It is an example of us being dead in sin and coming to life by salvation. During spring, we see all different animals coming out to play after hiding out for the winter. What are some animals or insects you see during spring?

"Our poem is about a bee, and we will sing a song about a spider!

Sing "The Itsy Bitsy Spider."

"Let's make a spider on a web!

On black construction paper, using white washable paint (tempera works well), paint one of your student's palms and fingers (NOT thumb), and press it in the middle of the page. (Think about the legs of the spider and the body of the spider. The palm is part of the body, and the fingers are its legs). Then, wash off that hand. Repeat this with the other hand making sure you overlap the palms (body of spider), and that the legs are going the opposite direction from the first handprints.

Using liquid washable glue, make a web with the spider on it. Take the salt and sprinkle it on the glue like you would glitter. Add googly eyes.

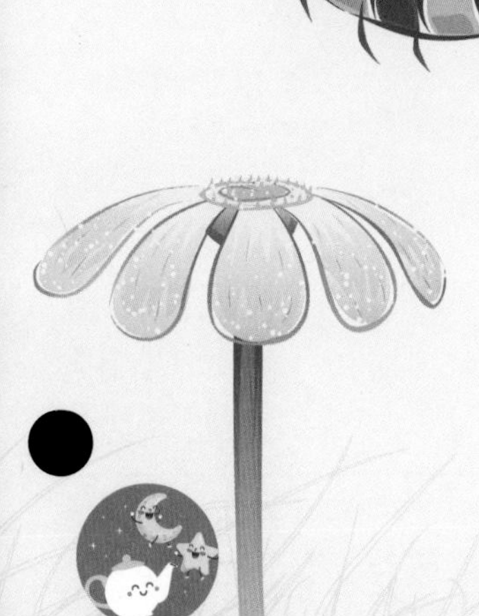

I Am a Busy Bee

I am a honey bee, buzzing away,
we are buzzing, are buzzing, are buzzing,
over the blossoms the long summer day,
we are buzzing, are buzzing, are buzzing.
Now in the lily's cups, drinking my fill,
now where the roses bloom under the hill,
seeking the honey our hives to supply,
we are buzzing, are buzzing, are buzzing.

LESSON 26
Day 1

ABC'S AND MORE:

See Teacher Resource Page.

Chant the ABC chart.

Sing the ABC song.

"This week we will learn to write our Zz's!

Point to the capital Z.
Point to the lowercase z.

"This is the capital Z and this is the lowercase z. Let's write them!

Practice writing Z's and z's.

"Z: (across, slant back, across)
Start at the top line, go across to the right (across).
Slant back to the bottom line (slant back).
Go across the bottom line (across).

"z: (across, slant back, across)
Start at the middle line, go across to the right (across).
Slant back to the bottom line (slant back).
Go across the bottom line (across).

Trace the Zz's below.

MINI-BOOK Z:

See the Teacher Resource Page.

Do a picture walk.

Read the book to the student, pointing to each letter/word.

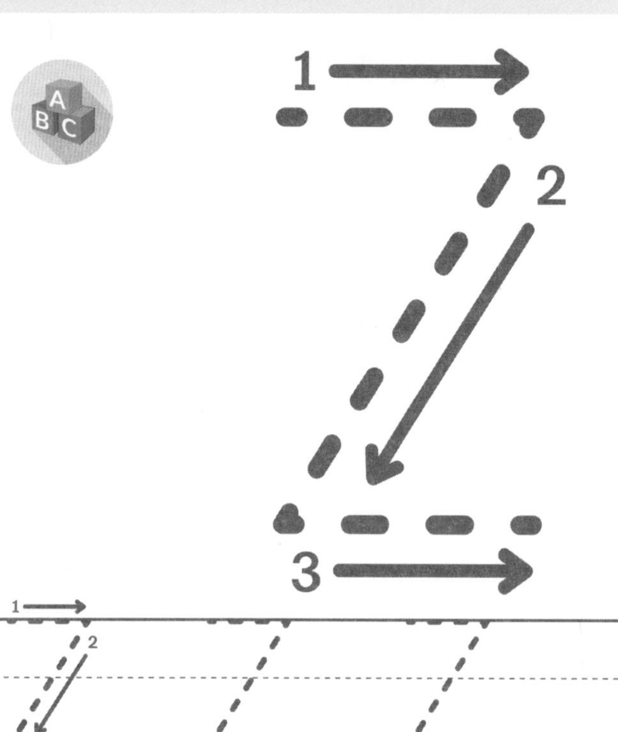

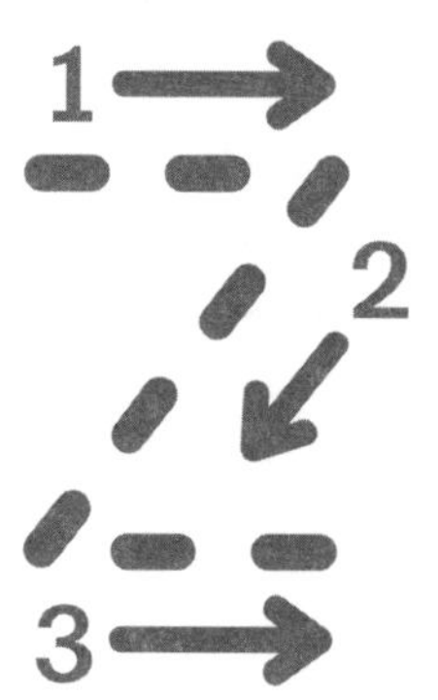

LESSON 26
Day 2

LIFE SKILLS:

Zippers, Snaps, Buttons, and Belts: This week focuses on teaching your child how to zip things up, snap a snap, button a button in a hole, and buckle and unbuckle a belt.

BIBLE:

Practice your memory verse on page 292.

“Remember how God sent His prophet Samuel to pick a new king for Israel? God told Samuel which of Jesse’s sons to pick. He picked David for a reason. David spent most of his time out in the fields keeping watch over his flock. He fought off bears and lions to keep his flock safe. Read 1 Samuel 17:34–36.

“You see, David had been out in the fields practicing using his slingshot, so if any other animal came after his sheep, he could kill it to save his sheep. Day after day, David practiced. You see, when God has a job for you, he puts you in a place where He can prepare you ahead of time. David was very good with his slingshot, because he had practiced and used it to fight off animals that were after his sheep. God was preparing David for a different battle.

Read 1 Samuel 17:2–11.

“This giant was huge, he was intimidating or frightening. It was as if the Israelites were shaking in their boots with fear. First Samuel 17 tells us that Jesse sent David to take food to his brothers who were fighting in the Israelite army and to the commander. He was also to see how his brothers were doing and report back to Jesse. When David got to the Israelite army lines, something happened. Let’s read it in verses 23–32.

“Here is where we see David’s faith. Most would look at David and only see courage and bravery, but David also had faith in what His God could do! He knew God had prepared him and he was not intimidated by Goliath, because He knew how powerful God is! We will look more into David and his faith tomorrow.

“Practice knocking over a plastic cup with a ball. Take six giant steps away from the cup. See how many you knock over after five tries. How was your aim? What if you stepped a little closer? Would that help? David had great aim because he practiced. Practice throwing a ball back and forth with someone.

RHYME TIME:

“Let’s read our poem again this week!

Read “I Am a Busy Bee” below.

“Our poem says the bees are buzzing over the blossoms. Blossoms is another word for flowers.

Make thumbprint bees. Using a yellow ink pad or yellow paint, paint their thumbs. Make several prints on the paper. Let it dry, then come back with a fine tip marker to add stripes and antennae.

I Am a Busy Bee

I am a honey bee, buzzing away,
we are buzzing, are buzzing, are buzzing,
over the blossoms the long summer day,
we are buzzing, are buzzing, are buzzing.
Now in the lily’s cups, drinking my fill,
now where the roses bloom under the hill,
seeking the honey our hives to supply,
we are buzzing, are buzzing, are buzzing.

LESSON 26
Day 2

ABC'S AND MORE:

Chant the ABC Chart.

Sing the ABC song.

Practice writing Z's and z's.

"Let's practice writing our Zz's today!

Point to the capital Z. Point to the lowercase z.

"This is the capital Z and this is the lowercase z. Let's practice writing them!

"Z: (across, slant back, across)
Start at the top line, go across to the right (across).
Slant back to the bottom line (slant back).
Go across the bottom line (across).

"z: (across, slant back, across)
Start at the middle line, go across to the right (across).
Slant back to the bottom line (slant back).
Go across the bottom line (across).

Trace the Zz's below.

MINI-BOOK Z:

Get the Zz Mini Book:

Highlight the Z's and z's in the book.

Read the letter Zz book to the student.

Zz
mini book

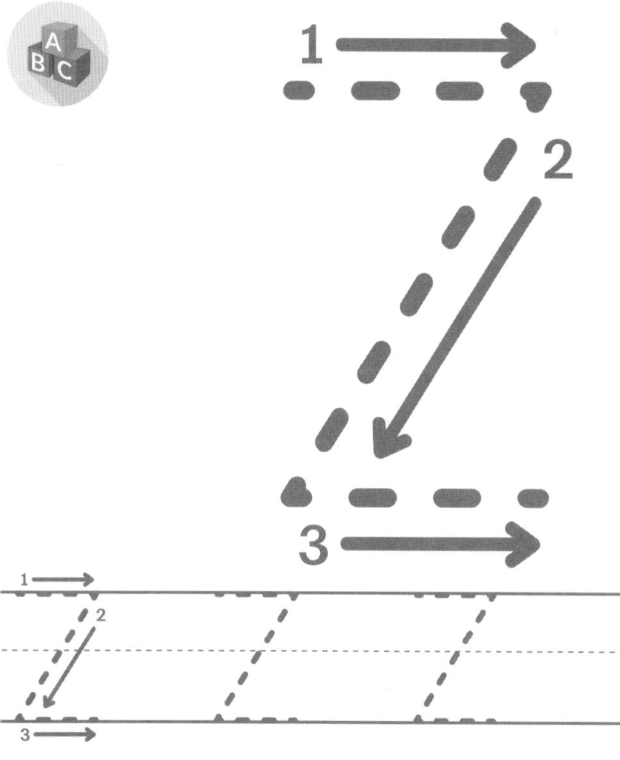

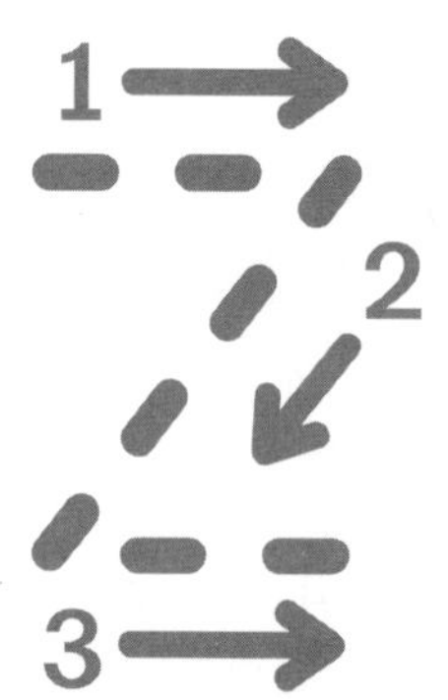

LESSON 26
Day 3

LIFE SKILLS:

Zippers, Snaps, Buttons, and Belts: Continue working on these fine motor activities using zippers, snaps, buttons, and belts.

BIBLE:

Practice your memory verse on page 292.

"Remember how David told Saul he would go fight the giant, Goliath? Well, Saul was worried about David. David did not have battlefield experience, or at least not the kind Saul's army had. Saul tried to put his armor on David to protect him.

"Put on your parent's long-sleeve shirt, a coat, and shoes and try to walk, jump, and throw a ball.

"Was that easy? No, it wasn't. It was even more difficult for David, because armor is so heavy. David couldn't fight Goliath with someone else's armor or in the same way someone else would. David had to use what he knew, which was his slingshot. Remember all the practicing David had done? Well, now it came time for him to show just what a great aim he had.

Read 1 Samuel 17:34–37.

"Goliath was boastful, which means he was proud and bragged a lot. He laughed at David. Goliath even teased David about him bringing "sticks" to fight him. But read what David told Goliath in 1 Samuel 17:45-47.

"When Goliath moved closer to attack David, David showed his faith in action by running toward Goliath, not away! He took a stone and his sling out and struck Goliath, the Philistine, right in the middle of his forehead. Goliath fell. You see, if David had not had such great faith in God and that God was on his side, he could have never run toward that giant. He would have never been able to tell him, "You come against me with sword and spear and javelin, but I come against you in the name of the Lord Almighty." David had great faith and he put his faith into action! We can have faith just like David. What are some ways you can show faith in God?

Help give examples.

"Let's make a faith box. Decorate this box on the outside.

"We will write down the things on post-its that we are having faith that God will handle in our lives, like prayers or needs we have. Then, each time God answers our prayers of faith, and shows us how He is faithful and hears us, we will remove it from our box.

Do the post-it note/faith box activity.

RHYME TIME:

"It's time to read our poem about the bee!

Read "I Am a Busy Bee" on page 293.

"Highlight the Z's and z's in the poem on page 293.

LESSON 26
Day 3

ABC'S AND MORE:

See Teacher Resource Page.

Chant the ABC chart.

Sing the ABC song.

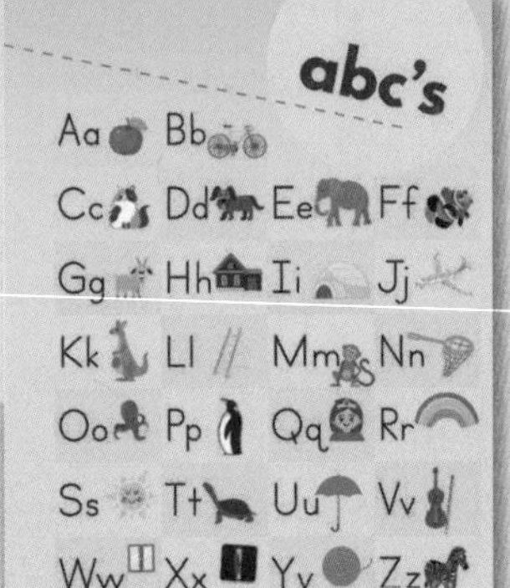

"Today, let's review how to write our Zz's.

Practice writing Z's and z's.

"Z: (across, slant back, across)
Start at the top line, go across to the right (across).
Slant back to the bottom line (slant back).
Go across the bottom line (across).

"z: (across, slant back, across)
Start at the middle line, go across to the right (across).
Slant back to the bottom line (slant back).
Go across the bottom line (across).

Trace the Zz's below.

MINI-BOOK Z:

Read the letter book again.

Advanced K — see if your child can read the book to you.

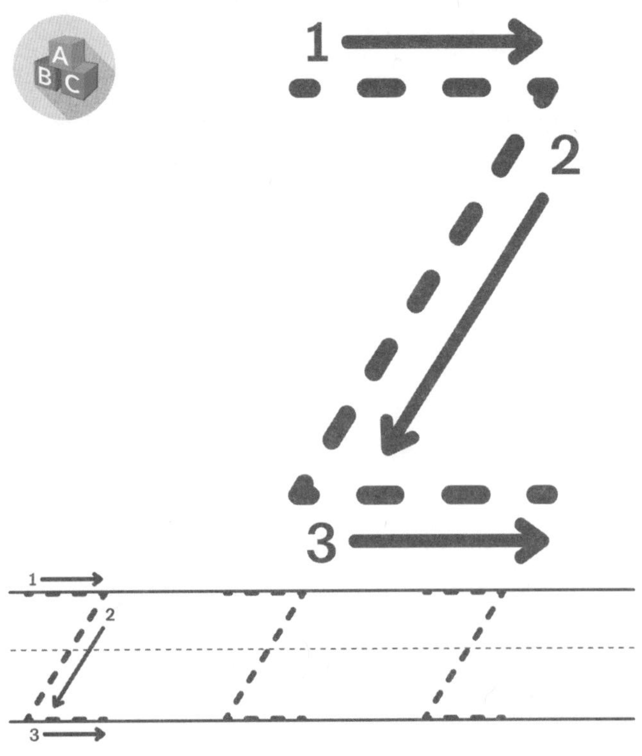

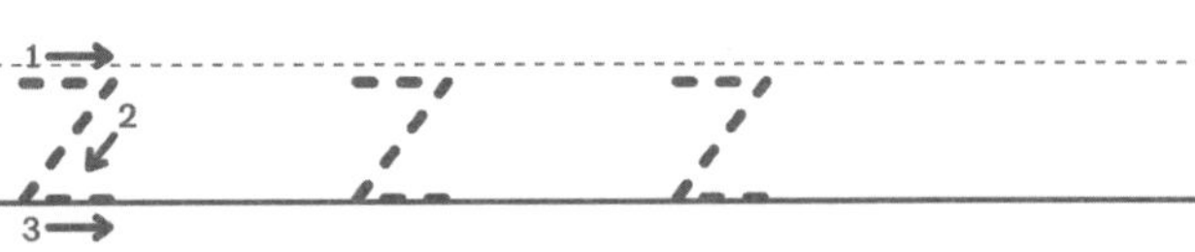

LESSON 27
Prep Page

Supply List

- ☐ Small hula hoop or large swim ring per person (day 1, life skills)
- ☐ Lego® figures (or other figures) or dolls (day 1, Bible)
- ☐ Bubbles (day 2, life skills)
- ☐ Large bubble wand (day 2, life skills)
- ☐ Art option 1: construction paper, stickers, cotton, paint, crayons/markers (day 3, Bible)
- ☐ Basket
- ☐ Plastic storage or some other container
- ☐ Yarn tied between two chairs and clothespins (optional) (days 2 and 3, ABC's and More)

Objectives

Rhyming and review letters using ABC Chart

Skills/Concepts: social skills, personal space, waiting your turn/not interrupting

Memory Verse

Psalm 34:11

Come, my children, listen to me; I will teach you the fear of the LORD.

Extended Activities

Practice rhyming throughout the day. At each meal, you can think of words that rhyme with the food you are eating.

Make cards from a favorite story by drawing a picture for beginning, middle, and end.

Practice waiting your turn at the park, grocery store, etc.

Art option 2: small items to represent each day of creation (land animals, sea animals, plants/trees, people, etc.), basket/container

LESSON 27
Day 1

LIFE SKILLS:

"Social manners we can also work on are how we act when others are talking. If I am talking with my friend, and there is something you need to tell me or say to me, you should wait until we are done talking or until there is a break in our conversation. Then, you can say, "Excuse me." Wait until I recognize you, and then you can speak. Another thing you can do if you need me is to place your hand on my arm. I will then place my hand on your hand, so you know that I know you are there and need me. When I can, I will stop and speak with you. Let's practice this.

Role play this with the child.

Discuss and explain "personal bubbles."

"Another thing we need to work on is personal space. Most people have this pretend "bubble" around them, and if you get in their "bubble" it makes them uncomfortable. Uncomfortable in this sense means to feel awkward or uneasy.

"If you invade someone's bubble it makes them uncomfortable. Keep others' space in mind. We have a game to help you understand.

"We are going to play the "IN MY BUBBLE" Game.

Using the hula hoop or swim ring, each person puts it over them and holds it in place around their middle. You want to scatter about the playing space and run around, but try to not pop each other's bubbles. You must keep moving. Then, play it again where you try to pop each other's bubbles by invading their bubble.

BIBLE:

Read chapter 3 of 1 Samuel, then reread it, having your child act out the part of Samuel and you being Eli. Have them narrate with actions the story of Samuel, using Lego® figures (or other figures like army men) or dolls.

"Our memory verse this week, Psalm 34:11, says:

Echo read the verse. Add motions.

Come, my children, listen  to me; I will teach  you the fear of the LORD.

"Samuel had a fear of the Lord, didn't he? This was not a fear like if you are scared or afraid. This type of fear is a respect or reverence. Samuel knew that to be called by God was a special job and he respected God just as we should show respect to God. What does respect mean? Respect is a reverence or deep admiration. We can show respect to others as well as for things, like our home. How can we show respect to our home?

(By taking care of it and not breaking things.)

"How can we show respect to parents?

(By obeying what is asked, by caring about what they say.)

LESSON 27
Day 1

ABC'S AND MORE:

"Before we do our poem, we need to do ABC's and More activities.

See Teacher Resource Page.

Chant the ABC chart.

Sing the ABC song.

ORDER: Using the ABC Cards, ask the student to try to put them in order like the ABC chart, but without looking at the chart to help them.

RELAY: Lay the cards out around the room randomly. Call out a letter and see how quickly they can get to it. You can also call out the pictures and have them yell the letter and then go grab the letter. See if they can beat their time each day.

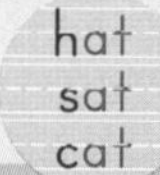

RHYMING WORDS:

"Today, we will talk about words and their sounds. Words that sound the same at the end are called rhyming words or words that rhyme.

"Words like cat . . . hat . . . bat . . . sat . . . all sound the same at the end. Words that sound the same at the end rhyme. Listen carefully as I say them more slowly this time.

Say the words slowly, stretched out, when you see them all capitalized.

"CAT HAT BAT SAT
Can you tell me what sound you hear at the end of each word?

See if they can.

"Listen — the sound at the end of CAT is AT. Listen to this: CAT, HAT. At the end I hear AT, do you hear that? Let's practice. I will say some words and you repeat me.

LESSON 27
Day 1

"CAT HAT . . . Did those words rhyme?

"CAT SAT . . . Did those words rhyme?

"I am going to try to trick you now . . . so listen.
CAT BAM . . . Did those words rhyme?

Keep going, whether they hear it or not. You may repeat it if they said no and really stress the ending chunk.

"LAKE BAKE . . . Did those words rhyme?

"FROG BEE . . . Do those words rhyme?

RHYME TIME:

"Our poem (or song) this week helps us with rhyming words. It is called "Down by the Bay."

Read "Down by the Bay" below.

Make silly rhymes by replacing "fly" in the poem with the options on the right below.

Down by the Bay

Down by the bay,
where the watermelons grow,
back to my home
I dare not go.
For if I do,
my mother will say,
"Did you ever see a fly
wearing a tie?"
down by the bay.

NOTE: The highlighted portions can be swapped out for the following rhymes:

Bear combing his hair?
Moose kissing a goose?
Whale with a polka dot tail?
Llamas wearing pajamas?
Snake baking a cake?
Hog riding on a frog?
Moose pulling a caboose?
Train going down a drain?
Time when you couldn't make a rhyme?

(or any others you might make!)

LESSON 27
Day 2

LIFE SKILLS:

"I am having a conversation with *(insert action figure's name)*, and you are wanting to tell me something. While *(insert action figure's name)* and I are speaking, show me what you should do. Remember how you place your hand on my arm and I will place my hand on yours? Let's try this now.

(Role play with the action figure.)

"Remember how people have a personal "bubble" and if you get inside of it then you make them feel uncomfortable? We will play a game to help you with this.

Don't pop my bubble game: You will blow bubbles close to yourself, but keep moving slowly around the area. The other person wants to pop all the bubbles you blow, but they do not want to invade your personal "bubble" or they cannot count that bubble. Once they pop ten bubbles outside of your personal "bubble" they become the blower and you become the popper. Be sure to move slowly. They should try to stay out of your bubble. (If playing with more than one, you can have those who invade your personal "bubble" sit down and the last one standing with you gets to be the blower.)

LESSON 27
Day 2

"Can you think of a way to show respect to a friend? What about when we practiced speaking today and waiting your turn? Does that show someone respect? Yes, because we are showing we respect them enough to listen to what they have to say.

BIBLE:

Read Genesis 1. Emphasize each day and what was made each day.

Get your Creation Cards on the following page and cut them out. Review what happened each day. Sequence the Days of Creation using the Creation Cards. Keep the cards for the next lesson.

ABC'S AND MORE:

"Before we do our poem, we need to do our ABC's and More activities.

Review all the letters on the ABC chart.

Chant the ABC chart.

Sing the ABC song.

PICK ONE of the activities using the ABC cards:

- ☐ *Hop to the letter called out.*
- ☐ *Match to the ABC chart.*
- ☐ *Use a piece of yarn tied between chairs with letters clipped with clothespins on the line. Have them crab walk to collect the letters as you call them out or as they say what they are.*

RHYME TIME:

Read "Down by the Bay" on page 302. Don't forget to make your own silly rhymes.

RHYMING:

"Words that sound the same at the end are called rhyming words.

Say these words slowly with a pause between them.

"Words like man . . . ran . . . fan . . . can . . . all sound the same at the end. Words that sound the same at the end rhyme. Listen carefully as I say them more slowly this time.

Say the words slowly, stretched out, when you see them all capitalized.

"MAN RAN FAN CAN
Can you tell me what sound you hear at the end of each word?

See if they can.

"Listen — the sound at the end of MAN is AN. Listen to this: CAN, FAN. At the end I hear AN. Do you hear that? Let's practice . . . I will say some words and you repeat after me

"SAM JAM . . . Did those words rhyme?

"BIG FAN . . . Did those words rhyme?

"I am going to try to trick you now . . . so listen. POT BOT . . . Did those words rhyme?

"SIT MAN . . . Did those words rhyme?

"LOG CAT. . . Do those words rhyme?

Give praise for effort or success!

Name

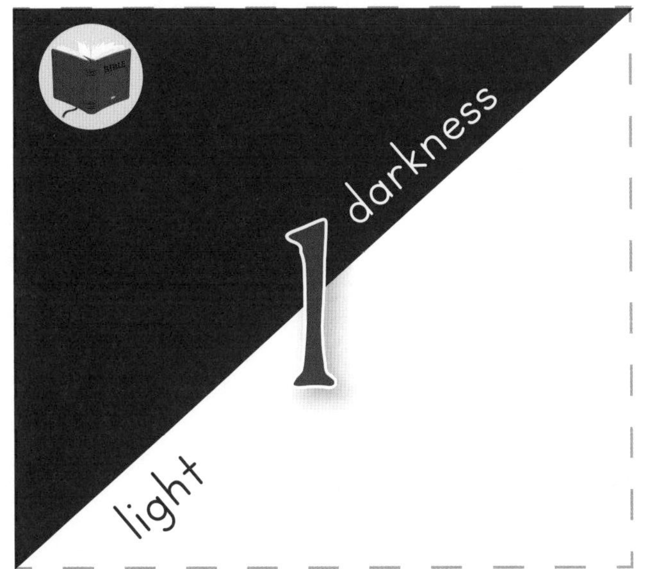
darkness
1
light

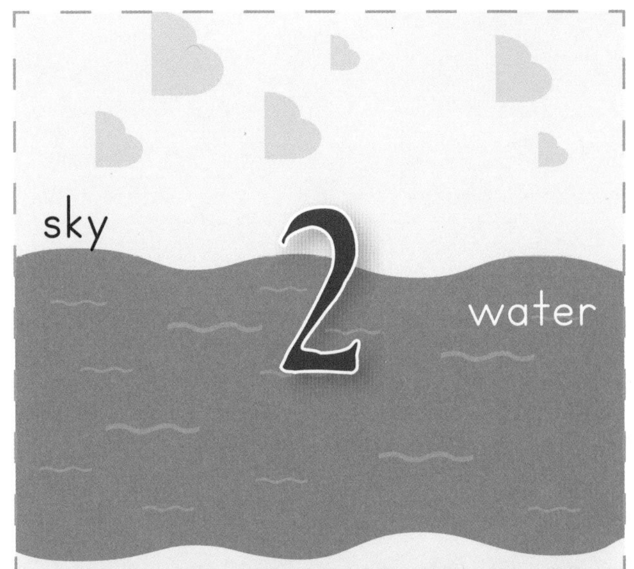
sky
2
water

land
3
plants

moon
stars
sun
4

birds
5
fish

people
6
animals

Blank Page for cutting.

LESSON 27
Day 3

LIFE SKILLS:

Try to find a time when you are in a public place for them to practice not interrupting while you or someone else is talking. You might remind them about putting their hand on your arm. Be sure to praise them for being patient and showing respect by waiting their turn.

Pick one of the games from this week to play again.

BIBLE:

Reread Genesis 1.

Get your Creation Cards and sequence the days of creation again.

Art option: 6 Days Illustrated

Using a piece of construction paper, fold it vertically in to make thirds. Then, open it back and fold it in half horizontally. This should give you six equal rectangles, one for each day of creation.

Illustrate the six days of creation. Help your child be sure they get it in the correct sequence. You can use the page horizontally or vertically. Let them be as creative as they want, using cotton, stickers, paint, crayons, etc., or as simple as they want with only a pencil and paper.

Review your memory verse on page 300.

“How do we show respect for things we have been blessed with?

(Take care of them, keep up with them.)

“Right — so each time we give respect to someone or something it requires us to take action. Sometimes, it isn’t easy to show respect to others or things. When this happens, we can pray and ask God to help us. God is faithful to help us when we need it. Is there anyone or anything you might be having a difficult time giving respect to that we can pray about?

RHYME TIME:

“Let’s review our poem.

Read “Down by the Bay” on page 302. Don’t forget to make your own silly rhymes.

“Let’s read it again and you can pick a different rhyme if you want.

ABC’S AND MORE:

Review all letters on the ABC chart.

Chant the ABC Chart.

Sing the ABC song.

PICK ONE of the activities using the ABC cards:

- ☐ *Hop to the letter called out.*
- ☐ *Match to the ABC chart.*
- ☐ *Use a piece of yarn tied between chairs with letters clipped with clothespins on the line. Have them crab walk to collect the letters as you call them out or as they say what they are.*
- ☐ *Sort letter cards by letter shapes. This will be in the pre-K letter category, but here is an example. Curved line letters: C, O, U, S; Stick letters (could use straight sticks to make them): A, E, F, H, I, K, L, M, N, T, V, W, X, Y, Z; Combo of curves and sticks: B, D, G, J, P, Q, R*

LESSON 27
Day 3

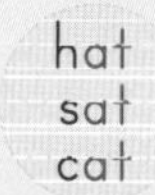

RHYMING WORDS:

NOTE: This is an introduction to rhyming. Please follow the steps below to help your child, but keep in mind this may take a little time to learn.

"Words that sound the same at the end rhyme.

Say these words slowly with a pause between.

"Words like sit . . . kit . . . fit . . . bit . . . all sound the same at the end. Words that sound the same at the end rhyme. Listen carefully as I say them more slowly this time.

Say the words slowly, stretched out, when you see them all capitalized.

"SIT FIT KIT
Do you hear the same ending? Can you tell me what sound is at the end?

If yes, praise them; if no, then praise them for being eager to learn, and move on.

"We will play the Rhyme Me Game. First, you will say a word and I will see if I can give you a word that rhymes with your word. Then, I will say some words and you see if you can say a word that rhymes with my word.

Optional words to use: can, jam, fit, cat, bug, mop, lake

See if you can match the words below.

NOTE: Go over these with them as you say each picture before they try to rhyme.

Match the picture with the one that rhymes with it. Draw a line to the picture that rhymes.

cat

frog

hog

cake

snake

rat

LESSON 28
Prep Page

Supply List

- ☐ Yarn tied between two chairs, clothespins (optional)

Look Ahead

Needed for next week: paper and art supplies for sketching

1 daisy (optional)

Objectives

Rhyming and review letters using ABC chart

Skills/Concepts: following 3-step directions

Memory Verse

The Ten Commandments

Exodus 20:1–17

LESSON 28
Day 1

LIFE SKILLS:

“Being a good listener is an important concept in conversation, as well as learning to follow instructions. What is conversation? Conversation is when two or more people are talking back and forth with each other. If we are not listening, then we might miss out on something we need to know or do. We will practice being a good listener this week. We have some games and activities we will play to help you be a good listener.

“Following directions is sometimes difficult, isn’t it?

“We will practice following three-step directions. I will tell you three things to do at once.

“Listen carefully.

“Put your dirty clothes in the hamper, get dressed, and brush your teeth. Now, you have three things to do. 1. Dirty clothes to hamper. 2. Get dressed. 3. Brush teeth. Tell me what the three things you are going to do are.

Repeat as needed.

BIBLE:

“Speaking of listening, when Moses and the children of Israel left Egypt and were in the desert of Sinai, Moses would go up Mount Sinai to hear from the Lord. We will read in Exodus 20:1–17 about what God told Moses.

“God gave Moses an important set of laws called the Ten Commandments. If Moses had not listened to God, he would not have been able to share the Ten Commandments with the children of Israel or with us.

Using page 312, we will color and go over the first four commandments today. We will work on memorizing these over the next two weeks. Save for future lessons.

NOTE: We have tried to make this in easier language so your child can remember them. If you do not prefer this wording, please feel free to use the version you want your child to know.

Read 1–4 of the Ten Commandments on the following page with the motions.

RHYME TIME:

Read “Down by the Bay.”

Down by the Bay

Down by the bay,
where the watermelons grow,
Back to my home,
I dare not go.
For if I do,
my mother will say,
“Did you ever see a fly
wearing a tie?”
down by the bay.

Name ______________________

Lesson 28
Day 1

The Ten Commandments
Exodus 20:1–17

1	Love God with all your heart.	
2	Do not let anything become more important than God.	
3	Respect God's name.	
4	Honor God by resting on the Sabbath.	
5	Love your parents.	
6	Do not hurt anyone.	
7	Be faithful to your husband or wife.	
8	Do not steal.	
9	Always tell the truth.	
10	Do not want what others have.	

Keep for future lessons.

LESSON 28
Day 1

ABC'S AND MORE:

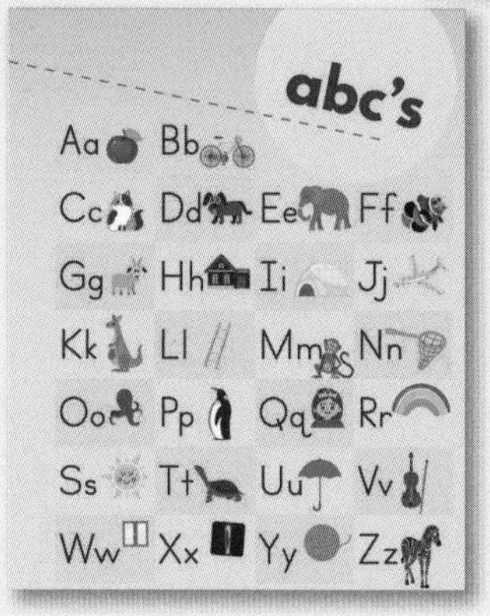

Review all the letters.

Chant the ABC chart.

Sing the ABC song.

PICK ONE of the following activities today:

ORDER: Using the ABC Cards, ask the student to try to put them in order like the ABC chart, but without looking at the chart to help them.

MEMORY CHALLENGE: After they have the cards out in order like their ABC chart, have them close their eyes or move away while you flip over ten cards randomly. They have to come back and tell you which cards they are before they can flip them over to check them.

RELAY: Lay the cards out around the room randomly. Call out a letter and see how quickly they can get to it. (If you have been using sounds for Advanced K, *you may also call out a sound and see if they can find the matching letter for that sound.) You can also call out the pictures and have them yell the letter and then go grab the letter. See if they can beat their time each day.*

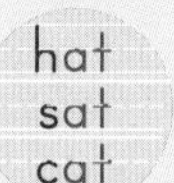

RHYMING WORDS:

Do the matching rhyming words on the next page.

NOTE: Go over these with them as you say each picture before they try to rhyme.

eagle

beagle

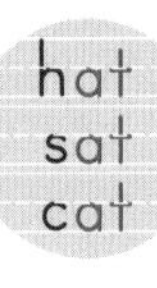

Draw a line to match the picture with the one that rhymes with it.

rake

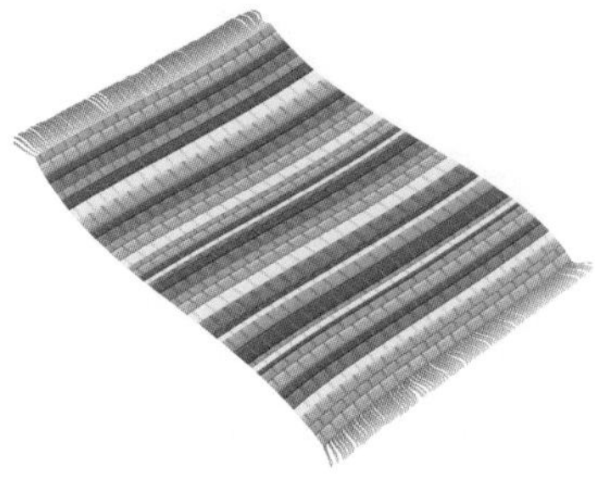

rug

pen

fan

cat

hen

bug

hat

man

bake

LESSON 28
Day 2

LIFE SKILLS:

"Being a good listener is an important concept in conversation as well as in learning to follow instructions. The Bible says in Colossians 3:17: "And whatever you do, whether in word or deed, do it all in the name of the Lord Jesus, giving thanks to God the Father through him." In this verse, it says in word or deed. Word means in what we say, or in our conversation, and deed means our actions. So, let everything we say and do be done in the name of the Lord. Listening is an action. It requires us to focus and give our attention to someone else.

"Listen closely as I give you directions to do something.

NOTE: You may come up with your own three-step directions if this does not work for you.

"Go outside, jump up and down three times, then turn around, and sit down. Now, you have three things to do. (Hold up fingers for each as you say them.) 1. Go outside. 2. Jump up and down three times. 3. Turn around and sit down. Tell me what the three things you are going to do are.

NOTE: If they are super frustrated you may back off to two things at a time.

BIBLE:

Re-read Exodus 20:1–17.

"God gave Moses an important set of laws, Do you remember what they are called? Yes, the Ten Commandments.

"Review 1–4 of your Ten Commandments page and color commandments 5–7.

You might review page 311 or make up motions to help them remember.

RHYME TIME:

Read "Down by the Bay."

"Remember our poem from last week called "Down by the Bay"? This poem helps us with rhyming words.

Down by the Bay

Down by the bay,
where the watermelons grow,
back to my home,
I dare not go.
For if I do,
my mother will say,
"Did you ever see a fly
wearing a tie?"
down by the bay.

LESSON 28
Day 2

ABC'S AND MORE:

Review all letters.

Chant the ABC chart.

Sing the ABC song.

Write the letters K–R using your letter sheet.

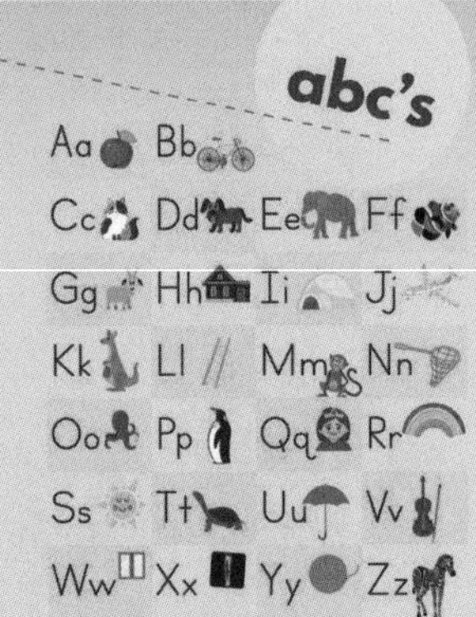

PICK ONE of the activities using the ABC cards:

- ☐ *Hop to the letter called out.*
- ☐ *Match to the ABC chart.*
- ☐ *Use a piece of yarn tied between chairs with letters clipped with clothespins on the line. Have them crab walk to collect the letters as you call them out or as they say what they are.*
- ☐ *Sort letter cards by letter shapes. This will be in the pre-K letter category, but here is an example. Curved line letters: C, O, U, S; Stick letters (could use straight sticks to make them): A, E, F, H, I, K, L, M, N, T, V, W, X, Y, Z; Combo of curves and sticks: B, D, G, J, P, Q, R*

hat
sat
cat

RHYMING WORDS:

"Remember words that rhyme sound the same at the end like sit, fit, mitt.

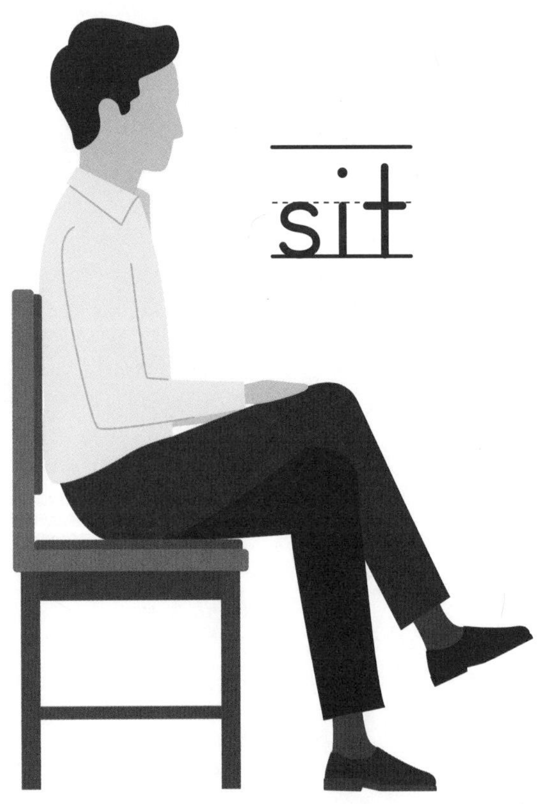

mitt

LESSON 28
Day 3

LIFE SKILLS:

"You have been doing a great job at listening this week! Being a good listener is something you can get better at over time. Listening is more important than talking. I cannot have a good conversation if I do not listen. Can you imagine talking with someone and they just kept talking and never listened to you? Would that make you feel frustrated? When we listen to others, it lets them know we value what they have to say. That makes everyone feel good about themselves too.

"Listen closely as I give you directions to do something.

"Put your socks in your drawer, get your school book, and meet me at the table. Can you tell me the three things I asked?

BIBLE:

Re-read Exodus 20:1–17.

"We are continuing to learn the Ten Commandments. Don't worry if you do not have them memorized yet as we will work more on that next week.

Read commandments 8–10 and color them on the 10 Commandments chart. Say each commandment three times today and repeat commandments 1–7 also.

RHYME TIME:

Review poem "Down by the Bay" on page 315.

ABC'S AND MORE:

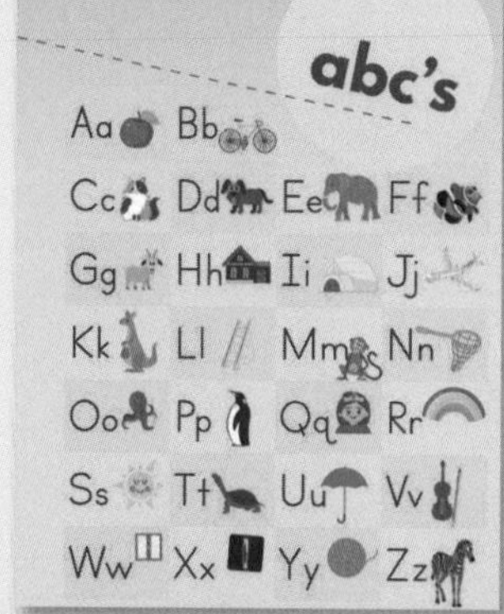

Review all your letters.

Chant the ABC chart.

Sing the ABC song.

Write the letters S–Z using your letter sheet.

PICK ONE of the activities using the ABC cards:

- ☐ *Hop to the letter called out.*
- ☐ *Match to the ABC chart.*
- ☐ *Use a piece of yarn tied between chairs with letters clipped with clothespins on the line. Have them crab walk to collect the letters as you call them out or as they say what they are (or a scooter board/skateboard with them on their back is good too) or have them shoot the letters with a NERF gun.*
- ☐ *Sort letter cards by letter shapes. This will be in the pre-K letter category, but here is an example. Curved line letters: C, O, U, S; Stick letters (could use straight sticks to make them): A, E, F, H, I, K, L, M, N, T, V, W, X, Y, Z; Combo of curves and sticks: B, D, G, J, P, Q, R*

hat
sat
cat

RHYMING WORDS:

"Remember words that rhyme sound the same at the end like frog, log, jog.

"Can you think of other words that rhyme with this group?

LESSON 29
Prep Page

Supply List

- ☐ Paper/sketchbook (daily, Rhyme Time)
- ☐ Art supplies for sketching (daily, Rhyme Time)
- ☐ Dishes (day 3, Rhyme Time)
- ☐ 1 daisy

Look Ahead

This week they are encouraged to go in nature and sketch. Please try to do this or provide nature items for them.

Objectives

Rhyming & review letters using ABC chart

Skills/Concepts: questions or statements

Putting away dishes

Memory Verse

The Ten Commandments

Exodus 20:1–17

Extended Activities

Sort other household items, such as pantry items.

Teach them how to wash/dry by hand and put the dishes away.

LESSON 29
Day 1

LIFE SKILLS:

"Just as important as listening is for conversation, asking good questions to help you understand is also important. You can be understanding of other's opinions and situations by asking questions. To be understanding means you are kind to others because of their situation. We will practice questions versus statements.

"Questions use words like why, who, how, when, what, where, and even requests like "May I?"

"If you want a glass of milk, you should ask the question: "May I have a glass of milk, please?" This is the correct way of asking. Some people say, "Can I" when they should say "May I" instead. Try to remember to use question words that will ask for something.

"A statement tells us something. An example of a statement is "The sky is blue." This tells me or makes a statement that the sky is blue. It is not a question. If you said, "There is the milk," I would not know you would like a glass of milk. If you asked the question, "May I have a glass of milk?" then I would know you wanted a glass of milk. We will practice this.

"Look around the room. What can you tell me or make a statement about in this room? What can you ask me or request of me about something in this room?

(The lights are on, there is a pencil on the table, etc. What color are the walls? Will you pass me the pencil? Where is my book? Will you hand me the remote?)

BIBLE:

Read Exodus 20:1–17 about what God told Moses.

"Who did God give the Ten Commandments to? (*Moses*)

"Do you remember the mountain that Moses was on when God gave him the Ten Commandments? (*Sinai*)

"Here are the first four commandments. Echo read them and then add motions to help you remember them.

Review the Ten Commandments chart from Lesson 28 on page 311.

RHYME TIME:

"Let's read our poem this week, "Over Field and Meadow."

Read "Over Field and Meadow" on the next page.

If you have a field, meadow, or creek nearby, go there with a sketch pad and have them sketch something they see or hear in nature. If you are not near anything, try to find a bird outside to sketch.

Name

Over Field and Meadow

Over field and meadow where the daisies grow,
up and down I wander, singing as I go.
They who see me roving, think me all alone,
but the birds are with me. Hark! Their merry tunes.

How can I be lonely where the lambkins play?
Up and down I wander, singing all the way.
How can I be lonely on the sunny banks,
while the murmuring waters raise a song of thanks?

LESSON 29
Day 1

ABC'S AND MORE:

Review all letters.

Chant the ABC chart.

Sing the ABC song.

Match uppercase and lowercase letters on the next page.

PICK ONE of the activities using the ABC cards:

- ☐ *Hop to the letter called out.*
- ☐ *Match to the ABC chart.*
- ☐ *Use a piece of yarn tied between chairs with letters clipped with clothespins on the line. Have them crab walk to collect the letters as you call them out or as they say what they are.*
- ☐ *Sort letter cards by letter shapes. This will be in the pre-K letter category, but here is an example. Curved line letters: C, O, U, S; Stick letters (could use straight sticks to make them): A, E, F, H, I, K, L, M, N, T, V, W, X, Y, Z; Combo of curves and sticks: B, D, G, J, P, Q, R.*

hat
sat
cat

RHYMING WORDS:

"Remember that words that rhyme sound the same at the end, like cat, hat, bat.

Complete Rhyming Words activity on page 324.

cat

bat

hat

Name

Match the capital and lowercase letters by drawing a line between the two letters.

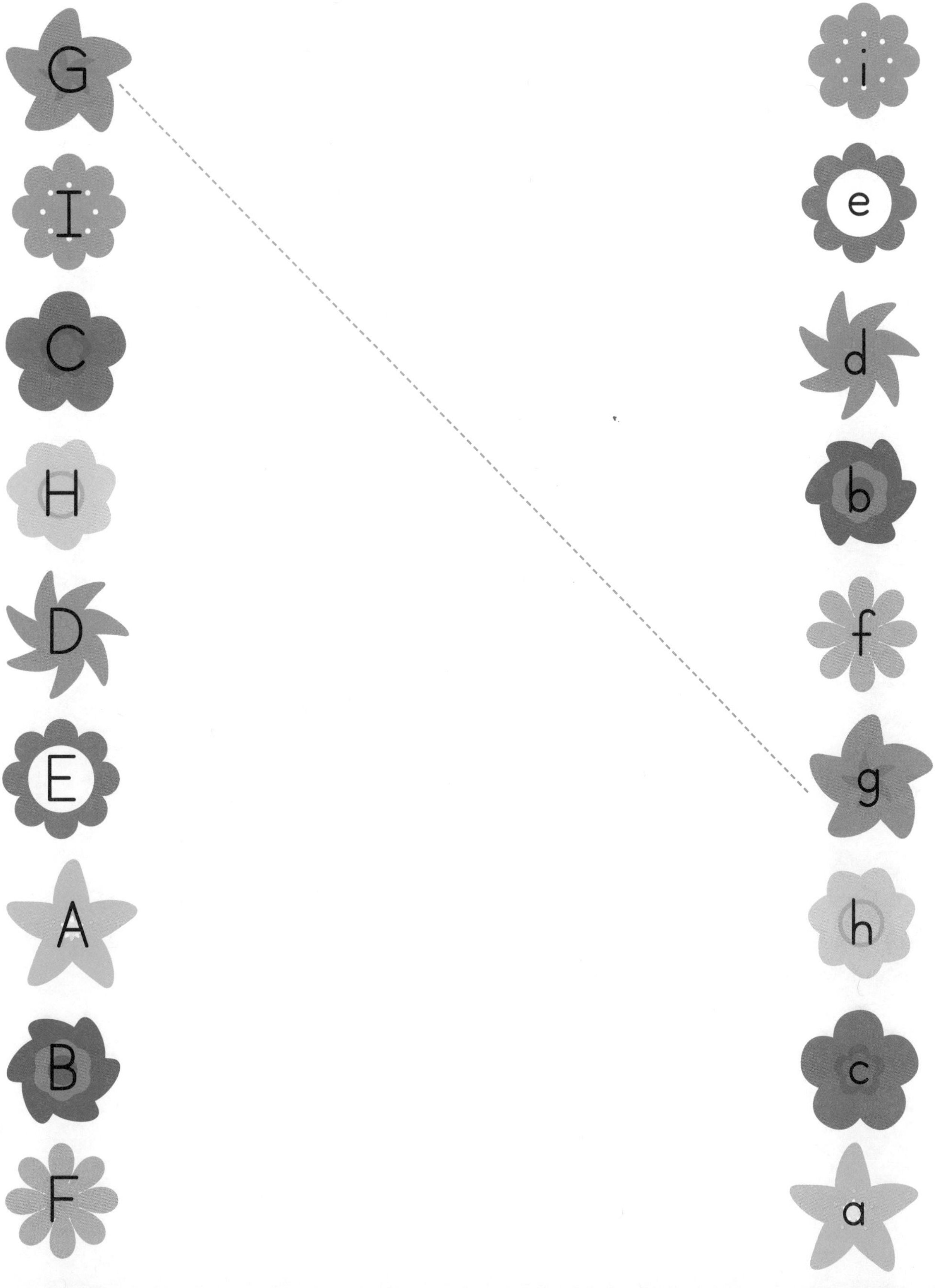

G	i
I	e
C	d
H	b
D	f
E	g
A	h
B	c
F	a

Lesson 29
Day 1

Name

hat
sat
cat

Rhyming Words - Match the words that rhyme.

LESSON 29
Day 2

LIFE SKILLS:

"If your friend responded in a mean tone, but then you found out they were sick and did not get good rest, would that help you in being understanding? Yes, it helps you understand why they reacted the way they did. It does not make it right, but it helps you show kindness because they are sick, right?

"Remember that statements tell something, and questions ask something.

"We will play the Statement or Question game.

"Line up at the start line (wall or spot outside).

"If what I say is a statement, you may take one step forward. If it is a question, you may take two steps forward. If you get it wrong, you have to take one step back.

(Mark a finish line.)

"The sky is blue.

(If you need to discuss or prompt, please do so.)

"What color is my hair?

"May I have a glass of water?

"My dog barks loudly.

"I need to get the mail.

"Will you hand me the box?

"How many cookies did you bake?

"Can you see me?

"I like pizza.

(Continue if needed.)

BIBLE:

Read Exodus 20:1–17 about what God told Moses.

"Here are the first seven commandments. Echo read them. Then add motions to help you remember them.

Review with Ten Commandments chart from Lesson 28 on page 311.

RHYME TIME:

"Let's read "Over Field and Meadow" again.

Read "Over Field and Meadow" on page 321.

Spend time outdoors sketching in nature.

LESSON 29
Day 2

ABC'S AND MORE:

Review all letters.

Chant the ABC chart.

Sing the ABC song.

Match uppercase and lowercase letters on the next page.

PICK ONE of the activities using the ABC cards:

- ☐ *Hop to the letter called out.*
- ☐ *Match to the ABC chart.*
- ☐ *Use a piece of yarn tied between chairs with letters clipped with clothespins on the line. Have them crab walk to collect the letters as you call them out or as they say what they are.*
- ☐ *Sort letter cards by letter shapes. This will be in the pre-K letter category, but here is an example. Curved line letters: C, O, U, S; Stick letters (could use straight sticks to make them): A, E, F, H, I, K, L, M, N, T, V, W, X, Y, Z; Combo of curves and sticks: B, D, G, J, P, Q, R*

hat sat cat

RHYMING WORDS:

"Remember that words that rhyme sound the same at the end, like cat, hat, bat.

"I will say two words and if they rhyme, you give me a thumbs up. If they do not rhyme, you give me a thumbs down.

"Cat-hog, man-tan, cake-rake, junk-spin, map-zip, jug-jig

Race to Space Rhyme Time: Look at the rockets below and mark out the picture that does not rhyme.

Race to Space

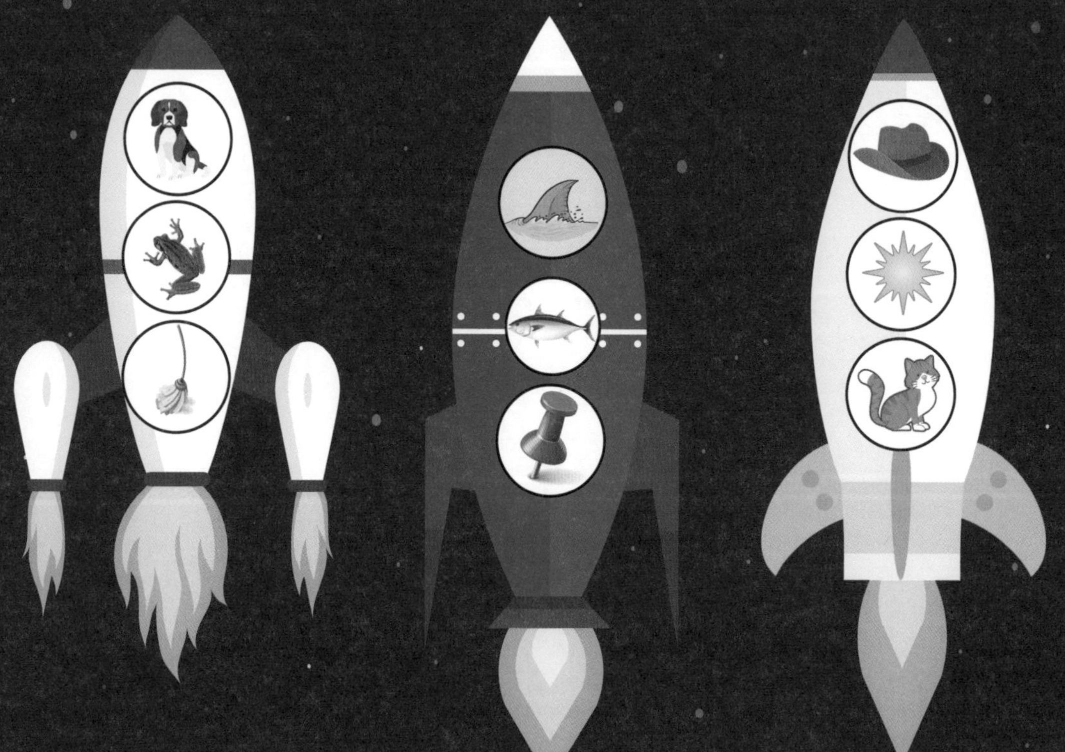

Name

Match the capital and lowercase letters by drawing a line between the two letters.

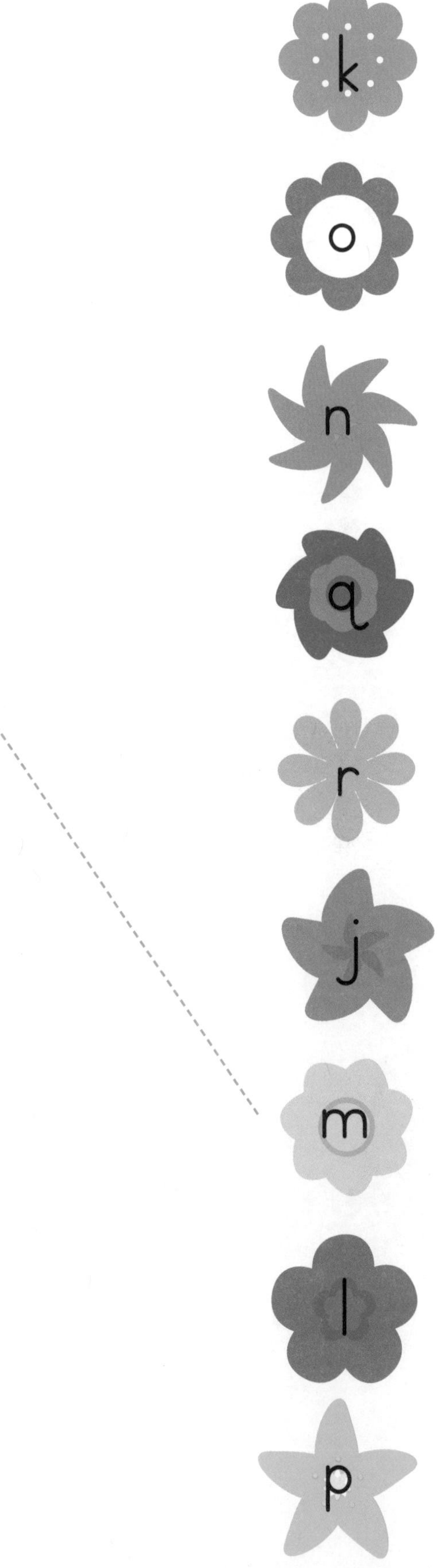

LESSON 29
Day 3

LIFE SKILLS:

"Sometimes we need to be more understanding of others. We can do this by responding with kindness even when others are not. We might not know what just happened and why the other person is responding in an unkind way, but we can show them kindness in spite of their attitude. Remember, statements tell something, but questions ask something.

"Look at the picture below. I will ask questions for you to answer.

"How many train cars do you see? (not counting the engine)

"What farm animals are on the train?

"Now you make a statement about the picture.

BIBLE:

Read Exodus 20:1–17 about what God told Moses.

"Here are the Ten Commandments. Echo read them, then add motions to help you remember them.

Review with Ten Commandments chart from Lesson 28 on page 311.

RHYME TIME:

"Let's read this week's poem again.

Read "Over Field and Meadow" on page 321.

Find a real daisy or look one up and have them sketch their own using the original as a guide.

LESSON 29
Day 3

ABC'S AND MORE:

Review all letters.

Chant the ABC chart.

Sing the ABC song.

Match uppercase and lowercase letters on the next page.

PICK ONE of the activities using the ABC cards:

- ☐ *Hop to the letter called out.*
- ☐ *Match to the ABC chart.*
- ☐ *Use a piece of yarn tied between chairs with letters clipped with clothespins on the line. Have them crab walk to collect the letters as you call them out or as they say what they are.*
- ☐ *Sort letter cards by letter shapes. This will be in the pre-K letter category, but here is an example. Curved line letters: C, O, U, S; Stick letters (could use straight sticks to make them): A, E, F, H, I, K, L, M, N, T, V, W, X, Y, Z; Combo of curves and sticks: B, D, G, J, P, Q, R*

RHYMING WORDS:

"Remember that words that rhyme sound the same at the end, like cat, hat, bat.

"I will say two words and if they rhyme, you give me a thumbs up. If they do not rhyme, you give me a thumbs down.

cake - rake, map - zip

Now, see if you can circle either thumbs up or thumbs down on the examples below. Thumbs up if they rhyme. Thumbs down if they don't rhyme.

"Cat-hog, man-tan, cake-rake, junk-spin, map-zip, jug-jig

If the two pictures in the box rhyme, circle the thumbs up. If not, circle the thumbs down.

Lesson 29
Day 3

Name

Match the capital and lowercase letters by drawing a line between the two letters.

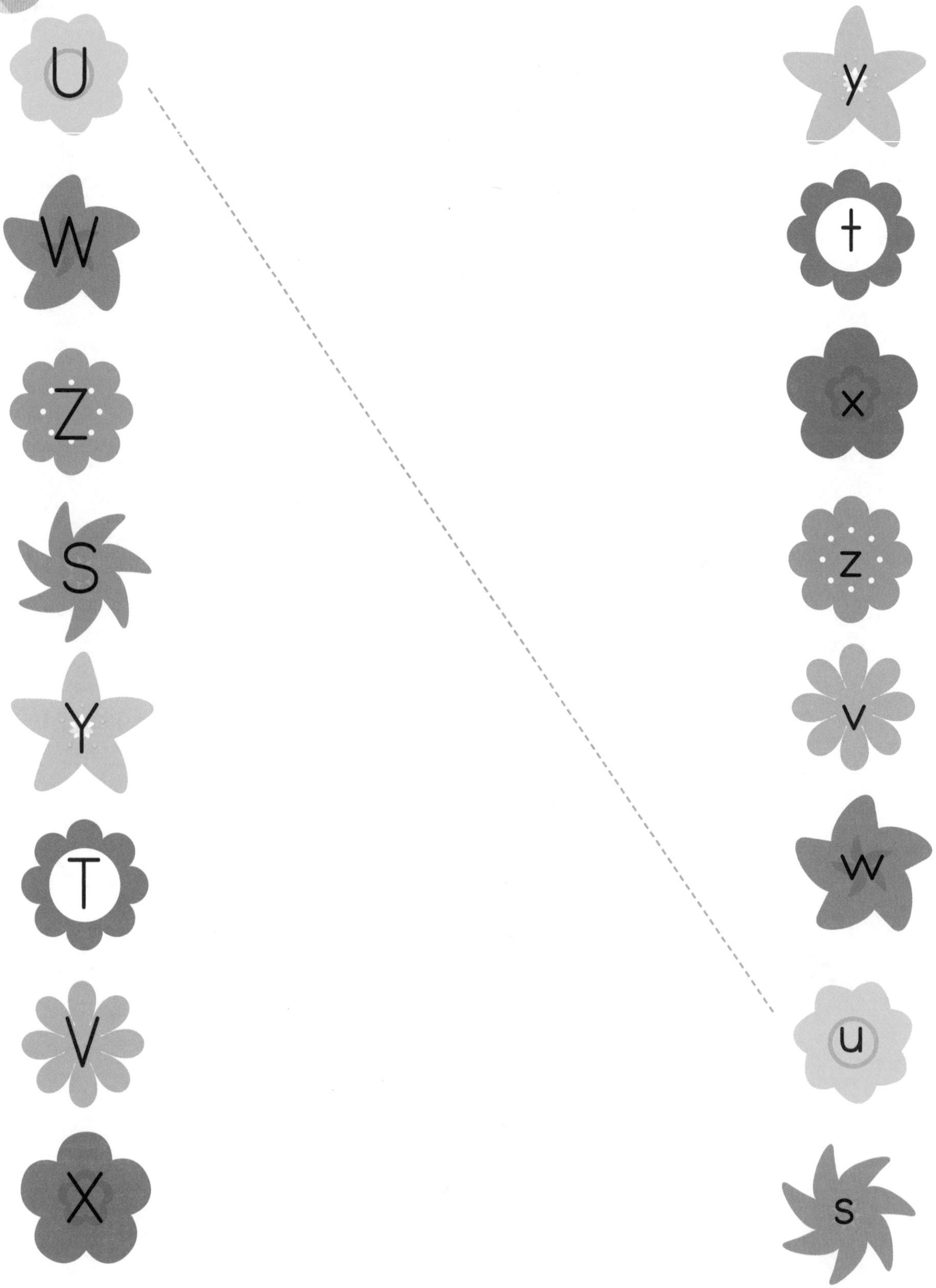

U

W

Z

S

Y

T

V

X

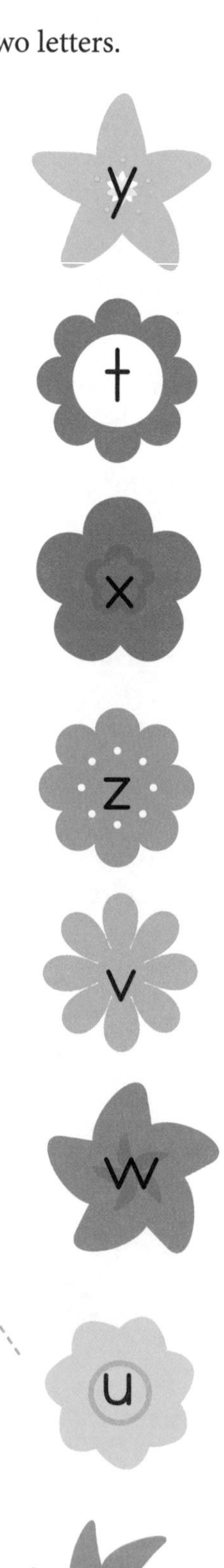

LESSON 30
Prep Page

Supply List

- ☐ Electronic games (optional) (day 3, life skills)
- ☐ Ball (small for tossing) (day 2, life skills)
- ☐ Blindfold (day 1, life skills)
- ☐ Book (day 1, life skills)

Look Ahead

Plan for labeling 5 pieces of clothing for next week. See prep page Lesson 31.

Objectives

Beginning sounds and ABC chart

Skills/Concepts: communication, electronic manners

Memory Verse

Proverbs 11:17

Those who are kind benefit themselves, but the cruel bring ruin on themselves

Extended Activities

Pretend to be a reporter. Watch a reporter. Video the student's interview or report.

LESSON 30
Day 1

LIFE SKILLS:

"Communication is saying something so that another person can understand it. Communication is not only words and their meaning but your facial expressions, body position, and how these make the listener feel. Communication is vital. Vital means necessary. Effective communication is vital, or necessary, in our lives. We have to use complete sentences in order to be understood correctly. Let's try this activity.

Place a book on the floor. Blindfold them in a space open enough for them to move. Do not give additional instructions.

"I will blindfold you, and you can only do what I say with my voice.

Wait on them to do each task before giving the next one. The following uses incomplete sentences on purpose. This is not a typo. Please say the phrases as listed.

"Two steps forward. Move circle. Touch your nose. Turn around and touch the ground.

Remove blindfold.

"Now, did you pick up the book off of the floor? (*Child: No*)

Probably confused.

"Hmmm . . . did I communicate what I wanted you to do? No, I left out important or vital information, didn't I? I told you to touch the ground, but I never said to get the book off of the floor, did I? I also did not use complete sentences. I said, "Move circle," but that didn't tell you much did it?

"Even saying two steps forward was leaving out words. So vital information was lost. This means I did not communicate well.

"Here are some picture clues that will help you to be a good communicator.

Review the Good Communicator sheet on the following page.

BIBLE:

"Our memory verse speaks about kindness. In Proverbs 11:17 it says:

Echo read the verse. Add motions.

Those who are kind 

benefit themselves,

but the cruel 

bring ruin on themselves.

"If we are kind, we will gain a good reputation. If we are cruel, we have ruined our character.

"There is a story in the Bible about a woman who received kindness because she was kind. We find this story in the Book of Ruth (1–4).

Name

Good Communicator

Keep your eyes focused on the person speaking.

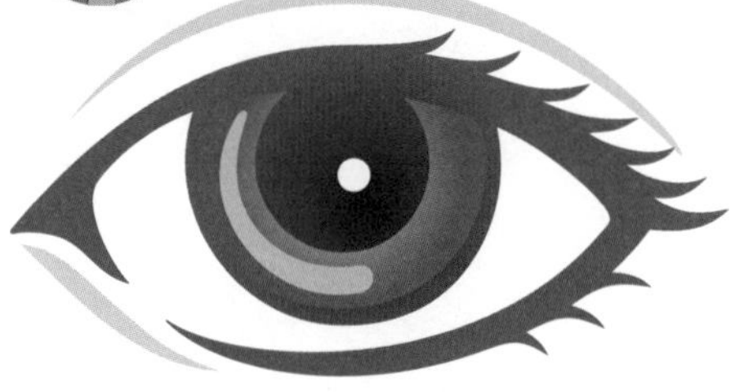

Listening Ears

Listening means you are taking in what the other person is saying and understanding their feelings.

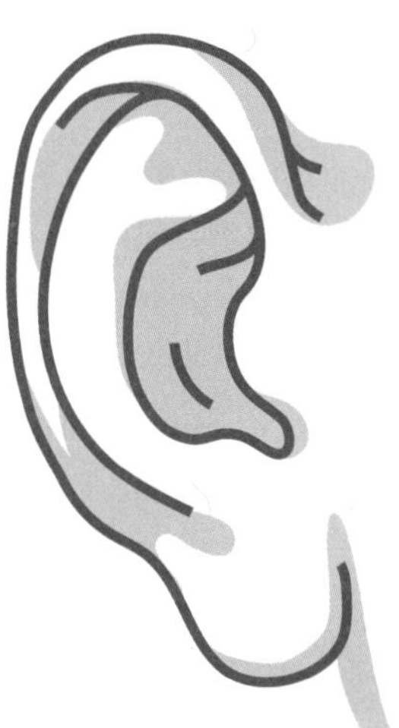

Eyes Focused

Keep your eyes focused on the person speaking.

Voice and Volume

I have to think about my tone of voice and my volume level. Is it the right tone and volume for where I am?

Hearts of Kindness

Respond to others in a respectful way even when I disagree.

Exploring Minds

Explore the story more by listening to the full story and gather the details.

Patiently Waiting

Patiently listening and understanding when someone is speaking. Not interrupting them.

LESSON 30
Day 1

"Naomi, an Israelite, lived in Moab with her husband Elimelech and their two sons.
After Elimelech's death, the sons both married Moabite women. Tragically, Naomi's sons died and she decided to return to Israel. When Naomi said goodbye to her daughters-in-law, one of them, Ruth, said she would go with Naomi, saying, "I have decided to go with you. Your people and your God will be mine too and when I die, I wish to be buried alongside you."
So together the two women went to Bethlehem and settled there.

"At harvest time, Ruth went gleaning in the fields. One day Boaz, the landowner, asked his servants, "Who is that woman?"
"Ruth, who lives with Naomi."
Boaz approached her and said, "Ruth! Stay by my servants and glean all the grain you like."
"Why are you being so kind to me?" she asked.
"I've heard how good you are to my relative Naomi." Ruth blushed and went on gleaning.

"That evening Naomi was delighted when Ruth told her about Boaz. She knew he would make Ruth a good husband. Later, Boaz married Ruth. (from the *Illustrated Family Bible Stories*, 66)

"You see, in this time in the Bible, the Israelite law stopped landowners from harvesting all of their fields. They were to leave the edges unharvested so foreigners, orphans, widows, and poor people would be able to gather leftover grain. There were many men who were not good and kind, and would not leave anything unharvested for these people. Boaz was one of the few who left part of his fields unharvested.

"Did you know Jesus is a descendant of Ruth and Boaz?

"Ruth was more than just a daughter-in-law. Ruth became Naomi's friend as well. Just like Jesus is our friend.

LESSON 30
Day 1

ABC'S AND MORE:

Chant the ABC chart.

Sing the ABC song.

Beginning Sounds: Please preview the ABC chart sounds video for instructions on how to correctly use and implement sounds with the ABC chart.

"I will say some words and you tell me what sound you hear at the beginning, or first.

"Here is an example. If I say ffffrog, the first sound I say is ffff. Did you hear that sound?

"Say the sounds you hear for these words:
Sand /s/
Can /c/
Man /m/
Fan /f/
Pan /p/
Lizards /l/

"Great job hearing the sounds!

RHYME TIME:

"Let's read our poem this week, "Lizards."

Say the highlighted words and have them tell you the sound they hear at the beginning of the words.

Lizards

Over in the meadow by the old mossy gate,
lived an old mother lizard and her little lizards eight.
"Bask," said the mother, "We bask," said the eight,
so they basked in the sun by the old mossy gate.

Over in the meadow by the old mossy gate,
basked an old mother lizard and her little lizards eight.
"Run," said the mother, "We run," said the eight,
so they ran to their homes from the old mossy gate.

LESSON 30
Day 2

LIFE SKILLS:

Review your communication chart briefly, hitting the main points for communication using the graphics. Play the following games to help hit home the points of communication:

Eyes Focused: (Toss ball as you sing.)

"I will toss this ball around, and your job is to keep your eyes on the ball at all times. Not on me. I will sing "Happy Birthday to You" while I toss the ball around. Let's see what great focus you have.

Tell a nursery rhyme and see if they can tell you what it was (Hey Diddle Diddle, Hickory Dickory Dock, etc.)

Meet and Greet:

"When meeting someone for the first time, there is a good way to greet them. You can shake their hand and say, "Hello, nice to meet you, my name is ____," and then wait for them to tell you their name. Let's practice this now.

BIBLE:

"Our memory verse speaks about kindness. In Proverbs 11:17 it says: "Those who are kind benefit themselves, but the cruel bring ruin on themselves." If we are kind, we will gain a good reputation. If we are cruel, we have ruined our character.

Review the memory verse on page 332.

"In our next story, we have a woman in the Bible named Esther. Esther was a queen, but she was also kind. There was a man who was cruel though. Let's read what happened in Esther 1–10.

"Esther was a queen and the wife of King Xerxes — we will call him King X. Esther's cousin, Mordecai, heard two men planning to kill King X. Mordecai told Esther and she told King X. King X sentenced the men to death. Later, a man under King X, named Haman, wanted everyone to bow down and worship him instead of God. Mordecai was a Jew and would only worship God, so he refused to bow down to Haman. This made Haman angry and he got King X to order the death of Mordecai and all Jewish people. Mordecai went to Esther again, begging her to speak to King X. Queen Esther went to King X and he listened to Esther. He got rid of Haman, and placed Mordecai as a leader in his kingdom.

"Without the help of Queen Esther, the Jewish people would have been killed. Queen Esther helped save God's people. Perhaps Esther wore fancy jewelry when she went to plead with King Xerxes. She would have needed to be in her best clothing and jewelry to distract the king, because to come to speak to him without his permission was breaking a law and she could have been killed. Instead, Esther had God on her side, and the king found favor with Esther.

LESSON 30
Day 2

RHYME TIME:

"Let's read our poem again this week.

Lizards

Over in the meadow by the old mossy gate,
lived an old mother lizard and her little
lizards eight.
"Bask," said the mother, "We bask," said the
eight,
so they basked in the sun by the old mossy
gate.

Over in the meadow by the old mossy gate,
basked an old mother lizard and her little
lizards eight.
"Run," said the mother, "We run," said the
eight,
so they ran to their homes from the old
mossy gate.

"The mother lizard told her little lizards to "bask." The word bask means to lie or lounge. So they basked or lounged or laid in the sun. I bet that felt good.

ABC'S AND MORE:

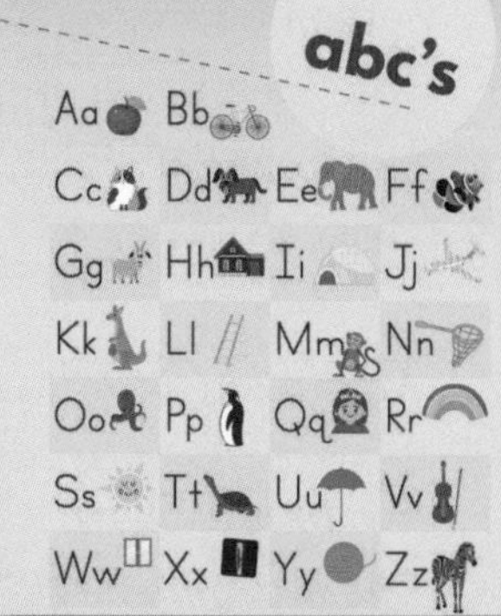

Chant the ABC chart.

Sing the ABC song.

Beginning Sounds

"I will say some words and you tell me what sound you hear at the beginning, or first.

"Here is an example. If I say sssun, the first sound I say is /s/. Did you hear that sound?

"Say the sounds you hear for these words:
cat /c/
mat /m/
ocean /o/
house /h/
llama /l/
goose /g/

"Great job hearing the sounds!

LESSON 30
Day 3

LIFE SKILLS:

"Sometimes it is difficult to wait and let someone else talk. We have to give our attention for the time they are speaking. This can be difficult, but if we wait, we are showing the other person how much we value what they have to say.

Meet and Greet: Practice meet and greet

Electronics Down: Practice electronics communication manners as indicated below.

(If your child does not play electronics, you may skip this.)

"Another important communication skill that falls in line with manners has to do with our electronic toys, like a cell phone or tablet. When you are playing on a cell phone, tablet, or video game and someone enters the room or begins speaking to you, you should stop your game and give your attention to the speaker.

"If you are worried about messing up your game, most games will allow you to continue after a time, right where you ended. Just press the button to get you home or make the electronic go into sleep mode. Let's practice this now.

Practice this for a few weeks with gentle reminders.

BIBLE:

Review the memory verse on page 332.

"The Apostle Paul was known for witnessing and encouraging Christians. He made friends with a couple, who were like missionaries, whose names were Aquila and Priscilla. Priscilla was a great help to Paul's ministry as well as to her husband in his ministry. We know that she worked alongside them both to witness and tell others about Christ.

Read the story in Acts 18:1–3.

"The role Aquila and Priscilla played in furthering the Kingdom of God and continuing to disciple others was amazing. They faced many who opposed them, and they did not become discouraged or give up. We know that in this time it was rare for women to be recognized, but we know that Priscilla played an important role because she is mentioned here. This is an example of how we can all be the hands and feet of Jesus and be disciples. We are all called to disciple others.

"Just as Paul found friendship in Aquila and Priscilla, we have a friend in Jesus.

RHYME TIME:

"Let's read our poem again.

Read "Lizards" on the next page.

Say the highlighted words in the poem and have them tell you the sound they hear.

"The lizards basked by a mossy gate. Mossy means covered in moss. Moss is a small, flowerless green plant that lacks true roots. It grows in damp areas. Look on the bridge, do you see moss?

Name

Lizards

Over in the meadow by the old mossy gate,
lived an old mother lizard and her little lizards eight.
"Bask," said the mother, "We bask," said the eight,
so they basked in the sun by the old mossy gate.

Over in the meadow by the old mossy gate,
basked an old mother lizard and her little lizards eight.
"Run," said the mother, "We run," said the eight,
so they ran to their homes from the old mossy gate.

LESSON 30
Day 3

ABC'S AND MORE:

Chant the ABC chart.

Sing the ABC song.

Beginning Sounds: Please preview the ABC chart sounds video for instructions on how to correctly use and implement sounds with the ABC chart.

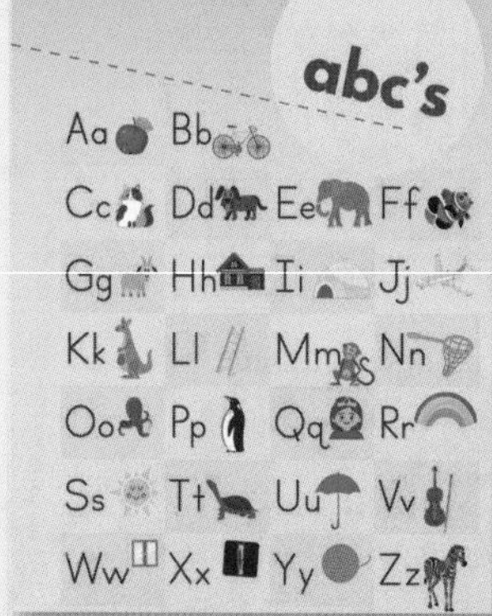

"I will say some words and you tell me what sound you hear at the beginning, or first.

"Here is an example. If I say yarn, the first sound I say is /y/. Did you hear that sound?

Say the sounds you hear for these words:

"Say the sounds you hear for these words:
violin /v/
dog /d/
zoo /z/
nail /n/
queen /q/
jam /j/

"Great job hearing the sounds!

LESSON 31
Prep Page

Supply List

- ☐ Deck of cards (Go Fish) (day 2, life skills)
- ☐ Board game(s) (day 1, life skills)
- ☐ 5 pieces of clothing (shirt, pants, socks, hat) labeled with kindness, compassion, humility, patience, and gentleness (day 2, Bible)
- ☐ Ball (day 1, Rhyme Time)
- ☐ Yarn/rope (day 1, Rhyme Time)
- ☐ Cardstock or small poster board (daily, Bible)

Look Ahead

Next week you will need a puzzle with not too many or few pieces.

Objectives

Beginning sounds and ABC chart

Skills/Concepts: social skills – good sport, taking turns

Memory Verse

Ephesians 4:32

Be kind and compassionate to one another, forgiving each other, just as in Christ, God forgave you.

Extended Activities

Ball toss — Toss a ball through a hula-hoop, trash can, or bucket.

LESSON 31
Day 1

LIFE SKILLS:

"We are going to play different games this week and practice being a good sport. Being a good sport means that we are kind even when we lose. We realize that it is a game and it is for fun. We do not become angry and throw things or stomp away if we are losing. We are also kind to the person who does win, and we can congratulate them.

Practice this by playing games. Choose a game to play like Horse (basketball), soccer, board game, etc.

"It is also important to take turns. We can practice taking turns getting a drink at a water fountain or even playing a game. We can even practice taking turns pushing buttons at the elevator. There are a lot of ways we can practice taking turns. Let's play Go Fish so we can practice taking turns.

(If you have a family board game, this is a great way to exhibit more patience when playing with more than two players. Games like Sorry®, Trouble®, Chutes and Ladders®, etc.)

BIBLE:

"In Ephesians 4:32 it says:

Echo read the verse. Add motions.

Be kind  and compassionate

to one another, forgiving each other,

just as in Christ 

God forgave you.

The Bible mentions the word *kind* a lot. It must be important to be in there so many times. We have discussed kindness before, and it means to be caring or loving toward others. We are to show kindness toward others. Think of the story of the Good Samaritan.

LESSON 31
Day 1

Read the story from Luke 10:25–37.

"The Good Samaritan showed kindness by loving a neighbor. When we use the word "neighbor" here, it doesn't mean our actual neighbor next door, but any others. We will make a Kindness Board. This will be a way for you to show ways you can be kind to others.

Use cardstock or small poster board to help them add a scene of kindness each day this week.

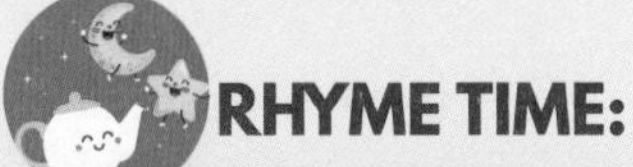

RHYME TIME:

"Let's read our poem this week, "To and Fro the Ball."

Use a ball tied to yarn to have it swing like a pendulum. Use the same or another ball to spin on the ground.

To and Fro the Ball

To and fro the ball is swinging,
like the church bell freely ringing.
Now it's turning round and round,
freely turning on the ground.

LESSON 31
Day 1

ABC'S AND MORE:

Chant the ABC chart.

Sing the ABC song.

Chant sounds of the ABC chart.

Please review the ABC chart sounds video for instructions on how to correctly use and implement sounds with the ABC chart.

Beginning Sounds:

Lay out the ABC cards.

❝ I will say a word and you find the letter it begins with.

❝ I will say some words and you tell me what sound you hear at the beginning, or first.

❝ Jet

Let them get the Jj jet card.

❝ Now, jet begins with what letter? *(J)*

❝ Listen to this word — jam. Does this word also begin with a j? *(yes)*

❝ Turtle

Let them get the Tt turtle card.

❝ What letter does turtle begin with? *(T)*

❝ Listen to this word — sand. Does sand also begin with a T? *(no)*

❝ Cat

Let them get the Cc cat card.

❝ What letter does cat begin with? *(C)*

❝ Listen to this word — canopy. Does canopy begin like cat? *(yes)*

❝ So it begins with a C too!

❝ Let's try one more. Rainbow

Let them get the Rr rainbow card.

❝ What letter does rainbow begin with? *(R)*

❝ Listen to this word — trampoline. Does trampoline start with an R like rainbow? *(no)*

❝ Do you know what letter trampoline begins with?

(See if they can answer T; if not, it's okay. You can prompt them, to see if they hear the sound.)

LESSON 31
Day 2

LIFE SKILLS:

"Do you remember what it means to be a good sport?

Help them recall the ways to be a good sport.

Practice being a good sport by playing games like Horse (basketball), soccer, board games, etc.

Taking Turns:

"It is also important to take turns. Let's play Go Fish so we can practice taking turns.

Practice using family board games. You can also have them take turns riding a bike or swinging on a swing.

BIBLE:

Review memory verse on page 342.

Read Colossians 3:1–17.

"Here, the Apostle Paul is telling the church, which includes you and me, how we are to live as we are made new in Christ. He tells them in verse 12: "Therefore, as God's chosen people, holy and dearly loved, clothe yourselves with compassion, kindness, humility, gentleness and patience."

**Put the clothing that is labeled on the child. As you put them on tell them what trait they are putting on.*

"Verse 12 says to "clothe" ourselves, but it doesn't mean to actually do what we have done and put on clothing. What is something clothing does? *(Covers us.)* By clothing ourselves with these traits, we are covering ourselves with compassion, kindness, gentleness, humility,

and patience. So, when we speak, we should use words that are kind, compassionate, gentle, humble, and patient. When we act, we should act out of a kind and compassionate heart. This is how God wants us to live. We will struggle, but with His help, we can do it!

"Add to your Kindness Board ways that you can be kind and compassionate.

RHYME TIME:

"Let's read our poem for this week again.

To and Fro the Ball

To and fro the ball is swinging,
like the church bell freely ringing.
Now it's turning round and round,
freely turning on the ground.

Use a ball tied to yarn to have it swing like a pendulum. Use the same or another ball to spin on the ground.

LESSON 31
Day 2

ABC'S AND MORE:

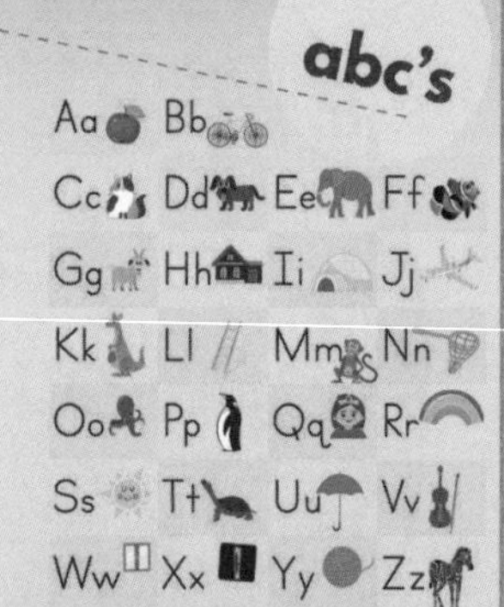

Chant the ABC chart.

Sing the ABC song.

Chant sounds of the ABC chart.

Beginning Sounds:

Lay out the ABC cards.

“I will say a word and you find the letter it begins with.

“Apple

Let them get the Aa apple card.

“Now, apple begins with what letter? *(A)*

“Listen to this word — ax. Does this word also begin with an A? *(yes)*

“Monkey

Let them get the Mm monkey card.

“What letter does monkey begin with? *(M)*

“Listen to this word — mail. Does mail also begin with a M? *(yes)*

“So, monkey and mail begin with an M.

“Penguin

Let them get the Pp penguin card.

“What letter does penguin begin with? *(P)*

“Listen to this word — drum. Does drum begin like penguin? *(no)*

“Let's try one more. Octopus

Let them get the Oo octopus card.

“What letter does octopus begin with? *(O)*

“If octopus begins with an O, what does ostrich begin with? *(O)*

LESSON 31
Day 3

LIFE SKILLS:

> "What are ways you can be a good sport?

Help them recall the ways to be a good sport.

Practice being a good sport by playing games like Horse (basketball), soccer, board games, etc.

Taking Turns:

> "It is also important to take turns. Let's play Go Fish again to practice taking turns.

Continue to practice taking turns through games and activities.

Add to My Picture: Make artwork by taking turns. Each person adds one thing at a time. So, if you draw a circle, the next person might draw eyes. Then, the other person could draw a nose or another hole to make a bowling ball instead of a head. Continue drawing until you have a complete masterpiece! You cannot become upset over how the other person changes the drawing. Be creative and have fun!

BIBLE:

Review memory verse on page 342.

Read Acts 28:1–10.

> "Here we have a story of the islanders of Malta being kind to the Apostle Paul. Let's re-read it and see what things they did to help Paul and show him compassion and kindness.

(built a fire, welcomed them, chief official showed hospitality, honored them, gave them supplies they needed)

> "What are some ways you can show compassion and kindness to others like the islanders of Malta showed compassion and kindness to Paul? Draw those on your Kindness Board.

RHYME TIME:

> "Let's read this week's poem.

To and Fro the Ball

To and fro the ball is swinging,
like the church bell freely ringing.
Now it's turning round and round,
freely turning on the ground.

Use a ball tied to yarn to have it swing like a pendulum. Use the same or another ball to spin on the ground.

LESSON 31
Day 3

ABC'S AND MORE:

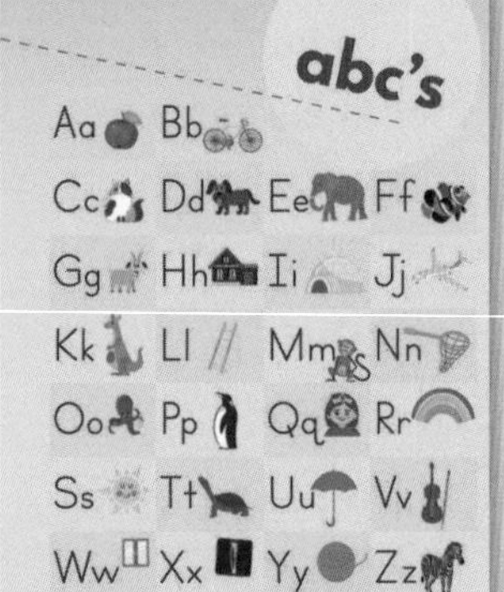

Chant the ABC chart.

Sing the ABC song.

Chant sounds of the ABC chart.

Beginning Sounds:

Lay out the ABC cards.

“I will say a word and you find the letter it begins with.

“Dog

Let them get the Dd dog card.

“Now, dog begins with what letter? *(D)*

“Listen to this word — alligator. Does this word also begin with a D? *(no)*

“Ladder

Let them get the Ll ladder card.

“What letter does ladder begin with? *(L)*

“Listen to this word — llama. Does this word also begin with a L? *(yes)*

“So ladder and llama begin with an L.

“Igloo

Let them get the Ii igloo card.

“What letter does igloo begin with? *(I)*

“Listen to this word — net. Does this word begin like igloo? *(no)*

“Let's try one more. Window

Let them get the Ww window card.

“What letter does window begin with? *(W)*

“If window begins with a W, what does wagon begin with? *(W)*

Practice writing the letters A–Z.

LESSON 32
Prep Page

Supply List

- ☐ Puzzle (kids) (day 2, life skills)
- ☐ Blank paper to draw on (day 2, Bible)
- ☐ Large shirt (day 3, life skills)
- ☐ Broom (day 3, life skills)
- ☐ Dusting supplies (day 3, life skills)
- ☐ Blocks on table (day 1, Bible)
- ☐ Blank paper to draw on (day 3, Bible)

Look Ahead

You will be grocery shopping during Week 33.

There is a special project in Week 34 — either a Fellowship Dinner or alternate — see lesson, Day 1.

Objectives

Beginning sounds and ABC chart

Skills/Concepts: cooperation – working together & communicating

Memory Verse

1 Corinthians 13:4–8

Love is patient, love is kind. It does not envy, it does not boast, it is not proud. It does not dishonor others, it is not self-seeking, it is not easily angered, it keeps no record of wrongs. Love does not delight in evil but rejoices with the truth. It always protects, always trusts, always hopes, always perseveres.
Love never fails…

Extended Activities

Make a stained-glass window. Draw an outline of a window (rectangular or arched) and then fold the paper so you only cut out the middle part where the glass of the window would be. Use torn strips of colored tissue paper glued in overlapping strips to make the stained-glass part of the window.

LESSON 32
Day 1

LIFE SKILLS:

"This week we will practice communicating while working together! This skill is called cooperation. When we cooperate with others, we use our communication skills, as well as consider the other person's ideas and combine them with ours. We want to be a cooperative person, which means we work with others to complete a task.

Two or more players: Set up a table with the blocks on it. It would be good if you built a sample of what they are to make for them to copy, or draw a picture. If you have enough kids to make a team, that would even be better for them to compete.

Team Building: We will use the blocks to make a house (or if your child is good at this, make something more difficult, such as a basic airplane or bird). We each get to add one piece at a time. We can communicate to help each other out, but everyone has to agree on how (or even what) to make it. Only one person can be at the table at a time and no one can yell at them once they are at the table. You can only move one block on or off what you are building at a time. (This is a relay building project.)

Once completed ask:

"Was this fun?
What was difficult?
How could you make it better?
Were you good at working with someone else and cooperating to build something?

BIBLE:

"Do you know what the greatest thing we can have is? LOVE. In 1 Corinthians chapter 13 it talks about love and what that means. Let's read it now.

Read 1 Corinthians chapter 13 from your Bible.

"Notice verse 13 says the greatest of these is love. Why do you think love is so important?

Read 1 Corinthians 13:4–8.

There is a helpful chart located on the following page for them to memorize the basics of 1 Cor. 13:4-8. Save for future lessons.

"Love does a lot of things! Love is amazing. Let's echo-read those verses as we will memorize them over the next two weeks.

Echo read the hearts on the next page.

Name

1 Corinthians 13:4–8

Love is patient

1. love willingly waits

Love is kind

2. we just talked about kindness in our last lesson

Love does not envy

3. it does not want what others have

Love does not boast

4. it is humble

Love is not proud

5. it does not feel superior or better than others

Love does not dishonor others

6. love shows respect

Love is not self-seeking

7. love cares about the needs of others first

Love is not easily angered

8. it shows self-control

Love does not keep a record of wrongs

9. love forgives

Love does not delight in evil

10. love does not get joy from failings of others and it does not take part in sin

Love rejoices in truth

11. love upholds what is true and pure

Love protects

12. love will guard you

Love trusts

13. love will believe you

Love hopes

14. love will have faith that there is something better

Love perseveres

15. love never quits

Love never fails

16. Wow . . . never gives up, never gives in

LESSON 32
Day 1

RHYME TIME:

"Let's read our poem this week, "The Church Door and Window."

Read "The Church Door and Window" on the next page.

If you live near a church with bells, go visit during the ringing of the bells.

"What sound do you hear at the beginning of Bim, bam, baum? *(B)*

"What letter makes that sound? *(B)*

ABC'S AND MORE:

Chant the ABC chart.

Sing the ABC song.

Chant sounds for the ABC chart.

"The last few weeks we have worked on hearing sounds at the beginning of words. Now you will find the letter that matches the beginning sounds of the pictures.

Complete matching beginning sound/picture activity below.

Match the letter to the beginning sound of each picture.

E

G

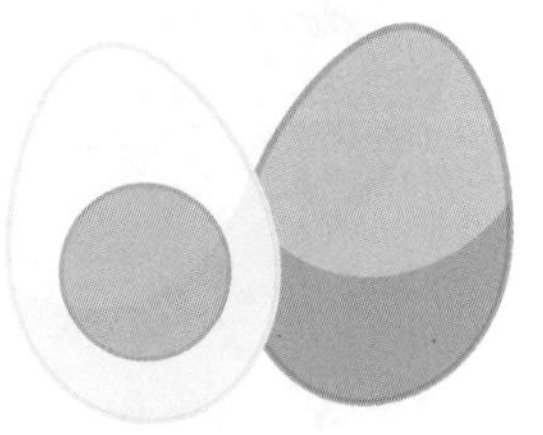

J

B

The Church Door and Window

The light within the window gleams,
all through the little church it streams.
Behold the door is open now,
that all within the church may go,
and every one who enters there,
to be attentive must prepare.
Now, hearken! While the organ's tone,
through solemn aisles is born along,
Lo, la, la!
And the bell upon the tower,
calls in lovely tones the hour,
Bim, bam, baum!
The tuneful bell, the organ's swell,
Lo, lo, la, la!
Must every heart with rapture thrill,
Bim, bam, baum!

LESSON 32
Day 2

LIFE SKILLS:

"Do you remember what it means to cooperate with others? *(Working together.)* Yes, when we cooperate with others, we use our communication skills and work with others to complete a task.

Pieces of the puzzle game: Two or more players: Set up a table with the puzzle box and all of the pieces. Each player can connect one piece at a time — only one player at the table at a time. You might come up with a strategy for one person to sort out the straight/side pieces, or corners, etc.

After doing it this way, take it apart, and try it with all players working together at the same table at the same time.

"Which way was easiest — working alone and taking turns or working together at one time?

Review: Help them if they have forgotten.

"Do you remember your phone number or address?

BIBLE:

"Why do you think love is so important? How can you show someone love?

Read 1 Corinthians 13:4-8 and help them memorize the hearts on the chart.

"Love does a lot of things doesn't it? Can you remember any of the things about love?

Read the 1 Corinthians 13:4–8 chart, and then have the student draw a picture or act out ways of how they can show others the first four on the list.

RHYME TIME:

"Let's read our poem this week again.

Read "The Church Door and Window" on page 353.

"What sound do you hear at the beginning of lo, la, la? *(L)*

"Which letter makes that sound? *(L)*

"Our poem begins with "The light within the window gleams." What do you think gleams means? Gleams means that the light inside the window is glowing or shining. So, if a water droplet on a leaf is gleaming, it means it is shining.

LESSON 32
Day 2

ABC'S AND MORE:

Chant the ABC chart.

Sing the ABC song.

Chant sounds of the ABC chart.

Beginning Sounds:

"Find the letter that matches the beginning sound of the pictures.

Complete matching beginning sound/picture activity below.

Match the letter to the beginning sound of each picture.

C 

M 

R 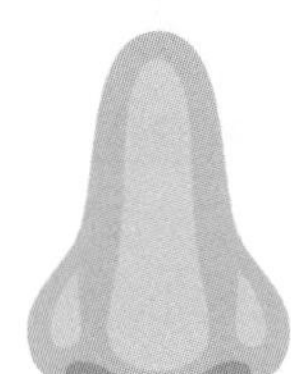

N 

I 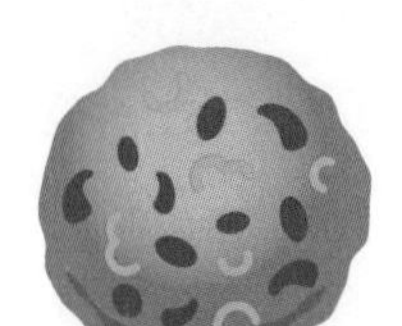

T 

LESSON 32
Day 3

LIFE SKILLS:

"How can you cooperate with others?

Work together, communicate

"We will both get inside this shirt.

Or you can choose two children to be inside a shirt.

"We will try to do some chores around the house, like sweeping and dusting, while we are sharing a shirt. If we do not work together, or cooperate, then we will not get done very quickly or do a good job. If we can communicate and work together, then we can get this done quickly!

BIBLE:

"How have others shown love to you? How do you know when someone loves you?
Our actions tell others how we feel about them, just like how others treat you lets you know how they feel about you! God loved you so much that He gave His only Son to die on a Cross for your sins. He wanted to give you the gift of eternal life. That is amazing love.

Read 1 Corinthians 13:4-8 and help them memorize the hearts on the chart. Have the student draw a picture or act out ways of how they can show others 5–7 on the list.

RHYME TIME:

"Let's read our poem again.

Read "The Church Door and Window" on page 353.

"What sound do you hear at the beginning of lo, la, la? *(L)*

"Which letter makes that sound? *(L)*

"There is a line in our poem that says, "Through solemn aisles is born along." This is talking about the organ's sound being spread throughout and down the aisles of the church. The word *solemn* here means quiet and formal. So here "through solemn aisles is born along" is telling us that the aisles of the church are quiet and formal.

LESSON 32
Day 3

ABC'S AND MORE:

Chant the ABC chart.

Sing the ABC song.

Chant sounds of the ABC chart.

Beginning Sounds:

"Find the letter that matches the beginning sound of the pictures below.

Complete matching beginning sound/picture activity below.

Match the letter to the beginning sound of each picture.

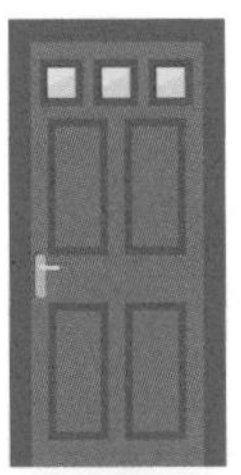

LESSON 33
Prep Page

Supply List

- ☐ Calculator
- ☐ Grocery list
- ☐ Money for groceries

Look Ahead

Look at Lesson 34, day 1, life skills to understand the fellowship dinner.

Look at Lesson 34, day 3, Bible to understand the art project.

Objectives

Ending sounds and ABC chart

Skills/Concepts: good stewards – staying on budget: grocery shopping, electricity, water, tithing

Memory Verse

1 Corinthians 13:4–8

Love is patient, love is kind. It does not envy, it does not boast, it is not proud. It does not dishonor others, it is not self-seeking, it is not easily angered, it keeps no record of wrongs. Love does not delight in evil but rejoices with the truth. It always protects, always trusts, always hopes, always perseveres.
Love never fails…

Extended Activities

Pretend store: Role play customer and cashier. Price items at 1, 2, or 3 cents.

LESSON 33
Day 1

LIFE SKILLS:

Good Stewards:

"You are going to go grocery shopping! We will need to get a calculator and stay on budget. A budget is a set amount of money we use to make a plan for our money. If we use our grocery budget on toys, then we will not have enough food. We have to make a plan. The Word of God has many examples for being a good steward.

Malachi 3:8–12; Matthew 25:14–30.

"A steward is a person who manages property or money. God blesses us and we should care for and manage what he has blessed us with. Stewardship goes beyond managing our money. It even means managing our time, so we have time to fellowship with God too!

Shopping: Give your child a list of a few items you need from the store and a set amount of money. Help them use a calculator for adding as they go to make sure they stay in budget. If they go over, help them decide what is needed most or what can wait. You might want to have them make one recipe and have them be in charge of those groceries.

BIBLE:

"Jesus loves us, and that helps us love others.

Read John 15:1–17.

"Do you know what a vine does for a branch of fruit? It carries the food and water it needs so the fruit can grow. This is what Jesus does for us. He is the vine, and He gives us what we need. He loves us so much. Love comes from a heart that is connected to Jesus, just as the branch of fruit is connected to a vine.

Read 1 Corinthians 13:4–8. Use the heart chart as we continue to memorize them this week.

Read the 1 Corinthians 13:4–8 chart from Lesson 32 again. Then have the student draw a picture or act out ways of how they can show others 8–10 on the list.

RHYME TIME:

"Let's read our poem this week, "The Child's World."

Read "The Child's World" on the next page.

"Did you hear any rhyming words? I will read the second stanza again.

The wonderful air . . .

"Tell me if you hear any words that rhyme.

Name

Lesson 33
Day 1

The Child's World

Great, wide, wonderful, beautiful world,
with the wonderful waters around you curled,
and the wonderful grass upon your breast,
world, you are grandly and beautifully dressed.

The wonderful air is over me,
and the wonderful wind is shaking the tree,
it walks on the water, and whirls the mills,
and talks to itself on the top of the hills.

Say, friendly earth, how far do you go,
with the wheat fields that nod and the rivers that flow,
with cities and garden and cliffs and isles,
and people upon you for thousands of miles.
Ah! You are so great, and I am so small,
I tremble to think of you, World, at all,
and yet when I said my prayers today,
a whisper within me seemed to say —

You are more than the earth, tho' you are such a dot.
You can love and think, and the world cannot.

LESSON 33
Day 1

ABC'S AND MORE:

Chant the ABC chart.

Sing the ABC song.

Chant sounds of the ABC chart.

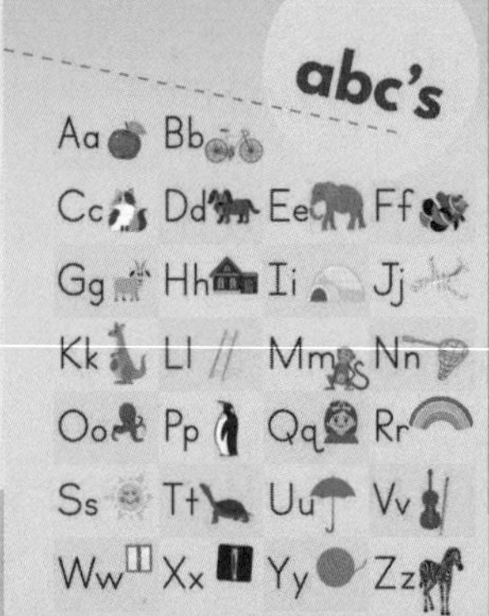

Ending Sounds:

"I will say some words and you tell me what sound you hear at the end or last.

"Here is an example. If I say mess, the last sound I say in messss is /s/.

If they do not get it, do these as examples and over-emphasize the ending sound. Then, make up words that have definite ending sounds for them to try on their own. Be careful to not choose words with the same beginning and ending sounds.

"Say the sounds you hear at the END for these words:
ham /m/
buzz /z/
mat /t/
clap /p/
cob /b/
dog /g/

Complete matching ending sound/picture activity below.

Circle the letter that makes the END sound for each of these images.

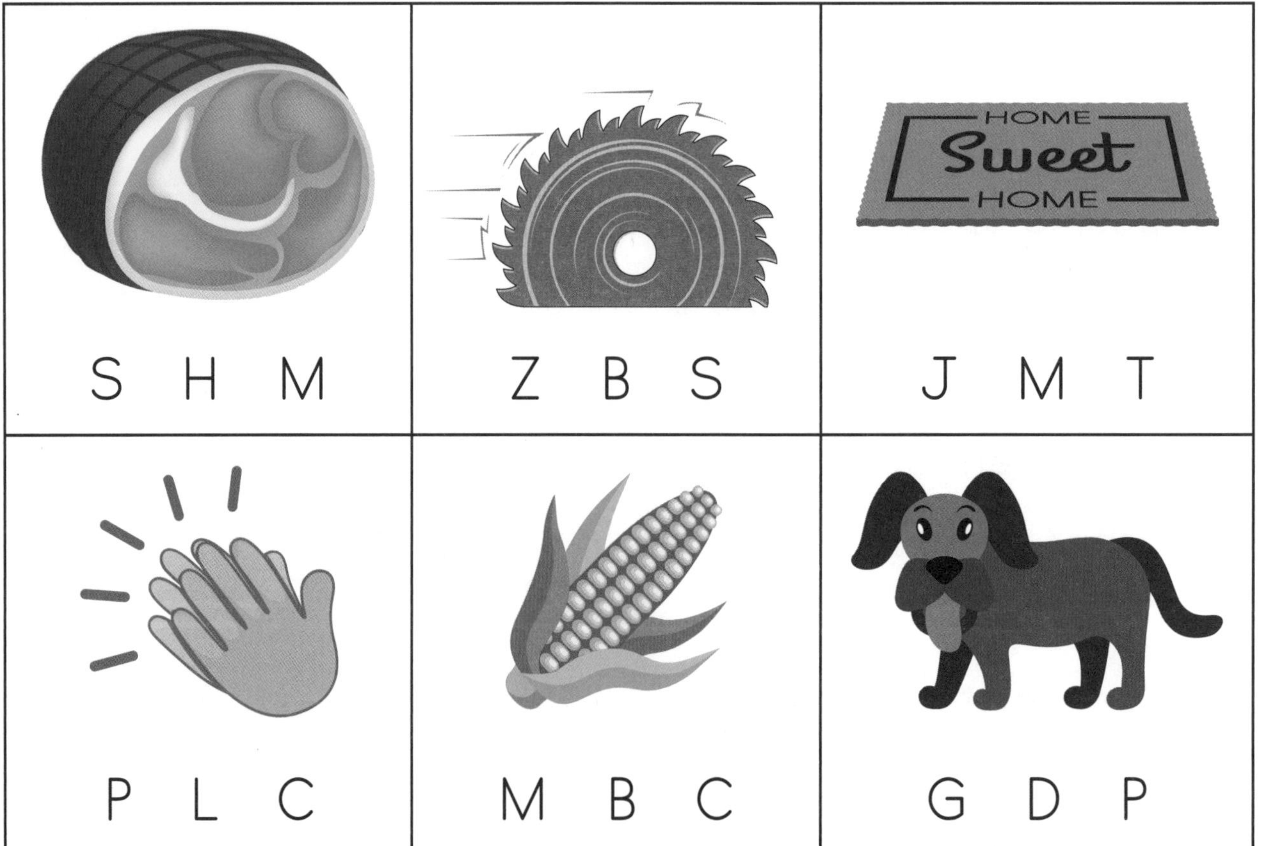

LESSON 33
Day 2

LIFE SKILLS:

Good Stewards:

"Remember, the Word of God has many examples for being a good steward. A steward is a person who manages property or money. God blesses us and we should care for and manage what He has blessed us with. One way for us to be good stewards is to be mindful of electricity and water. If we are brushing our teeth, we can turn off the water while we brush so we are not wasting water we do not need. If we are not using a light in a room, we should turn it off. Little things like this really add up and help our family's budget as well as help others. Some people do not have water like we do. We can show we are grateful by being mindful and not wasting water.

BIBLE:

"Jesus loves us, and that helps us love others.

Read Luke 19:1–10.

"You see, Jesus loves those that no one else loves. Zacchaeus was unkind, unpleasant, and unlovable, but he still wanted to see and meet Jesus. He wanted to be loved too. Jesus went out of His way to reach out to Zacchaeus, and by Jesus' love toward Zacchaeus, his heart was changed.

Read 1 Corinthians 13:4–8.

Read the 1 Corinthians 13:4-8 chart from Lesson 32 again. Have the student draw a picture or act out ways of how they can show others 11–13 on the list.

Echo-read the heart chart again.

RHYME TIME:

"Let's read our poem again.

Read "The Child's World" on page 361.

"Did you hear any rhyming words? I will read the third stanza again.

Read the first four lines, starting at friendly earth.

"Tell me if you hear any words that rhyme.

LESSON 33
Day 2

ABC'S AND MORE:

Chant the ABC chart.

Sing the ABC song.

Chant sounds of the ABC chart.

Ending Sounds:

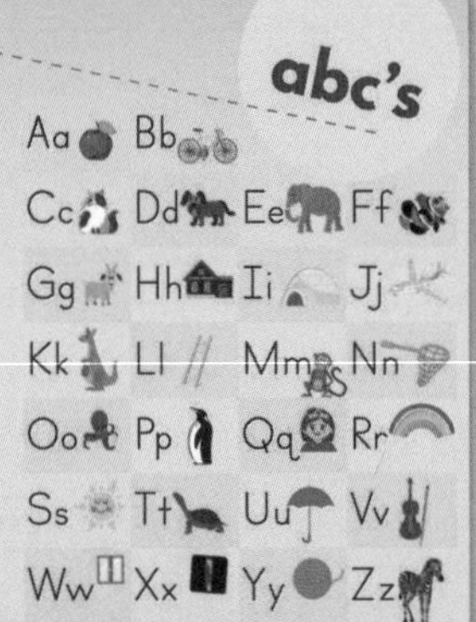

"I will say some words and you tell me what sound you hear at the end or last.

"Here is an example. If I say "part," the last sound I say in parT is /t/.

"Say the sounds you hear at the END for these words:
graze /z/
dove /v/
bop /p/
clock /k/
tree /e/
fall /l/

Complete matching ending sound/picture activity below.

Circle the letter that makes the END sound for each of these images.

 G Z R	 O V D	 B M P
 O L K	 T E R	 A L F

LESSON 33
Day 3

LIFE SKILLS:

Good Stewards:

"What are ways you can be a good steward?

"Are you helping turn off lights that we are not using?

"Are you helping not to waste water?

Turn on all the lights in the house, then show them the electrical meter and watch it spin. Then, turn off all lights, and go back and watch it spin. What do they notice? Discuss how we can be better at conserving energy.

BIBLE:

"Jesus loves us, and that helps us love others.

"We talked about the story of the Good Samaritan and how he stopped to help the man on the side of the road (Luke 10:26–37).

"I want you to notice those in need around you. We don't want to be so busy that we cannot stop and help someone. It could be an elderly person at the grocery store who needs help loading groceries. We can see and act when others are in need. By doing this, we are showing a love that puts others first — the kind of love that is not self-seeking.

Read 1 Corinthians 13:4–8 again.

Read the 1 Corinthians 13:4-8 chart from Lesson 32 again. Ask the student to draw a picture or act out ways of how they can show others 14–16 on the list.

Echo-read the heart chart again.

RHYME TIME:

"Let's read our poem this week, "The Child's World."

Read "The Child's World" on page 361.

LESSON 33
Day 3

ABC'S AND MORE:

Chant the ABC chart.

Sing the ABC song.

Chant sounds of the ABC chart.

Ending Sounds:

"I will say some words and you tell me what sound you hear at the end, or last.

"Here is an example. If I say "ham," the last sound I say in ham is /m/.

"Say the sounds you hear at the END for these words:

watch out for cow . . . over-emphasize w.

leaf /f/

bag /g/

map /p/

*cow /w/

box /x/

yell /l/

Complete matching ending sound/picture activity below.

Circle the letter that makes the END sound for each of these images.

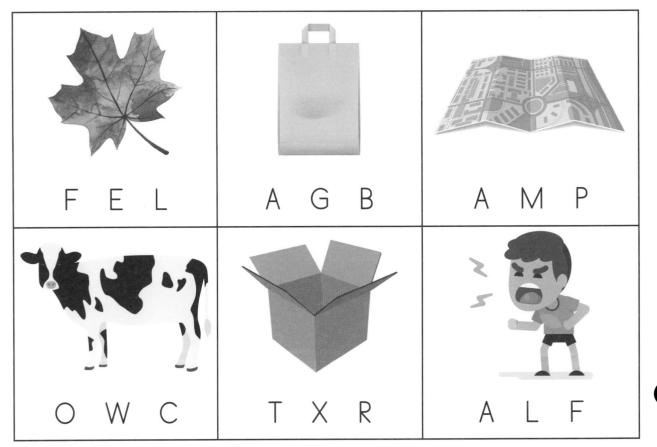

F E L	A G B	A M P
O W C	T X R	A L F

LESSON 34
Prep Page

Supply List

- ☐ Cardstock, art supplies to write with, glitter, stickers, paints, mod podge, fabric, cotton (optional, day 3, Bible)
- ☐ Supplies for fellowship dinner or picnic (day 1, life skills)
- ☐ Supplies for this dinner or picnic will be determined by the teacher. Decorations or other items are optional.

Look Ahead

Next week you will need things like ketchup packets, straws, etc. for opening.

Objectives

Ending sounds and ABC chart

Skills/Concepts – Hospitality and planning

Memory Verse

Matthew 22:37–39

Jesus replied: "'Love the Lord your God with all your heart and with all your soul and with all your mind.' This is the first and greatest commandment. And the second is like it: 'Love your neighbor as yourself.'"

Extended Activities

Review any concepts needed.

Read at least one book per day.

Pick a vocabulary word from the book and put it into everyday terms to build a connection.

LESSON 34
Day 1

LIFE SKILLS:

"Have you ever heard of a host or hostess? A host is someone who receives or entertains guests. If a boy is the one receiving and entertaining guests, he is a host. If a girl is the one receiving and entertaining guests, she is a hostess. So, you would be a (host/hostess). When we do this, we are showing hospitality. Showing hospitality or being hospitable means to be welcoming of guests and making them feel comfortable. We will be having a dinner this week. You will be the host/hostess and will plan a menu. I will help you, but what we serve will be your choice, as will the theme.

NOTE: Have some fun with this and give support so your child feels confident. If you are uncomfortable being a host, then maybe have it at a park or a picnic outdoors. Also be sure to check for food allergies/sensitivities of your guests.

"Let's learn what things you can do to be a good host/hostess and show hospitality:

"How to be hospitable:

1. Greet the guests with a smile and a greeting. For example, "Hello, thank you for coming to our home."
2. If they have coats or belongings, show them a safe place they can place those while they visit.
3. Introduce them to other guests by saying the person's name and then telling them who this person is. Example: "Sally, this is Ted. Ted, this is my friend Sally."
4. Try to have an area for all guests to talk and feel comfortable.
5. At the meal, when saying the blessing, either ask a parent ahead of time to say it or you say it, so you do not make others feel uncomfortable.
6. Try to find things to talk about and make sure all your guests are being included.
7. As guests leave, thank them for coming. Example: "Thank you for joining us this evening. We hope to have you again."
8. Clean up. Good hosts/hostesses always help in cleaning up.

Dinner/picnic Planning — do this over the week:

- ☐ *If you want a theme, help your child come up with a theme for the dinner.*
- ☐ *Help them make a list of who to invite.*
- ☐ *Make a menu (let them draw the pictures and you write the words).*
- ☐ *Grocery shop for the items.*
- ☐ *Plan how many people and how much food you need. (You can keep it simple with snacks, like popcorn, cookies and punch, or ice cream.)*
- ☐ *Have student help prepare the food.*
- ☐ *You can also discuss budget for this and what kinds of things you can do to stay in budget (shop for things on sale, use coupons, etc.).*

NOTE: You can make place cards for seating or go simple — make this your own and have fun! Even if it turns into a park play date with PB&J and fruit cups, this is a great time to learn how to be hospitable and build relationships with others.

LESSON 34
Day 1

BIBLE:

"A relationship is a connection with a person or thing. My relationship with you is ________ (father/daughter, mother/son, teacher/student, etc.). Relationships are vital, or important, to our lives as Christians. A relationship with Christ is the most important relationship we can have. Do you remember the story about Mary and Martha? They had invited Jesus to their home, but Martha was busy working while Mary sat at the feet of Jesus listening to Him. Jesus told Martha that Mary had chosen the best part by fellowshiping with Him.

"This is how we can grow in our relationships with others when we open our homes and fellowship with them.

"As Christians, our focus should first be on Jesus and our relationship with Him. Then, we should show love to others and build relationships with others.

"Our memory verse will be from Matthew 22:37–39:

Echo read the verse. Add motions.

Matthew 22:37–39

Jesus replied: "'Love  the Lord your God with all your heart  and with all your soul  and with all your mind.' This is the first and greatest commandment. And the second  is like it: 'Love  your neighbor as yourself.'"

LESSON 34
Day 1

RHYME TIME:

"Your choice! This week, think back on the songs, poems, and rhymes you have learned the last few weeks. Pick your favorite(s) to practice, and say them at your dinner.

ABC'S AND MORE:

Chant the ABC chart.

Sing the ABC song.

Chant sounds of the ABC chart.

Ending Sounds:

"I will say a word from the pictures below and you tell me the letter it ends with.

"Sun. What letter do you hear at the end of sun? *(N)*

"Listen to this word — fun. Does this word also end with an n? *(yes)*

"Box. What letter do you hear at the end of box? *(X)*

"Listen to this word — cake. Does this word also end with an x? *(no)*

"Net. What letter do you hear at the end of net? *(T)*

"Listen to this word — bat. Does this word also end with a T? *(yes)*

"Red. What letter do you hear at the end of red? *(D)*

"Listen to this word — sad. Does this word also end with a d? *(yes)*

"Pig. What letter do you hear at the end of pig? *(G)*

"Listen to this word — dog. Does this word also end with a g? *(yes)*

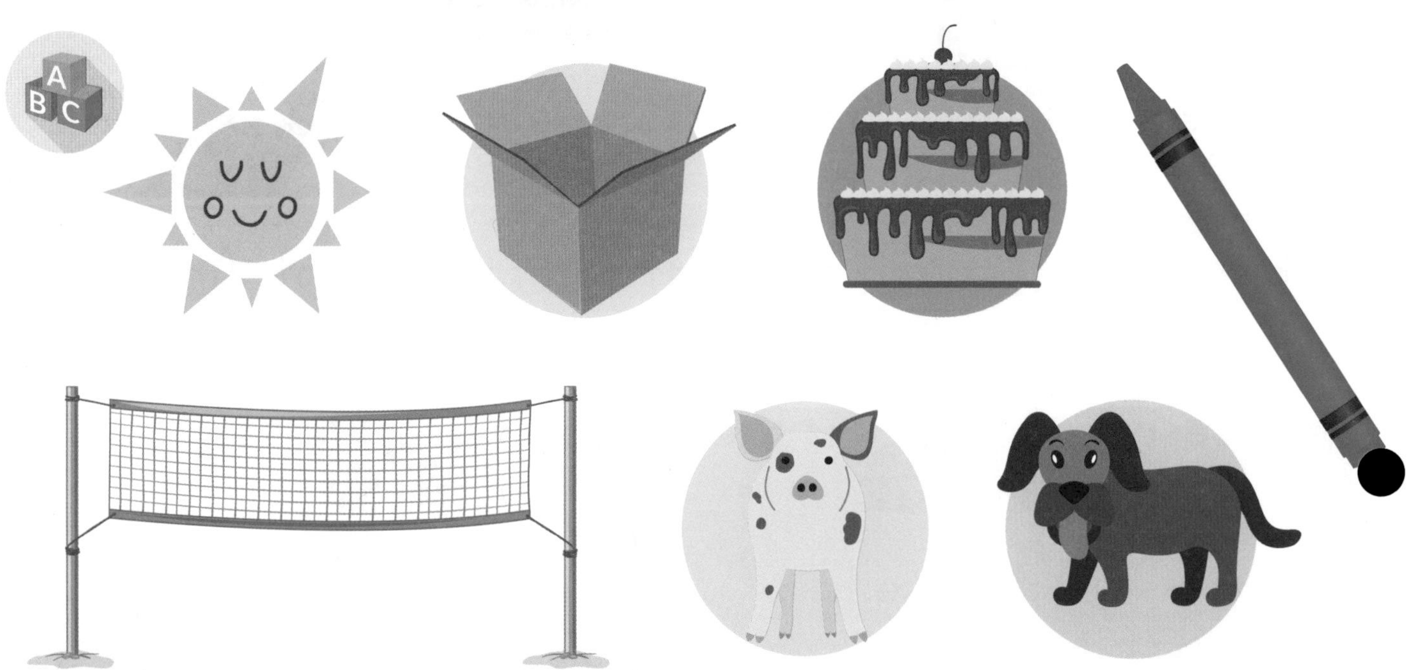

LESSON 34
Day 2

LIFE SKILLS:

"Remember, a host or hostess is someone who receives or entertains guests. When we do this, we are showing hospitality. Showing hospitality or being hospitable means to be welcoming of guests and making them feel comfortable.

Review how to be a good host/hostess and role play this each day so your child feels comfortable in the situation when it comes.

Review what things you can do to be a good host/hostess and show hospitality.

BIBLE:

"Our relationship with Christ is the most important relationship we can have. Another relationship that is vital for us is one with other Christians. Fellowshipping with others that believe like we do helps encourage us and the other person. One way we can do this is by playing with others or having a dinner like you are doing!

Read Philippians 2:1–5.

"Here we find good instruction for how we should act when we fellowship with others. We should value others above ourselves, show love, and encourage one another. We can do this by making sure each person feels like they are included.

"Matthew 22:37–40 says: "Jesus replied: "'Love the Lord your God with all your heart and with all your soul and with all your mind.' This is the first and greatest commandment. And the second is like it: 'Love your neighbor as yourself.' All the Law and the Prophets hang on these two commandments."

"We are to put others before our own wants. That is difficult at times, but with God's love and His help you can do it! How can you show your guests love?

(By being kind, welcoming them, making them feel comfortable, playing with them, etc.)

Practice your memory verse on page 369.

RHYME TIME:

"Practice the song/poem/rhyme you have chosen to share with your guests at the fellowship dinner.

LESSON 34
Day 2

ABC'S AND MORE:

Chant the ABC chart.

Sing the ABC song.

Chant sounds of the ABC chart.

Ending Sounds:

“Sack. What letter do you hear at the end of sack? *(C or K is acceptable.)*

“Listen to this word — block. Does this word also end with a C/K? *(yes)*

“Mouse. What letter do you hear at the end of mouse? *(S)*

“Listen to this word — snake. Does this word also end with an S? *(no)*

“Bulb. What letter do you hear at the end of bulb? *(B)*

“Listen to this word — job. Does this word also end with a B? *(yes)*

“Ball. What letter do you hear at the end of ball? *(L)*

“Listen to this word — well. Does this word also end with an L? *(yes)*

“Ram. What letter do you hear at the end of ram? *(M)*

“Listen to this word — cat. Does this word also end with an M? *(no)*

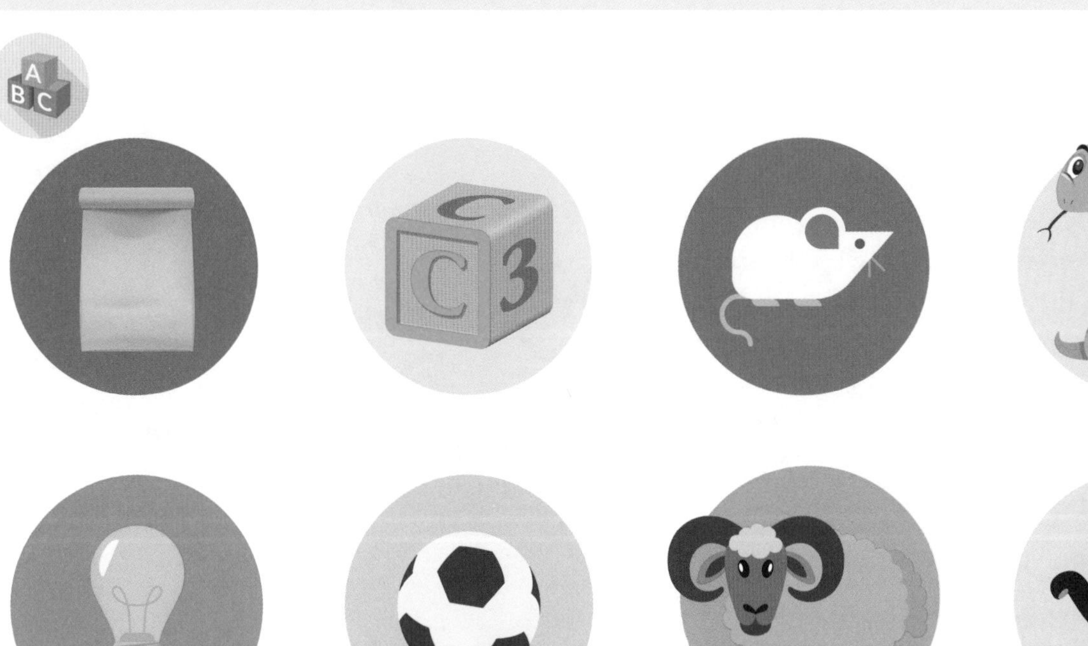

LESSON 34
Day 3

LIFE SKILLS:

"Do you remember what a host or hostess is?

Someone who receives or entertains guests.

"Do you remember how you can show hospitality?

By welcoming guests and making them feel comfortable.

Dinner Planning — Continue planning and preparing for this.

BIBLE:

"JOY: There is a saying that in order to have JOY, we have to put Jesus first, others second, and yourself last. We will make artwork for each letter to remind us that we are to put Jesus first, as the greatest commandment says to love God with all our heart, soul, and mind. Then, others above our own wants by loving our neighbors, and then what you want yourself.

Make the letters JOY on a piece of cardstock using any art supplies you want. You can make bubble letters and have them use stickers, glitter, paints, etc., or you can have them use mod podge with fabric and cover wooden letters of JOY. Or you can have them use objects, like cotton, fabric, etc. to make the shapes of the letters. Be creative and have fun!

Read Matthew 22:37–40.

Review your memory verse on page 369.

RHYME TIME:

"Practice the song/poem/rhyme you have chosen to share with your guests at the fellowship dinner.

LESSON 34
Day 3

ABC'S AND MORE:

Chant the ABC chart.

Sing the ABC song.

Chant sounds of the ABC chart.

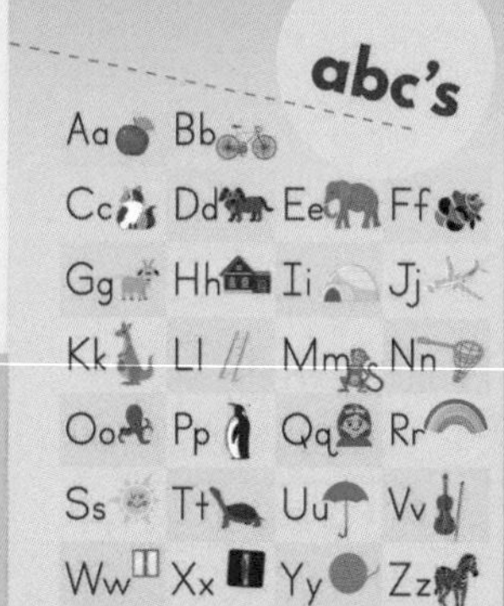

"I will say a word from the pictures below and you tell me the letter it ends with.

Ending Sounds:

"Pen. What letter do you hear at the end of pen? *(N)*

"Listen to this word — sun. Does this word also end with an N? *(yes)*

"Mop. What letter do you hear at the end of mop? *(P)*

"Listen to this word — sang. Does this word also end with a P? *(no)*

"Bed. What letter do you hear at the end of bed? *(D)*

"Listen to this word — glad. Does this word also end with a D? *(yes)*

"Ladder *(Stress the r.)* What letter do you hear at the end of ladder? *(R)*

"Listen to this word — maker. Does this word also end with an R? *(yes)*

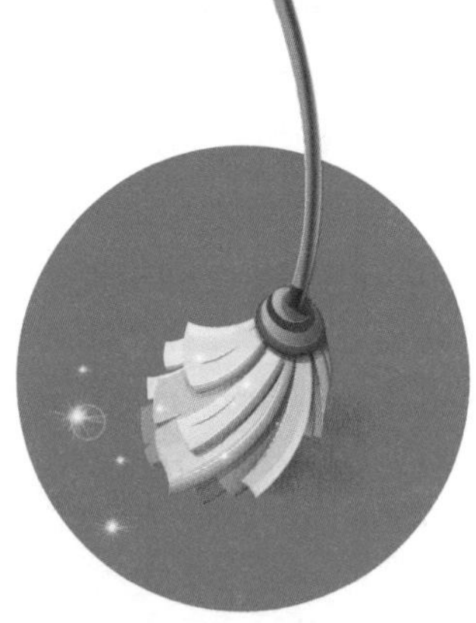

LESSON 35
Prep Page

Supply List

- ☐ Ketchup packets (daily, life skills)
- ☐ Straws in wrappers (daily, life skills)
- ☐ Juice boxes (if you use any) (daily, life skills)
- ☐ Milk cartons (if you use them) (daily, life skills)
- ☐ Any other containers that your child might be able to learn to open (daily, life skills)
- ☐ Optional: Play-Doh® or real dough (cinnamon rolls or crescent rolls)

Look Ahead

Wow, this course is almost done. Be thinking of areas your child still needs some work as you will be focusing on those next week.

Objectives

Ending sounds and ABC chart

Skills/Concepts – opening containers and straws

Memory Verse

Matthew 19:26

Jesus looked at them and said, “With man this is impossible, but with God all things are possible.”

Extended Activities

Review any concepts needed.

Read at least one book per day.
Pick a vocabulary word from the book and put it into everyday terms to build a connection.

LESSON 35
Day 1

The last two weeks of this course are for continuing to build up the confidence of your child. Please focus on any areas you feel they might be struggling with, but mostly focus on praising and building them up. It is fun to do a "caught being good" type initiative. Create a storage container and each time the student is caught doing something good, add a pom pom ball into their container. Let the student decorate the container. Prizes do not have to be toys or something tangible. Prizes might be a special movie with popcorn, day at the park, ice cream with Mom and Dad, etc. Use this time to focus on building up your child.

LIFE SKILLS:

*Opening Containers and Straws: Teach your child how to open *ketchup packets, straws in wrappers, juice boxes, milk cartons, or any other containers you could teach them to open. Opening things, such as learning to open a bag of chips, requires fine motor control as well as a simple explanation. You can also show them how to zip/unzip a plastic baggie. Think about the things in your daily lives and help them in learning to open and close these items.*

**For ketchup packets, you might want to put on old clothing or place a towel over them and do this outside.*

BIBLE:

"Even if we have things we cannot do . . . all things are possible with God! God is not limited like we are.

"Our memory verse, Matthew 19:26, says:

Echo read the verse. Add motions.

Jesus  looked at them and said, "With man this is impossible , but with God all things are possible ."

"In Exodus 14 we know that God performed all kinds of miracles in the Bible. Once there was a Pharaoh ("pharaoh" was the name given to the king of Egypt). This particular Pharaoh troubled the Israelites, and he made them slaves for his people. Moses, with the help of God sending the plagues, convinced Pharaoh to let the children of Israel go free. The children of Israel left with Moses, but as they grew in number and began to move toward the Promised Land, Pharaoh had second thoughts. He wanted the Israelites to keep working for him as slaves. So, Pharaoh and his army went after the children of Israel. God had provided Moses and the Israelites a cloud to follow by day and a pillar of fire to follow at night, which led them to the Red Sea. Can you imagine what it would be like to stand at the edge of a sea with nowhere to run and hide? Nowhere to escape from Pharaoh and his army? It would be scary. Now, the Israelites began crying out to Moses asking why he had brought them there to die and saying how it would have been better for them to have remained slaves back in Egypt. Moses reassured everyone that God would handle the situation.

LESSON 35
Day 1

God spoke to Moses and told Moses to hold out his staff over the Red Sea and that He would push back the waters so they could escape. Moses held his staff over the sea, and suddenly, the waters rolled back and made a path on dry ground! Then, once the Israelites were on the other side, the Egyptians were coming through the path too. God told Moses to raise his staff over the sea again. As Moses raised his staff over the sea, the waters of the Red Sea came crashing back together and swept away all the Egyptians.

"Let's read our poem this week, "The Snail.""

"Can you creep like a snail out of its shell?

Use books or the Internet with a parent to find pictures, or find slugs and snails outside.

"What differences do you see between a slug and a snail?

The Snail

Hand in hand you see us well,
creep like a snail out of his shell.
Always nearer, always nearer,
ever closer, ever closer.
Who would think this tiny shell,
would have held the snail so well.

Hand in hand you see us well,
creep like a snail out of his shell.
Ever wider, ever wider,
ever farther, ever farther.
Who would have thought this tiny shell,
would have held the snail so well.

LESSON 35
Day 1

ABC'S AND MORE:

Chant the ABC chart.

Sing the ABC song.

Chant sounds of the ABC chart.

Ending Sounds:

"The last few weeks we have worked on hearing sounds at the end of words. Now you will find the letter that matches the ending sounds of the pictures.

Match each letter with the picture's ending sound.

T

G

N

P

M

B

LESSON 35
Day 2

LIFE SKILLS:

Practice opening containers and straws.

Continue teaching how to open things.

Remember to build up your child and focus on areas where they need improvement.

BIBLE:

"There might be things we cannot do, but with God all things are possible! God is not limited like we are.

Review your memory verse on page 376.

"John 9:1–11 tells of a man who had been blind from birth. When Jesus and His disciples saw the man, the disciples asked Jesus if this man had sinned or if his parents had sinned. Jesus told them that neither he or his parents had sinned, and that his blindness had happened so that the glory of God might be displayed in Him. Let's read this story from our Bible.

"Have you ever played in the mud? What do you do to dirt to make mud? Have you ever put mud on yourself? If you have put mud on yourself, do you think that mud would heal any sickness or disease? Well, this man was not healed because of the mud, but he was healed because of Jesus. Once again, we have a miracle. God chose to heal this man so that He would be glorified. This man had been blind his whole life, but now he could see. He was obedient and did what Jesus told him to do, and because of his obedience and faith he was healed! With God, all things are possible!

RHYME TIME:.

"Let's read our poem this week again.

Read "The Snail" on page 377.

Optional: Use Play-Doh® to make a snail or use cinnamon roll or bread dough to make snails and bake.

LESSON 35
Day 2

ABC'S AND MORE:

Chant the ABC chart.

Sing the ABC song.

Chant sounds of the ABC chart.

Ending Sounds:

"The last few weeks we have worked on hearing sounds at the end of words. Now you will find the letter that matches the ending sounds of the pictures.

Match each letter with the picture's ending sound.

F

D

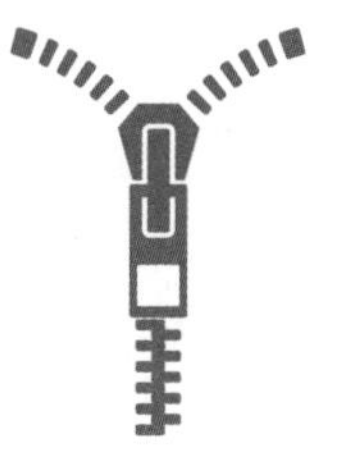

K

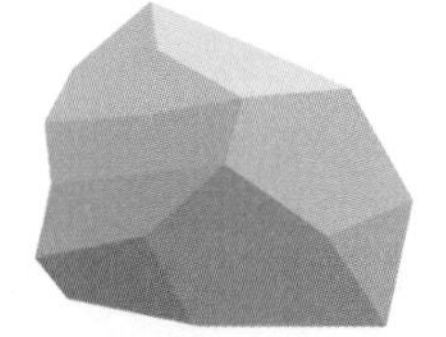

L

R

LESSON 35
Day 3

LIFE SKILLS:

Review opening containers and straws.

Continue teaching how to open things.

BIBLE:

"There might be things we cannot do, but with God all things are possible! God is not limited like we are.

Review your memory verse on page 376.

"Do you remember the story about Mary and Martha? The two sisters had Jesus to their house and Martha worked while Mary sat at Jesus' feet. Well, they had a brother named Lazarus. Jesus performed another miracle! Read about it in John 11:1–44.

"Can you imagine your brother or sister dying and then Jesus coming and telling them to get up and come back out of their grave? That would be amazing! You see, when God shows up, great and mighty things happen. Jesus performed miracle after miracle. He proves that with God all things are possible!

RHYME TIME:

"Let's read our poem for this week.

Read "The Snail" on page 377.

Look for signs of snail and slug trails outside. (You can also look them up online to see the slime trail.) Slime or mucus from snails and slugs helps them by providing protection, helping them stick to things like leaves, and keeping their skin moist.

LESSON 35
Day 3

ABC'S AND MORE:

Chant the ABC chart.

Sing the ABC song.

Chant sounds of the ABC chart.

Ending Sounds:

"The last few weeks we have worked on hearing sounds at the end of words. Now you will find the letter that matches the ending sounds of the pictures.

Match each letter with the picture's ending sound.

S

Z

LESSON 36
Prep Page

Supply List

- ☐ Anything they might need for practicing tying shoes, sewing a button, making a bed, etc.

Look Ahead

Celebrate! You're almost done. Congratulations! Be proud!

Objectives

Ending sounds and ABC chart

Skills/Concepts – understanding first, second, third

Memory Verse

John 1:1

In the beginning was the Word, and the Word was with God, and the Word was God.

LESSON 36
Day 1

LIFE SKILLS:

Continue "caught being good" initiative.

"What is your address?

"What is your phone number?

Review and practice any skills they still need work on.

BIBLE:

"God ordered things. He ordered the days of creation we read about in Genesis. John 1:1 tells us "In the beginning was the Word, and the Word was with God, and the Word was God." God was and is the beginning. This concept is sometimes difficult for us, because we only see through human eyes. Genesis 1:1 says "In the beginning God. . . ." This again tells us that God was already there. Revelation 1:8 says that He is the alpha and omega. Those are big words for "beginning" and "ending." Revelation also says He is the God who is, who was, and who is to come. This all tells us that God is here, He was there in the beginning of creation, and that He is coming back for us. What an amazing God who created everything! God truly is amazing! God is infinite, or never ending. That is difficult for us to fully grasp, but we know that God's Word is true, and we have faith in what it says. Just like a rainbow is a full circle that has no beginning or ending points, that is how God is. He always is there and is the beginning and the ending.

"The last verse we will memorize for this course is John 1:1:

Echo read the verse. Add motions.

In the beginning was

the Word , and the

Word was with God ,

and the Word was God.

RHYME TIME:

"This week is YOUR PICK! You get to choose your favorite poem/rhyme and song. I encourage you to make a video of you reciting your favorite poem(s)/rhyme(s)/song(s). This is a great way to share with family and for a keepsake. I hope you have enjoyed all the songs, poems, and rhymes you have learned!

LESSON 36
Day 1

ABC'S AND MORE:

Chant the ABC chart.

Sing the ABC song.

Chant sounds of the ABC chart.

Match the items below that begin with the same sound.

Practice writing all lowercase letters a-z today.

Match the items that begin with the same sound.

LESSON 36
Day 2

LIFE SKILLS:

Continue "caught being good" initiative.

"What is your address?

"What is your phone number?

Practice any skills they still need work on from this course.

BIBLE:

"God ordered things and creation. The first man He created was Adam. Through Adam came all people. Later, God put on flesh, and Jesus entered the world. Only through Jesus can we come to heaven. First Corinthians 15:47 says, "The first man was of the dust of the earth; the second man is of heaven." Jesus came to earth as a baby. Later, He died on a Cross for our sins. On the third day after His death, He was resurrected, which means He was brought back to life. He returned to heaven, and one day will come back for us! Draw a picture illustrating the first, second, and third main events of Jesus' life.

(Birth, Death, Resurrection)

Practice your memory verse on page 384.

RHYME TIME:

"This week is YOUR PICK! You get to choose your favorite poem/rhyme and song. I encourage you to make a video of you reciting your favorite poem(s)/rhyme(s)/song(s). This is a great way to share with family and for a keepsake. I hope you have enjoyed all the songs and poems and rhymes you have learned!

LESSON 36
Day 2

ABC'S AND MORE:

Chant the ABC chart.

Sing the ABC song.

Chant sounds of the ABC chart.

Match the items below that begin with the beginning sound.

Practice writing all capital letters A–Z today.

Match items that begin with the same sound.

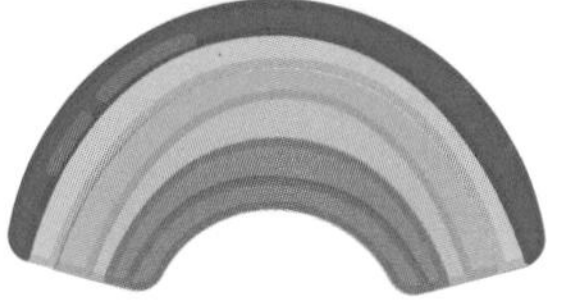

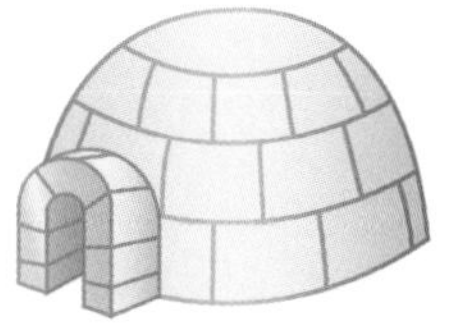

LESSON 36
Day 3

LIFE SKILLS:

Continue "caught being good" initiative.

"What is your address?

"What is your phone number?

Practice any skills they still need work on, like tying shoes, sewing a button, making a bed, getting all the shampoo and conditioner from their hair, etc.

BIBLE:

"We are given several instructions in the Bible. One instruction we are given is to seek first the kingdom of God and His righteousness. Matthew 6:33 says, "But seek first his kingdom and his righteousness, and all these things will be given to you as well." When we seek something, we are trying to find it. The main thing we should be pursuing or going after is the kingdom of God and righteousness. "Righteousness" is another word for right living. If we are seeking God's kingdom, we will be trying to add people to it, and we will be living right according to God's Word. Ways we can seek the kingdom of God are by reading His Word, praying, and witnessing to others. The next part of the Scripture tells us that then we will be given all these things. The Scripture was discussing clothing and food, or the needs that we have. We know that God blesses us with the things we need when we are seeking His kingdom and righteousness.

"What is the first thing we are to seek?

"Who blesses us with what we need?

Review your memory verse on page 384.

RHYME TIME:

"This week is YOUR PICK! You get to choose your favorite poem/rhyme and song. I encourage you to make a video of you reciting your favorite poem(s)/rhyme(s)/song(s). This is a great way to share with family and for a keepsake. I hope you have enjoyed all the songs and poems and rhymes you have learned!

LESSON 36
Day 3

ABC'S AND MORE:

Chant the ABC chart.

Sing the ABC song.

Chant sounds of the ABC chart.

Do the match the ending sounds activity below.

Scramble the ABC Cards on the ground and have them put them back in order like the ABC chart without looking at the ABC chart.

Match items that end with the same sound.

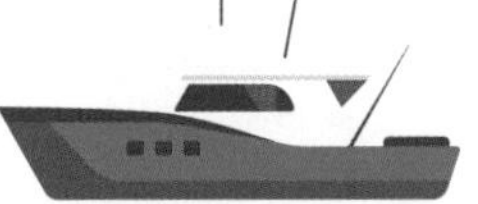

DIPLOMA

this certificate of graduation is presented to

....

by

....

Book Suggestions:

All Lessons:

10 Minute Bible Journey, 101 Favorite Bible Stories, Big Thoughts for Little Thinkers set, *My Creation Bible*

Lesson 1:

When You See a Rainbow by Master Books

Lesson 3+:

Dinosaur Fun, Dinosaurs for Little Kids: Where Did They Go? by Ken Ham from Master Books

Lesson 5:

The Creation Story for Children by Master Books, *Six Short Days, One Big Adventure* by Master Books

Lessons 7–8:

44 Animals of the Bible would be good for picking an animal each day that is in your area for them to use their senses to find (birds chirping, frogs singing, etc.). *It's Designed to Do What it Does Do* by Master Books, *Life Before Birth* by Master Books, *The Work of Your Hand* by Master Books.

Lesson 9:

Nine Fruits of the Spirit set by Master Books

Lesson 12:

It's Designed to Do What it Does Do by Master Books, *The Very Hungry Caterpillar* by Eric Carle

Lesson 23:

Master Books suggestion for birds is *God's Design for Life Beginners, The Complete Zoo Adventure, Big Book of Animals*

You can also get a bird guide from the game and fish commission/wildlife conservation in your area.

Lesson 27:

Buddy Davis: Dinosaurs, Genesis, and the Gospel DVD and *Six Short Days, One Big Adventure DVD* from Master Books.

Bibliography:

Mason, Dale. *10 Minute Bible Journey*. Green Forest, AR: Master Books, 2017.

Illustrated Family Bible Stories: Over 200 beautifully illustrated events from the Old and New Testaments. New Leaf Press edition. Green Forest, AR: New Leaf Press, 2014. (Originally published by Parragon Publishing, Ltd. in 2008.)

CARRIE BAILEY is a Christian homeschool mom to three boys. She has a degree in early childhood education and has also taught students with special needs in the public school system. She and her husband, Jesse, work in their church serving in many capacities from media to curriculum decisions. Carrie has a passion for helping others on their journey and encouraging other moms.

In addition to *Simply K*, she has written *Stepping Stones*, a book for teaching preschoolers, and has teamed up with author Angela O'Dell on *Math K* in the popular *Math Lessons for a Living Education* series from Master Books.

TEACHER RESOURCE

See Instructional Video 1 for chanting the ABC chart, writing, and course introduction. See Instructional Video 2 for adding in alphabet sounds later.

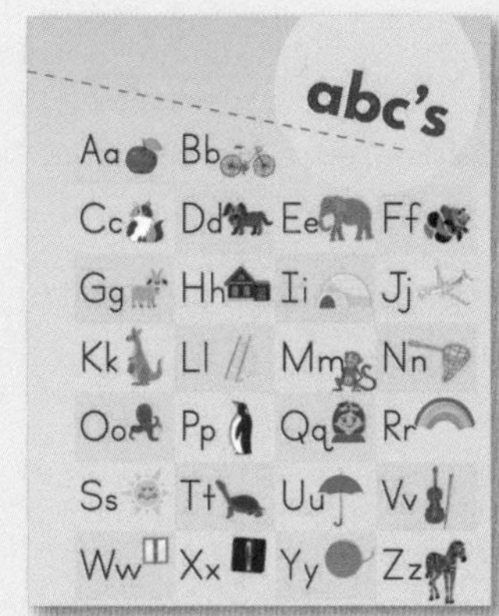

Remember: This is you modeling steps for independent student use later on. Please use them as a guide as this sets a foundation to build upon.

Sounds will not be taught until later on in this course.

 See the instructional videos here:

https://www.masterbooks.com/classroom-aids

Advanced K: Begin sounds on Lesson 8.

LETTER TRACING

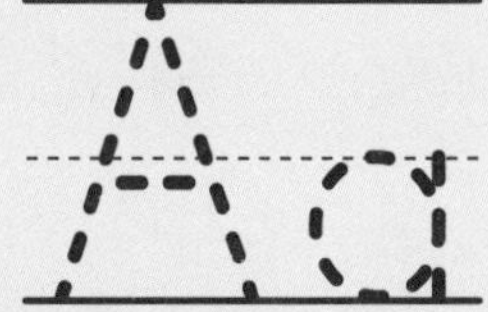

Lessons 1-26 focus on one letter per week. In each day's lesson, you will see a prompt:

Practice writing A's and a's.

To teach the student the proper way to make the letter noted, follow this sequence:

1. Model the proper letter strokes on a piece of paper by writing the letter as you say the steps.

Note: It is very important for you to use the letter writing cues each time you do these steps. The cues are found for each letter on the back of this page as a reference sheet.

2. Air write the letter really big together using the cues.
3. Have the student write the letter on a larger surface (a dry erase board or plain paper in a page protector without lines). If needed, assist them by placing your hand over theirs.
4. Say the letter tracing cues (in parentheses) and the writing instructions for each letter.
5. Then have the student trace the letter tracers for the day's lesson.

These steps are presented in Instructional Video 1.

Additional tracing practice sheets for upper and lowercase letters are included in the back of the book. It is recommended that you place them in plastic sleeves or laminate them for use daily.

MINI-BOOK

Day One

Go through each page of the mini-book and ask them what they think each picture is. If they are wrong, please correct them gently, by saying, "that is a great option, but this is a ________."

Read the front cover, pointing to each letter and saying its name, but not sounds yet. Then, go through each page, reading it as A, a, apple. A, a, astronaut. A, a, alligator…and so on.

Day Two

Read the mini-book, pointing to each word or the letter as you go along. Then, use a highlighter to make a dot on the Aa's in the book.

Day Three

Have them watch as you read the book again.

Advanced K: See if the child can read the book to you.

TEACHER RESOURCE

A: (slant up, slant down, across in the middle)
a: (over around, up, and down)

B: (down, up around, around)
b: (down, up, around)

C: (over around, leave it open)
c: (over around, leave it open)

D: (down, up, curve around)
d: (over around, up, down)

E: (down, out, out, out)
e: (out, over around, leave it open)

F: (down, out, out)
f: (curve up, down, across in the middle)

G: (over around, in)
g: (over around, up, down and curve)

H: (down, down, across in the middle)
h: (down, up and over)

I: (down, across, across)
i: (down, dot)

J: (down and curve, across)
j: (down, curve dot)

K: (down, slant in, slant out)
k: (down, slant in, slant out)

L: (down, over)
l: (down)

M: (up, slant down, slant up, down)
m: (down, up and over, up and over)

N: (up, slant down, up)
n: (down, up and over)

O: (over around and close)
o: (over around and close)

P: (down, up, around)
p: (down, up, around)

Q: (over around and close, slant out)
q: (over around, up, down, curve)

R: (down, up, around, slant out)
r: (down up and over)

S: (curve back, curve forward)
s: (curve back, curve forward)

T: (down, across)
t: (down, across)

U: (down, curve up)
u: (down, curve up, down)

V: (slant down, slant up)
v: (slant down, slant up)

W: (slant down, slant up, slant down, slant up)
w: (slant down, slant up, slant down, slant up)

X: (slant forward, slant back)
x: (slant forward, slant back)

Y: (slant down, slant up, down)
y: (slant back, slant in)

Z: (across, slant back, across)
z: (across, slant back, across)

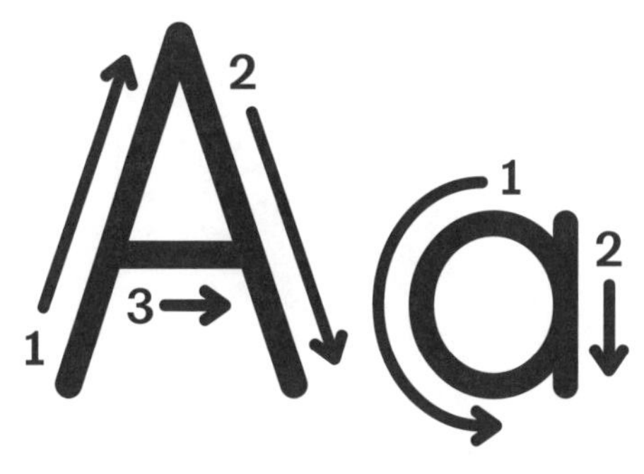

Aa

mini book

fold

A a astronaut

A a antelope

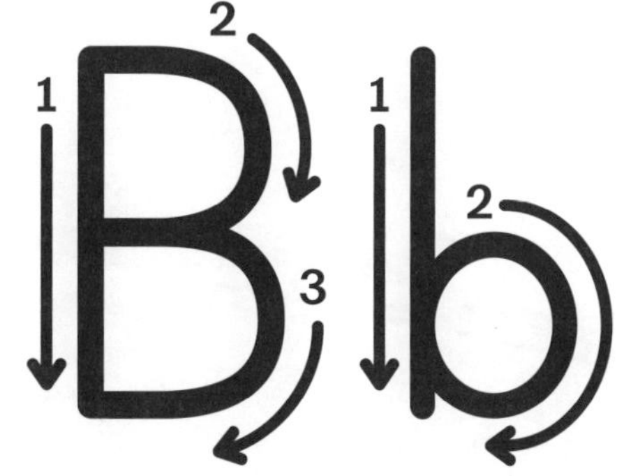

Bb

mini book

B b baby

B b bicycle

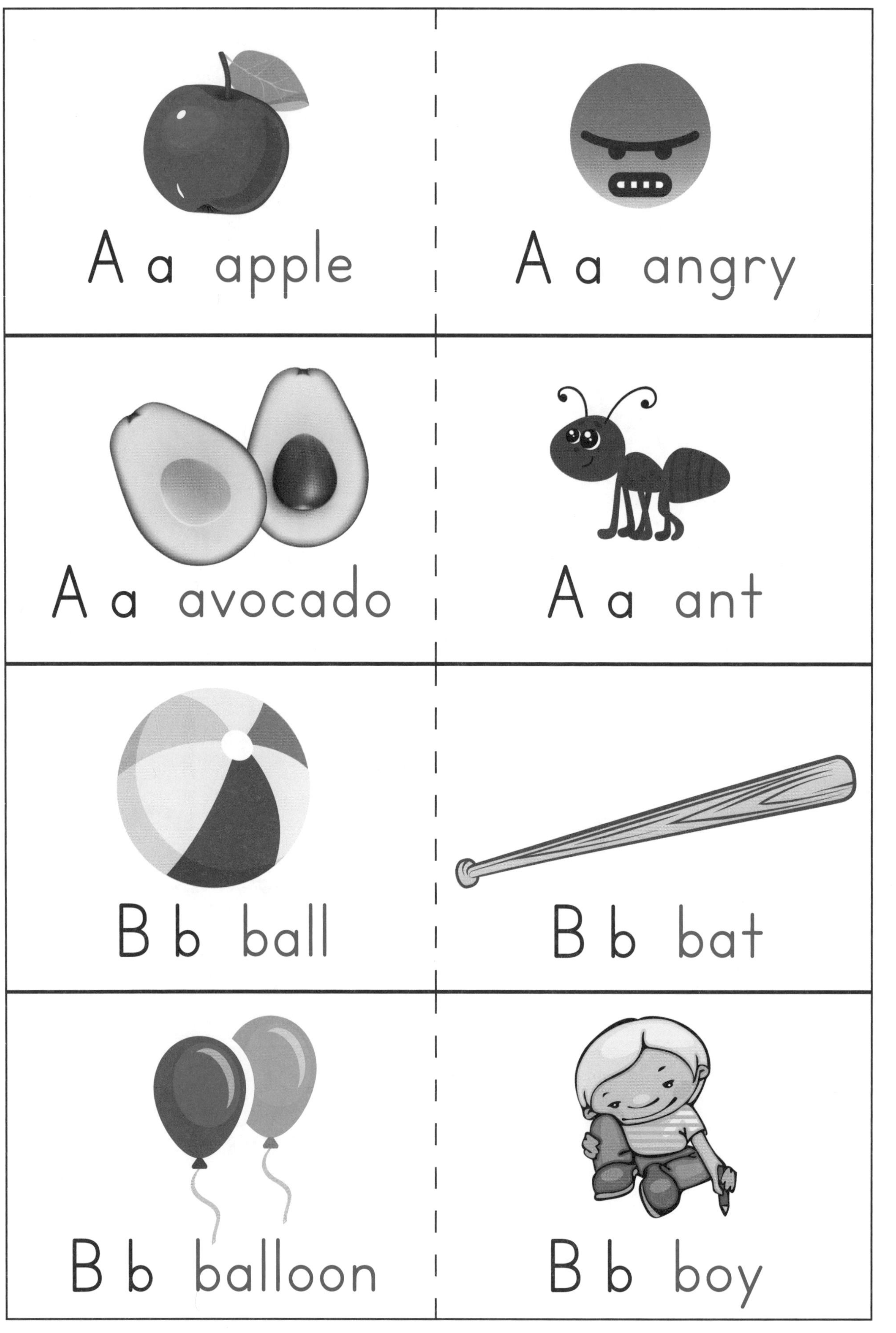
A a apple
A a angry
A a avocado
A a ant
B b ball
B b bat
B b balloon
B b boy

Cc
fold
Cc
mini book
Cc camel
Cc cake
Dd
Dd
mini book
Dd donkey
Dd doll

C c cat

C c camera

C c car

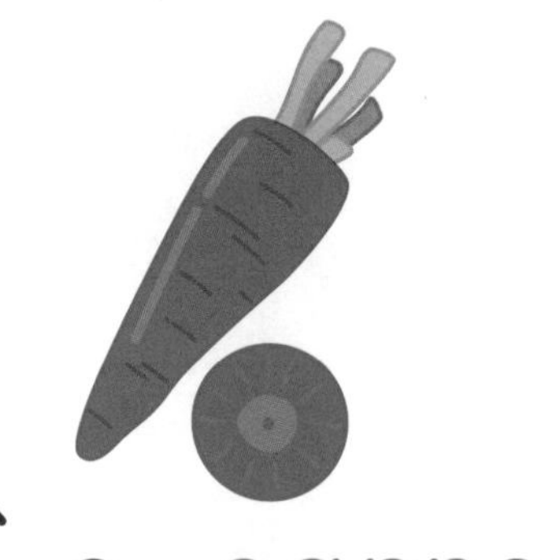

C c carrot

D d donut

D d dog

D d duck

D d dinosaur

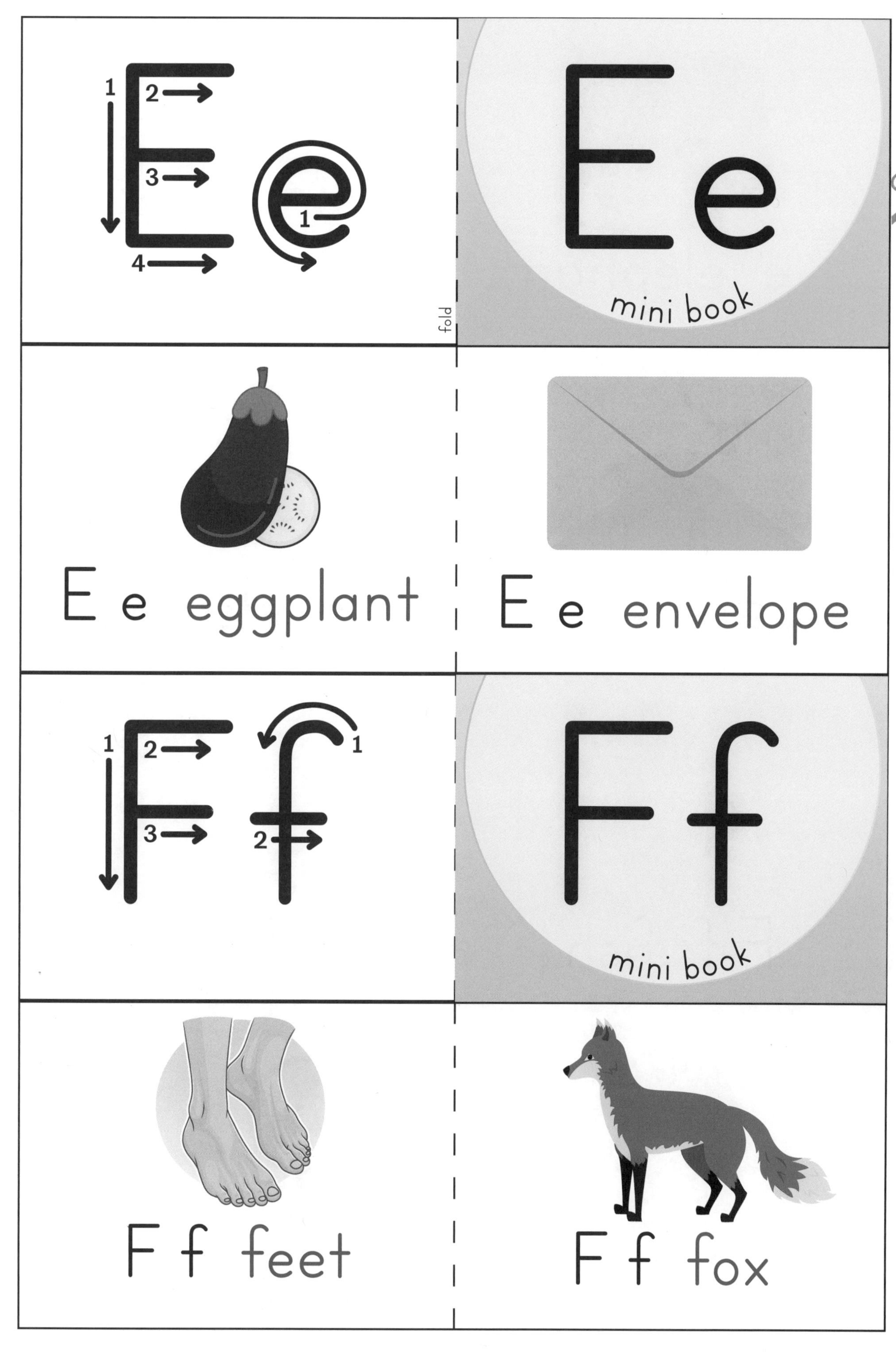

1
2
3
4
Ee
1
fold
Ee
mini book
E e eggplant
E e envelope
1
2
3
Ff
1
2
Ff
mini book
F f feet
F f fox

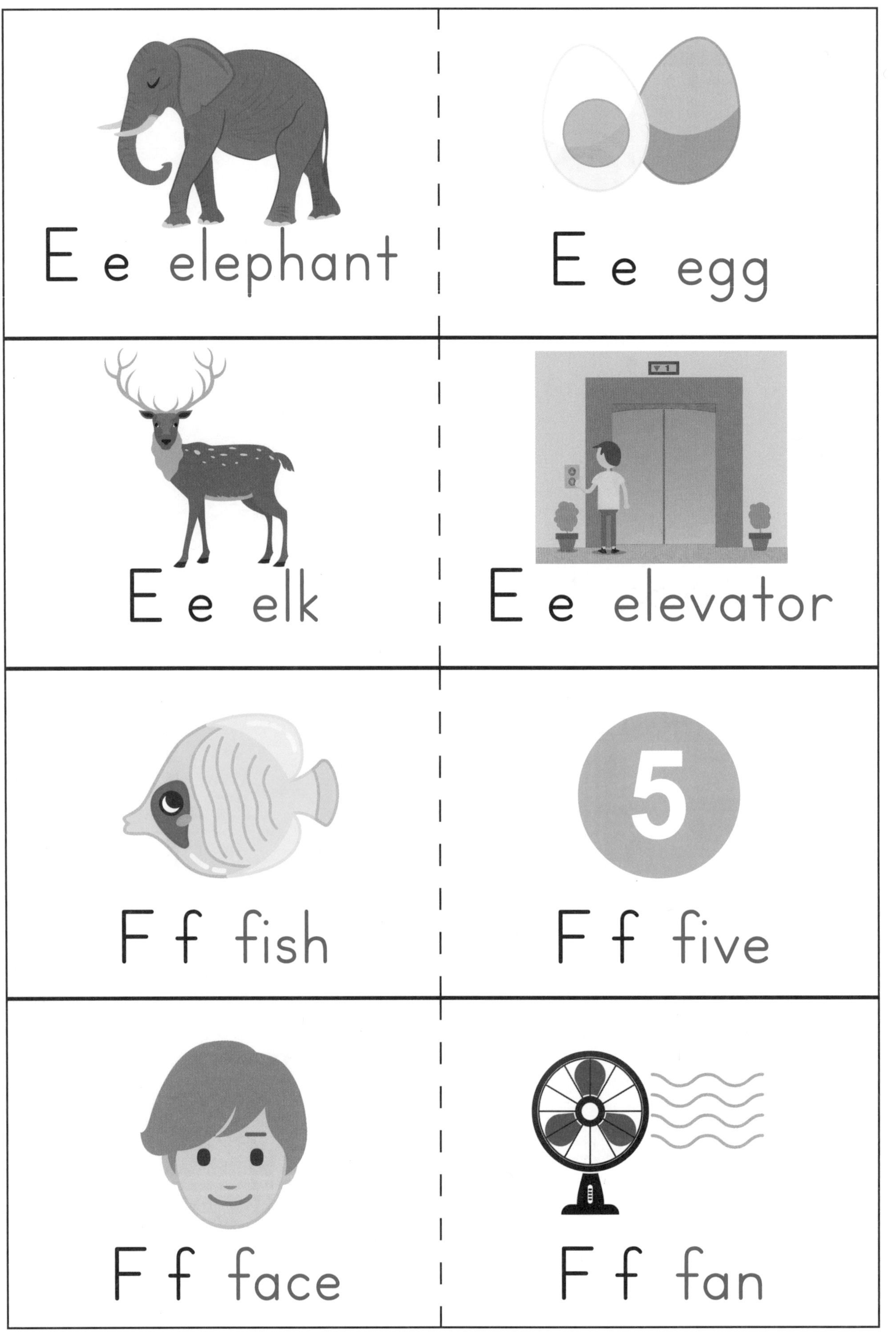
E e elephant
E e egg
▼1
E e elk
E e elevator
5
F f fish
F f five
F f face
F f fan

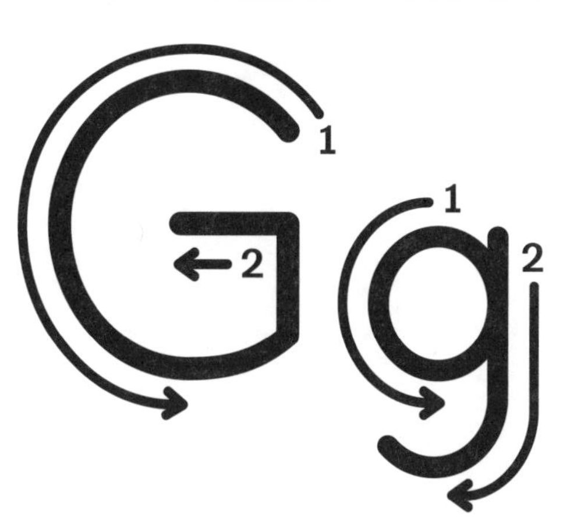

fold

G g girl

G g game

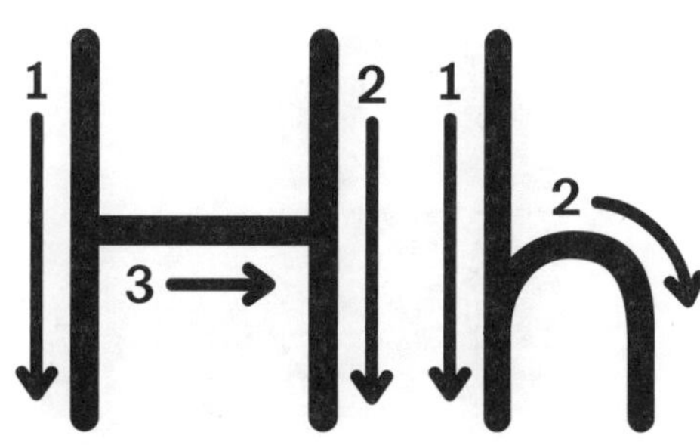

Hh

mini book

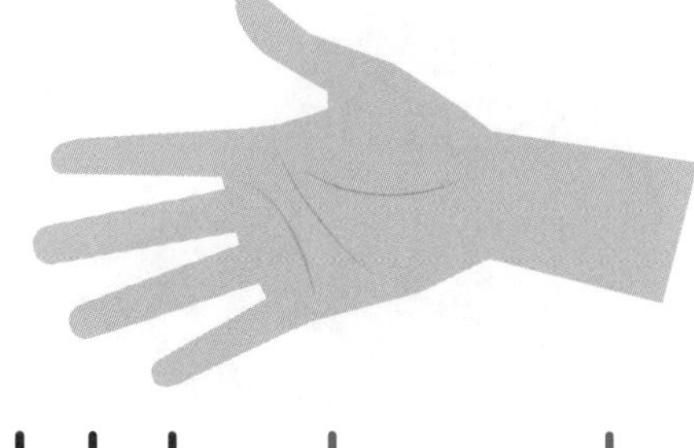

H h hand

H h honey

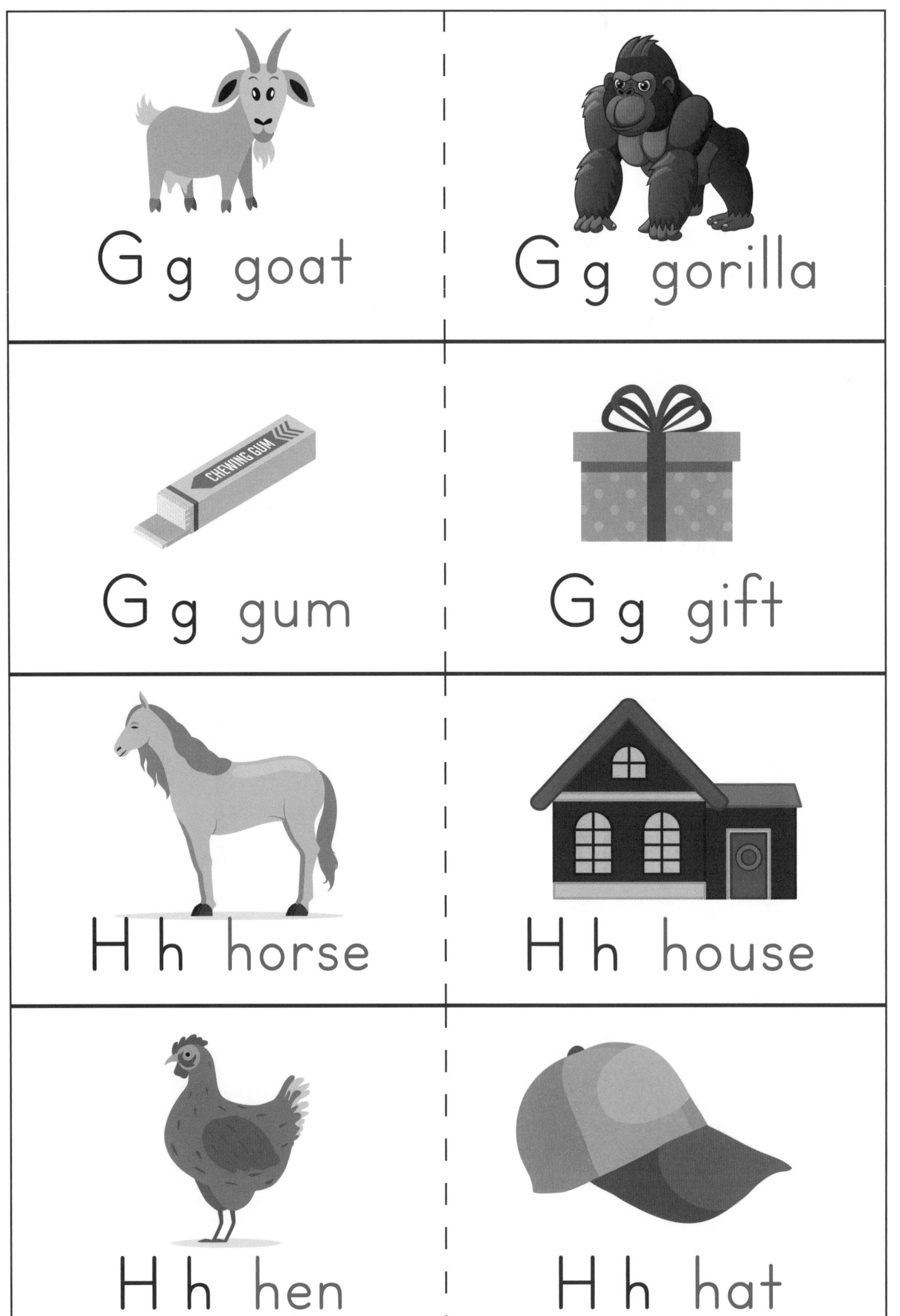
G g goat
G g gorilla
CHEWING GUM
G g gum
G g gift
H h horse
H h house
H h hen
H h hat

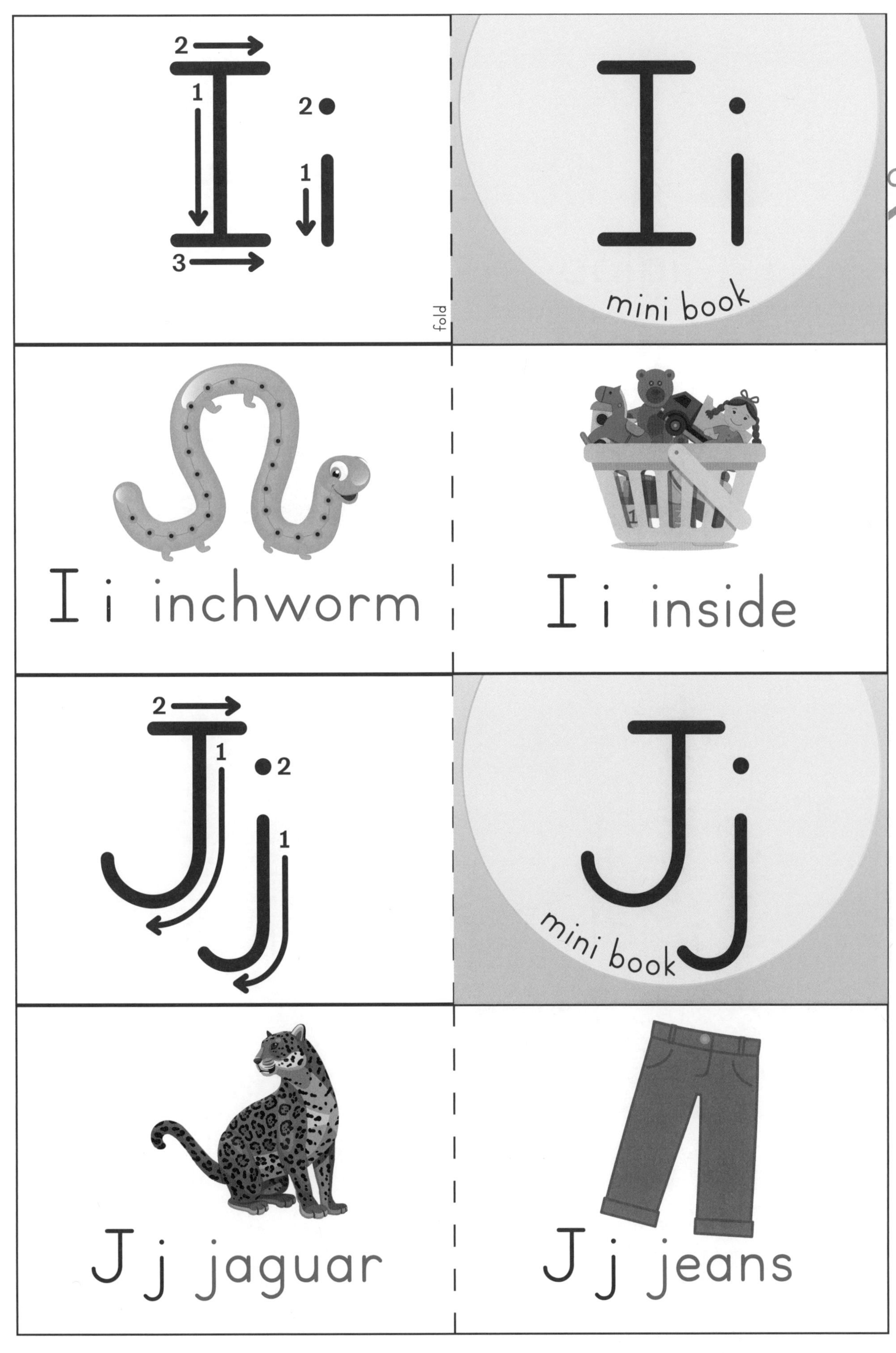

Ii
mini book
fold
Ii inchworm
Ii inside
Jj
mini book
Jj jaguar
Jj jeans

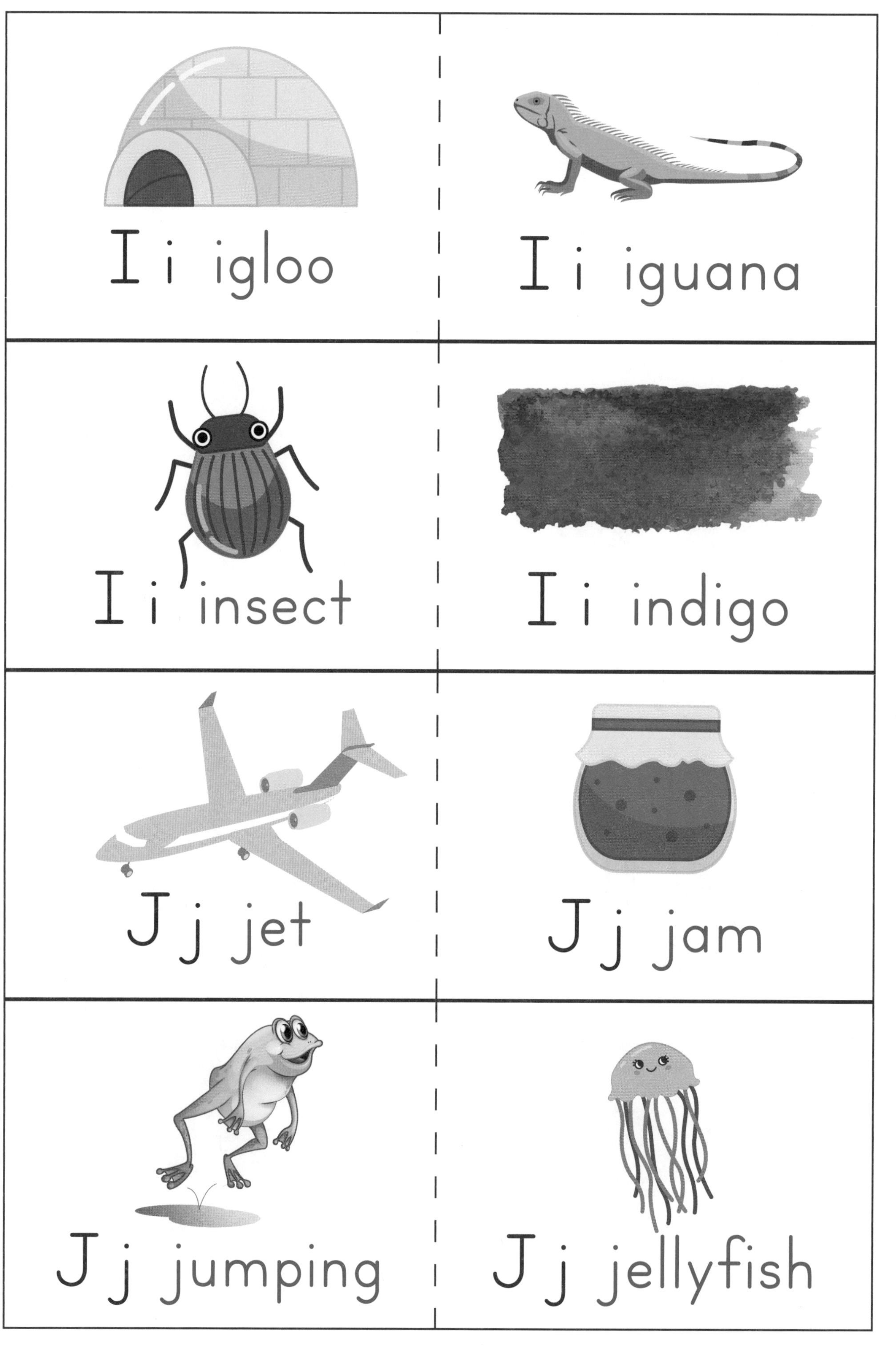
I i igloo
I i iguana
I i insect
I i indigo
J j jet
J j jam
J j jumping
J j jellyfish

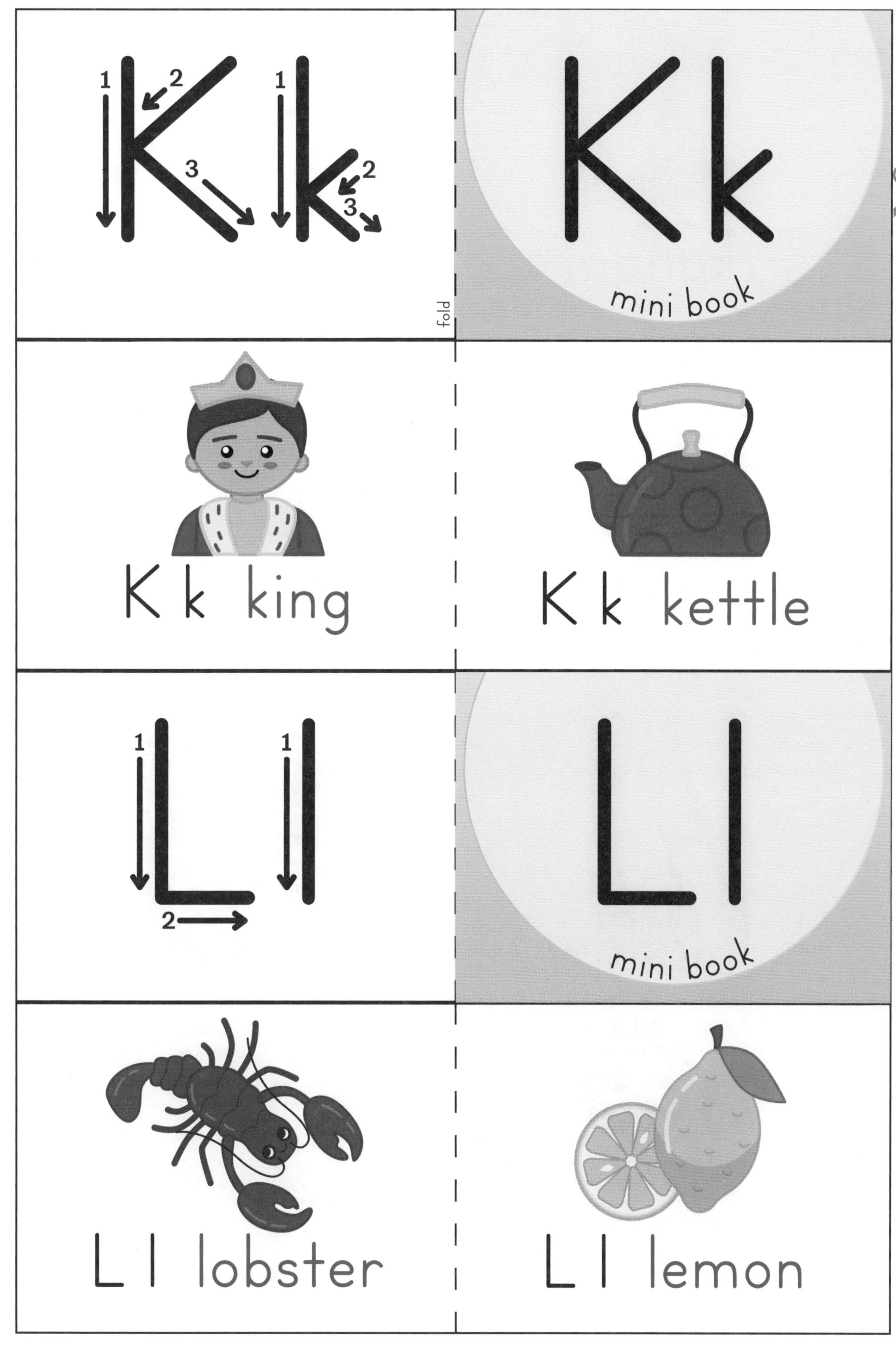
1
2
3
1
2
3
Kk
Kk
mini book
fold
K k king
K k kettle
1
1
2
Ll
Ll
mini book
L l lobster
L l lemon

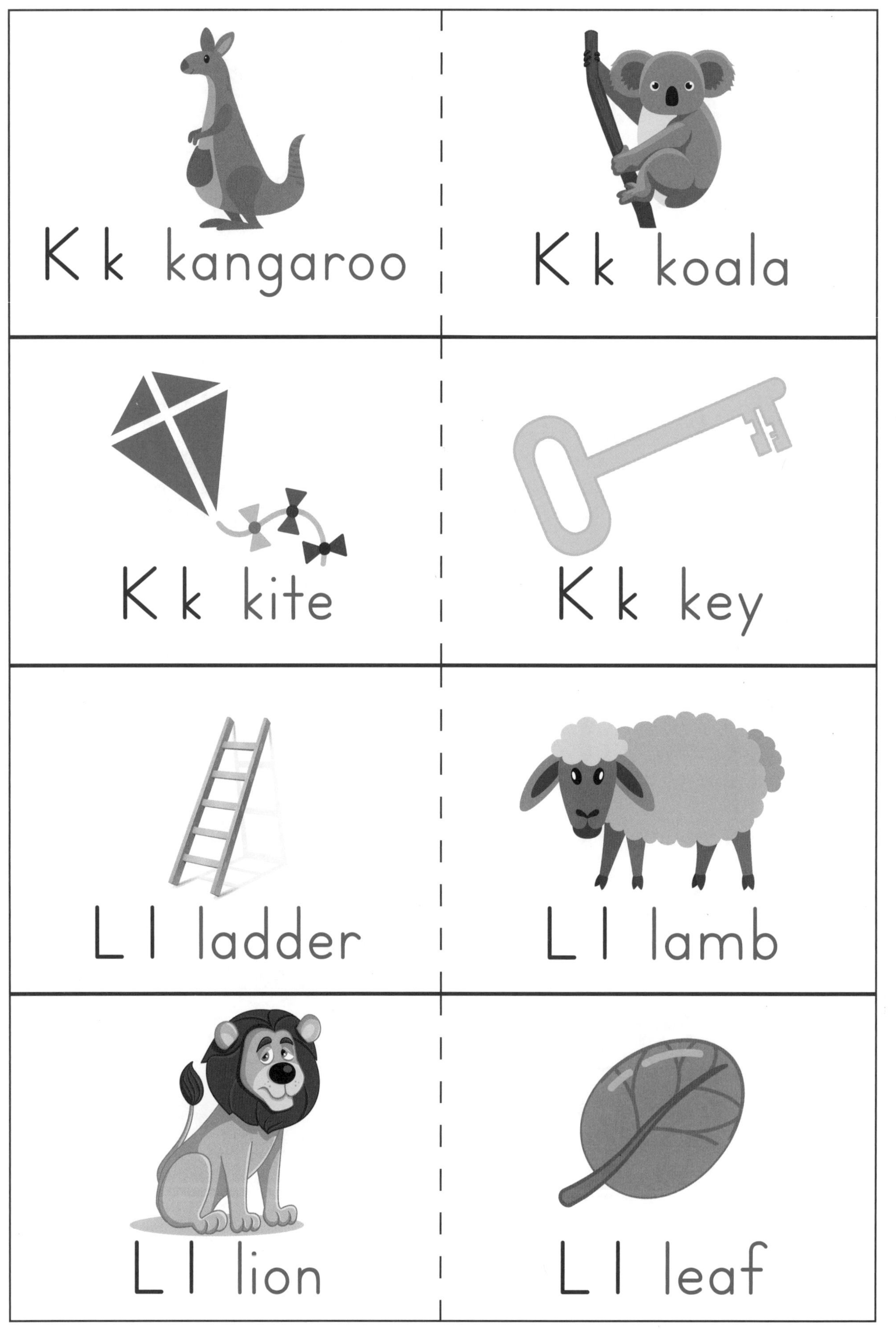
K k kangaroo
K k koala
K k kite
K k key
L l ladder
L l lamb
L l lion
L l leaf

Mm

fold

Mm

mini book

M m moon

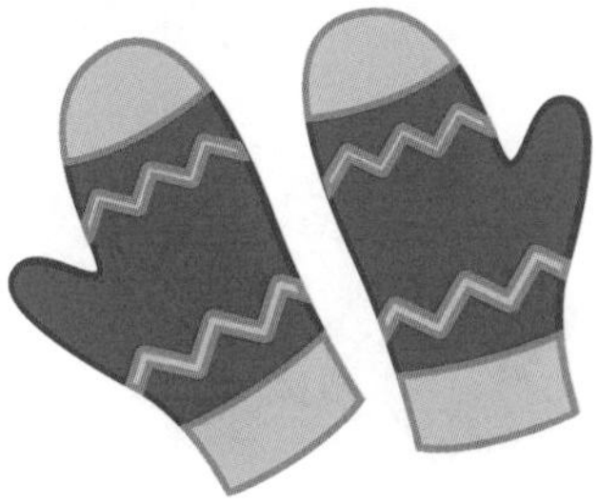

M m mittens

Nn

Nn

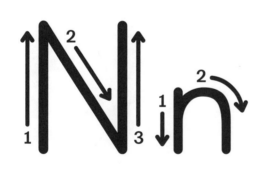

mini book

N n notes

N n net

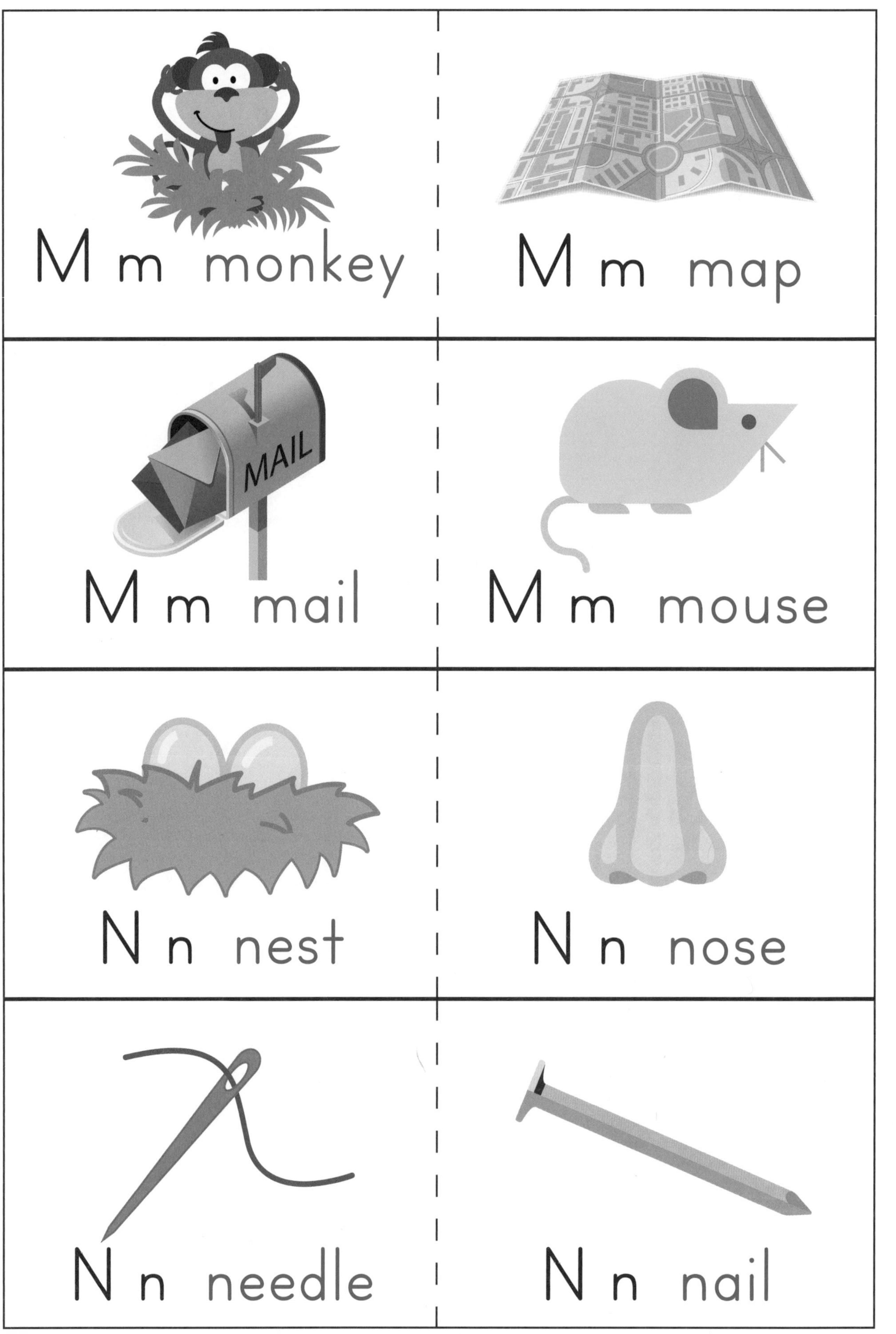
M m monkey
M m map
MAIL
M m mail
M m mouse
N n nest
N n nose
N n needle
N n nail

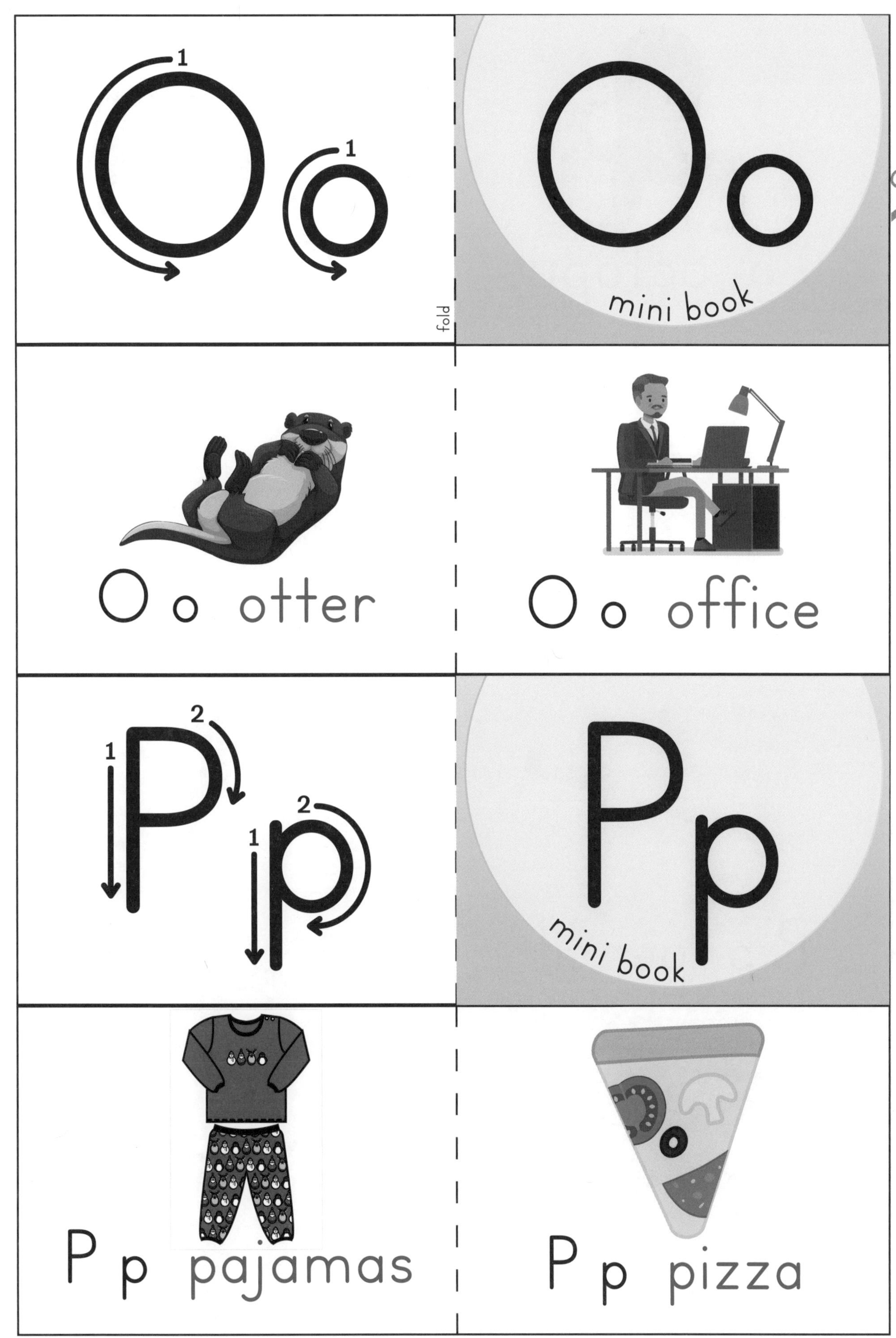

1
Oo
1
fold
Oo
mini book
O o otter
O o office
2
1
Pp
2
1
Pp
mini book
P p pajamas
P p pizza

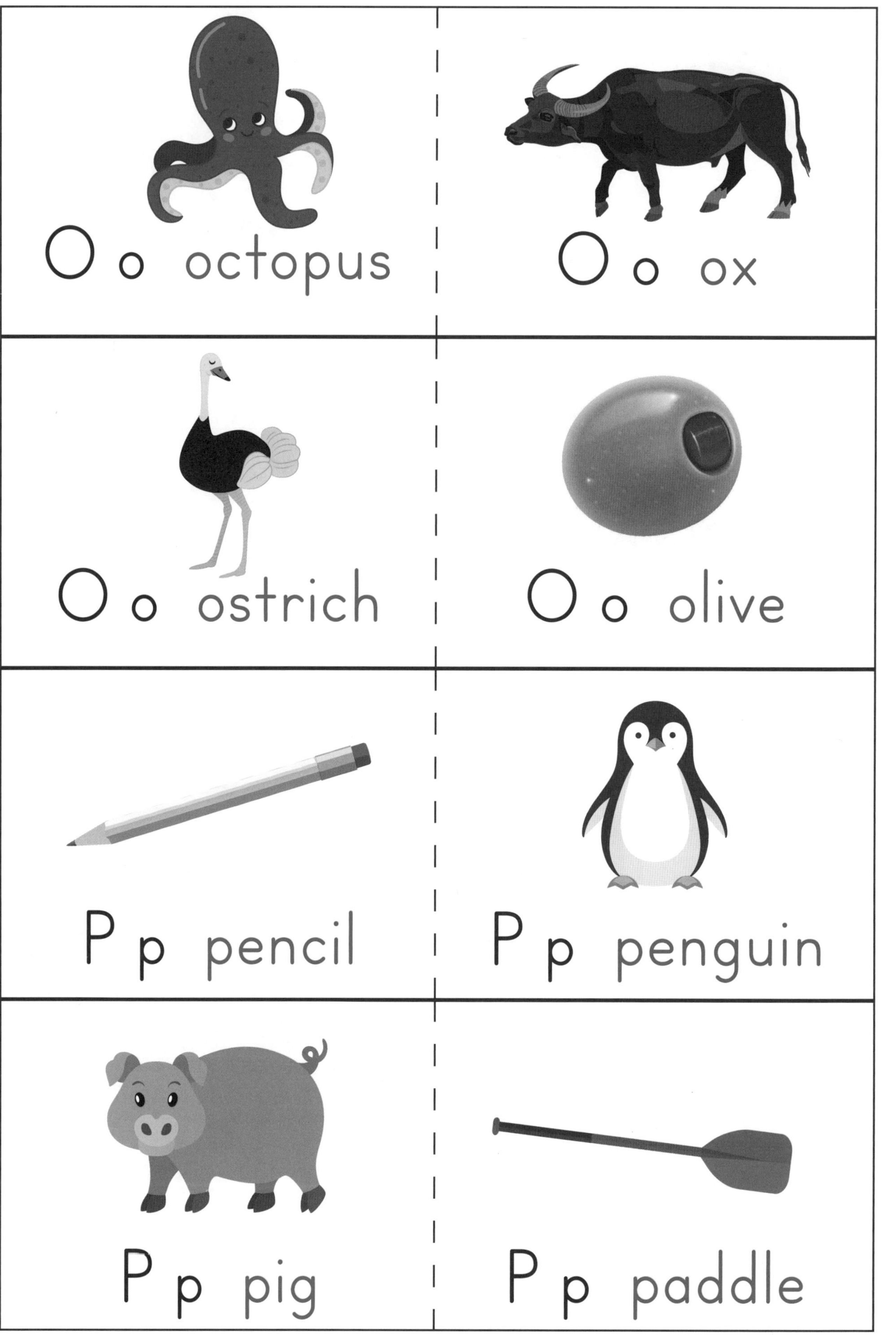
O o octopus
O o ox
O o ostrich
O o olive
P p pencil
P p penguin
P p pig
P p paddle

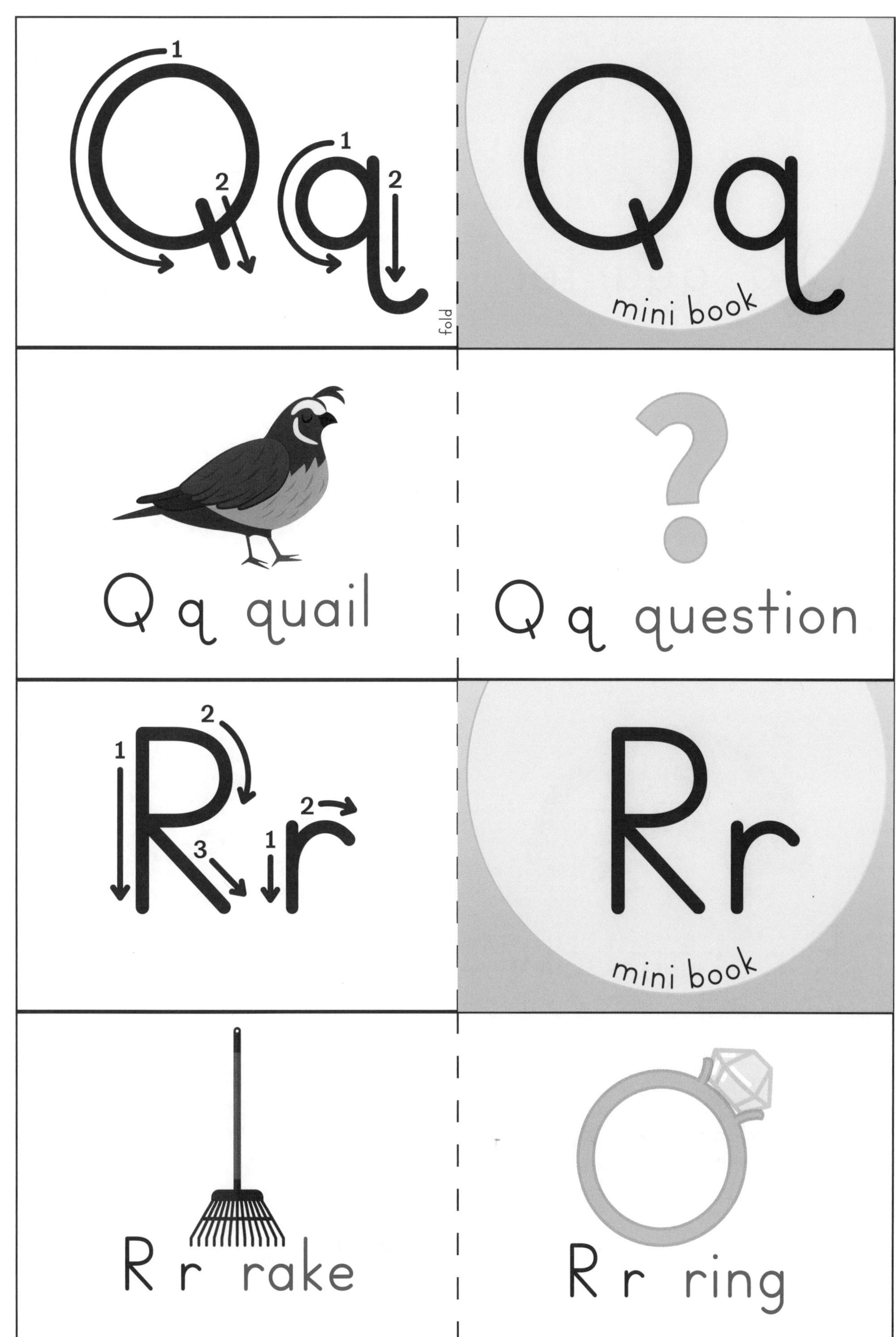
Qq
fold
Qq
mini book
Q q quail
Q q question
Rr
Rr
mini book
R r rake
R r ring

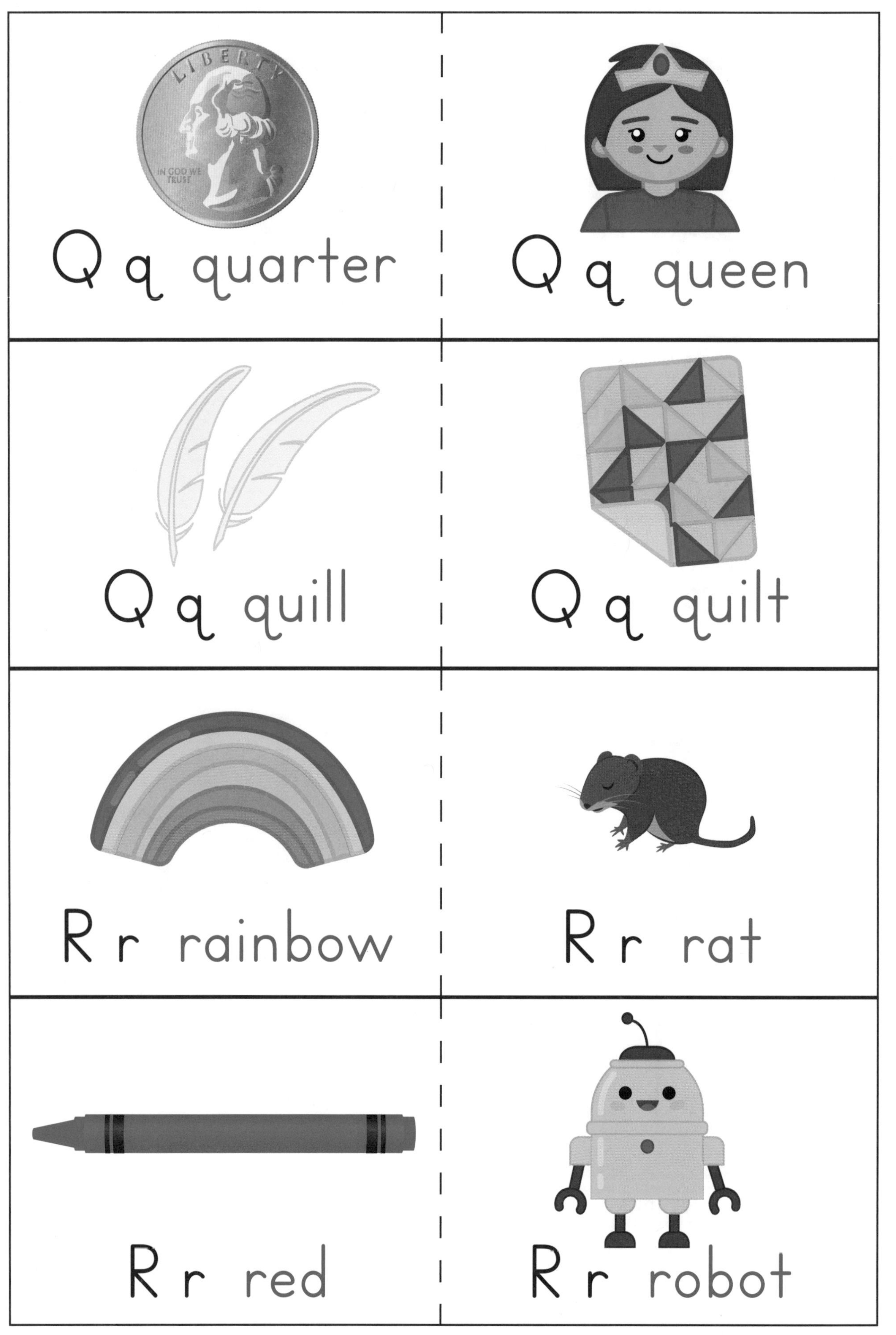
LIBERTY
IN GOD WE TRUST
Q q quarter
Q q queen
Q q quill
Q q quilt
R r rainbow
R r rat
R r red
R r robot

1
Ss
1
fold
Ss
mini book
S s seal
S s sailboat
2
1
T
1
2
t
Tt
mini book
T t tent
T t tulip

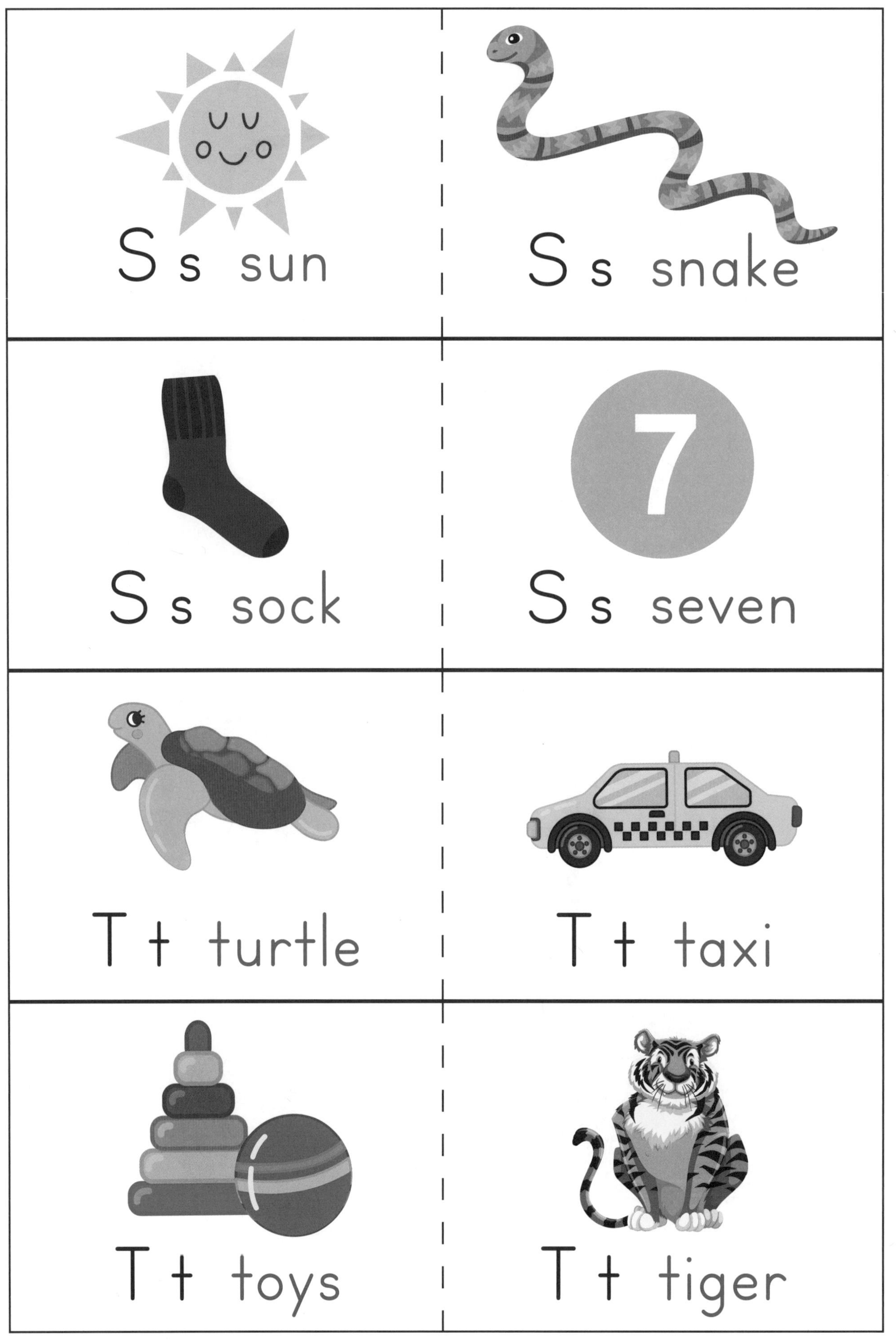
S s sun
S s snake
S s sock
7
S s seven
T t turtle
T t taxi
T t toys
T t tiger

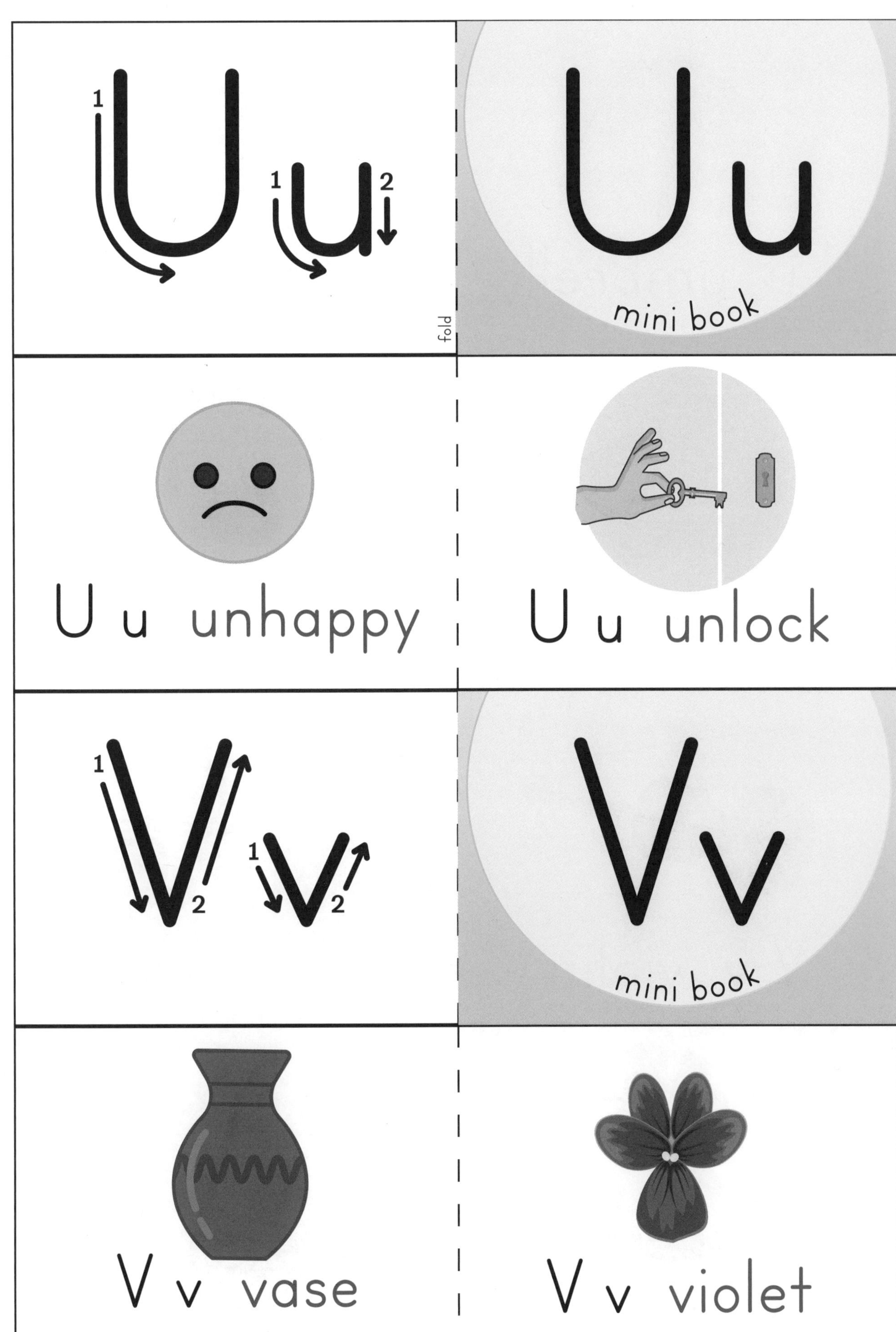
Uu
fold
Uu
mini book
U u unhappy
U u unlock
Vv
Vv
mini book
V v vase
V v violet

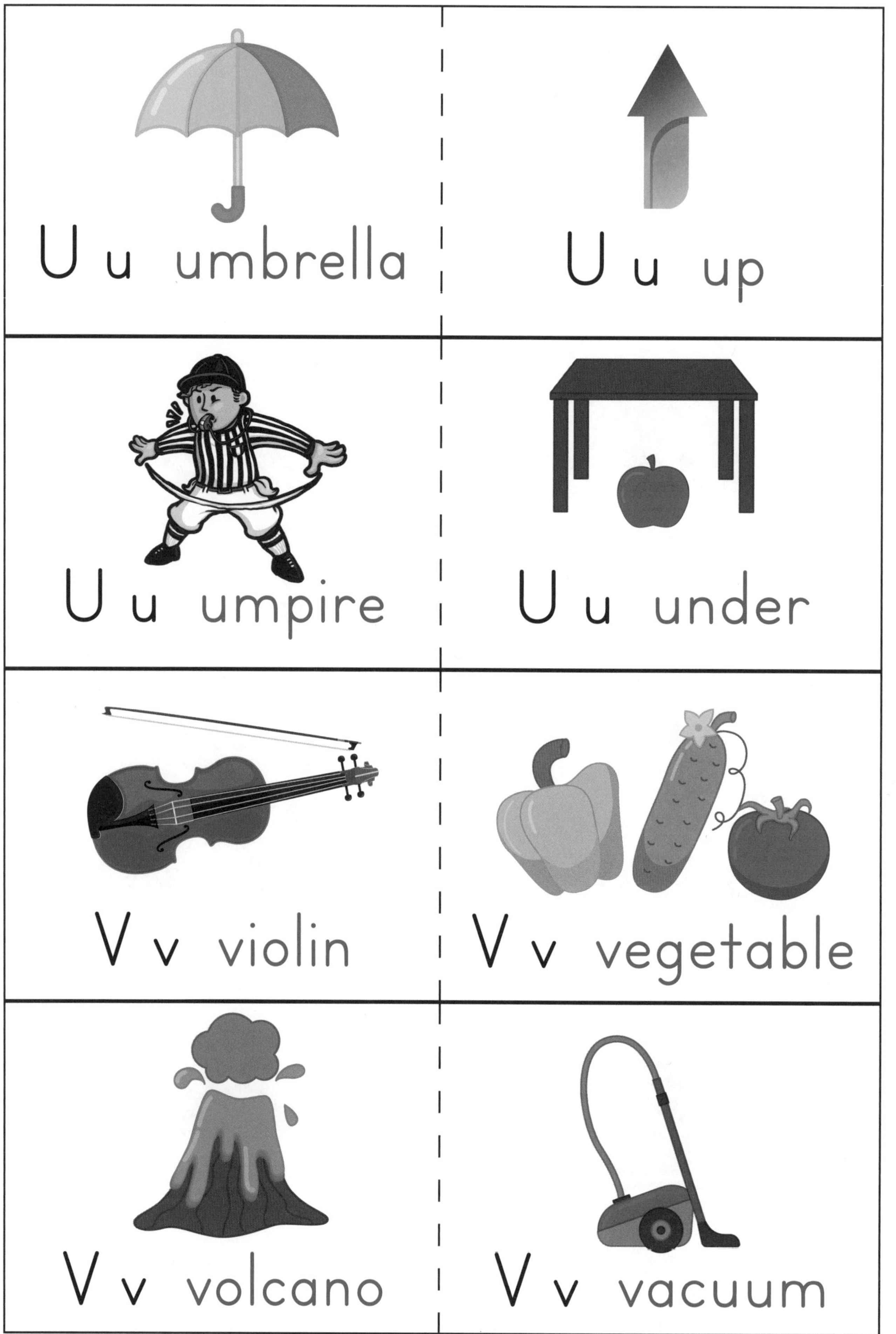
U u umbrella
U u up
U u umpire
U u under
V v violin
V v vegetable
V v volcano
V v vacuum

1
2
3
4
1
2
3
4
fold
Ww
mini book
W w wasp
W w water
1
2
1
2
Xx
mini book
6
X x siX
X x aX

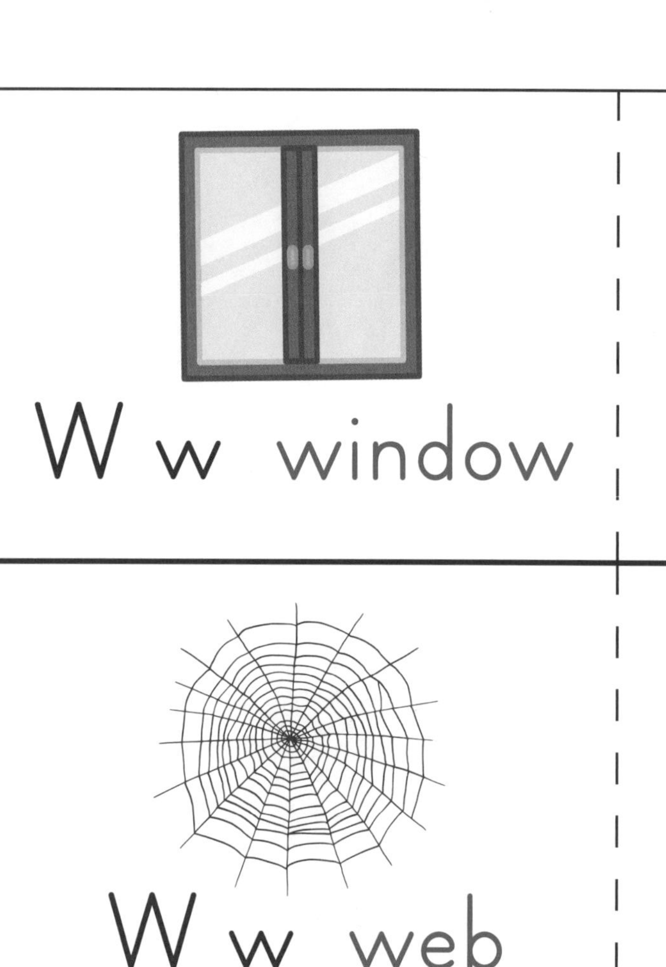

W w window

W w walnut

W w web

W w well

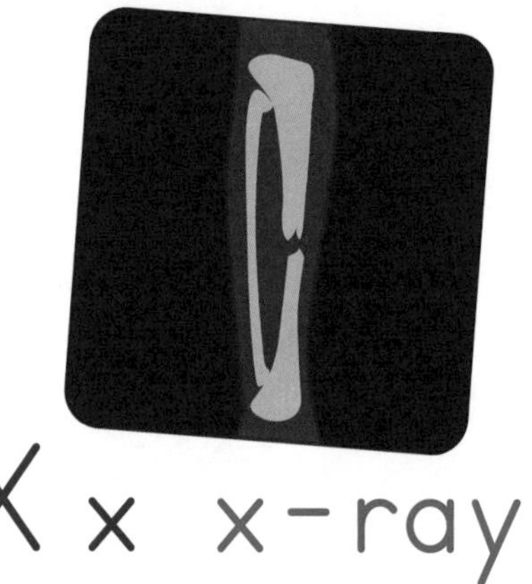

X x x-ray

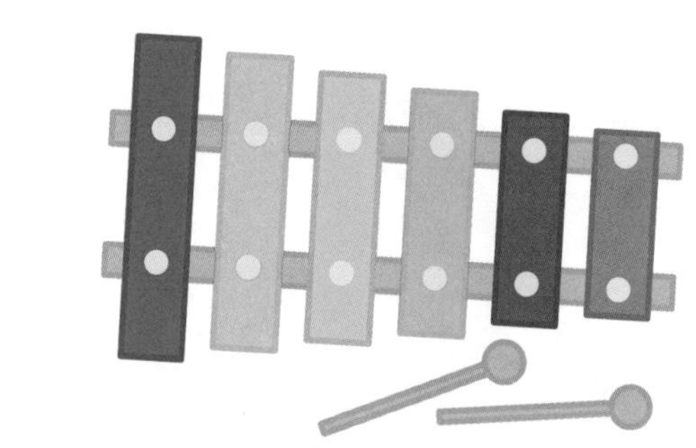

X x xylophone

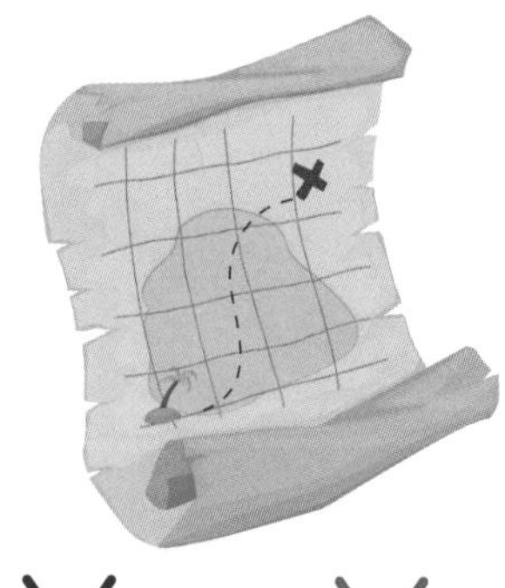

X x X

X x miX

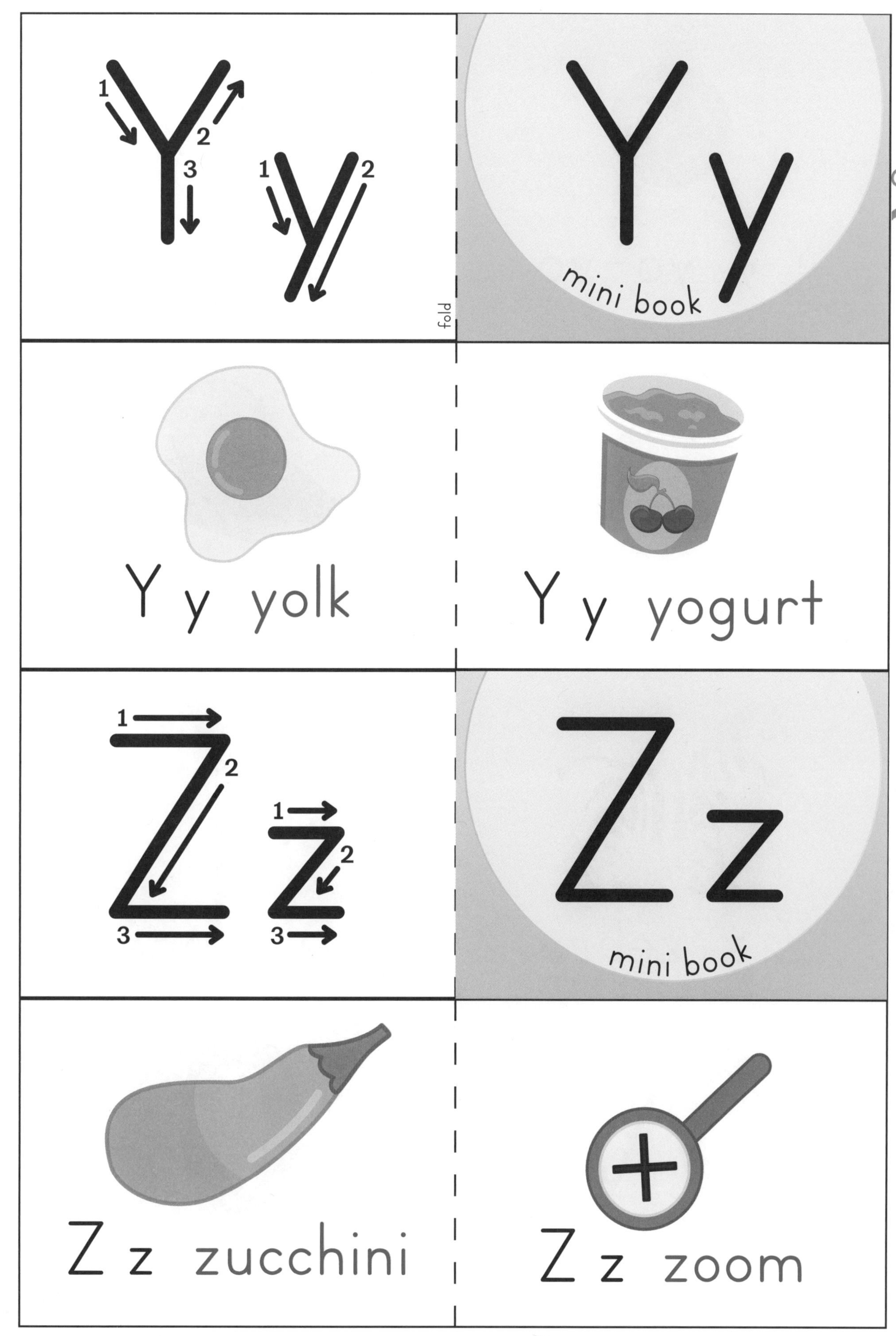
1
2
3
1
2
Yy
fold
Yy
mini book
Y y yolk
Y y yogurt
1
2
3
1
2
3
Zz
mini book
Z z zucchini
Z z zoom

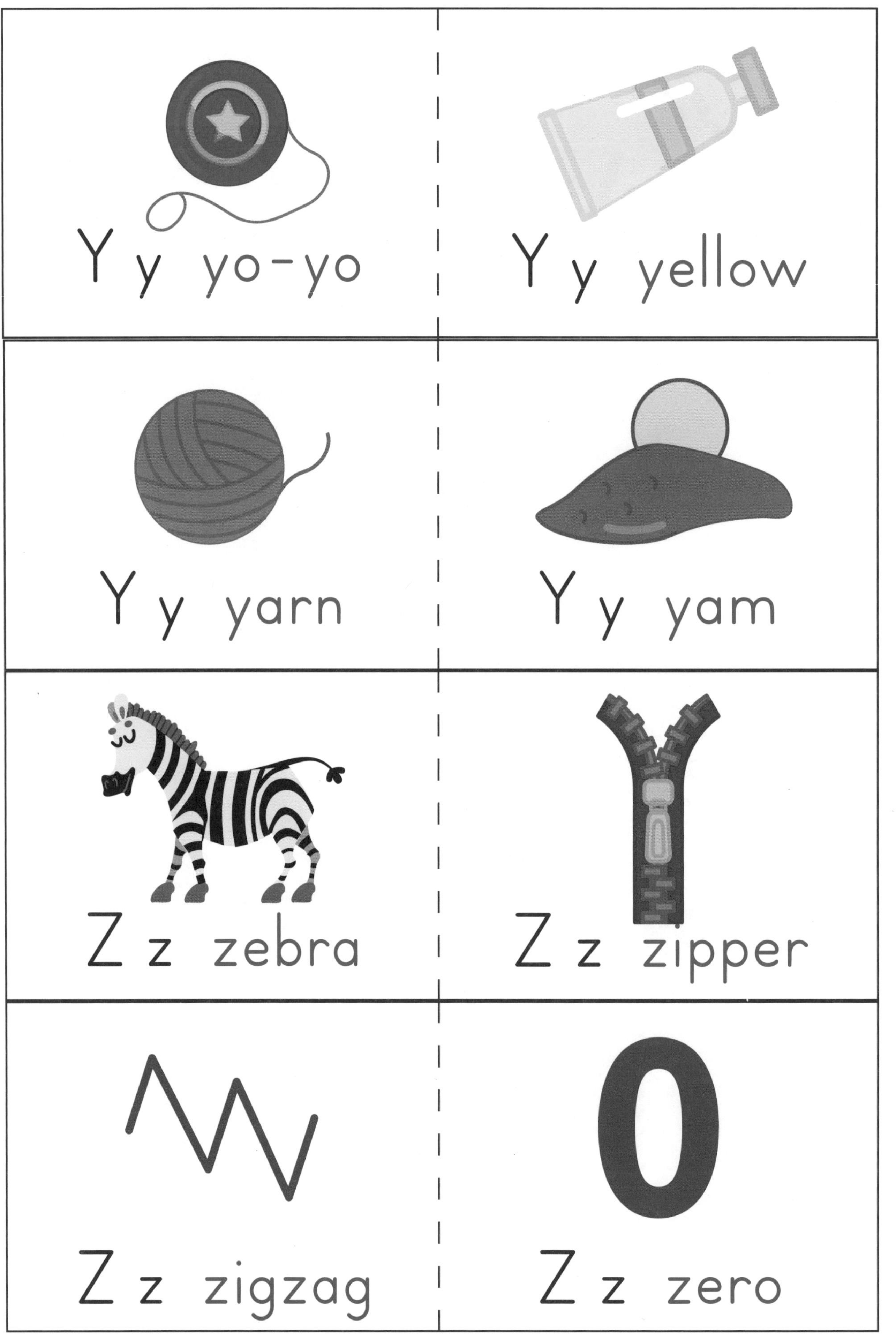

Y y yo-yo
Y y yellow
Y y yarn
Y y yam
Z z zebra
Z z zipper
Z z zigzag
0
Z z zero

emotions

emotions chart

weather

today is?

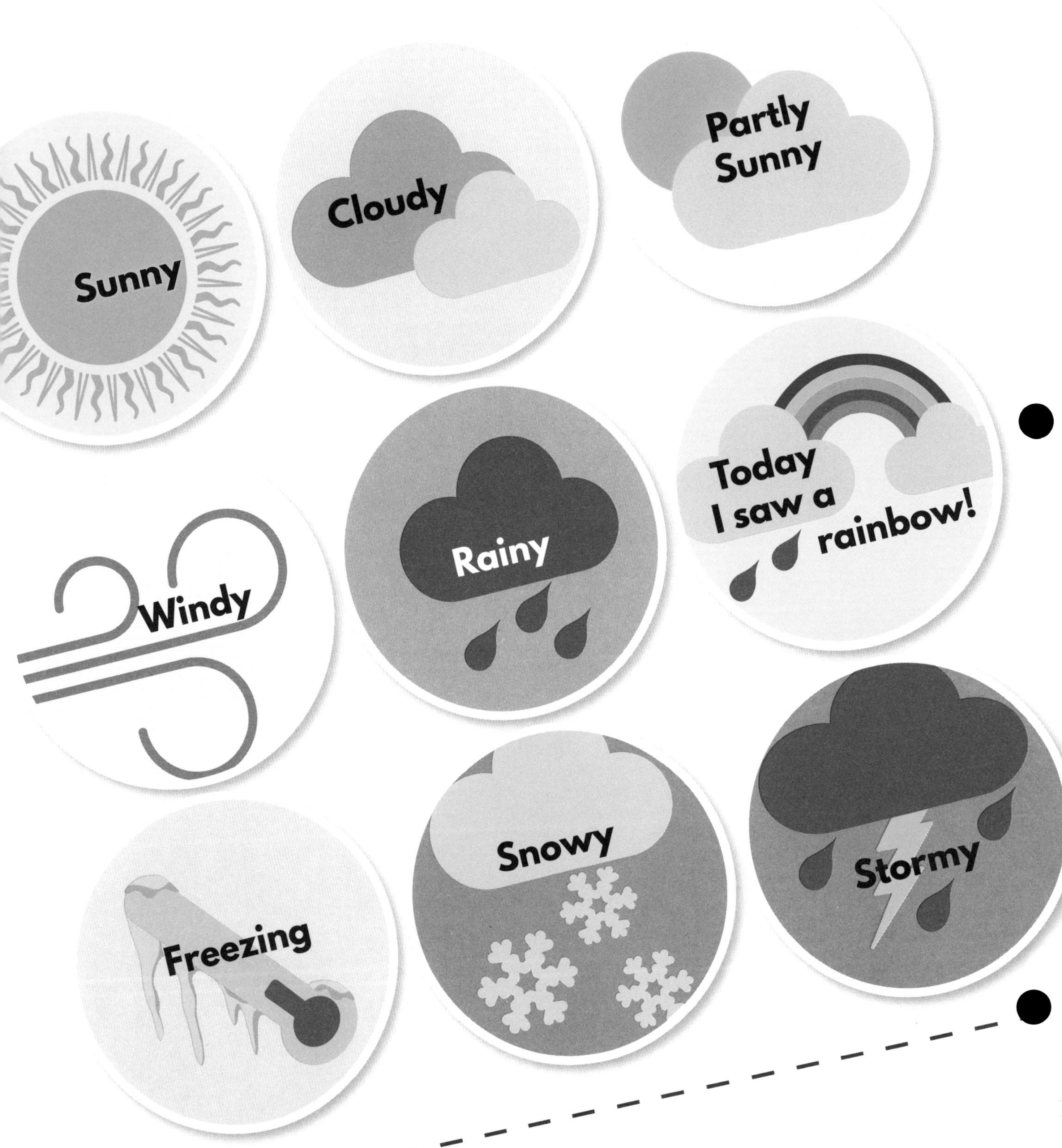
Sunny
Cloudy
Partly Sunny
Windy
Rainy
Today I saw a rainbow!
Freezing
Snowy
Stormy

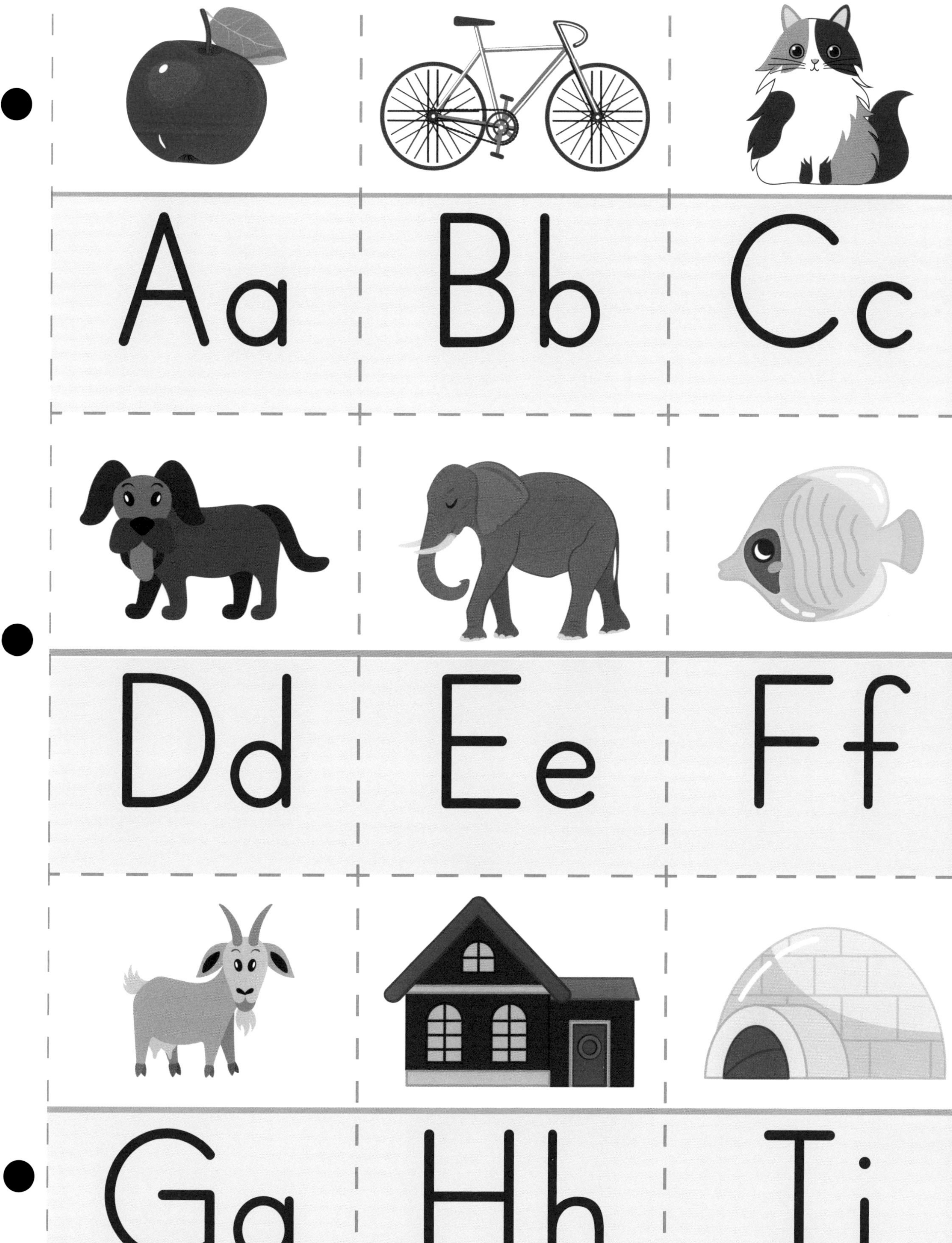
Aa
Bb
Cc
Dd
Ee
Ff
Gg
Hh
Ii

Jj
Kk
Ll
Mm
Nn
Oo
Pp
Qq
Rr

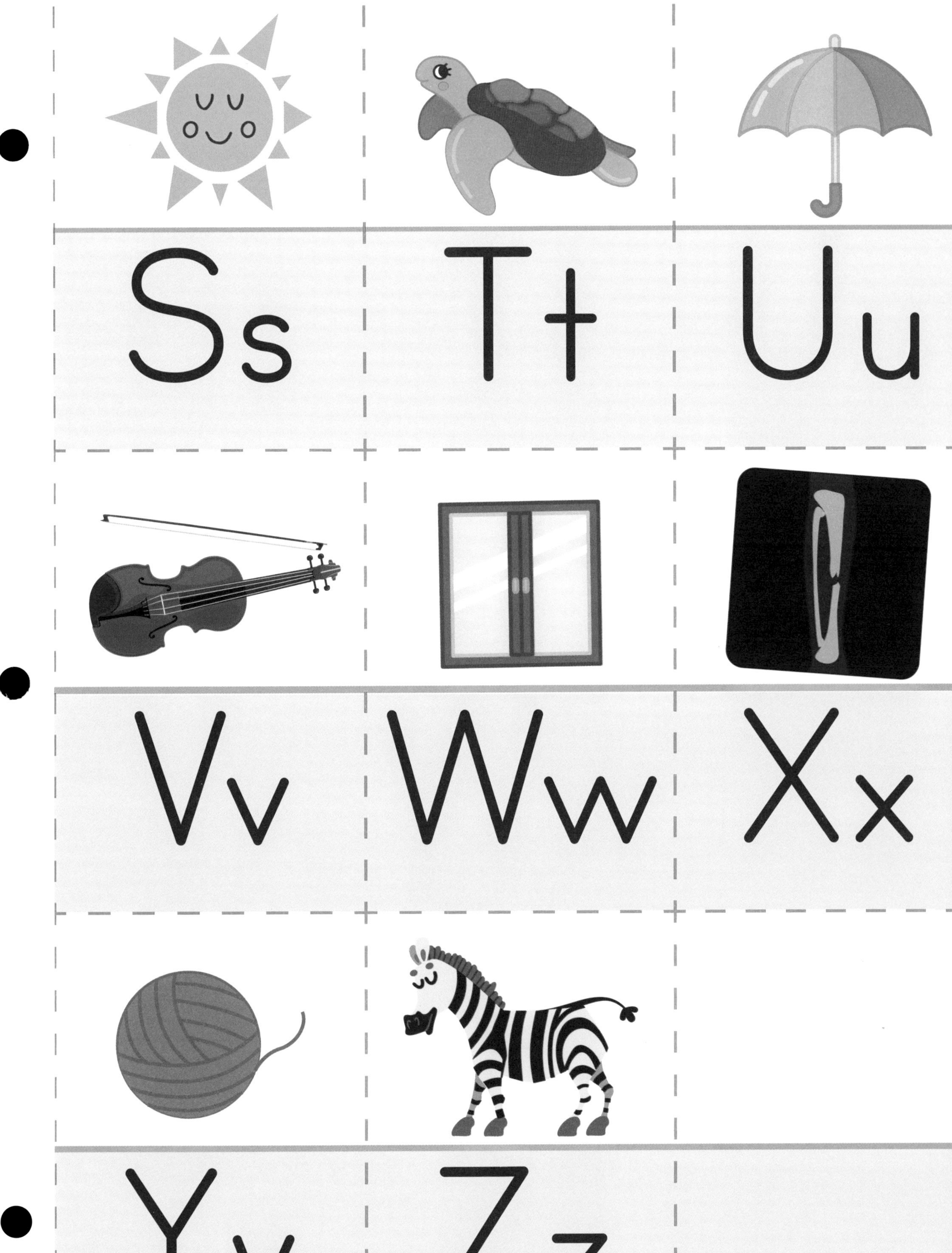
Ss
Tt
Uu
Vv
Ww
Xx
Yy
Zz